&

73
Squadron

39
Squadron

MOD, DDC Brand & Licensing Manager: Pauline Aquiline email 09/02/2022 Approval to use Squadron Insignia/Badges (only inside the book NOT on Front & Rear Covers)

World War 2 - NORTH AFRICA & ITALY
1940 – 1945. 'One Man's Story'

Author: Philip Lamb

AuthorHouse™ UK
1663 Liberty Drive
Bloomington, IN 47403 USA
www.authorhouse.co.uk
UK TFN: 0800 0148641 (Toll Free inside the UK)
UK Local: 02036 956322 (+44 20 3695 6322 from outside the UK)

Because of the dynamic nature of the Internet, any web addresses or links contained in this book may have changed since publication and may no longer be valid. The views expressed in this work are solely those of the author and do not necessarily reflect the views of the publisher, and the publisher hereby disclaims any responsibility for them.

Any people depicted in stock imagery provided by Getty Images are models, and such images are being used for illustrative purposes only. Certain stock imagery © Getty Images.

This book is printed on acid-free paper.

ISBN: 978-1-6655-9918-4 (sc)
ISBN: 978-1-6655-9919-1 (e)

Print information available on the last page.

Published by AuthorHouse 10/20/2022

authorHOUSE®

Front Cover:
Lamb L. B. – LAC SN: 1012281, forced landing of Hurricane - 73 Squadron at **AIN EL GAZALLA**.

Rear Cover:
Hangers at **EL ADEM**, what was left after 3 hours of bombing. 13/3/1942 – Tobruk; **ALEXANDRIA**, Hospital ship being bombed by Axis aircraft; shared Graveyard for **ALLIED, Italian,** and **German** service men.

The Year is 2022

Over 82 years ago, my father signed up to join the RAF at the Gloucester Labour Exchange.

&

104 years ago, 73 Squadron was formed at Upavon, Wiltshire

About the book:

The book sets out on a journey through enlisting to basic training, and then to war. Then, when RAF 73 Squadron was reformed after Dunkirk at RAF Debden the Squadron was mobilized and posted to North Africa. The Ground Crew Personnel were transported via troop and naval ships to Alexandria, Egypt. The pilots and Squadron's Hurricanes were transported on HMS Furious to RAF Takoradi (African Gold Coast). The planes then flown across Africa to Heliopolis, Egypt on selected routes where refueling could be carried out.

The book contains several Battles, starting with the sea battle against the Italian fleet at Cape Spartivento 30/11/1940, battles at and for Tobruk 1941 and 1942 and the battles at El Alamein 1942, the final battle which saw the start of the demise of the German/Italian Axis Force.

The book makes great use of the RAF Records held at National Archives. RAF 73 & 39 Squadrons Operational Record Reports (AIR's) for 1940, 1941, 1942, 1943 and 1944, daily records of events as they took place. Also included is the personal diary which my father kept during 1943. The book is embellished with photographs taken at the time during the war, along with postcards and tourist attraction photographic information. Finally concluding with a brief history of my father through his career and working life.

INTRODUCTION

During my younger years and being of the inquisitive type; I would ask my father on numerous occasions to tell me about his experiences whilst in the Royal Air Force and his postings to **North Africa** and **Italy**, during the **Second World War** with **73 Squadron & Detachment to 39 Squadron**.

On most occasions, I was told that "there wasn't a story to tell, and anyway I don't think it will interest you". In other words, "I don't want to talk about it". (As one gets older one can understand that.) This could not be further from the truth.

To try and imagine what the men went through during the Second World War is hard to comprehend or contemplate. It is only during the last 80 plus years where other conflicts have taken place, which required the British Military to embark on new battles across the world that the measure of conflict can now be established and today is known as PTSD *[Post-Traumatic Stress Disorder]*.

However, there were times when, given half a chance, I would listen to conversations between my father and some of his old friends and comrades, when they happened to get together over a pint or two; where they would share their experiences/stories and have a laugh and joke about, what they termed as the '**Good Old Days'**.

Some of their stories were hilarious and there were some that brought (for a split second) a deathly hush into the room. With the help of those memories, my father's diary, notebooks, and photograph's taken at the time I felt that the time had arrived, to sit down and place into writing the records of events based on these diaries and photograph's and to provide one man's account of those events that took place in **North Africa and Italy during the Allied Campaign 1940-1944**.

The book has primarily been compiled using the written evidence provided by my father's diary & notes **1940- 1944** and the records provided by the **Royal Air Force, Headquarters Air Command and Disclosures, Ministry of Defence – Air Historical Branch (RAF), Museum's, Library's** and in association with records kept at the **Public Records Office, Forces War Records, The National Archives at Kew Gardens**, a book titled **The History of 73 SQUADRON – Parts 1, 2 and 3 written by Don Minterne,** Mr. Malcolm Barrass, Mr. Frank Haslam, plus today's **IT** availability, through **Google** via **WIKIPEDIA** and finally **MOD - RAF St Athan, South Wales**.

Whilst every effort has been made to provide a true and factual account of one man's war as it was then. I apologies in advance for any misrepresentation of any facts.

This book is dedicated to the men who fought for **King and Country** and thus provide a world in which we could all live together as one, and in peace. To my father, his pals (as he always called them) and the Squadrons to which they were assigned.

73 Squadron -' Tutor Et Ultor' [Protector and Avenger] &
39 Squadron - 'Die Noctuque' [By Day and Night]

Footnote:
On a personal note, this book would not have happened, been possible had it not been for the continued support and encouragement over the last twenty-five years from my wife Jane, my son Mark, my daughter Emma-Jane, our eldest granddaughter Chloe, plus all remaining family members and enthusiastic friends; one in particular Jim Erskine who like my family encouraged me to continue and complete the book. His final comment to me was 'It's an historical document and should be put out there for all to read'. Finally, I would like to thank Damien Lewis – Author for his encouragement and support along with his Endorsement of my book, and Robin Philip, Squadron Leader (Rtd) for 'proofreading the manuscript' along with his Book Review.

CONTENTS

Acknowledgements:
Bibliography:

Book Endorsement

As an author myself I am aware of the time, work, effort and research that goes into producing a manuscript on any given subject in preparing the work for publishing. 'One Man's Story' is one such manuscript that uses the World War 2 memorabilia, which had been collected through 1940 to 1946 by Leo Bernard Lamb – RAF 1012281, along with Official Military Records from that time.

It's a story that follows him from signing up in May 1940, through the many battles across North Africa, including Tobruk (2) 1941 and 1942. The crucial battle at El Alamein 1942 and then on to Italy – September/October 1943, landing at Salerno. Finally, his Orders for Home Embarkation (ASAP) in March/April 1944 (due to injuries sustained).

As an author I'm always intrigued to witness new author's coming forward with stories that relate to their family. Stories which otherwise would be lost in time. I am very happy to endorse the book as I have witnessed the books development and a story which should be told.

Endorsement by: *Damien Lewis - Author*

Book Review of 'One Man's Story' written by Philip Lamb

As the name suggests it is the story of Leo Bernard Lamb, the author's father, primarily from his time in 1940 when, as a civilian, he volunteered to join the RAF till his demob in 1946. It tells of his early training in England before he was posted to 73 Squadron as an armament fitter. Shortly after his arrival on the Squadron they were sent to North Africa. The ground crew, such as himself, travelling by ship. Whilst on route the ship was involved in a fierce naval sea battle against the Italian Fleet whilst in the Mediterranean. Leo's time in North Africa was mainly with his own 73 Squadron but it did also include a short detachment to 39 Squadron, who were also in North Africa. In October 1943 the Squadron was transferred to Italy. During his time in Italy serving with the Squadron he was injured, hospitalized, and subsequently sent back to the UK and later demobbed.

The book not only tells the story of LAC Lamb but also includes the history of 73 Squadron and 39 Squadron from their inauguration until 1945. There are many original photographs from LAC Lamb's time in North Africa and Italy and there are also photographs of original documents during the same period. Also included are daily reports from Squadron official records from the beginning of November 1940 to December 1943 mainly regarding LAC Lamb.

A great deal of research has gone into the writing of this book with the result that it gives a very accurate picture of LAC Lamb's life during the second World War and also of the very trying times that Britain faced both in North Africa and also in Italy.

In conclusion this is a must-read book for any World War 2 RAF historian. The book has been written lovingly over a number of years by a very proud son who has gone to great lengths to ensure its accuracy.

Book Review by: *Robin Philip, Squadron Leader (Rtd)*

Chapter 1

A. Brief Summary – Start of World War 2

The Second World War started in 1939, with the Germans invading Poland. To try and protect the countries on the European continent, Great Britain had sent over/dispatched the British Expeditionary Force.

The Germans under Adolf Hitler pressed their march forward into the bordering countries on the European continent, which resulted in the BEF being trapped at Dunkirk, resulting in some 338,000 allied troops and 128,000 French troops having to be evacuated back to the British Isles during May 1940. The Dunkirk evacuation, codenamed 'Operation Dynamo', otherwise known as the 'Miracle of Dunkirk', is where the allied troops between 26 May and 4 June 1940 were taken from the beaches and harbour of Dunkirk. The operation commenced after large numbers of Belgian, British, and French troops had been cut off and surrounded by German forces.

There were many who fought a rear-guard action to ensure that the troops on the beaches at Dunkirk could be saved and repatriated back to good old 'Blighty'.

The evacuation and retreat from Dunkirk, is well documented, and this book will not make any other references to those early periods of World War 2 – particularly because, these events were not related to the North African and Italian campaigns of World War 2.

Prior to evacuation of troops from Dunkirk, Great Britain under the guidance of Winston Churchill was preparing for a long battle. Initially intended to prevent the Germans from invading Great Britain, which resulted in the now famous and well - documented 'Battle of Britain'.

B. Leo Lamb – Specific Recruitment

Towns and cities across the United Kingdom and Commonwealth were all getting ready for what would turn out to be another long and arduous world war. To ensure more men and women were required to enlist, local papers would print editorials such as those in the local Gloucester Paper, *The Citizen*.
On 7 May 1940, a small paragraph stated: - *"R.A.F. Training speed up production to be better". A drastic speed up in the training of men for the R.A.F. and the production of aircraft is to begin immediately.*

Again, and in the same paper on 9 May 1940 appeared the following paragraph on the front page.
New Proclamation will mean calling up of 2,500,000 more men. Age groups affected are from 19 to 36. Ascending Registration to remain. A new proclamation calling up all men from 19 to 36 was signed by the King to-day. It affects all those who have to-day reached the age of 19 but have not reached 37 – in other words all men born between May 10, 1903, and May 9, 1921, both dates inclusive. No call update as yet, due date set for 28 May 1940.

Later, in June 1940 the enrollment date was set for men aged 28.

The Citizen, Saturday, 15 June 1940, page 5 column 4:
Men of 28 Register TO-DAY: [Throughout the country 300,000 Expected to sign up]
*To-day in Gloucester, as in other parts of the country, it was the turn of the 28's to register for Military Service.
Before nightfall, 300,000 men will have visited their local employment exchanges all over the country and signed up for King and Country.*

Registration times were arranged according to initials in the same way as before, namely: A to B 12:30pm to 1:00pm; C to E 1:00pm to 2:00pm; F to J 2:00pm to 3:00pm; K to O 3:00pm to 4:00pm; P to S 4:00pm to 5:00pm; T to Z 5:00pm to 6:00pm.

The men registered to-day, all born in 1911 were the first to be affected since the Second Royal Proclamation. No 20's registered to-day. They will do so next Saturday at the same time as 1910 class men – the 20's.

As it is expected that 320,000 will register next week this will bring the total "on the books" to about 2,800,000. The New Proclamation covers men up to the 36 class. The 27's who registered on May 25, were the last to be covered by the Old Proclamation.

It is estimated that to-day's class will produce more married men than the other classes so far registered. Labour Exchange officials were astonished at the number of men among the 27's.

In Gloucester during this period, all recruitment was taking place at the Labour Exchange, which was in Northgate Mansions, 110 Northgate Street, Gloucester.

Having looked at the various registration dates I can now confirm that my father Leo Bernard Lamb registered on 25 May 1940.

Leo Bernard Lamb

Having registered he would then have had to wait the delivery of his letter from the Ministry of Defence (Royal Air Force), which would confirm his selection and to where he was to assemble. In July 1940 (actual date unknown), the postmen of the day delivered his brown envelope, marked OHMS (On His Majesty's Service) through the letterbox.

His letter would have told him of his selection, and where he was to report. Included within the envelope would have been a rail warrant/pass to allow him to get from Gloucester to Warrington Station. From there he would have been taken in military vehicles, quite possibly a three-ton Bedford lorry to RAF Padgate – Recruiting's Centre 3.

Prior to him receiving his 'marching orders' my dad would have gone to see family and friends to say his farewells, and no doubt some of them would have said, "This will make a man of you, Leo."
On reflection, I wonder what they would have said when he eventually arrived home, some 4 + years later.

C. Leo B. Lamb Early Recruit Training: RAF Padgate

My father was sent in the first instance to 3RC Padgate, which at the time was in the district known as Poulton with Fearnhead near to Warrington.

Main Entrance to Royal Air Force Padgate
The above Image has been provided by Cheshire Archives & Local Studies Record Office – Cheshire Image Bank c01024. Approval and image received via email from Hannah Bate (Archives Assistant; date 01/03/2022), who has given consent and approval to use in the book.

Padgate Camp was set up as a National Recruiting &Training Centre initially for RAF recruits enlisting to join up for World War 2. The camp known as 3 RAF Recruit Centre opened in April 1939. On arriving at the Recruit Centre all recruits would be giving the rank of **AC2**.

During July 1940, and from the research carried out at the National Archives of the RAF Padgate – Operations Record Book **AIR 29/497** the base operated four wings plus the addition of the Base Headquarters. When looking through the AIR's it is clear to see that the turn-over of trainees IN and OUT was quite exceptional through all four wings.

On arrival they would have been given tea and biscuits and a welcome from a flight lieutenant or squadron leader. All very civilized, but things would soon change. Their hair would be cut short, issued with a 1250 (identity card), given a service number 'his was 1012281' and issued a uniform. They would move in line through the store and the equipment assistants would throw the various items at them in a most un-Grace Brothers manner. Every item would have to be marked with his number, using stencils provided.

To get prepared for travelling to fight in foreign lands, vaccinations would be given out with the flight sergeant probably warning them 'Don't any of you men faint.'

From my father's RAF records, he arrived at 3RC Padgate on 25 July 1940 (from records Mustering ACH.GD.25.7.40) to begin his initial training, which would consist of the following: -
- how to salute an officer
- how to report to your superiors
- how to look after your equipment
- how to march. (Square bashing)

In addition to that above, physical exercises were part of the day-to-day routine to ensure that the enlisted men were fit and ready for battle, wherever that may take place.

It is not clear from the service records as to which 'Wing' he was allocated, 1, 2 or 3. However, on 25 July 1940 (the date on which he arrived) the following can be confirmed: -

- Wing 1: 1,081 trainees arrived.
- Wing 2: intake of 580 recruits.
- Wing 3: intake 663 recruits with 34 rejected.
- Wing 4: passing out parade inspected by Station Commander.
- Headquarters: yellow, 08.25 hours; white, 08.40 hours; passing out parade took place in wings 1 and 4 on, parade ground; inspection by Station Commander.

OPERATIONS RECORD BOOK

R.A.F. Form 540

of (Unit or Formation) HEADQUARTERS, No. 3 RECRUITS CENTRE.

Page No. One.

No. of pages used for month/day

Place	Date	Time	Summary of Events	References to Appendices
PADGATE.	3.7.40.		Message received from Police, all troops warned against attack by Parachutists. Transport and striking force turned out and proceeded to Burtonwood. All Clear given at 06.20 hours.	
	4.7.40.		Convoy of six vehicles and one motor-cycle arrived en route for Carlisle, accommodated for night.	
	8.7.40.		Despatch Rider Letter Service commenced between Market Drayton and Carlisle on alternate days. Hooton, Sealand, Hawarden, serving into Padgate via W. Kirby. Ringway and Altrincham serving into Padgate via Wilmslow.	
	9.7.40.		Air Raid warning Red 10.30 hours, White, 10.58.	
	12.7.40.		Convoy of 36 vehicles arrived en route for the North. 72 airmen and 2 officers accommodated for the night.	
	13.7.40.		Convoy of 9 vehicles arrived, 12 airmen accommodated for the night.	
	14.7.40.		Convoy of 10 vehicles arrived, 18 airmen, 1 officer and 1 civilian driver accommodated for night.	
	15.7.40.		Air Raid Warning Red 13.16 hours. All Clear 13.55 hours. Striking Force turned out.	
	16.7.40.		Yellow received, 00.31. White 01.23. Aircraft heard overhead, searchlights in operation.	
	17.7.40.		Yellow, 01.45 hours. White 02.35.	
	18.7.40.		Convoy of 5 vehicles arrived, accommodated for night. Passing out Parade of No. 1 and No. 4 Wing on No. 4 Wing Parade ground.	
	19.7.40.		Yellow received 01.10 hours. White, 02.55 hours.	
	20.7.40.		Yellow received, 02.53 hours. White 03.00 hours.	
	22.7.40.		Yellow received, 18.40 hours. White 18.53 hours.	
	23.7.40.		Air Raid Warning Red 01.42, Green 02.00, White 02.10.	
	25.7.40.		Air Raid Warning Yellow 01.45, White 01.49 hours.	
	24.7.40.		Air Raid Warning Aircraft passed over the Camp. Searchlights in operation. Green & Red ... Searchlights switched off. Red, 02.05. Striking Force assembled.	

Headquarters, Recruits Centre 3
Continued: -

Place	Date	Time	Summary of Events	References to Appendices
PADGATE.	24.7.40.		White, 02.55 hours. Yellow, 03.05, White 03.37 hours.	
	25.7.40.		Yellow, 08.25 hours. White 08.40. Passing out Parade took place in Nos. 1 and 4 Wings, Parade Grounds. Inspection by Station Commander.	
	28.7.40.		Purple received 00.10 hours. White 01.45 hours. Aircraft heard overhead. 0.30 searchlights in operation. Purple, 02.25. White 03.00 hours.	
	29.7.40.		Purple received 00.10 hours.	
	30.7.40.		White 00.40 hours.	
	31.7.40.		Purple 00.50 hours. White, 01.05. Aircraft heard overhead, searchlights in operation. Purple 01.15, White 01.30 hours. Despatch Rider Letter Service Trunk Section between Market Drayton and Carlisle commenced daily schedule in both directions.	

Group Captain,
Commanding No. 3 Recruits Centre.
PADGATE.

Wing 1, Recruits Centre 3

R.A.F. Form 540.
See instructions for use of this form on E.R. and A.C.I.,
para. 1049, and War Manual, Pt. II., chapter XX., and
Notes in R.A.F. Pocket Book.

OPERATIONS RECORD BOOK

Page No. 1

No. of pages used for this One
month
JULY 1940.

of (Unit or Formation) No. 1 Wing, No. 3 Recruits Centre.

Place	Date	Time	Trainees	Trainers In	Trainers Out	Trans Stage	Drill Course		Summary of Events	References to Appendices
PADGATE.	1.7.40	am	947			116	170	13	F/O. R.L.Haines (Adjt. No.1 Wing) promoted A/Fl.Lieut.	
	2.7.40	am	954	186	9	117	167	13		
	3.7.40	am	773		186	117	167	13		
	4.7.40	am	940	172	1	117	167	11		
	5.7.40	am	680		260	118	168	11	No. 9 Drill Course commenced.	
	6.7.40	am	643		37	118	167	9	No. 4 Course completed. 31 Posted.	
	7.7.40	am	1049	406		118	168	9		
	8.7.40	am	1049			118	161	9	No. 5 Course completed. 48 Posted.	
	9.7.40	am	958		90	131	150	10	Air Raid Warning sounded 10.30 hrs. Raiders passed 10.50 hrs. No aircraft sighted.	
	10.7.40	am	952		6	131	150	8		
	11.7.40	am	952			131	170	11		
	12.7.40	am	906		56	121	160	11	No. 10 Drill Course commenced.	
	13.7.40	am	963	57		122	196	10	No. 6 Course completed. 15 Posted.	
	14.7.40	am	963			122	192	10		
	15.7.40	am	963			122	192	9	Air Raid Warning 13.16 hrs. Raiders passed 13.58 hrs. No aircraft sighted.	
	16.7.40	am	963			121	176	13	No. 6 Course completed. 26 Posted.	
	17.7.40	am	961		2	123	176	11		
	18.7.40	am	954		27	123	185	10		
	19.7.40	am	778	58	234	122	190	5	No. 11 Drill Course commenced.	
	20.7.40	am	974	204	28	122	226	6		
	21.7.40	am	974		2	122	226	6		
	22.7.40	am	972			122	227	6	Air Raid Warning 01.42 hrs. Raiders passed 02.00 hrs. No aircraft sighted.	
	23.7.40	am	970		2	122	192	6	No. 7 Course completed. 56 Posted.	
				1073	950					

Wing, Recruits Centre 3
Continued: -

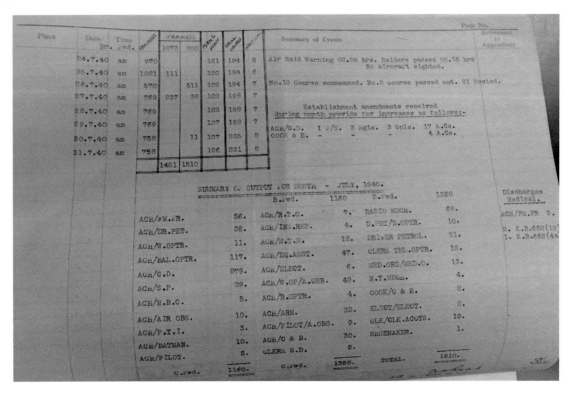

Place	Date Br.fwd.	Time	Trainees	Trainers In 1073	Trainers Out 950	Trans Stage	Drill Course		Summary of Events	References to Appendices
	24.7.40	am	970			121	194	5	Air Raid Warning 02.05 hrs. Raiders passed 02.35 hrs. No aircraft sighted.	
	25.7.40	am	1081	111		120	194	6		
	26.7.40	am	570		511	122	194	7	No.12 Course commenced. No.8 Course passed out. 21 Posted.	
	27.7.40	am	769	237	38	122	198	7		
	28.7.40	am	769			122	198	7	Establishment amendments received during month provide for increases as follows:-	
	29.7.40	am	769			127	193	7	ACH/G.D. 1 F/S. 3 Sgts. 3 Cpls. 17 A.Cs.	
	30.7.40	am	758		11	127	235	8	COOK & B. - - - 4 A.Cs.	
	31.7.40	am	758			126	231	8		
				1491	1510					

SUMMARY OF OUTPUT FOR MONTH - JULY, 1940.

	B.fwd.	1160	B.fwd.	1359	Discharges Medical.	
ACH/FM.FR.	56.	ACH/R.T.O.	7.	RADIO MECH.	68.	ACH/FM.FR 3.
ACH/DR.PET.	35.	ACH/INS.REP.	4.	D.PET/B.OPTR.	10.	2. K.R.652(19)
ACH/W.OPTR.	11.	ACH/M.T.M.	12.	DRIVER PETROL.	21.	1. K.R.652(4a)
ACH/BAL.OPTR.	117.	ACH/EQ.ASST.	47.	CLERK TEL.OPTR.	12.	
ACH/G.D.	879.	ACH/ELECT.	6.	MED.ORD/MED.O.	13.	
ACH/S.P.	29.	ACH/W.OP/A.GNR.	42.	M.T.MECH.	4.	
ACH/M.B.C.	5.	ACH/R.OPTR.	4.	COOK/C & B.	2.	
ACH/AIR OBS.	10.	ACH/ARM.	32.	ELECT/ELECT.	2.	
ACH/P.T.I.	3.	ACH/PILOT/A.OBS.	9.	CLK/CLK.ACCTS.	19.	
ACH/BATMAN.	10.	ACH/C & B.	30.	SHOEMAKER.	1.	
ACH/PILOT.	5.	CLERK G.D.	5.	TOTAL.	1510.	
	C.fwd.	1160.	C.fwd.	1359.		

Wing 2, Recruits Centre 3

OPERATIONS RECORD BOOK

R.A.F. Form 540

of (Unit or Formation) .... No. 2 Wing, No. 3 Recruits Centre, Padgate.

No. of pages used for ... this ... month

Place.	Date.	Time.	Summary of Events.	References to Appendices.
PADGATE.	1940 July			
	1.		The strength of No.2 Wing is officers 4 : Airmen (Staff) 104: Recruits 788.	
			Intake of 264 recruits. 979 recruits posted to various units.	
	2.		Intake of 792 recruits. 533 recruits posted out.	
	3.		Intake of 594 recruits. 182 recruits posted out.	
	4.		Intake of 330 recruits. 330 recruits posted out.	
	5.		Intake of 870 recruits. 1194 recruits posted out.	
	6.		Intake of 493 recruits. 538 recruits posted.	
	8.		Intake of 348 recruits. 403 recruits posted out.	
	9.		Intake of 430 recruits. 38 recruits posted out.	
	10.		Intake of 329 recruits. 330 recruits posted to No. 5 R.C., West Kirby.	
	11.		Intake of 435 recruits. 503 recruits posted away.	
	12.		Intake of 513 recruits. 463 recruits posted to various units.	
	13.		Intake of 926 recruits. 907 recruits posted away.	
	15.		Intake of 518 recruits. 592 recruits posted away.	
	16.		Intake of 522 recruits. 445 recruits posted away to various units.	
	17.		Intake of 371 recruits. 320 recruits posted away.	
	18.		Intake of 377 recruits. 382 recruits posted away.	
	19.		Intake of 687 recruits. 660 recruits posted away.	
	20.		Intake of 420 recruits. 539 recruits posted away.	
	21.		66 recruits posted away.	
	22.		Intake of 549 recruits. 667 recruits posted away.	
	23.		Intake of 493 recruits. 393 recruits posted to 1 Wing, Seighall Massie.	
	24.		Intake of 636 recruits. 511 recruits posted away.	

Wing 2, Recruits Centre 3
Continued: -

Place.	Date.	Time.	Summary of Events.	References to Appendices.
PADGATE.	1940 JULY 25.		Intake of 580 recruits. 743 recruits posted to various units.	
	26.		Intake of 431 recruits. 887 recruits posted away.	
	27.		Intake of 402 recruits. 410 recruits posted away.	
	29.		Intake of 502 recruits. 336 recruits posted to 4 Wing, 6 R.C., Wilmslow.	
	30.		Intake of 614 recruits. 603 recruits posted away.	
	31.		Intake of 667 recruits. 436 recruits posted away.	
			Good weather has been experienced during the month, and the health of staff and recruits has been excellent.	
			There is nothing further to report for the month of JULY 1940.	
			Flight Lieutenant.	

Wing 3, Recruits Centre 3

OPERATIONS RECORD BOOK

Page No. One

of (Unit or Formation) No. 3 Wing, No. 3 Recruits Centre — No. of pages used for day

Place	Date 1940	Time	Summary of Events					References to Appendices
Padgate	July		Disposal of recruits during July 1940					
			Intake	Rejected	Deferred	Posted	Remain	
	1		1059	14	264	383	1058	
	2		972	27	178	726	1099	
	3		879	40	298	759	881	
	4		933	30	255	355	1192	
	5		886	12	284	897	887	
	6 7		654	5	200	569	827	
	8		695	18	281	348	875	
	9		712	16	265	412	896	
	10		884	32	247	329	1170	
	11		861	26	253	438	1318	
	12		923	11	275	513	1442	
	13 14		929	28	280	1000	1069	
	15		728	52	261	518	1055	
	16		696	40	276	493	942	
	17		715	21	262	400	951	
	18		711	52	267	377	996	
	19		699	25	233	664	773	
	20 21		667	22	65	464	889	
	22		799	13	222	349	904	
	23		953	27	168	493	1209	

Wing 3, Recruits Centre 3
Continued: -

Place	Date 1940	Time	Summary of Events					References to Appendices
			Disposal of recruits during July 1940 continued					
Padgate	July		Intake	Rejected	Deferred	Posted	Remain	
	24		821	21	158	636	1016	
	25		663	24	232	580	832	
	26		642	25	165	456	790	
	27 28		725	7	23	402	1073	
	29		894	65	257	501	143	
	30		871	26	334	617	1037	
	31		355	42	222	670	916	

Received information on 26th July 1940 that 339 Army tradesmen Electricians and N.C.O's were reporting for trade test. Accommodation and posting out to various RAF units on attachment to RAF for five months. The soldiers started arriving at Padgate on 27th July and the following numbers were received rejected and posted up to and including 31st July 1940. Total received 257. Posted to RAF units 249. Rejected.

The weather throughout the month was FAIR

[signature]

Squadron Leader.
Commanding No. 3 Wing No. 3 Recruits Centre

2/8/40

Wing 4, Recruits Centre 3

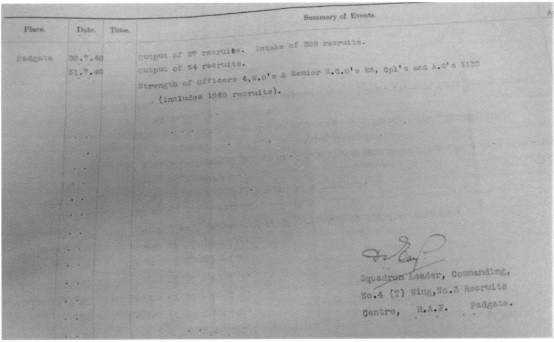

OPERATIONS RECORD BOOK

R.A.F. Form 540

of (Unit or Formation) No.4 (T) Wing, No.3 Recruits Centre, Padgate.

Place.	Date.	Time.	Summary of Events.	References to Appendices.
Padgate.	1.7.40		Strength of Officers 4, W.O.& Senior N.C.O's 25, Cpls.& AC's 848 (includes 782 recruits)	
	2.7.40		Intake of 397 recruits. Output 1 airman (discharged)	
	3.7.40		Output of 15 recruits.	
	4.7.40		5 Senior N.C.O's (Drill Instructors) attached to No.3 S.of T.T., BLACKPOOL.	
	5.7.40		Output of 24 recruits.	
	7.7.40		Intake of 86 recruits.	
	8.7.40		Output of 30 recruits.	
	9.7.40		Output of 25 recruits.	
	10.7.40		Output of 94 recruits.	
	11.7.40		"Passing out" inspection of 178 recruits by Station Commander.	
	12.7.40		Output of 169 recruits.	
	13.7.40		Intake of 342 recruits. Output of 9 recruits.	
	15.7.40		Output of 9 recruits.	
	18.7.40		"Passing out" inspection on No.4 Wing Parade Ground of 296 recruits No.4 Wing - 220 recruits of No. 1 Wing, by Station Commander.	
	19.7.40		F/Lieut.P.W.Evans proceeded on attachment to Officers'School, LOUGHBOROUGH attending No. 20 Course. F/O.O.H.Brown appointed Wing Adjutant vice F/Lieut.P.W.Evans (detached on course) Output of 323 recruits.	
	20.7.40		Output of 61 recruits.	
	23.7.40		Output of 1 recruit.	
	24.7.40		Intake of 309 recruits.	
	25.7.40		"Passing out" inspection of 392 recruits by Station Commander.	
	26.7.40		Output of 313 recruits.	

Wing 4, Recruits Centre 3
Continued: -

Place.	Date.	Time.	Summary of Events.	A
Padgate	30.7.40		Output of 97 recruits. Intake of 309 recruits.	
	31.7.40		Output of 54 recruits. Strength of Officers 4, W.O's & Senior N.C.O's 25, Cpl's and A.C's 1133 (includes 1068 recruits).	

Squadron Leader, Commanding,
No.4 (T) Wing, No.3 Recruits
Centre,   R.A.F.   Padgate.

Note: Contains public sector information licensed under the Open Government Licence v3.0

After his arrival on the 25 July 1940, my dad along with all the recruits arriving on the day, would have had to have a medical, would have been weighed and measured and given a sight test, a reflexes test, aptitude tests involving shapes and patterns and a colour-blindness test, primarily for those who were going on to become a pilot.

Then on 27 July 1940 – my father along with all other recruits, was transferred to **3W 5RC RAF West Kirby** for more in-depth training on the selected trade that they would be working in. He would have probably travelled by train to West Kirby, and they were all most likely locked in the non-corridor carriages so that no one could escape. On arrival at the camp, they would've been taken to the stores to be kitted out with blankets, sheets and pillowcases and then marched (you marched everywhere at West Kirby) to their billet.

RAF West Kirby:

RAF Station Badge

RAF Station Standard

MOD, DDC Brand & Licensing Manager: Pauline Aquiline email 09/02/2022 Approval to use Squadron Insignia/Badges (only inside the book NOT on Front & Rear Covers) Standard photograph supplied by Mr. Alan Carter – RAF West Kirby Association.

Royal Air Force West Kirby - Camp Entrance
The above Image has been provided by (Mr. Alan Carter of the RAF West Kirby Association) who has given his consent and approval to use in the book.

The base opened as No. 5 Recruits Centre on 25 April 1940 and was located at **Larton**, in Cheshire, located approximately 3 miles (4.8 km) from West Kirby village, from which it took its name. The camp entrance as shown below was on **Saughall Massie Road**, almost opposite **Oldfield Lane**. RAF West Kirby was set up at the beginning of the Second World War, as a basic training camp, to train new recruits into the Royal Air Force. Known as a "square bashing camp" in the vernacular.

The base was re-designated as No. 1 Personnel Despatch Centre on 17 September 1941. Reformed at West Kirby on 1 September 1946 and was re-designated No. 5 School of Recruit Training on the 1 November 1948. The final Passing Out Parade took place on the 20 December 1957 and West Kirby closed on the 1 January 1958.

The first recruits arrived on the 16 May. During 1940, RAF West Kirby later became the Personnel Dispatch Centre for kitting out the airmen and women for service overseas. It was also used as the main assembly point for the Polish Pilots coming to England after the fall of Poland in 1939. The Polish Pilots went on to play a significant role in the Battle of Britain, flying as members of RAF squadrons (often Polish squadrons of the RAF).

The camp was the initial starting point for many personal and became the main training base for service overseas. It was also instrumental in the formation of two RAF Beach Reconnaissance Units, No's 68 and 69 RAF Beach Units who were set up in April 1943, who went on to see service on D-Day in Sicily, Italy (Salerno) 1943 and Normandy 1944.

The following photographs ['a' to 'f' to Final Pass Out Parade ['g'] give a flavour of what life was like in the Royal Air Force in preparation for posting to your allotted Squadron up to and during World War II.

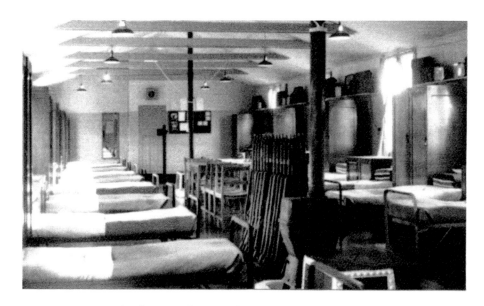

Typical Barrack Hut already for Inspection [a]

Putting Recruits through their Drill [b]

Typical 'Physical Exercise/Gym Work' [c]

Drill Work and Marching – Parade Ground [d]

Some more Drill Work – Even when it's raining [e]

Fixed Bayonet – Combat Drill Training [f]

Typical Passing Out Parade [g]

Images [a] to [g] have been provided by (Mr. Alan Carter of the RAF West Kirby Association) who has given his consent and approval to use in the book, email dated 08/03/2022.

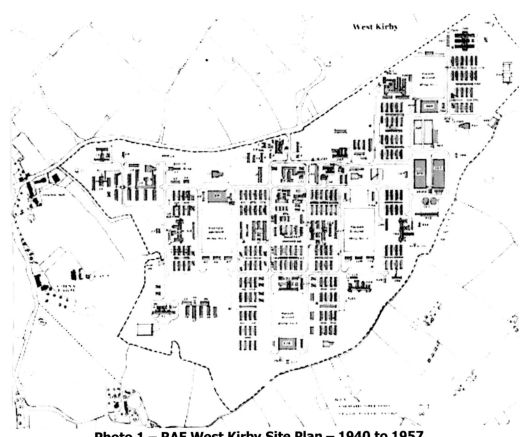

Photo 1 – RAF West Kirby Site Plan – 1940 to 1957

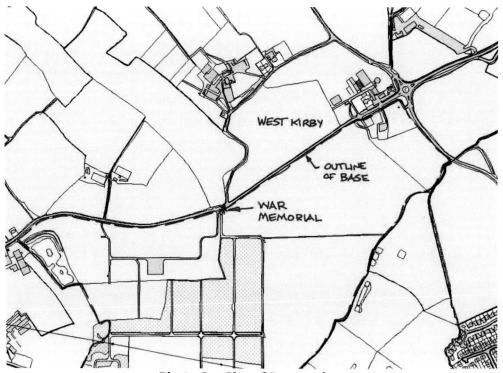

Photo 2 – Site of Base today

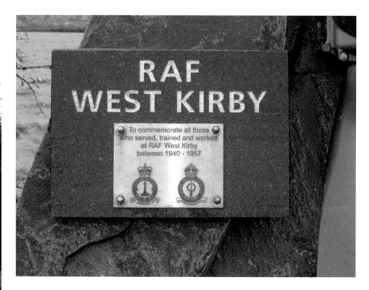

Photo 3   **Photo 4**
Commemoration stone and plaque near the old site entrance to RAF West Kirby
Images 1, 2, 3 & 4 have been provided by (Mr. Peter Jackson-Lee) who has given his consent and approval to use in the book, email dated 08/02/2022.

Whilst based at the camp, the recruits would be put through their initial training for the RAF, which included first learning RAF parade ground drill with rifles, intensive physical fitness training, training in ground combat and defence under the guidance of Non-Commissioned Officers (NCOs) along with some education about the RAF and its history. The RAF Regiment were not formed until 1 February 1942.

The Recruits would have been asked what their preferred trade would be and once decided OR appointed to, would then once at their appointed squadron be given the initial training to ensure that their skill set was good and if not transferred too somewhere else where they would have received their "trade training". In addition to this they would have all received the basic introduction to RAF Military Life.

Men while undergoing their basic training at West Kirby were accommodated in wooden barrack huts, each one housing about twenty men. Because West Kirby was a basic training camp with no airfield, discipline was very much stricter than in any normal RAF operational or trade training camp. If in your first few weeks at camp, the only way to get off camp legally was by attending church and boarding the special buses to the church of your denomination.

In peace time recruits would spend a period of eight weeks on their training at West Kirby before being posted on to their "trade training" camp elsewhere in the United Kingdom. In my father's case and looking through his Service Record he arrived at RAF Padgate on the 25 July 1940 then two days later was posted across to RAF West Kirby, on the 27 July 1940. Then on 17 August 1940 he was posted to 73 Squadron based at RAF Debden.

The squadron had returned from Northern France where they played their role in fending off the German attacks and in doing so, help the BEF and French troops to evacuate to the UK via Dunkirk. RAF Debden was being used primarily to help squadrons rebuild in readiness for further action and deployment as well as train the new recruits into their chosen profession within the RAF.

Royal Air Force Records: LAC Lamb L. B. – Service No. 1012281

At this time of crisis in the world, men of all creeds and nationalities were signing up to 'as they say' DO THEIR BIT for King and Country. Having gone through the basic training it was now time for getting ready for deployment to North Africa. It is unquestionably extremely difficult to contemplate, even understand what thoughts were going through his head and all those like him that had signed up. There must certainly have been elements of fear of the unknown, in trepidation of what they were letting themselves in for. Particularly when you are going off to foreign lands, leaving your loved ones behind not knowing if you/they would ever see them again?

Like most service men and women there were many that got married (prior to their departure's), going on the briefest of honeymoons, then a kiss and hugs before saying their final goodbyes. Please write to me and I will write back when I can. What their loved one's thought is also difficult to comprehend. Only that with God's HELP they will return to us one day, and hopefully in one piece. As we now know there were many that didn't and made the ultimate sacrifice. God Bless you all, thank you and RIP, duty served and completed.

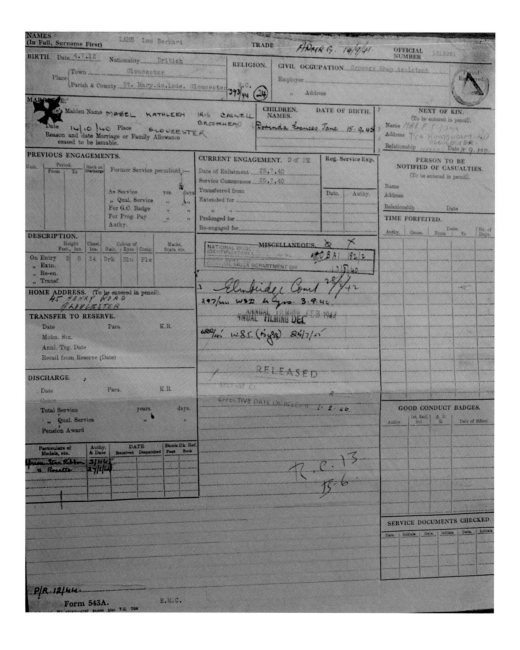

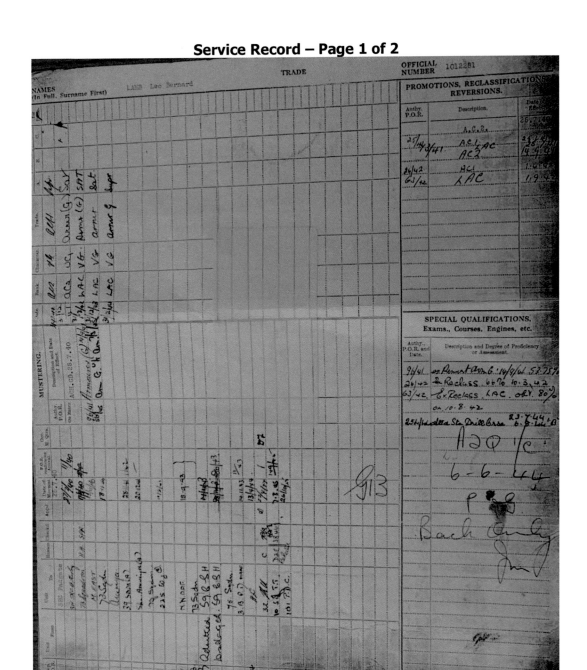

Footnote:

The above two (2) pages of my father's Service Record, whilst being a record of movements, etc of his service during World War 2, is not a fully complete record, as records were never fully updated during the war since communications were lost or misplaced. This is in no way a criticism of the staff collating the records of thousands of personnel, it was what it was.

From the official *Service Record Document - Form 543A,* Leo Bernard Lamb signed up to join the Royal Air Force on 25 May 1940. He was one of many who had decided that the time had come to give of their services for the war effort and stop the Germans come what may.

During the next two to three months and prior to deployment abroad it was a case of getting use to and coming to terms with the military way of life. To some if not most, a new and alien way of life. However, without this training and indoctrination one would not be able to survive, and this would be never more evident than when confronted with the vagaries of war. You were sent to train in readiness to fight for King and Country so that the world could be freed from the evil despot; namely, Hitler.

On completion of his training, L. B. Lamb – SN 1012281 was posted to RAF Debden where 73 Squadron was preparing to move abroad. Destination somewhere in the Middle East. The actual destination being known only to the Commanding Officers, the Allied Supreme Command, and the War Office.

The following Chapters of this book endeavour to give an insight in to what was experienced through the North African and Italian Campaigns looking the through the eyes of one man.

At the end of **World War II** those that survived and equally as important those who made the 'Ultimate Sacrifice' were awarded **British Campaign Medals** and my father was no exception and the Medals he received are detailed below.

<u>From left to right the Medals awarded are as follows</u>: -
- **The 1939-45 Star [Overseas war-service]**
- **The Africa Star [10 June 1940 to 12 May 1943]**
 & Clasp [North Africa 1942-43]
- **The Italy Star {11 June 1943 t0 8 May 1945**
- **The Defence Medal [Head of George VI]**
- **The 1939-45 War Medal [Crowned Head of George VI]**

Chapter 2

73 Squadron deployment from Great Britain to Alexandria (North Africa) – November 1940.

A. R.M.S. Franconia – Brief History:

S.S. Franconia (HMT Troop ship) 5 March 1927

The above Image has been provided by (Australian National Maritime Museum Image Ref: 0017492. Approval given by Inger Sheil – Assistant Curator via email dated 07/03/2022). Credit: Australian National Maritime Museum collection, gift from the Estate of Peter Britz. [There being NO Copyright Restrictions.]

S.S. Franconia was built in 1923 by John Brown Clydebank, Yard No. 492 and she was fitted with engines that were manufactured by the shipbuilder.

The ship was registered, as Port of Registry – Liverpool. Propulsion was by Steam Turbines, twin screws which gave 13500shp. The ship was launched on Saturday, 21 October 1922 and her primary role was as a Passenger Vessel sailing in the North Atlantic and cruising. The ship's size was as follows: - Tonnage: 20155grt, Length: 624 feet and Breadth: 73 feet.

In its life as a cruise ship the S. S. Franconia was owned by the following companies: -
- Cunard Steam-Ship Company, Liverpool
- 1934 Cunard-White Star Ltd., Liverpool
- 1950 Cunard Steam-Ship Co., Liverpool
- Status: Arrived for Scrapping on the 18 December 1956.

The Ministry of Defence [MOD] in September 1939 requisitioned the ship for the carrying of and transporting of troops to wherever they were needed, and the ship went through an extensive refit, which took place in Liverpool.

Having been requisitioned by the MOD and refitted one of the First Duty's that S.S. Franconia carried out was transporting troops to Malta and while travelling in convoy with the *Alcantara* and *Empress of Australia* was involved in a collision, which resulted in the Franconia having to undergo major repairs in Malta.

One of the next roles that S.S. Franconia carried out was to help in the evacuation of the British Expeditionary Force [BEF} from Dunkirk, Northern France during which she was damaged by air raids whilst carrying 8,000 troops. On completion of her repairs and throughout the remainder of the war, she continued as a troop ship, travelling to India via Cape Town and the Middle East. She assisted and took part in the invasions of Madagascar, North Africa, and Italy. With the USA joining in World War 2 [after the Japanese bombed the American Fleet at Pearl Harbour] she carried American troops from New York to the Mediterranean. From the time of her requisition in 1939 S.S. Franconia covered 319,784 nautical miles and carried 189,239 troops.

In late October 1940, RAF 73 Squadron were preparing for deployment to North Africa leaving RAF Debden on the 13 November 1940. On arrival at Birkenhead, Liverpool the troops and airmen who had amassed on the quayside, got orders to board the SS Franconia in readiness to set sail and join the convoy heading for Gibraltar, and then onto Alexandria, Egypt.

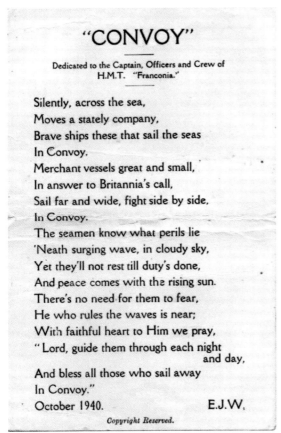

HMT Franconia 'Handed Out' on board

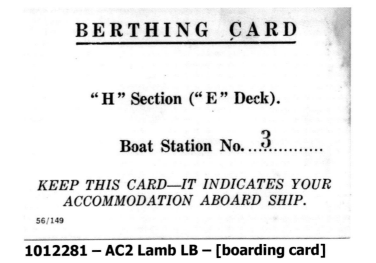

1012281 – AC2 Lamb LB – [boarding card]

As previously stated, the S.S. Franconia now fully laden with troops and RAF personnel set sale to join up with the convoy heading for the Middle East of which HMS Manchester was part of that convoy.

B. HMS Manchester:

HMS Manchester (C15) 1942.jpg
The above Image taken prior to 1 June 1957 and is in the Public Domain.
HMSO has declared that the expiry of Crown Copyrights applies Worldwide.

The Ships History:
HMS Manchester was built and manufactured by Hawthorn Leslie at their Hebburn shipyard with her keel laid down on 28 March 1936. She was launched on the 12 April 1937 and commissioned on the 4 August 1938. The ship came to a sorry end when she was scuttled [after being torpedoed by 2 by Italian MAS – motor torpedo boats] on the 13 April 1942 off Cap Bon, Tunisia.

The Ships General Characteristics:
Class & Type: Town Class – Light Cruiser
Displacement: 11,930 tons **full load**
Length: 591 ft 6 in
Beam: 64 ft 9 in
Draught: 20 ft 6 in
Propulsion:
- Four-shaft Parsons geared turbines
- Four Admiralty 3-drum boilers
- 82.500 shp (61.5 MW)

Speed: 32 knots

Range: 7,320 nmi at 13 kn (24 km/h)
Complement: 750 Officers and crew
Sensors & processing systems:
- Type 279 air warning radar
- Type 273 surface warning radar
- Type 284 fire control radar
- Type 285 fire control radar.

Armament: Original configuration:
- 12 x 6-inch Mk XXIII guns in triple turrets (4 x 3)
- 8 x 4-inch Mk XVI guns (4 x 2)
- 8 x 0.50-inch AA machine guns
- 6 x 21-inch torpedo tubes (2 x 3) deck mounted, later removed

Aircraft carried:
- Two Supermarine Walrus aircraft
- 1 Catapult (Removed in the latter part of WWII)
- Aircraft fitted with British 0.303 Vickers K gun, which could fire 950 rounds per minute

Pennant No.: C15

Battle Honours: Norway 1940 – Spartivento 1940 – Arctic 1942 – Malta Convoys 1942

Supermarine Walrus I General Statistics:

Engine: Bristol Pegasus VI radial engine
Power: 750 hp
Crew: Four
Wingspan: 45 ft 10 in
Length: 37 ft 3 in
Height: 15 ft 3 in
Maximum Speed: 135 mph
Service Ceiling: 17,100 ft to 18,500 ft
Maximum Range: 600 miles
Armament: 1 x 0.303 in Vickers K gun in the nose, and 1 or 2 K guns in the beam positions
Bomb Load: 600 lb of bombs or 2 Mk VIII depth charges

The Vickers K also known as the GO or VGO, was a gas operated light machine gun and was fed from a 100-round double-row pan magazine. The design of the K gun was based on the Vickers-Berthier infantry machine gun and replaced the outdated Lewis of the First World War. The gun being mounted in flexible mounts as the fixed version was unsuccessful, it also had an inferior rate of fire to that of the 0.303 Browning, which was used as a fixed gun in British Aircraft of the day.

HMS Manchester was fitted with Supermarine Walrus aircraft, which were launched from the ship using a catapult system. The system was installed near mid-ships on the ship and was set to launch on the Port Side of the ship. When required the aircraft would be launched, carry out their patrol and then return to the ship. After carrying out reconnaissance flights the aircraft would return to the ship and land on the sea from where they would be hooked up and winched aboard and placed back onto the launching gear in readiness for its next mission.

The Supermarine Walrus very rarely carried out the role it had been designed for – 'spotting' falling shells during a naval engagement. During the sea battle at Cape Spartivento 27 November 1940, the aircraft from *HMS Renown and HMS Manchester* were used as spotter aircraft, and that on 29 November 1940 *HMS Gloucester* were used as spotter aircraft at the sea battle at Cape Matapan. With the combination of the presence of carrier borne aircraft and the development of 'radar', spotter aircraft like the Walrus were not needed and phased out.

73 Squadron Mobilization:

From records sourced the transport ship SS Franconia on arriving at Gibraltar 13 November 1940, transferred the RAF personnel onto HMS Manchester, of which my father was one. HMS Manchester had orders to transport the RAF personnel to Alexandria, Egypt. As my father was an armourer/gunner fitter it is quite conceivable that his training was put to good use during the voyage on maintaining the Walrus guns.

Name Unknown – Photo taken on board HMS Manchester during convoy to North Africa.

During the voyage to Alexandria HMS Manchester received orders to join with other ships of the fleet to engage and attack the Italian fleet. The **Battle of Cape Spartivento** otherwise known as **the Battle of Cape Teulada** in Italy on 27 November 1940. The sea battle was brought about because the Italian fleet along with the Germans were constantly attacking the British Convoys, which were taking supplies of all kinds to Malta, which was under siege.

The two opposing fleets were made up of the following: -

Commanders and Leaders

British Fleet – James Somerville   **Italian Fleet** – Inigo Campioni

Strength

British	Italian
1 Carrier	2 Battleships
1 Battleship	6 Heavy cruisers
1 Battlecruiser	14 Destroyers
1 Heavy cruiser	
5 Light cruisers	
1 Anti-Aircraft Cruiser	
14 Destroyers	
4 Corvettes	
4 Freighters	

Casualties and losses

British	Italian
7 Killed	1 Destroyer damaged
1 Heavy cruiser damaged	1 Heavy cruiser slightly damaged
1 Light cruiser slightly damaged	

The ensuing sea battle like all the battles [sea or on land] have all been well recorded and like the Battle of Cape Spartivento is one of many that can be attributed to those who took part and moreover to commemorate those who gave of their life. There are many sources for research into the sea battle and it is not intended to elaborate or expand any more than is necessary other than record my father's attendance and receipt of his Certificate.

For those present at the battle and in whatever capacity, all received certificates to commemorate the battle that had taken place. My father received his all signed by Captain H.A. Packer, Royal Navy. A copy of his certificate is set out below.

Certificate: 1012281 – L. B. Lamb (AC2)

C. Sequence of Events during Transportation from Great Britain to Alexandria, Egypt

From records researched, HMS Manchester along with SS Franconia along with other ships of the convoy to Gibraltar and then onto Egypt

Year – 1940: Actions/operations undertaken by HMS Manchester - November through to December.

November:
Nominated for service in Mediterranean to reinforce the Fleet at Alexandria after Italy entered the war.
15th Took passage to join Mediterranean Fleet and carried troops to Malta. Destroyers JAGUAR and KELVIN provided escort for passage to Gibraltar
23rd Escorted Malta convoy of three merchant ships to Gibraltar with HMS SOUTHAMPTON as Force F (Operation COLLAR).
25th Met up with HMS RENOWN, HMS ARK ROYAL, HMS SHEFFIELD, and destroyers of Force H off Gibraltar to cover passage to Malta and for the return of HMS RAMILLIES and HM Cruiser BERWICK from Alexandria to Gibraltar.
27th Took part in engagement at long range with two Italian battleships and six cruisers with escorts, which all withdrew (Battle of Cape Spartivento).

(Note: Vice Admiral Sir James Somerville's decision not to pursue the enemy ships but to safeguard the convoy was the subject of a Board of Enquiry which found in his favour. For details see Naval Staff History HMSO – 2002).

28th Disembarked troops in Malta and went to Alexandria with Mediterranean Fleet.

30th HMS Manchester arrived in Alexandria and the ground crew of 73 Squadron disembark and move to RAF Heliopolis, Egypt

December:

2nd Passage to Gibraltar

8th Passage from Gibraltar escorted by HM Destroyers KASHMIR, KELVIN, JERSEY and JUPITER.

11th Arrived at Plymouth and took passage to Scapa Flow.

13th Re-joined Horns Fleet at Scapa Flow.

As for the RAF Pilots and the Hurricanes of 73 Squadron *[refer to Chapter 3]* for further details. These were being transported on the Aircraft Carrier HMS Furious and taken to the British Gold Coast (now Ghana). They arrived on the 27 November 1940 *[uncannily the very day on which the Battle of Spartivento took place]*.

The pilots and aircraft were unloaded and taken to RAF Takoradi where they were made ready to fly across Africa to Heliopolis, Egypt. Refer to Chapter 3 for further details.

HMS Manchester – Ship's Log's for November and December 1940

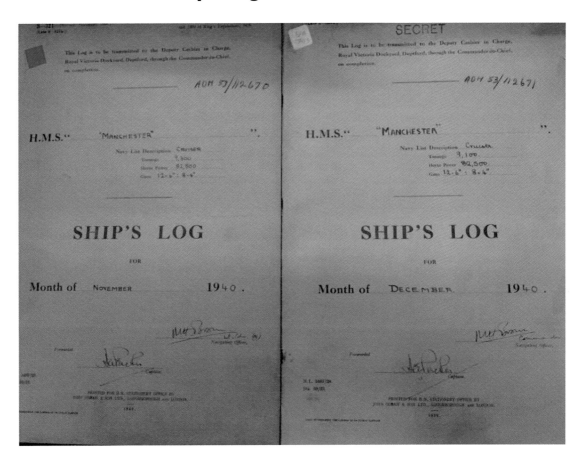

Extracts from HMS Manchester Ship's Log – November 1940

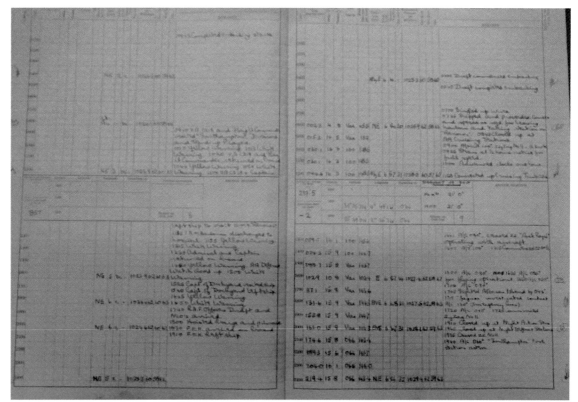

24 & 25 November 1940

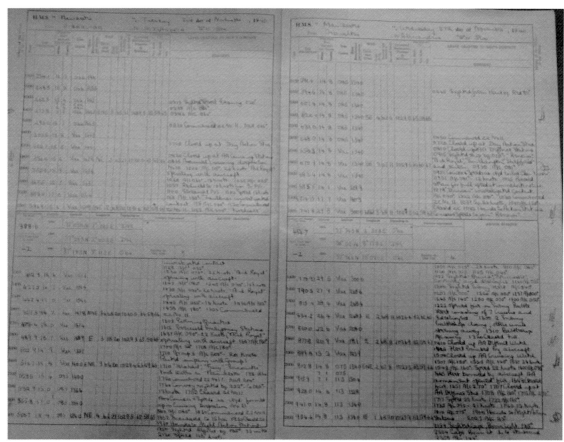

26 & 27 November 1940

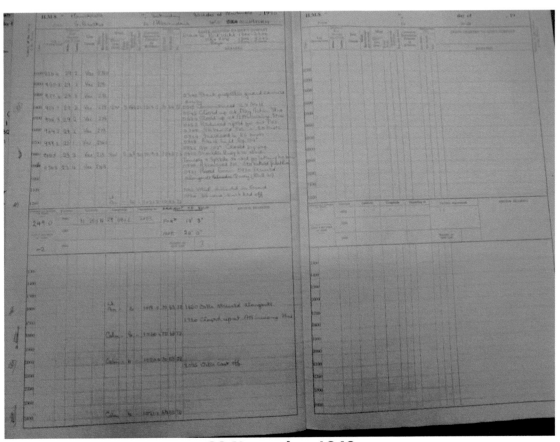

28 & 29 November 1940

30 November 1940

H.M.S. " Manchester ", Saturday 30th day of November, 1940

From G. Gibraltar To Alexandria ...11 ALEXANDRIA

Time	Log (Patent type) Miles	Tenths	True Course	Mean Revolutions per minute	Wind Direction (true)	Force (0-12)	Weather and Visibility	Sea and Swell	Corrected Barometric Pressure in Millibars	Dry Bulb	Wet Bulb	Sea	REMARKS
0100	826.4	29	2	Var	278								
0200	850.2	29	2	Var	278								
0300	877.6	29	2	Var	278								0340 Starb. propeller guard carried away.
0400	901.7	29	2	Var	278	SW	3	8662		1014.5	70	64	72	0315 Commenced Z.Z No.11 0545 Closed up at Day Action Stns
0500	935.3	29	2	Var	278									0650 Closed up at A.A Cruising Stns. 0850 Reduced speed for out P.V's
0600	964.2	29	2	Var	278									0700 Streamed P.V's - 20 Knots. 0714 Increased to 25 Knots
0700	989.2	25	1	Var	284									0818 Ras el Tin Lt. bg. 104° 0825 A/c 102° Ceased zig-zag.
0800	010.5	23	3	Var	215	SW	2	b8	30	1019.3	70	63	73	0830 Shoulder Buoy to stb. Courses & Speeds as reqd. for entering harbour
0945	036.3	23	4	Var	216									0900 Recovered P.V's 0911 Inhaul Breakwater 0921 Passed Boom. 0950 Secured
1000														alongside Mohammedieh Quay (Brth 41).
100														1010 V.A.L.F arrived on board. 1020 D.B coils switched off.
200						Lt. Air	-	bc	-	1021.2	70	63	73	

Enlarged extract from 30 November 1940

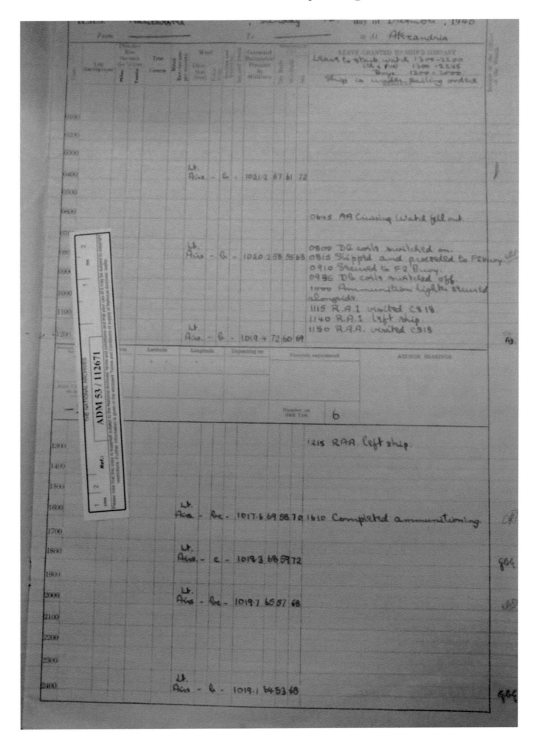

1 December 1940

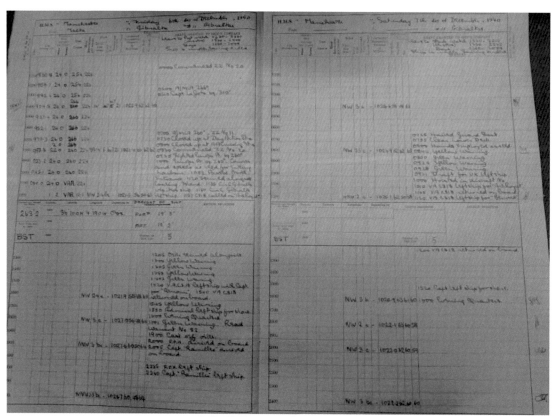

2 & 3 December 1940

6 & 7 December 1940
Note: Contains public sector information licensed under the Open Government Licence v3.0

Chapter 3

A. HMS Furious:

HMS Furious
[The aircraft shown towards the aft of the ship are 4 Hurricanes]
The above Image was taken prior to 1 June 1957 and is in the Public Domain.
HMSO has declared that the expiry of Crown Copyrights applies Worldwide.

HMS Furious as the ship was to be named was built by Armstrong Whitworth, Wallsend with her keel being laid down on 8 June 1915. She was to be of the Class Type *Courageous-class battlecruiser* and was launched on 15 August 1916 and commissioned on 26 June 1917.

General characteristics are as follows: -

Displacement: 19,513 long tons 'normal' and 22,890 long tons 'deep load'
Length: 786 ft 9 in, Beam: 88 ft, Draught: 24 ft 11 in, Speed: 31.5 knots and Penant Number 47 with the ship's motto being ***Ministrat arma furor,* "Fury supplies arms".**
The design of the ship included 18 Yarrow boilers, which produced 90,000 shp (67.113 kw). The propulsion was through 4 shafts: 4 geared steam turbines. The ship had a compliment of 737 officers and ratings.
The ship had been originally designed to support the Baltic Project and championed by the First Sea Lord of the Admiralty, Lord Fisher. The ship was very lightly armoured and designed with a main battery of only two 18-inch guns.

After a major refit/conversion, the ship in September 1925 *[still under the name of HMS Furious]* was reclassified as an aircraft carrier. The ship was now fitted with a continuous flight deck size of which was 576 ft long x 92 ft wide, over three-quarters of her length. The deck itself was not flat but tilted upwards aft to fore, which allowed the landing aircraft to slow down.

General revised characteristics are as follows: -

Displacement: 22,500 long tons and 26,500 long tons 'deep load'
Length: 786 ft 9 in, Beam: 88 ft, Draught: 27 ft 3 in, Speed: 30 knots, Range: 7,480 nmi; with a ships Compliment of 795 (1939) Officers and ratings. The ship also carried 36 aircraft, primarily for the use to keep the ship safe.

After her conversion the ship was used extensively for trials of naval aircraft and later as a training carrier. In the early period of WW2, the carrier spent time hunting German raiders in the North Atlantic along with escorting convoys.

This changed dramatically in 1940 with the first of what would be numerous aircraft ferry missions, one of which was to redeploy 73 Squadrons Hurricane aircraft (some 55 initially) along with their pilots. Some of the aircraft were in crates (in kit form) and some already constructed and ready to fly off once they arrived at their destination. On this occasion the destination being RAF Takoradi – Africa's Gold Coast.

In later months HMS Furious would transport further Hurricanes to RAF Takoradi, which were very much needed to help fight the German/Italian Axis Forces in North Africa.

B. RAF Takoradi:

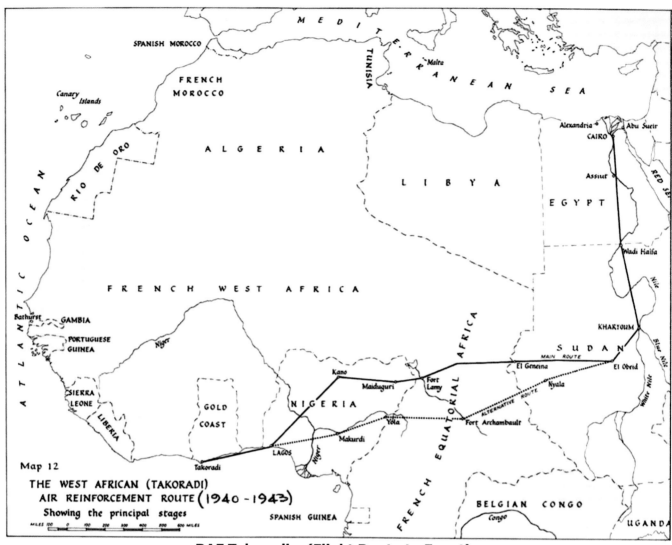

RAF Takoradi – (Flight Route to Egypt)
No known Copyright Restrictions found.

During 1940 the Prime Minister – Winston Churchill and his military advisers turned to an underdeveloped, 3,700-mile air route from Takoradi in the British colony of the Gold Coast (now Ghana) to Cairo, Egypt. The route would allow both fighter and bomber aircraft to be transported to Takoradi.

On the 14 July 1940 a Royal Air Force advance party of twenty-four officers and men arrived at Takoradi. The group being led by Group Captain H. K. Thorold, who, after his experiences as Maintenance Officer-in-Chief to the British Air Force in France was unlikely to be dismayed by any difficulties in Africa.

Thorold was quick to confirm that Takoradi was a fine selection as a base. The advance party were set to work building the necessary facilities such as roads, gantries, hangars, workshops, storehouses, offices and living accommodation. These activities were not confined to the port and Thorold was then charged to turn the primitive landing-grounds into efficient staging posts and perfecting wireless communication along the whole route. Wireless communication would become a very useful tool along the 3,600-mile route.

By now French Equatorial Africa had joined de Gaulle, and that the pilots had the consolation of knowing that they were flying all the way over territory, which diplomatically was well disposed.

As the starting point of the Allied trans-African supply line to Egypt the route became known as the West African Reinforcement Route (WARR).

RAF Takoradi was one of the most important bases for the RAF and on 5 September 1940 the first shipment of Hurricanes and Bristol Blenheim (light bomber) aircraft were delivered in crates. The crates would be unloaded, and aircraft parts unpacked, assembled, and made airworthy for their flight to Cairo.
As previously stated, the journey was over 3,700 miles and would take six days to complete, which allowed time to rest as well as refuelling. A pilot at the time, Nelson Gilboe described Takoradi assembly plant *'as cut out of dense forest with monkeys playing in nearby trees.'*

Each flight of Hurricanes flying from Takoradi to Cairo would be escorted by the Bristol Blenheim's. The journey was plagued with problems, in the Sahara Desert portion of the route, sand would take a severe toll on the aircraft engines. There were no maps of the route, and many pilots used ominously burned-out aircraft on the ground as their guide.

Despite the challenges, between August 1940 and June 1943, over 4,500 Bristol Blenheim's, Hurricanes, and Spitfires were assembled at Takoradi and ferried to the Middle East via this same route.

The flight route across Africa would take in Lagos, Oshogbo, Kano, Maiduguri, Fort-Lamy, El Geneina, Khartoum, Wadi Halfa then to Cairo.

From the tiny point in Western Africa, they leaped to the first staging post at Lagos, 380 miles away. From Lagos, Nigeria to Kano over dense jungle [still in Nigeria] 520 miles over equatorial forest. Between Kano and El Geneina, already in Sudanese barren desert plains some 960 miles with refuelling stops at Maiduguri in the heart of Africa, El Fasher, El Obeid, on the long way this time facing typical sandstorms of East Central Africa, until reaching Khartoum the Sudanese capital.

The journey proceeded, this time along the majestic sinuous Nile River 520 miles through strategic refuelling points at Sueir, and stretching out 560 miles to Wadi Haifa, Luxor and finally after five days over the perilous jungle and thunderstorms of Equatorial Africa, barren and desolate landscapes of the semi deserted southern Sudan, then came in sight, the greatness of the Pyramid, the historical intriguing city of Cairo, the outpost of Middle East Command.

Whilst Takoradi was in the first instance used as the main starting point for flights from Takoradi to Cairo, Egypt; other routes were also planned and opened and put quickly into operation across Africa to maintain a constant delivery of aircraft and stores to the front line, as supplies of both were dwindling due to the continued fighting being carried out across North Africa.

Takoradi route was one gigantic ferry flight operation in WWII. More than 5,000 aircraft of several different types were ferried across that route from 1940 to 1943.

The RAF set up recovery teams *[especially skilled group of engineers and technicians to recover crashed aircraft]* along the route. These teams would use specially designed tractors and trailers, which became precious tools in the hands of those men.

Many aircraft crashed due to mechanical problems or simply running out of fuel due to the difficulty in locating their next staging post. Of those aircraft that crashed *(and there were many)* they were spotted and, as soon as they were, the specialist team of engineers was sent out to recover both aircraft and hopefully its pilot. *[Pilots too were in short supply.]*

Despite the state of any aircraft found, they were dismantled and once recovered all aircraft parts were sent back to the nearest RAF Maintenance Team situated along the flight route, and there the aircraft parts would be reassembled to make one aircraft ready to fly again.
[The RAF, at this time, were in such severe shortages of supplies and parts that engineers were required to use parts from several aircraft to build a new serviceable one.]

The above actions were also to be played out on the front line where the fighting was taking place, and any/all spare parts that could be salvaged were used on aircraft to ensure that the aircraft were kept flying.

Chapter 4

73 SQUADRON & 39 SQUADRON - THEIR RECORDED HISTORY.

Before delving into the campaign that was being fought in North Africa during the Second World War, we must firstly look back through the origin and history of the squadrons; 73 Squadron and 39 Squadron themselves.

A: 73 SQUADRON:

73 Squadron was formed at Upavon, Wiltshire on 1st July 1917 as 73 Squadron R. F. C. and was to be primarily a fighter unit. In January 1918, 73 Squadron was equipped with Sopwith Camels and once operational was moved to France to fight on the Western Front during the First World War. During this period, the squadron flew fighter patrols and bomber escort missions over the Western Front. In March 1918, the German offensive resulted in the squadron undertaking large numbers of ground attack sorties *(in support of the Tank Corps)* and during the final Allied attack was engaged in low-level flying sorties to give as much needed air support for the armoured forces. This continued until the end of the war in 1919. In February 1919, the squadron returned home, and, on the 2nd of July 1919, the squadron was formerly disbanded.

After almost two decades the squadron was reformed. This was mainly in response to the growing concern as to what was happening in Eastern Europe. The squadron was reformed on 15th March 1937 at Mildenhall, again as a fighter squadron, flying the Hawker Fury. In June of that same year the Hawker Fury's were to be replaced with Gladiators, which were then flown until conversion to Hurricanes, in July 1938.

In September 1939 No.73 was one of two Hurricane squadrons that moved to France with the Advanced Air Striking Force. After months of inconclusive action, the storm broke in May 1940, and the squadron was soon involved in desperate battles over Allied airfields. The squadrons prime position was to protect the Allied airfields. During the German attack in May 1940 the squadron helped to cover the Allied airfields and bases; and gradually falling back as the Allied airfields were being overrun by the advancing German forces. On the 18th of June 1940, the squadron was finally forced to retreat, back to Britain.

Having retired back to England on 18th June 1940, the squadron was immediately involved in preventing (like so many other squadrons at the time) the Germans advancing over the Channel and was instrumental in undertaking and carrying out night-time fighting during the 'Battle of Britain'.

In this early period of the war the squadron were fortunate to have the services of Flying Officer E. J. 'Cobber' Kain, the famous New Zealand 'Ace', among its members. Unfortunately, he lost his life in an air accident. A great loss to all. During the Battle of Britain, the RAF were seriously short of suitable night fighters. To fill the gap, No.73 Squadron now based at RAF Debden from 5th September 1940 used its Hurricanes at night, but single seat non-radar equipped fighters made very poor night fighters, and this experiment ended on 20th October 1940, in preparation for a move to the Middle East.

After operating as a night fighter squadron during the Battle of Britain, from 5th September to 20th October 1940, 73 Squadron was to be made ready for their planned move to the Middle East, which would see them take part in the campaigns in North Africa, in Italy and in Greece, before ending the war in the Balkans.

On the 20th of October 1940, the operations that had been entrusted to the squadron, ceased. This was to allow the squadron the time to prepare for transfer to the Middle East.

At this time no direct air route was open through the Mediterranean to North Africa, which meant that the squadrons hurricanes and pilots were shipped to 'TAKORADI' on the Gold Coast. On completion of the preparations in readiness for transfer, the Hurricanes and Pilots of 73 Squadron were transported by the carrier 'HMS FURIOUS' to Takoradi on the African Gold Coast and once unloaded the squadrons Hurricanes were then flown across North Africa to Egypt where they were to be re-joined with their ground crew. The ground crew were transported on RMT Franconia to Gibraltar and then transferred to HMS Manchester, who would then transport the ground crew to Alexandria. During the voyage to Alexandria, HMS Manchester was ordered, along with other ships of the convoy ships to take part in a sea battle with the Italian Navy off Cape Spartivento, Sardinia. A battle that saw the allied forces sinking some of the Italian Fleet, with the remainder of the Italian Fleet heading back to port.

Once in North Africa the squadron took part in the entire campaign in the Western Desert, Tunisia and the eastern Desert, helping cover the supply routes to Tobruk and taking part in the development of highly effective ground-attack methods during the later stages of the fighting.

The main duties of the squadron during its period of stay in North Africa, was to provide defensive patrols over shipping on the supply route to Tobruk. Night patrols and ground-attack missions occupied the squadrons Hurricanes throughout the campaign in the Western Desert and Tunisia. Whilst based in North Africa the 73 Squadron converted from Hurricanes to Spitfires in June 1943, and in October of that same year they were moved to Italy where their role was to provide, once again, defensive patrols for shipping, etc.

In April 1944, they officially became a fighter-bomber unit, and began to operate over the Balkans, at first from bases in Italy.

In December 1944 part of the squadron was moved to Greece to take part in the fighting against the Communist resistance group that was attempting to seize power. In January 1945, they returned to Italy, before in April 1945 moving on to Yugoslavia, where it remained until the end of the war.

Aircraft of 73 Squadron – 1938 to 1947:

July 1938 – January 1942:	Hawker Hurricane I
September – November 1941:	Curtiss Tomahawk IIB
December 1941 – June 1942:	Hawker Hurricane IIA and IIB
June 1942 – July 1943:	Hawker Hurricane IIC
June 1943 – October 1944	Supermarine Spitfire VC
July – November 1944:	Supermarine Spitfire VIII
October 1943 – November 1947	Supermarine Spitfire IX

Location of 73 Squadron 1937 to 1945:

November 1937 – September 1939:	Digby
September 1939:	Le Havre/Octeville
September – October 1939:	Norrent Fontes
October 1939 – April 1940:	Rouvres
April 1940:	Reims/Champagne
April – May 1940:	Rouvres
May 1940:	Reims/Champagne
May 1940:	Rouvres
May 1940:	Reims/Champagne
May 1940:	Villeneuve-les-Vertus
May – June 1940:	Gaye
June 1940:	Echemines
June 1940:	Raudin
June 1940:	Nantes
June – September 1940:	Church Fenton
September – November 1940	Castle Camps
November – December 1940:	Takoradi
December 1940:	Heliopolis
December 1940 – January 1941	Sidi Haneish
January – March 1941:	Gazala West
March – April 1941:	Bu Amud
April 1941:	El Gubbi
April – September 1941:	Sid Haneish
September 1941:	Amriya
September 1941 – February 1942	Port Said / Gamil
October – December 1941:	Detachment to Kilo 8
December 1941 – April 1942	Detachment to Shandur
February 1942:	El Adem
February 1942:	Gasr-el-Arid
February 1942:	Gambut II
February – March 1942:	Gasr-el-Arid
March – April 1942:	Gambut I
April – May 1942:	Gambut Main
May 1942:	El Adem
May – June 1942:	Gambut Main
June 1942:	LG.115
June 1942:	LG.76
June 1942:	Qasaba
June 1942:	El Daba
June – July 1942:	Burg-el-Arab
July 1942:	LG.89
July 1942:	El Ballah
July – August 1942:	Shandur
August – November 1942:	LG.85
November 1942:	LG.21
November 1942:	LG.13
November 1942:	LG.155
November 1942:	Gambut West
November 1942:	El Adem

November 1942:	El Magrum
November 1942 – January 1943:	Merduma
January 1943:	Alemel Chel
January 1943:	Tamet
January – February 1943:	Bir Dufan
February 1943:	Gasr Garabulli
February – March 1943:	El Assa
March – April 1943:	Nefatia South
April 1943:	Gabes Main
April 1943:	Sfax / El Maoui
April 1943:	Kairouan / Alem
April 1943:	Monastir
April – October 1943:	La Seballa II
October – December 1943:	Montecorvino
December 1943 – September 1944:	Foggia Main
September 1944 – April 1945:	Canne
September – December 1944	Detachment to Hassani
April – May 1945:	Prkos
May – July 1945:	Brindisi

Squadron Codes: TP, R, P, E, C

Duty:
Fighter Squadron, Advanced Air Strike Force: 1939 - 1940
Fighter Command: 1940
Fighter Squadron, North Africa: 1940 - 1943
Fighter Squadron, Italy, and the Balkans: 1943 – 1945

Due to the Communists attempt to control Greece (in the wake of the German evacuation and withdrawal), a large detachment from 73 Squadron (December 1944) was sent to assist the then Government of Greece from being overthrown by the Communists. Having completed their assigned duties, the squadron eventually returned to Italy at the end of January 1945.

In April 1945, they mainly operated from Yugoslavian soil until the end of the war, and in July 1945 they moved to Malta.

Summary of Research:

From the diaries and records kept by *Lamb L. B. - Service No. 1012281*, it is possible to follow his trail, not only throughout the North African campaign but also the Italy campaign during the period of the war 1940-1944.

From the additional research material available, further, and better details have emerged when looking through the National Archives records for 73 Squadron, 39 Squadron under RAF Records AIR 27, and Naval 'Ship Logs' Records, which are kept at Kew Gardens. In addition to these are the records held at RAF Headquarters Air Command, RAF Disclosures, RAF St Athan (now MOD St Athan), Ministry of Defence, the book – The History of 73 Squadron Parts 1, 2 and 3 – written by Don Minterne, RAF Museums, Public Records Office, and Library's all of which have helped to provide the picture and the story told.

Summary of Historic Background of 73 Squadron:

As a footnote, and to complete the historic background of 73 Squadron it is necessary to establish the outcome of the squadron itself. As previously stated, the squadron moved to and was based in Malta. From the base in Malta, they were then transferred to Cyprus, where they converted in preparation to receive and fly Vampires. The change over from Spitfires to Vampires took place between September and October 1948.

They retained the use of Vampires for the next six (6) years, and it was not until December 1954 that Venoms replaced these. (The actual introduction of the Venom FB.1 started in November 1954).

In March 1957, they converted over to flying Canberra's and these were flown right up to the time of the squadron's eventual disbandment, which took place in Cyprus on the 3rd of February 1969.

RECORD OF PLANES OPERATED DURING THE - FIRST & SECOND WORLD WARS AND IN PEACE TIME.
73 SQUADRON

Aircraft Equipment:	Period of Service:	Representative Serial:
Sopwith Camel	July 1917-Feb 1919	D8164
(Squadron disbanded; 2nd July 1919)		
Hawker Fury II	May 1937-July 1937	K8277
Gladiator I	June 1937-July 1938	K7965
Hawker Hurricane I	July 1938-Jan 1942	N2358 (Z)
Curtiss Tomahawk IIB	Sept 1941-Nov1941	AN301
Hawker Hurricane IIA, IIB	Dec 1941-June1942	BD930 (R)
Hawker Hurricane IIC	June 1942-July 1943	BN131 (P)
Supermarine Spitfire VC	June 1943-Oct 1944	JK991 (E)
Supermarine Spitfire VIII	July 1944-Nov 1944	JF560
Supermarine Spitfire IX	Oct 1943-Nov 1947	MA630 (C)
Supermarine Spitfire F.22	Nov 1947-Oct 1948	PK518 (F)
Vampire F.3	Aug 1948-April 1950	VT855 (B)
Vampire FB.5	April 1950-May 1953	VZ318 (R)
Vampire FB.9	Nov 1951-Dec 1954	WR214(K)
Venom FB.1	Nov 1954-March 1957	WR314(W)
Canberra B.2	March 1957-Aug 1962	WD988
Canberra B.15	June 1962-Feb 1969	WH977

(Squadron disbanded; 3rd February 1969)

Brief History of 73 Squadron:

On 15 March 1937 73 Squadron reformed and was equipped with Hawker Fury's, they then relocated to RAF Digby and were then re-equipped with Gloster Gladiators before later being equipped with Hawker Hurricanes.

At the breakout of World War 2, 73 Squadron along with No. 1 Squadron were deployed to North-East France as part of an advanced RAF Air Striking Force. In the early stages of the conflict the squadron controlled the Cherbourg Peninsula and in October 1939 moved to Rouvres. At this time in the history of 73 Squadron the squadron was blessed with some amazing, outstanding pilots. To name but two; F/O E. J. 'Cobber' Kain, who unfortunately was killed in a flying accident on 7 June 1940. Another 'ace' at the time was F/O Newell 'Fanny' Orton.

After the German air attacks on 10 May 1940 the squadron were set the task to provide cover over Allied airfields and bases and by the 17 June 1940 the squadron had withdrawn from France. During the evacuation the squadron lost 40 ground crew when RMS Lancastria was sunk off the coast of St. Nazaire.

During the Battle of Britain 73 Squadron had been redeployed to RAF Debden and from 5 September until late October 1940 the squadron regrouped and refitted in readiness for a deployment to the Middle East.

The squadron's orders came through that they were being deployed to North Africa – Heliopolis, Egypt and in November 1940 the ground crew were taken to Birkenhead, Liverpool where they embarked-on SS Franconia *(Refer to Chapter 2)* in readiness for sailing to Gibraltar. A stopping point in the Mediterranean. The squadrons Pilots and aircraft were to be transported on HMS Furious *(Refer to Chapter 3)*, to RAF Takoradi *(Refer to Chapter 3)*.

On arrival at Gibraltar the squadrons ground crew were transferred onto HMS Manchester for the remainder of their journey to Alexandria, Egypt. It was during their voyage to Egypt that HMS Manchester was given orders to join the fleet being prepared to fight the Italian Navy at Cape Spartivento *(Refer to Chapter 2)*.

The squadron took part in the series of campaigns in the Western Desert and Tunisia, helping cover supply routes to Tobruk and taking part in ground-attack operations. December 1942 saw the squadron record their 300th victory when F/S Beard shot down a JU88 over the sea of Benghazi. In addition to Tobruk the squadron also provided cover and ground-attack during the battles at El Alamein. One of the most important battles of the war in North Africa, and one that the Axis Forces would not recover from.

In June 1943 the squadron converted to Spitfire and in late September early October 1943 were posted to Italy, landing at Salerno. On landing the squadron would be deployed to one of the captured Italian airfields near Foggia (Foggia Main).

Not only were the squadron providing cover and ground-attack during the Italy campaign, they also, in April 1944 began operating over the Balkans, in a fighter-bomber role. In December 1944 a proportion of the squadron were deployed to Greece to assist in fighting the Communist resistance attempting to seize power. In January 1945, the squadron returned to Italy and in April moved to Yugoslavia, where it remained until the end of the war moving to Malta in July 1945. Initially near Hal Far, the squadron soon moved to Takali.

B: 39 SQUADRON:

The inclusion of 39 Squadron in the telling of my father's memoirs is that on the 28 November 1941 he was sent on detachment to the Squadron, which saw them move to Amriya on the 20 December 1941 until his redeployment back to 73 squadron on or around January 1942.

39 Squadron was formed at Hounslow on 15 April 1916, as a home defence unit. Flights of B.E.s were detached to Suttons Farm, Hornchurch, and nearby Hainault Farm to guard the eastern approaches to London and in August of that year the squadron headquarters were moved to Woodford, Essex and a further detachment was based at North Weald. When the Germans supplemented their *Zeppelin* attacks by formations of Gotha bombers, the squadron replaced its inadequate B.E.s with Bristol Fighters and in November 1918 moved to France. Five days later the Armistice came, and the squadron was disbanded on 16 November 1918.

On 1 July 1919, 37 Squadron at Biggin Hill was renumbered 39 Squadron and remained a cadre until moved to RAF Spitalgate in February 1923 to be equipped with D.H.9As as a day bomber unit.
In December 1928, the squadron left for India and began patrol duties on the North-West Frontier with Wapiti in February 1929. Harts were received in November 1931 and were replaced by Blenheim's in August 1939 before the squadron moved to Singapore, shortly before the outbreak of World War II.

In April 1940, the squadron returned to India en-route for the Middle East but was diverted to Aden when Italy's entry into the war became imminent. Bombing raids were made on targets in Italian East Africa until November, when the squadron moved to Egypt.

Converting to Maryland's in January 1941, the squadron began strategic reconnaissance missions in April 1941. In August, some Bristol Beaufort's were received for anti-shipping operations, which began on 17 September but Maryland's continued reconnaissance flights until January 1942. Torpedo - bomber missions against enemy convoys were mounted from advanced bases in Egypt and Libya while a detachment was based in Malta. On 20 August 1942, this detachment joined others of 86 and 217 Squadron to become 39 Squadron, the residue of 39 in Egypt joining 47 Squadron.

Anti - shipping and mine laying operations with Bristol Beaufort's continued, until they were replaced by Bristol Beaufighter's in June 1943. Sorties ranged over the Central Mediterranean, first from North Africa and later from Sardinia. Night intruder missions over northern Italy supplemented shipping strikes along the French and Italian coasts and a move in July 1944 to Italy extended these activities to the Balkans but in December the squadron began to receive Marauders. Operations with these began on 7 February 1945 and in October 1945 39 Squadron moved to the Sudan where it began to re-equip with Mosquitoes. On the 8 of September 1946, the squadron disbanded.

On the 1st of April 1948, No. 39 Squadron reformed at Nairobi as a Tempest squadron but disbanded again on 28th February 1949. On the 1st of March 1949, the squadron was reformed at RAF Fayid with Mosquito night fighters for the defence of the Suez Canal. In March 1953, the squadron was re-equipped with Meteors and moved to Malta in January 1955, where it disbanded on 30 June 1958.

69 Squadron was renumbered 39 Squadron and, on the 1 July 1958, transferred to RAF Luqa, Malta. The squadron's Canberra's were engaged on photographic reconnaissance duties while attached to NATO until September 1970, when the squadron moved to the UK. On the 28 May 1983, the squadron was finally disbanded, and its tasks being taken over by No. 1 Photographic Reconnaissance Unit.

RECORD OF PLANES OPERATED DURING THE - FIRST & SECOND WORLD WARS AND IN PEACE TIME.

39 SQUADRON

Aircraft Equipment:	Period of Service:	Representative Serial:	
B.E.2c, B.E.2e	April 1916 - Sep 1917	B4482	
B.E.12, B.E.12a	Aug 1916 - Sep 1917	A6326	
Bristol F.2b	Sep 1917 - Nov 1918	B1350 (3)	
(Squadron disbanded; 16th November 1918)			
D.H.9A	Feb 1923 - Dec 1928	J7819 (5)	
Wapiti-IIA	Feb 1929 - Dec 1931	J9381 (4)	
Hart	Nov 1931 - Jul 1939	K2088 (1)	
Blenheim I	Aug 1939 - Jan 1941	L8387 (XZ-F)	
Blenheim IV	Dec 1940 - Jan 1941		
Maryland I	Jan 1941 - Jan 1942	AH214	
Beaufort I-II	Aug 1941 - Jun 1943	W6519 (Y)	
Beaufighter-X	Jun 1943 - Feb 1945	NT889 (F)	
Marauder-III	Dec 1944 - Sep 1946	HD607 (F)	
Mosquito-FB.26	Feb 1946 - Sep 1946	KA154	
(Squadron disbanded; 8th September 1946)			
Tempest-F.6	Jun 1948 - Feb 1949	NX284	
(Squadron disbanded; 28th February 1949)			
Mosquito-NF.36	Mar 1949 - Mar 1953	RI233 (G)	
Meteor-NF.13	Mar 1953 - Jun 1958	WM363	(H)
(Squadron disbanded; 30th June 1958)			
Canberra-PR.3	Jul 1958 - Nov 1962	WE144 (D)	
Canberra-PR.9	Oct 1962 - Jun 1982	XH171 (M)	
Canberra-PR.7	Oct 1970 - Mar 1972	WJ825	
(Squadron disbanded; 28th May 1983)			

Brief History of 39 Squadron:

The squadron after being disbanded in November 1918, was reformed in 1923, and in 1939 re-equipped with more modern Bristol Blenheim, twin-engine monoplane bombers. As the threat of war increased, it was decided to strengthen British defences in the Far East by moving 39 Squadron to Singapore. Nine Bristol Blenheim's from 39 Squadron setting off on 6 August 1939. The whole trip was a disaster, with six aircraft wrecked, and three men killed, which included Wing Commander Burton Ankers, commander of the 2nd Indian Wing Stationed at RAF Risalpur. His Bristol Blenheim had caught fire and crashed after being struck by lightning.

In April 1940 the squadron returned to India, *en-route* to the Middle East, but was diverted to Aden when Italy's entry into the war became imminent. [Then on 10 June 1940, after withholding formal allegiance to either side in the battle between Germany and the Allies, *Benito Mussolini* dictator of Italy, declares war on Great Britain and France.]

39 Squadron were quickly committed to action against Italian East Africa, carrying out its first combat mission of the war on 12 June 1940.

The squadron continued with their operations against the Italian forces until 24 November 1940, when it was ordered to transfer to Egypt to help support the planned offensive in the Western Desert (Operation Compass). The first aircraft left for Helwan on 29 November 1940. Whilst operating in the Western Desert detachments of the squadron Bristol Blenheim's operated with 45 and 11 Squadrons. [11 Squadron being deployed to Greece]. To replace its Bristol Blenheim IVs, 39 Squadron received Martin Maryland bombers, originally built for the French Air Force and the first RAF squadron to operate Maryland's.

The Maryland aircraft, having a long-range capability were used as reconnaissance aircraft by 39 Squadron, with the squadron being heavily deployed during the Battle of Crete. During this time the squadron claimed at least two Junkers Ju 52 transport aircraft shot down during its operations.

During August-September 1941, the squadron partly converted to the Bristol Beaufort torpedo bomber for anti-shipping operations. The squadron however still retained a flight of Maryland's until January 1942. In the early days of the Bristol Beaufort's joining 39 Squadron, they were armed with bombs but from January 1942 it added torpedo attack to its role. Prior to January 1942, in late 1941 the unit was split up with one flight moved to RAF Luga, Malta and then six months later this flight was combined with others from 86 and 217 squadrons to eventually form a new 39 Squadron.

In 1943, the now newly formed 39 Squadron re-equipped with Bristol Beaufighter aircraft and took on the role of ground attack and moved back to Egypt then onto Italy.

Whilst stationed in Egypt the squadrons' role took on more duties, namely, sending rocket-armed aircraft to participate in the RAF operations during the Greek Civil War. Then in December 1944 the squadron re-equipped with Martin Marauders, flying medium bombing missions in support of Tito's Partisans.

In 1946 the squadron once again were re-equipped, this time with de Havilland Mosquitos but disbanded later in the year.

Chapter 5

A. 73 SQUADRON LOCATIONS – World War 2

[Northern France]

Location:	Date:
Digby	November 1937 to September 1939
Le Havre / Octeville	September 1939
Norrent Fontes	September-October 1939
Rouvres	October 1939 to April 1940
Reims / Champagne	April 1940
Rouvres	April /to May 1940
Reims / Champagne	May 1940
Rouvres	May 1940
Villeneuve-les-Vertus	May 1940
Gaye	May to June 1940
Echemines	June 1940
Raudin	June 1940
Nantes	June 1940
Church Fenton	June to September 1940
Castle Camps	September to November 1940

B. NORTH AFRICA & ITALY – (November 1940 to January 1944.)

During the next four to five years the Squadron would be involved in many battles and would have to fight to retain their positions, retreat when ordered to, and then press forward again to recapture their previous positions. This would happen on numerous occasions and would be a cause for much frustration of the ground crews and troops.

When the order for retreat was given the groundcrew would have to destroy all serviceable equipment prior to retreating so that the enemy would not be able to use any of the equipment having to be left behind. *[This would also be the same scenario for the enemy]*

When supplies and spares were in short supply the ground crews would, wherever possible, strip their own damaged or lame aircraft plus captured enemy aircraft (where salvage was possible) and use or convert parts so that they could ensure that those planes capable of flying were kept flying.

Without the ingenuity of the ground crews at the time, many of the Royal Air Force 'Kites' as they were commonly known as would never have flown again. **(Wherever possible the enemy planes were stripped bare of all usable parts in readiness for use on any serviceable captured aircraft.)**

73 Squadron Movement Record:

[As prepared by Lamb L.B. - 1012281. End of December 1940 through to January 1944]

North Africa 1940 – 1941:
Location:

Heliopolis	to	Dekhala
(At Dekhala for Christmas with lads)		
Dekhala	to	Sidi Haneish
Sidi Haneish	to	L.2 Sollum
L.2 Sollum	to	Bu Amud
Bu Amud	to	Gazala
Gazala	to	El Adem
El Adem	to	Bu Amud
Bu Amud	to	Martuba
Martuba	to	Barce

Retreat.

Barce	to	Mechili
Mechili	to	Gazala - South
Gazala-South	to	Bu Amud
Bu Amud	to	Bir el Gubi - Tobruk

Remained in Tobruk during siege.
Left Tobruk by S.A.R.N.U.R., HMSAS Southern Isles.

Tobruk	to	Alexandria by sea.	28 May 1941
(Arrived at Alexandria, 30 May 1941.)			
Alexandria	to	Bir Hooker (Stayed for three days).	
Bir Hooker	to	Alexandria (Six days leave).	
Alexandria	to	Sidi Haneish	12 June1941.
Sidi Haneish	to	Gamil / Port Said	2 October 1942
Gamil	to	Amriya [From 28 November 1941 to January 1942]	

(On detachment to 39 Squadron; went flying in Maryland for three hours).

Amriya	to	Margut	
Margut	to	Amriya	
Amriya	to	Edku	
Edku	to	Amriya	

(Away for Christmas again; had Christmas with 53 RSU-Repair and Servicing Unit)

Amriya	to	El Gamil	
El Gamil	to	Gazala	
Gazala	to	Heliopolis	(By air, five hours flying)

(Flew from Gazala to El Adem)

(The above movement details have been taken from the diary written at the time, by L.B. Lamb whilst stationed in North Africa.)

North Africa 1942:

Location:

El amil	to	Gazala	*January 1942
Gazala	to	El Adem	*February 1942
El Adem	to	Gambut No. I	*March 1942
Gambut No. I	to	Gasr el Arid	
Gasr el Arid	to	Gambut No. II	
Gambut No. II	to	Gambut Main	*April 1942
Gambut Main	to	El Adem	
El Adem	to	El Gubbi (Tobruk)	
El Gubbi (Tobruk}	to	Gambut Main	*May 1942
Gambut Main	to	Sidi Aziz	
Sidi Aziz	to	B.L.G. 75	
B.L.G. 75	to	B.L.G. 76	*June 1942
B.L.G. 76	to	Sidi Haneish	
Sidi Haneish	to	Qasaba	*June 1942
Qasaba	to	El Daba	
El Daba	to	L.G. 20	
L.G. 20	to	B.L.G. 39	} 5 July; Advance.
B.L.G. 39	to	B.L.G. 154	}
B.L.G. 154	to	Burg el Arab 39	}
Burg el Arab	to	L.G. 89	}
L.G. 89	to	El Ballah	*July 1942
El Ballah	to	Shandur	*August 1942
Shandur	to	El Bassa	

(Flew by Hudson to El Bassa, six hours and back, flying to Shandur)

El Bassa	to	Shandur	
Shandur	to	L.G. 85 - Amriya	24 August 1942
L.G. 85	to	Burg el Arab	
Burg el Arab	to	L.G. 85	
L.G. 85	to	L.G. 89	24 October 1942
L.G. 89	to	Burg el Arab	
Burg el Arab	to	L.G. 21 *(10 miles West of Daba)*	
L.G. 21	to	L.G. 155 *(South of Sidi Barrani)*	
L.G. 155	to	Martuba	
Martuba	to	El Adem	
El Adem	to	Martuba	
Martuba	to	Barce	
Barce	to	Magrum *(West of Benghazi)*	
Magrum	to	Martuba	

(Left, 27 November 1942; arrived 23 December 1942. Christmas with Squadron for the first time. Not much of one.)

(The above movement details have been taken from the personal diary written at the time, by L.B. Lamb whilst stationed in North Africa.)

* Dates taken from The Squadrons of the Royal Air Force & Commonwealth 1918 - 1988, by James J. Halley.

PILOTS & AIRMEN not in M.E. up to: 24 May 1943

Name:	Name:
P/O Lamb	LAC Cropper
P/O Holdenly	P/O Shark - U.S.
Sgt. Webster	LAC Webster
Sgt. Willis	LAC Reid
2 No. French Pilots	AC Bouco
F/LT Smith	LAC Leo Longfellow
P/O Green F.	LAC Mack

S/Ldr. Ward - Killed, 17 June 1942 *(Drowned in Hospital ship; bombed and sunk off Alex.)*
F/O Wolley - Killed, 17 June 1942.

Sgt. Wright - POW.	Sgt. Stone
Sgt. Dolan	Sgt. Hill
Sgt. Logan - POW.	
F/Sgt. Johnson	

(3 No. French Pilots at Sidi Heneish; July 1941.)

Sgt. Baker	
P/O Chandler	
Sgt. Caster	F/LT Houghton
Sgt. Hopkins	P/O Barker
P/O Beaumont	Sgt. Stephenson
F/LT Brotherton	F/LT Miller - November 1942.
P/O Thomson	Sgt. Harris
F/LT Shelley	Sgt. Packman - 14 July 1942.
Sgt. Green	Sgt. Casman (Sebala)
Sgt. White	Sgt. Murray – 20 June 1943.
P/O Smyth	F/Sgt. Johnston

North Africa & Italy 1943 - 1944:

Location:			Date:
Martuba	to	Alem el Chel	2 January 1943
Alem el Chel	to	Sidi Haneish	11 January 1943
Sidi Haneish	to	Tamet	13 January 1943
Tamet	to	Bir Dufan	22 January 1943
Bir Dufan	to	Castle Verdi	

(Near Gasr Garabulli. 36 miles from Tripoli. Arrived 4 February 1943.)
(Leaving Castle Verdi 14 February, passed through Tagiura via Tripoli, Davia, Sabathra.)

El Asasa	to	Nafatia {15 February arrived 20 March 1943}	
Nafatia	to	Gabes	9 April 1943
Gabes	to	El Maoui / Sfax	12 April 1943

(Passed through El Alem 19 April 1943)

El Maoui / Sfax	to	Kairouan	19 April 1943

(Left at 09.00 hrs and arrived at 14.30 hrs: same day.)

Kairouan	to	Monastir	21 April 1943

(Left at o8.30 hrs and arrived at 10.00 hrs; same day.)

Monastir	to	La Sebala No.II, near Tunis.	29 May 1943

(Arrived the same day, 2 - 933 kites from Cairo by road.)

La Sebala No. II	to	La Sebala No. I	27 July 1943
La Sebala No. I	to	Bizerta *(Arrived 21 September 1943)*	
Bizerta	to	Salerno *(Arrived 3 October 1943)*	

Lamb L.B. LAC -1012281:

Injures and Hospitalization:
Admitted to 59 British General Hospital, Mercattella, Southern Italy (14 November 1943)
Discharged on the 28 November 1943. (Shrapnel Wounds to leg/legs)

Salerno	to	Foggia *(Arrived 1 December 1943.)*
Foggia Main	to	No. 30 – Military Field Hospital 4 January 1944

Hospitalisation due to an allergic reaction to Penicillin?

No. 30 - M.F.H.	to	No. 1 – General Hospital, Naples 17 January 1944 (flown by plane)
No. 1 G.H., Naples	to	Foggia Main (20 March 1944)

Discharged back to 73 Squadron for immediate return to United Kingdom.
(Received three letters on 25:5:44; one from Mabel, one from Mother and one from Dadda)

Home Embarkation date 13 April 1944. Arrived at RAF St Athan, South Wales on 22 April 1944.

Note: Craig, D. - 1004960; 73 D.T.U.
Legend:
B.G.H. - **British General Hospital**
G.H. **-** **General Hospital**
M.F.H. - **Military Field Hospital**
R.S.U. - **Repair and Servicing Unit**

73 Squadron Military Movement Record: (1940 to 1945)

Location:	Date:
En route to Takoradi [HMS Furious]	November to December 1940
Heliopolis	December 1940
Sidi Haneish	December 1940 to January 1941
Gazala West	January to March 1941
Bu Amud	March to April 1941
Bir el Gubi [Tobruk]	April 1941
Sidi Haneish	April to September 1941
Amriya	September 1941
Port Said / El Gamil	September 1941 to February 1942
Detachment to Kilo 8	October to December 1941
Detachment to Shandur	December 1941 to April 1942
El Adem	February 1942
Gasr-el-Arid	February 1942
Gambut II	February 1942
Gasr-el-Arid	February to March 1942
Gambut I	March to April 1942
Gambut Main	April to May 1942
El Adem	May 1942
Gambut Main	May to June 1942
LG.115	June 1942
LG.76	June 1942
Qasaba	June 1942
El Daba	June 1942
Burg-el-Arab	June to July 1942
LG.89	July 1942
El Ballah	July 1942
Shandur	July to August 1942

LG.85	August to November 1942
LG.21	November 1942
LG.13	November 1942
LG.155	November 1942
Gambut West	November 1942
El Adem	November 1942
El Magrum	November 1942
Merduma	November 1942 to January 1943
Alemel Chel	January 1943
Tamet	January 1943
Bir Dufan	January to February 1943
Gasr Garabulli	February 1943
El Assa	February to March 1943
Nefatia South	March to April 1943
Gabes Main	April 1943
Sfax / El Maoui	April 1943
Kairouan / Alem	April 1943
Monastir	April 1943
La Sebala II	April to October 1943

Location:	Date:
Montecorvino	October to December 1943

(Salerno 1 December 1943 to Foggia on 2 December 1943)

Foggia Main	December 1943 to September 1944
Canne	September 1944 to April 1945
Detachment to Hassani	September to December 1944
Prkos	April to May 1945
Brindisi	May to July 1945

Squadron Codes: TP, R, P, E, C

Duty:
Fighter Squadron, Advanced Air Striking Force: 1939-1940
Fighter Command: 1940
Fighter Squadron, North Africa: 1940-1943
Fighter Squadron, Italy, and Balkans: 1943-1945

Statements made: During 1940 - 1941

i) *Operations such as these begin with a phase in which each commander struggles, on the one hand, to obtain information, and on the other to deny it to his enemy. One of the few advantages that soldiers experience in having a desert for their theatre of war is that the auditorium is empty. (Extract from a statement issued by G.H.Q., Cairo, June 19, 1940.)*

ii) *Graziani has taken command .... an attack must be expected. (Statement issued by G.H.Q.., Cairo, August 6, 1940)*

iii) *A successful attack was made against Massawa .... one of our aircraft failed to return. (R. A. F. Communiqué, issued in Cairo, July 14, 1940.)*

iv)   In the Western desert elements of our forces are now in contact with the enemy on a broad front. In an engagement South of Sidi Barrani, we have captured 500 prisoners.
        (General Wavell's first communiqué announcing his offensive into CYRENAICA, December 9, 1940.)

v)   We have taken twenty thousand prisoners with tanks, guns, and equipment of all types.
        (Cairo Communique, December 12, 1940.)

vi)   Early this morning our attack was launched on Tobruk.
        (Cairo Communiqué, January 21, 1941.)

vii)   The capture of Derna was completed this morning.
        (Cairo Communiqué, January 30, 1941.)

viii)   Benghazi is in our hands.
        (Cairo Communiqué, February 7, 1941.)

ix)   In all other sectors, our penetration into ABYSSINIA is enlarging.
        (Cairo Communiqué, April 1941.)

x)   Benghazi is indefensible from a military point of view.
        (Cairo Communiqué, April 3, 1941.)

C. TOBRUK

TOBRUK: (In Brief)

Tobruk was a much sought-after treasure as it had many attributes. It had a natural deep and protected harbour, which meant that even if the port were to be bombed, ships would still be able to anchor there and be safe from squalls, so the port could never be rendered wholly useless regardless of any military bombardment. This was of critical importance, as it made Tobruk an excellent place to supply a desert warfare campaign. Tobruk had been heavily fortified by the Italians prior to the invasion of Egypt in November 1940.

In addition to these prepared fortifications, there were several escarpments and cliffs to the south of Tobruk, providing substantial physical barriers to any advance on the port over land. It was also located on a peninsula, which allowed it to be defended by a minimal number of troops, something that the Allies used to their advantage when under siege.

Tobruk was strategically significant due to its location regarding the remainder of Cyrenaica. Any attackers from the East who had secured Tobruk could then advance through the desert to Benghazi, cutting off all enemy troops along the coast.

On the 21 January 1941 Tobruk was captured from the Italians and liberated after the assault of the Australian 6th Division under Major-General Iven Mackay, the Allied Forces of British, Australian, and Indian troops carried out a counterstrike, pocketing two of the Italian camps against the Mediterranean, forcing their surrender. This subsequently led to an Italian retreat to El Agheila.

This prompted the Italians to call on the Germans to send an army Corp, under the name of *Deutsches Africa Korps (DAK)*. Italy also sent several more divisions to Libya, the result of which was that the strengthened Axis Forces drove the Allies back across Cyrenaica to the Egyptian border, leaving Tobruk isolated and under siege.

SIEGE OF TOBRUK – Axis Forces 1941

The Battle for Tobruk is one that has been well documented and recorded, and one in which many Historians have gone to great depths to explain not only the Allied position, but also the Axis position under the then *Generalleutnant Erwin Rommel*, probably one of the greatest generals ever to wear a uniform.

Tobruk was fought over in two battles the first of which was in 1941, when Rommel tried to capture the stronghold and more importantly the fuel emplacements along with its harbour, which would be of immense benefit in fighting the war in North Africa, as the German supply routes were constantly under a huge pressure to deliver supplies and fuel to ensure that the German and Axis Force could maintain their push forward.

The British 8th Army along with forces from the Commonwealth held fast and sent Rommel packing. The one big frustration for Rommel at this time was the fact that he had no idea of any of the fortifications within the perimeter and town of Tobruk. When you consider that the Italians had built the fortifications no one from the Italian side could provide any plans or details to Rommel. He was one very frustrated and stressed-out Field Marshall.

Churchill had always stated that **'Tobruk must be held at all costs'** and that the German army must be defeated.

Hitler at the time had always seen Tobruk as a treasure to behold and of great importance to which Rommel had been given specific orders by Hitler that the German Army in North Africa under his control must prepare and assault the garrison at Tobruk and give Hitler the victory he required and in doing so provide a safer route for German supplies and much needed fuel, thus enabling the North African battles to continue at pace.

Air War:
The defeat of the Axis attacks in April 1941 had greatly improved the situation in Tobruk. However, the German *Fliegerkorps X* had dispatched 150 to 200 aircraft to Libya from Sicily in February, which flew frequent dive-bomber sorties by day and medium-bomber raids by both day and night on the docks, buildings, anti-aircraft sites, artillery positions and airfields, were proving extremely effective.

Hangars at El Adem after 3 hours of bombing and strafing.

Westland Lysander aircraft and all but the most essential ground crew of 6 and 73 Squadrons were withdrawn to Egypt. Ten Hawker Hurricane fighters were based at the port during the day and on 19 April, Hurricanes of 73 and 274 Squadrons intercepted a Stuka raid escorted by fighters. Two days later 73 Squadron were down to five operational aircraft with very tired pilots. By the 23 April, three more Hurricanes had been shot down with a further two more damaged and on the 25 April the squadron was withdrawn. The fighters of 274 Squadron stayed at Gerawla and 6 Squadron remained at Tobruk with a view to flying tactical reconnaissance sorties. Fighter cover could only be maintained at intervals by the last 14 Hurricanes in the desert. The Axis airfields in the Marchat Gazala, Derna and Benna, were bombed at dusk and night to limit Axis air attacks on Tobruk.

Battle of the Salient:

*(The meaning of the word **salient** is most noticeable or important, a piece of land or section of fortification that juts out to form an angle.)*

Having failed to capture Tobruk in March 1941, *Comando Supremo and OKW* agreed that Tobruk should be captured and that supplies should be accumulated before any advance into Egypt was resumed. Field Marshal Rommel thought that the only way Tobruk could be taken was by a deliberate attack, which could not be started until such time that support units had arrived in the area and that the Luftwaffe was reinforced, particularly with transport aircraft to carry ammunition, fuel, and water.

On the 27 April 1941 Major-General Friedrich Paulus, Deputy Chief of the General Staff, arrived from Oberkommando des Heeres *(OKH)* in Berlin, to question Rommel on his intentions and to impress on him that there was no additional help available and to forecast the defensive possibilities of the area should Sollum be lost to the Allies. Paulus also refused to allow the planned attack for the 30 April 1941 until he had studied the situation. On the 29 April 1941 the planned attack was to proceed. Nothing more ambitious was to be carried out, other than securing the Axis HOLD to the Egyptian frontier, from Siwa Oasis North to Sollum was envisaged.

The Allied garrison at Tobruk worked on improving their defences by sowing minefields with the first being planted to the South-West, between the outer and inner perimeters. Despite the Axis bombing, which continued daily, the garrison were boosted by the delivery of twelve tanks and 5,000 long tons of supplies within the month. During this time the Axis forces managed to sink two supply ships.

The Axis attack was going to be made from the south-west, either side of the hillock of Ras el Medauar, approximately two weeks after the previous attempt. The 5th Light Division to the right and the 15th Panzer Division on the left, even though they had only recently arrived in North Africa. At 8.00 pm on 30th April the divisions were to break into Tobruk's defences, followed by assault groups from the *Ariete* Division along with the 27th Infantry *Brescia* to roll up on the flanks. Whilst all this was taking place the German infantry would press forward to reconnoitre the area of Fort Pilastrino to ensure that the attack could continue to the harbour. If this were not the case, then the Italian infantry would dig in on the flanks and the tanks brought forward for an attack the next day.

The Axis forces found the going very tough as the 26th Australian Brigade along with 2 – 23rd and 2 – 24th Battalions in the line with the 4 – 28th Battalion in reserve at Wadi Giaida were well entrenched and expecting not only a ground attack and shelling from artillery but also an aerial attack from the Luftwaffe.

Although the Axis forces made good ground and created a small bridgehead as planned, the Australian infantry held out in pockets around the battlefield and after further reconnoitre by the Germans the Axis Forces decided that the night passed in confused fighting as the Germans tried to recognize and mop up at Ras el Medauar and attack south-westwards along the perimeter. The attack failed and by morning some of the posts held by the Australians were still holding out.

Under cover of a thick mist the German tanks moved eastwards instead of south-east and ran into a minefield where they were engaged by anti-tank guns and repulsed. They tried moving north but were prevented from doing so by further anti-tank fire. With no reserves left and the most advanced troops south of Wadi Giaida, tired and isolated in a sandstorm. Paulus judged that the attack had failed. However, Rommel decided to attack on the right to widen the breach. Further battles ensued with attacks and counterattacks. Eventually the German attack was stopped for the loss of five British tanks. In the evening the Australian 2-24th Battalion counterattacked Ras el Medauar but met determined resistance and was repulsed. ***During the Battle, 73 and 274 Squadrons had maintained standing patrols over the area and on the morning of 2 May, the fighting around Wadi Giaida continued in a dust storm, as German troops tried to trickle forward.***

The Axis attacks had overrun the perimeter defences on a 3-mile front, to a maximum depth of 2-miles and had captured high ground which would prove useful as a position to observe from. The Axis loss was 650 German and 500 Italian casualties. The German Regiments had captured most of the Australian positions. Paulus ordered that no more attacks be made unless the Allies were evacuating the port of Tobruk.

The **Rats of Tobruk**, which was made up of Australian, British, Indian, and Polish troops suffered at least 3,836 casualties with the 70th Division losing 2,153 casualties making the total 5,989. These casualty lists did not record the RAF casualties. The RAF lost 10 pilots and 6 ground crew all recorded from burials at the cemetery, and, in addition 6 pilots had been shot down in the harbour.

The Axis casualties from 15 February to 18 November were Italian 1,130 killed, 4,255 wounded and 3,851 missing. Libyan losses were 184 killed and German casualties for the same period were about 538 killed, 1,657 wounded, about 681 missing and from 74-150 Axis aircraft shot down.

As the siege came to an end the hospital ship *Gloucestershire* began making trips to pick up patients from Tobruk. During the first run the harbour was still under fire, though about 540 patients were collected and taken to Alexandria.

After the battle for Tobruk the Germans made fast that which they had gained **whilst the British 8th Army retreated along the road back toward Egypt]**. Hitler was pleased to know that the Germans had gained a victory at last. However, Rommel having got his revenge victory wanted to press on with the advantage, with the next goal being Egypt itself.

The British 8th Army had retreated to a place called El Alamein, where they would set up their defences in readiness for the pursuing German/Axis army. There are several Battles documented/recorded around Tobruk during this conflict, *Operation Crusader* by the Allies and *Operation Venezia* by the Axis Forces to name but a few.

Following the surrender, Rommel made an address to the Axis troops which was intercepted as an Enigma Decrypt. It stated the following: -

"Solders! The great battle of the Marmaric Coats has reached its climax with the rapid conquest of Tobruk. In all 45,000 prisoners were taken and more than 1000 tanks and almost 400 guns destroyed or captured. By your incomparable valour and tenacity, you have, in the long, bitter struggle of the last 5 weeks, given the enemy blow for blow. By your offensive spirit, the enemy lost the core of his field army, which stood ready to leap to the attack on us losing above everything his strong armoured forces. My particular appreciation goes to the leaders and the troops for these outstanding achievements."

"Soldiers of Panzer Army Africa! We must now destroy the enemy completely. We will not rest until we have annihilated the last remaining portions of the British 8th Army. In the next few days, I demand of you more great achievements so that we may reach our goal."

Over 32,000 Allied personnel were taken prisoner – the second-largest surrender of British-led troops after the fall of Singapore a few months earlier.

Shortly after the loss of Tobruk the Prime Minister - Winston Churchill went to the United States to see President Roosevelt. On returning to London, he faced a debate in the House of Commons on the conduct of the war, and a motion of No Confidence, which was easily defeated.

Tobruk continued to be used as a base while it was in Axis hands, with some shipping arriving there. In September, Allied Forces launched a raid, known as Operation Agreement, intending to destroy supplies and equipment in Tobruk, but it was a failure. At the time and in the Prime Ministers Personal Minute – Winston Churchill commented *'We certainly suffered very heavy losses for little or no result. One would have thought such an enterprise would have played its part in a battle combination rather than as an isolated episode' PREM 3/311. Extract from Serial No M.422/2 to First Lord, First Sea Lord.*

During this period, Allied Forces attacked Axis shipping sailing to Tobruk and, on 26 October, the Italian tanker *Proerpina* and cargo ship *Tergestea* were sunk by aircraft. The two ships are named in Enigma decrypt *HW 1/1015.*

47 Squadron took part in the attack on the *Proerpina* and the squadron operation record book can be found at *AIR 27/464/6.* At this moment in time, both 73 and 39 Squadrons were constantly on operational flying carrying out all types of sorties from reconnaissance to bombing and strafing of all types of Axis locations. *Refer to Chapter 6 for more details.*

Battle for TOBRUK – 1941 & 1942

The Axis Forces conducted the Siege of Tobruk *[some 8 months after the Italian surrender of 21 January 1941]*. Tobruk was finally recaptured by the German/Axis Forces in the Second Battle for Tobruk on 17 – 21 June 1942. At the time Winston Churchill commented *'The fall of Tobruk … in a single day was utterly unexpected'*. The Battle of Gazala had begun on 26 May 1942, with the Allied 8th Army defeated and driven East of Tobruk and boosted by their success the AXIS Forces pressed home their advantage to confront the Allied Forces in the main Battle for Egypt, but their advance was halted at the First Battle of El Alamein, the point at which the Allied Forces had retreated to.

During the Axis Siege of Tobruk Operation *Sonnenblume* (1 February – 25 May 1941), the ground crew of 73 Squadron along with other service men were transported into the Tobruk fortress and ordered to make ready for their evacuation. They were to be transported by ship from Tobruk to Alexandria, Egypt where they would regroup and make ready for the forthcoming battles.

Evacuation from Tobruk:
The evacuation was to be carried out by HMSAS Southern Isles [Pennant Nr. T29 (T469), which was one of four ships commandeered by the South African Government at the outbreak of war. The ships were owned at the time by the Southern Whaling & Sealing Co. Ltd. and were approximately 344 tons each. They were converted for Anti-Submarine and mine-sweeping operations and were each armed with 1 x 3lb Gun (forward), 20mm and machine-guns with a speed of 13 knots. Each had a complement of 20 – 25 Officers and ratings, all South African. On completion of the conversion, the ships left South African waters on 15 December 1940 sailing from Durban and went into service in the Mediterranean Sea in January 1941 and joined up with the Mediterranean 22nd Anti-submarine Group. The ship's role was to keep the harbours free of mines and submarines. The ship eventually returned to Durban in December 1944.

HMSAS Southern Isles:

The above Image provided by (South Africa Naval Museum – Commander Leon Steyn Curator) who give consent and approval to use in the book, plus extract from 'South Africa's Fighting Ships' by Alan du Toit.

The above Image provided by (South Africa Naval Museum – Commander Leon Steyn - Curator) who give consent and approval to use in the book, plus extract from 'South Africa's Fighting Ships' by Alan du Toit.

*The Southern Class, which were without doubt the most famous of the SANF's 'little' ships, were fine looking vessels, with the usual high bows of a whale catcher, sweeping down to the characteristic low freeboard amidships. The ships were placed under the 22ⁿᵈ Anti-Submarine Group, under the command of Lieutenant-Commander A F Trew, arrived at Alexandria, the eastern base of the British Mediterranean Fleet, on 11 January 1941, and were almost immediately put to work protecting the exposed supply route to Tobruk. (**Extract from 'South Africa's Fighting Ships' by Alan du Toit.**)*

From my father's records and notes he was evacuated from Tobruk by sea on board HMSAS Southern Isles, 28 May 1941, arriving in Alexandria on 30 May 1941.

War Decorations: *HMSAS Southern Isles*

DSC – Sub. Lt. L.B. Ribbink
DSM – P/O W.H. Dean, Ldg. Smn. H. Offer, Stoker (1st Cl.) A. Mooney, Ldg. Stoker H.M. Jewell
*CGM – Ldg. Stoker Rene' Sethern
MID – Lt. A.C. Matson, A.B.T.E.E. Overton, Signalman P.D. Kockett

Conspicuous Gallantry Medal:

Rene' Sethern has a story which is simply jaw dropping to say the least. On 30 June 1941, a small flotilla of ships including the South African minesweepers were on convoy from Mersa Mutrah approaching Tobruk in the midst of the fighting around Tobruk between the Allied Forces and the Axis Forces, with South Africans right at the centre of it defending Tobruk and El Alamein. As they close in on the coast the convoy comes under fire from German shore batteries and is also attacked by a number of German Stuka dive bombers, JU87's and Messerschmidt 109's. Enter HMSAS Southern Isles and its stoker Rene' Sethren. Five German JU-88's attacked the HMSAS Southern Isles, luckily with no real damage, then came a lull in the fighting, during which a JU-87 had been attacking a convoy merchant called the 'Cricket'. The plane was shot down by HMSAS Southern Isles. The convoy came under a fiercer attack from 50 enemy aircraft. The commander of the little ship described it as "the sky appeared to rain bombs." From the attack there were a number of casualties on the upper deck. In order to assist those fighting off the attacking Stuka aircraft stoker Rene' Sethren is sent up from his normal station shovelling coal in the engine room, a task he had carried out for a full 12 hours.

He is qualified as a reserve machine gunner, and he was urgently needed up on deck as his best friend who had been manning the ship's twin Lewis anti-aircraft machine gun was dead lying next to the gun. Rene' immediately took over the gun, standing on ammunition boxes to train his gun with non-stop volley firing against the attacking German aircraft. At this stage a German JU-88 joined the Stuka attack and strafed the ship's upper deck. Sethren is seen to fall after being hit be machine gun bullets from the JU-88 (he has 8 separate bullet wounds – read that again – shot 8 times). Notwithstanding his wounds he muscles up some superhuman strength and stands up and engages the attacking JU-88 with the Lewis gun. At the conclusion of the battle Rene' Sethren is found to have more than just the eight bullet wounds, in fact medics counted a total of 27 wounds in one arm, both legs and his side.

For his actions he is awarded the Conspicuous Gallantry Medal – the highest award won by a South African rating in World War 2, the only South African to be awarded this medal. Rene' Sethren received his gallantry decoration from King George V. His wounds are so extensive he spends 18 months recovering in hospital. The injuries sustained finishes his boxing as well as his sea faring days.

Before expanding on the El Alamein battles, we need to look briefly at the recapture of Tobruk from the Axis Forces by the Allied forces.

The Axis Forces now boosted by their taking of Tobruk pushed on to capture further ground and as stated in Rommel's address 'Annihilate' the British 8th Army, which had retreated under the orders of General Claude Auchinleck, back into Egypt stopping at El Alamein, and within 50 miles of Alexandria where the *Qattara Depression* was 40 miles south of El Alamein. The depression was impassable and would mean that any attack had to be frontal. Winston Churchill was extremely unhappy in how Auchinleck had commanded the desert army and the battles in which they fought. As a result of this his replacement was Lieutenant-General William Henry Ewart Gott, nicknamed "Strafer" was a *(Senior British Army Officer who fought in the First and the second World Wars)* and whilst travelling in a plane on his way to North Africa, the plane was shot down killing all on board. His replacement was to be Lieutenant- General Bernard Montgomery who then took command and led the 8th Army offensive.

Tobruk remained in Axis hands until 11 November 1942. The following victory at El Alamein, the 8th Army advanced again into Libya, taking back Tobruk unopposed on 13 November 1942.

After the recapture of Tobruk, salvage work in and around the area went on for months as witnessed in the Salvage Control Officer's Report for week ending 31 July 1943 is given below: -

Salvage Control Officer's Report:

1. OC 'G' Salvage Unit reported to this HQ today 31st inst. Balance ofnGI098 stores were drawn up and locations of HQ and two sections at DERNA confirmed
2. Col Collins was met during the week, and welfare of 'B' Units Bechuana personnel discussed. There were no complaints, and the natives are happy in their work.
3. Cast Iron and Non-Ferrous metals are now being returned in considerable quantities. Some 160 additional NOR labour is being utilised at RH to cope with incoming salvage. Co-operation by units is very good.
4. Arrangements for the collection of Jerricans by civilians have now been completed, every assistance is being given by the Political Officer and collection points have been agreed upon. Specimen Jerricans of the class required at Base have been available for exhibiting to Local Sheikhs, etc.
5. A considerable number of German Aircraft spares have been found in TOBRUK (MR 415436). These stores are underground, and still in their original cartons, several complete aircraft wings are in crates, and disposal now awaited.

Capt. GH Cassy – Salvage Control Officer

D. El Alamein

First Battle of El Alamein: (1-27 July 1942)

Belligerents

Axis	Allies
Italy	United Kingdom
Germany	India
	Australia
	New Zealand
	South Africa

Commanders and Leaders

Erwin Rommel	Claude Auchinleck
Ettore Bastico	

Strength

96,000 troops (56,000 Italian, 40,000 German	150,000 Troops
70 tanks initially (585 tanks later) and 500 planes	179 tanks initially (1,114 tanks later
	1,000+ artillery pieces
	1,500 + planes

Casualties and losses

10,000 killed or wounded	13,250 casualties
7,000 prisoners	

The First Battle was a battle fought in Egypt between the Axis Forces made up of German and Italian Forces, and the 8th Army - Allied Forces made up of Britain, British India, Australia, South Africa, and New Zealand. The Allied Forces prevented a second advance by the Axis Forces into Egypt. Axis positions near El Alamein were only 66 miles from Alexandria. This was considered to be far too close to the ports and cities of Egypt, which were occupied by the Allies and also dangerously close to the base facilities of the Commonwealth forces, especially the Suez Canal.

The Axis Forces were extremely low on supplies and in not having the good supply routes and infrastructure in place, along with the required backup support, were now too far from their base at Tripoli in Libya to remain at El Alamein indefinitely. From both sides' perspective, both sides needed to accumulate stores and supplies for more offensives. The Axis Forces more so than the Allied Forces.

In June 1942 the Allied Forces commanded by Lieutenant-General Neil Richie were defeated at Gazala in Eastern Libya, after which they further retreated from the Gazala line into north-western Egypt as far as Mersa Mutruh, approximately 100 miles inside the border. Richie had decided not to hold 'his' defences on the Egyptian border as this could only be held by infantry, with a strong armoured force behind them. Unfortunately for Richie, there were NO armoured units remaining for him to call upon.

Up until June 1942 Rommel had been receiving detailed information about the strength and movement of the Allied Forces from reports sent to Washington by Colonel Bonner Frank Fellers, the U.S. military attaché in Cairo. *[The American code had been stolen following a covert operation by Italian military intelligence at the American Embassy in Rome the previous year.]* Despite British concerns, the Americans continued to use the code until the end of June 1942. Confirmation that the code had been compromised came after the Australian 9th Division captured the German 621st Signal Battalion in July 1942.

On 25 June General Claude Auchinleck assumed direct command of the 8th Army, replacing Lieutenant-General Neil Richie after the 8th Army was defeated at Gazala. Auchinleck made an early decision not to seek a confrontation with Rommel at the Mersa Matruh position, as he concluded that his armour, now, was inferior to that of Rommel due to the defeat at and he would therefore not be able to stop Rommel breaking through. Auchinleck employed delaying tactics while withdrawing a further 100 miles to a more defensible position near El Alamein.

From June 1941 the British had intelligence advantage because ULTRA *(ULTRA - being the designation adopted by British military intelligence in June 1941 for wartime signals intelligence obtained by breaking high-level encrypted enemy radio and teleprinter communications at the Government Code and Cypher School (GC&CS) at Bletchley Park)* and along with local sources which exposed the Axis order of battle, its supply position, routes, and intentions. A reorganisation of military intelligence in Africa in July 1942 had also improved the integration of information received from all sources and the speed of its dissemination. With rare exceptions, intelligence identified ships destined for North Africa, their location and in most cases their cargoes, allowing them to be attacked. By 25 October 1942, *Panzerarmee Africa* was down to three days' supply of fuel, only two days' worth, which were east of Tobruk. After six more weeks, the 8th Army was ready and began the offensive against the Axis forces.

Both the Axis Forces and the 8th Army attacks and counterattacks were clearly now at a stalemate with little advance being gained by either side.

The time between the First and Second Battles of El Alamein was used by both armies to gain much needed supplies and equipment for the forthcoming Second Battle.

At this time in the war General Claude Auchinleck had been replaced by Lieutenant-General Bernard Montgomery. Previously Auchinleck had been replaced by Lieutenant-General William Gott who had been killed when his transport aircraft was shot down.

Second Battle of El Alamein: (23 October to 4 November 1942)

This battle of the Second World War took place near the Egyptian railway halt of El Alamein. The First Battle of El Alamein and the Battle of Alam el Halfa had prevented the Axis forces from advancing further into Egypt, in August 1942

British Plan: Operation Lightfoot

Montgomery's plan was for a main attack to the north of the line and a secondary attack to the south. With Operation Lightfoot, Montgomery intended to cut two corridors through the Axis minefields in the north, one corridor running south-west towards the centre of *Miteirya* Ridge, while the second was to run west. Tanks would then pass through and defeat the German Armour. Diversions at *Ruweisat Ridge* in the centre, and the south of the line would keep the rest of the Axis forces from moving northwards. Montgomery expected a 12 -day battle in three stages: the break-in, the dogfight, and the final breaking of the enemy. In readiness, two further operations were planned by Montgomery, these being Operation Bertram and Operation Braganza.

Axis Plan:

With the failure of the offensive at the Battle of Alam el Haifa, the Axis forces went onto the defensive although at this point their losses had not been excessive. The Axis supply line from Tripoli was extremely long. Even although captured British supplies and equipment had now been exhausted, but Rommel still decided to advance into Egypt.

During this time, the 8th Army were being supplied with men and materials as well as with trucks and the new Sherman tanks from the United States. Rommel continued to request equipment, supplies and fuel but the priority of the German war effort was the Eastern Front and very limited supplies reached North Africa.

Rommel fell ill in early September 1942 and arrangements were made for him to return to Germany on sick leave. His replacement was General der Panzertruppe Georg Stumme who transferred from the Russian front. But before leaving on the 23 September 1942, Rommel organised the defence and wrote a long memo, which outlined the current situation to the *Oberkommando der Wehermacht (OKW)* High Command of the Armed forces of Nazi Germany (created in 1938), once again requesting his essential needs.
Rommel's only hope of more supplies was for the Russian Red Army to be defeated in quick time, thus freeing men, and equipment. With Rommel away, the Panzerarmee dug in and waited for the attack by the 8th Army or the defeat of the Red Army at Stalingrad.

Whilst waiting for the outcome of the battle for Stalingrad, the Axis forces laid around 500,000 mines *(many of which were British, which had been captured at Tobruk)*, and to lure Allied forces vehicles into the minefields, the Italians dragged an axle fitted with tyres through the fields using rope to create what appeared to be well-used tracks.

Axis forces did not want the British armour to break out into the open as they had neither the strength of numbers nor enough fuel to match them in a battle, and that the battle had to be fought in their fortified zones and that any breakthrough defeated quickly. The Axis forward lines were stiffened by alternating German and Italian infantry formations, as the British deception confused the Axis as to the actual point/points of attack. The Axis forces split their armoured strength into a northern and southern group to allow quick intervention wherever an Allied attack/breakout would occur as they were never sure where an attack would take place.

The Second Battle of El Alamein would consist of Five Phases: -

Phase one: The break-in, 23 October to 24 October 1942
At 21:40 hours (Egyptian Summertime) on 23 October Operation Lightfoot began with a 1,000-gun Barrage of all areas. After 20 minutes of general bombardment, the guns switched to precision targets, and this continued for five and half-hours. Some 529,000 shells had been fired.

Phase two: The crumbling, 24 October to 25 October 1942
Dawn reconnaissance showed little change in Axis positions. Montgomery ordered that the clearance of the northern corridor should be completed and the armoured 10th Division push south from Miteirya Ridge. Rommel was still in a sanatorium in Germany and Hitler had decided that Rommel return to North Africa. On the 25 October Rommel flew to Rome to press for more fuel, and then to North Africa to resume command. Rommel's arrival boosted German morale but did little to change the course of the battle.

Phase three: <u>The Counter. 26 October to 1 November 1942</u>

Rommel on his return assessed the battle and casualties, particularly in the north after incessant artillery and air attack, had been severe. Rommel was convinced that the main assault would come in the north. However, he was determined to retake Point 29, one of many strategic points of the Battle Maps, and ordered a counterattack which came to nothing. Only a small success was had where the Italians recaptured part of Hill 28. Many of the attacks ordered by Rommel didn't fully materialise due to the lack of fuel.

Phase four: <u>Operation Supercharge, 2 November to 3 November 1942</u>

This phase of the battle began at 01:00 hours (Egyptian Summertime) on the 2 November. The objective to was to destroy enemy armour forcing them to fight in the open, reduce the Axis stock of petrol and attack and occupy Axis supply routes along with disintegrating the Axis army. As with Operation Lightfoot, Operation Supercharge started with a seven-hour aerial bombardment focused on Tel el Aqqaqir and Sidi Abd el Rahman, followed by a four and a half-hour barrage of 300 guns. The advance took place and met was met with stubborn resistance by the Axis forces. Brigadier Currie stated, 'that he believed the brigade would be attacking on too wide a front with no reserves and most likely have 50 percent losses.' The reply came back that Montgomery 'was aware of the risk and had accepted that casualties could be 100 percent in the 9th Armoured Brigade to make the breakthrough, however the risk was not considered as great as all that.' The Brigade had sacrificed itself upon the gun line and caused great damage but had failed to create the gap to pass through.

On the night of 2 November, Montgomery once again reshuffled his infantry to bring four brigades into reserve.

Phase five: <u>The break-out, 3 November to 11 November 1942</u>

Rommel on the night of the 2 November said he would have at most 35 tanks available to fight the next day and that his artillery and anti-tank weapons had been reduced by half of their strength. He ordered a fighting withdrawal.

Rommel proceeded to signal Hitler saying, 'The army's strength was so exhausted after its ten days of battle that it could not offer an effective opposition to the next Allied forces break-through.' And at 13:30 hours on 3 November Rommel received a reply from Hitler, which in broad terms stated, ***'that there was no other road than that of victory or death'. Adolf Hitler***

Casualties:

Panzerarmee, some 36,939 casualties were estimated, because of the chaos of the Axis retreat. British figures gave German casualties as 1,149 killed, 3,886 wounded and 8,050 captured. Italian losses were 971 dead, 933 wounded and 15,522 captured. By the 11 November 1942 Axis prisoners had risen to 30,000 men.

8th Army, some 13,560 casualties, of whom 2,350 had been killed, 8,950 wounded but 2,260 missing.

Post El Alamein:

There can be no denying that the Battles at El Alamein were a turning point in the defeat of the Axis Forces. However, whilst being a victory for the Allied Forces, Rommel did not give up hope until the end of the Tunisia Campaign. At the time Winston Churchill said and I quote ***"It may be said, that" 'Before El Alamein we never had a victory. After El Alamein we never had a defeat'.***

The Allies frequently had numerical superiority in the Western Desert, but never had it been so complete in quantity and quality. The artillery was superbly handled, and the air support was excellent, in contrast to the *Luftwaffe and Regia Aeronautica,* which offered little or no support to ground forces, preferring to engage in air-to-air combat. Air supremacy had a huge effect on the battles.

Montgomery wrote: -
The moral effect of air [on the enemy] is very great and out of all proportion to the material damage inflicted. In the reverse direction, the sight and sound of our own air forces operating against the enemy have an equally satisfactory effect on our own troops. Ab combination of the two has a profound influence on the most important single factor in war – morale.

At this moment in time, it became clear that there were other battles to fight but ultimately the Allies were now the dominant force and that it was only a matter of time that the Axis forces would be overrun and defeated. The Allied forces would continue to pursue the retreating Axis forces taking back the ground that had previously been relinquished to the Axis Forces, one of which being Tobruk, which fell quickly and easily, and without a great loss of life. *(Refer to section C. Tobruk of this chapter.)* The Allied Forces would press on their charge against the Axis forces until they were completely defeated, and no longer a threat, and that North Africa was now safely under the control of the Allies.

The next big challenge for the Allied Forces was the taking of Sicily and then Italy itself. *(Refer to Section E. Italy 1943 to 1944 of this chapter.)*

E. Italy 1943 to 1944:

Operation Avalanche – Invasion of Italy, September - October 1943

The Allied Forces having now driven the Axis Forces (Germany and Italy) from North Africa their next task was to push the them out of Italy, and in September 1943 the Allied Forces implemented Operation Avalanche. The following map shows how this plan was to be implemented, which included the relocation of the RAF Squadrons from North Africa to the area around FOGGIA, where there were a good number of Italian airbases, once captured could soon be put into use.

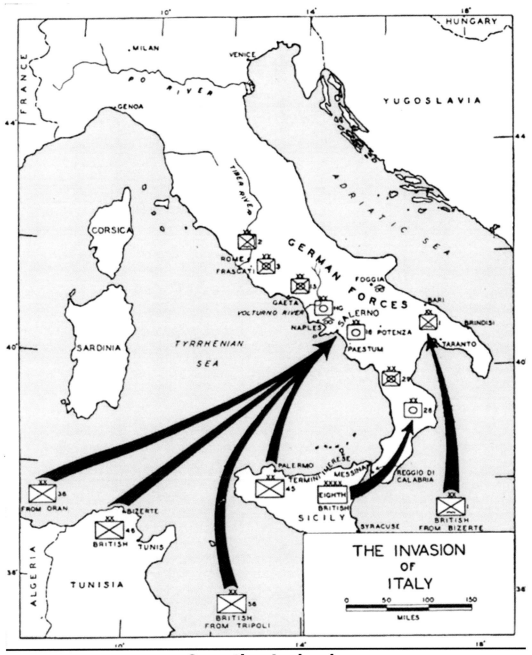

Operation Avalanche
The above Image is in the Public Domain in the United States of America – No Copyright in the USA. Source:
http://army.mil/cmh-pg/books/wwii/salerno/sal-prep.htm File: Invasionofitaly 1943.jpg
Email received from susannezoumbaris@nara.gov on the 5 April 2022 at 10:44 hours.
Providing the credits are set out then consent is approved.

Operation Avalanche:

This being the codename used by the Allies for the beach landings near the Port of Salerno. The battle for Italy was implemented to start on the 9 September 1943 as part of the Allied invasion of Italy. It is worth noting that after the Axis defeat in North Africa and the advance of the Allied Forces across North Africa, the Italians withdrew from the war the day before the Allied invasion started. Unfortunately for the Allies they landed in an area defended by the German's.

Under the command of the American General Mark W. Clark, the landings were carried out by the US Fifth Army, which comprised of the U.S. VI Corps, The British X Corps, and the U.S. 82nd Airborne Division, a total of nine divisions. The landings were supported by the newly formed RAF 68 and 69 Beach Unit Squadrons whose prime role was of 'reconnaissance'. The main goal of the Allies was to capture the Port of Naples to ensure that supply routes for the allies would be maintained, *[something the Axis Forces in North Africa found extremely difficult to maintain]* and to cut across to the east coast, trapping the German troops further south.

As the Allies continued their assault on the Germans at Salerno, it was essential that the Allies drew the German troops away from the landing ground, and Operation Baytown was put into operation. Operation Baytown is where the British 8th Army, after their victory in North Africa, was to land in Calabria in the 'toe' of Italy, on the 3 September 1943. At the same time simultaneous landings were to take place by the British 1st Airborne Division at the Port of Taranto *(Operation Slapstick)*. British General Bernard Montgomery predicted that Baytown would be a waste of effort, as he assumed the Germans would give battle in Calabria. If this failed, then the diversion would not work. *Montgomery was proved right*. The 8th Army, after Operation Baytown's failure marched 300 miles north to the Salerno area without meeting any opposition other than engineering obstacles.

As the Salerno landings continued, without Allied naval or aerial bombardment so as to achieve maximum surprise, the surprise was not achieved. With the first wave of troops approaching the shore at Paestum a German voice via a loudspeaker located somewhere on the landing area proclaimed in English *"Come on in and give up. We have you covered."* However, the troops attacked anyway.

Prior to the Italians withdrawing from the war, they had established artillery and machine-gun posts as well as scattering tanks throughout the landing zones, which made progress difficult, but the beach areas were captured. A counterattack by the 16th Panzer Division took place, causing heavy casualties were inflicted as the beachhead could not resist the concentrated attacks., but the attack was beaten off. The British and American forces progress was slow with still a 10-mile gap between them at the end of day one. On day two they had linked up and now occupied 35-45 miles of coastline to a depth of 6-7 miles.

Over the 12-14 September 1943 there were concerted counterattacks by six German divisions of motorized troops hoping to stem the attacks by the Allies and thus throw the Salerno beachhead into the sea before it could link up with the British 8th Army. With the Allied troops spread out too thinly, heavy casualties were inflicted as the beachhead could not resist the concentrated attacks. Outmost troops were withdrawn to reduce the perimeter and the new perimeter was able to hold with the assistance of naval and aerial support, even though the German attacks had reached almost to the beaches in places. During this period of the fighting the Allied fighter pilots would sleep under the wings of their planes just in case they had to beat a hasty retreat to Sicily.

Allied Strategy:

Following on from the defeat of the Italian Forces and the Afrika Korps in North Africa, there were disagreements in the Allied Camp as to the next best step of the war. Winston Churchill was of the strong opinion that Italy should be invaded, which he called the "underbelly of Europe". Popular support in Italy was on the decline, and he believed an invasion would remove Italy and the influence of the Italian Navy *(Regia Marina)* in the Mediterranean, which would open the sea up to Allied traffic and their supply routes.

In addition, it would tie down the German forces, keeping them away from the planned invasion of Normandy – Operation Overlord.

However, the American General, General George Marshall and much of his staff didn't want to undertake any operations that could delay the Normandy planned invasion. On closer examination of the proposed plans for Normandy, it became clear that Operation Overlord could not take place in 1943, and that the forces in North Africa should be used to invade Sicily in the first instance with no further commitment on follow-up operations.

Joint Allied Forces HQ – AFHQ were operationally responsible for all Allied land forces in the Mediterranean theatre, and it is they who would plan and command the invasion of Sicily and then the Italian mainland.

Operation Husky was the codename for the invasion of Sicily, which took place on 10 July 1943. Operation Husky was brought to fruition when the British Army set up a 'deception operation' Code Named – Operation Mincemeat', which was to hide and disguise an invasion in Sicily by putting the enemy on a wrong track. The Allied Forces allowed false information to be leaked to the German High Command, which detailed that Greece was to be the next country to be invaded. The outcome of the deception was that Hitler diverted troops from the eastern front and sent them to the Balkans.

During Operation Husky, however unfortunate many Axis forces were allowed to avoid capture by escaping to the Italian mainland. However, importantly a *coup* deposed Benito Mussolini as head of the Italian Government, which started a chain reaction of the Italians approaching the Allies with a view of making peace. The Allies believed that a quick invasion of Italy might hasten an Italian surrender and allow quick military victories over the German troops, now trapped in a hostile country. This proved not to be the case, and the Italian and German resistance proved strong and fighting in Italy continued even after the fall of Berlin. Battle of Berlin – 16 April 1945 to 2 May 1945.

The Allied Plan:

Operation Avalanche was the code name for the Allied landings near the Port of Salerno, executed on 9 September 1943 as part of the Allied invasion of Italy during World War II. Its primary role/objectives were to seize the Port of Naples to ensure that supply routes were kept open, and to cut across to the east coast thus trapping Axis troops further south.

The Italians withdrew from the war a day before the invasion, but the allies landed in an area defended by German troops.

The 82nd Airborne was used as a reserve force. This was only possible because *Operation Giant II* was cancelled. 1st British Airborne would land by sea near Taranto, on the "heel" of Italy as a diversion for Salerno, *Operation Slapstick.* The task ahead of the 1st British Airborne was to capture the port and several nearby airfields, link up with the 8th Army and then press north to join the 5th Army near Foggia.

The plan was deeply flawed due to poor reconnaissance and that NO naval action by way of bombardment was ordered. Finally, although tactical surprise was unlikely, Clark ordered that NO naval preparatory bombardment took place, this, despite the experience in the Pacific Theatre demonstrating that this was paramount and necessary.

In and around the area, approximately eight German divisions had been positioned to cover any possible landing sites.

Operation Avalanche
Part of the Invasion of Italy
Date: 9 – 16 September 1943
Location: Salerno, Italy
Result: Allied Victory

Belligerents

Germany

United States of America
United Kingdom
Canada

Commanders and Leaders

Germany: H. von Vietinghoff

United States: Mark W. Clark

Strength

35,000 Germans

170,000 servicemen

Casualties and losses

Germany:
840 killed
2,002 wounded
603 missing

United States:
5th Army:
788 killed
2,841 wounded
1,318 missing
U.S. Navy:
296 killed
422 wounded
551 missing
United Kingdom:
982 killed
4.060 wounded
2,230 missing
Royal Navy:
83 killed
42 wounded

RAF 73 Squadron: Relocation to Italy

The squadron having been greatly involved in the fighting and battles undertaken in and across North Africa were now to be used, along with other RAF Squadrons to take the fight into Italy. The squadron was now equipped with Spitfires as their previous aircraft "Hurricanes" were being used in other theatres/fields of air battles.

From the diary and recorded details kept by *LAC – Lamb L.B. 1012281* it is clear to see that 73 Squadron were to be shipped from North Africa – Tripoli, across to Italy, and in readiness for this moved down to the harbour on 30 September 1943 and then on the 1 October 1943 set sail for Italy [mainland] arriving at Salerno on the 3 October 1943. On the 4 October the ground crew of 73 Squadron moved to Foggia Main to await the arrival of the squadrons Spitfires. *(Refer to Chapter 6 of this book for further details.)*

LAC - Lamb L.B. 1012281 was transported to hospital with shrapnel wounds to his legs. He was admitted to **59 GCH** on the 14 November 1943 and discharged on the 28 November 1943 back to his squadron. It was never made clear as to why he sustained the injuries. However, what was made clear was that whilst in **59 GCH** he was given 'Penicillin' to which he had a massive reaction, and this required more critical and sustained treatment whilst in hospital.

On his return to his squadron from 59 GCH, he was then transferred in early January 1944 to **No. 30 MFH** with a further transfer to **No.1 General Hospital, Naples** where he stayed until 20 March 1944. He was then discharged and repatriated to his squadron with orders for immediate Home Embarkation, return to the United Kingdom. From that day on he wore a wrist band 'Medic Alert', which stated 'Allergic to Penicillin'.

From records kept by my father other movements took place during the war in Italy. The following applied to 73 Squadron when the squadron moved from North Africa to Italy and in Italy itself. These were as follows: -
- Bizerta [Tunisia] to Salerno [Italy] 3 October 1943
- Salerno [Italy] to Foggia [Italy] 1 December 1943
- Montecorvino [Italy] October to December 1943
- Foggia Main [Italy] December 1943 to September 1944
- Canne [Italy] September 1944 to April 1945

Several numbers of detachments took place where 73 Squadron and its ground crew received orders to take up temporary posts away from Italy and in Italy itself. These are as follows: -
- Hassani [Greece] September to December 1944
- Prkos [Yugoslavia] April to May 1945
- Brindisi [Italy] May to July 1945

Foggia Airfield Complex: World War II

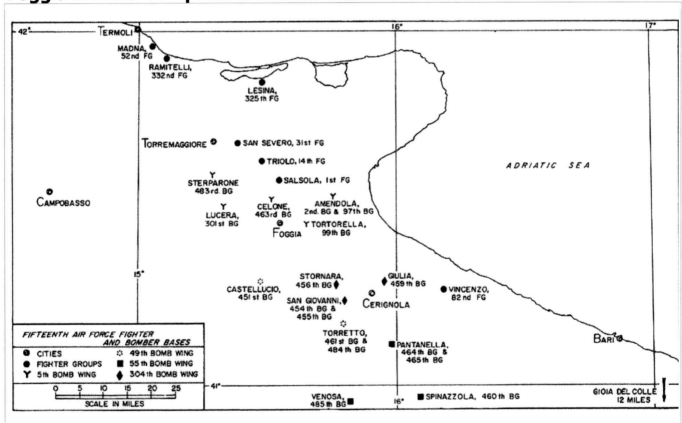

World War II military airfields in the Province of Foggia, Italy:
No known Copyright Restrictions found.

75

Foggia Airfield Complex:

Prior to and during World War II the Italians had built military airfields all located within a 25-mile radius of Foggia. On the surrender of Italy, the airfields were used extensively by the USAAF – 15th Air Force as part of the strategic bombardment campaign against Nazi Germany in 1944 and 1945, as well as the 12th Air Force along with the Royal Air Force during the Italian Campaign, 1943 – 1945.

The History of the Foggia Airfields:

Prior to the outbreak of World War II, the Italian Air Force *Regia Aeronautica* constructed a series of airfields in and around Foggia. They consisted of hard-surfaced runways, taxiways, and concrete hard standings with permanent buildings.

On completion of the Armistice between Italy and the Allied forces in September 1943 the airfields were seized by the German Luftwaffe. During the Axis control the airfields were heavily bombed by the USAAF and the RAF in 1943, before being seized by the British 8th Army in October 1943.

Having been captured, the facilities were repaired by the USAC of Engineers (COE) to make them fully operational for heavy bomber operations. The 15th USAAF and the RAF flew their operations and sorties from these bases as the weather in southern Italy was far better than that of England from where the 8th USAAF were conducting daylight strategic bombing of Occupied Europe and Nazi Germany. This meant that by using the Foggia Air bases the Allied heavy bombers could target a wider field of countries, such as, France, Germany, Austria, and the Balkans, which were not accessible from England.

It also allowed Foggia to become a major Allied command center for ground forces in southern Italy and naval forces in the Adriatic Sea, with numerous headquarters being assigned.

In addition to the captured airfields, several temporary and semi-permanent airfields were operated by both the 12th and 15th USAAF and RAF units. The airfields by and large consisted of grass or Pierced Steel Planking runways, parking and dispersal areas, and support structures quickly constructed out of wood. There were als tents along with a temporary steel control tower (where required). Six-man tents were used for billeting, lined up in rows with an orderly room and mess hall at one end, all of which were dimly lit by a central light bulb. The floor was generally grass but more commonly dirt. Eventually the men scavenged plywood for flooring. Wooden cots were used for beds and 55-gallon empty drums were converted into stoves and other items.

Previously used by the Italians and Germans the captured airfields were laden with wrecked enemy aircraft, parts of which soon becoming used in the support areas.

With the work ongoing to bring the captured airfields into operation by mid-1944 two dozen airfields were now operational supporting strategic bombing missions; escort missions; tactical fighter operations, reconnaissance, and air defence missions.

Albert Spear, Hitler's Minister for Armaments, declared: *I could see omens of the war's end almost every day in the blue southern sky when, flying provocatively low, the bombers of the American 15th Air Forces crossed the Alps from their Italian bases to attack German Industrial targets.*

At the end of the war in May 1945, most of the airfields were abandoned and the land returned to the owners, or the Italian Government.

Today, most of the airfields are long gone with little or no evidence of the lands former use. A few still exist as commercial airports with one still used by the Italian Air Force *(Aeronautica Militare)*.

The Airfields and Unit:

The airfield complex consisted of several major airfields with numerous axillary landing strips not listed.

- **Amendola Airfield** – Located approximately 16km northeast of Foggia. The base was used by the 15th USAAF, primarily for heavy bombardment units. Repaired by COE in September 1943 and put into use immediately. Last USAAF unit left in March 1946.
- **Bari Airfield** – Located approximately 7km west of Bari. The base was used by the 15th USAAF as a command-and-control facility, using the airfield for reconnaissance and liaison units. Last USAAF unit left in September 1945.
- **Canne Airfield** – Located approximately 2.2 miles South-east of Campomarino. The airfield was used by the RAF 241 Squadron flying Spitfires, December 1943 – May 1944. The base was afterwards used by parts of the Italian Anti-cobelligerent Air Force and Yugoslav Air Force until the end of the war.
- **Castelluccio Airfield** – Abandoned, located approximately 15km south of Foggia. Semi-permanent heavy bomber airfield used by the 15th USAAF. Built by the COE in early 1944. It had one PSP runway with extensive taxiway and hardstand parking areas. Steel control tower. Opened 15 March 1944. Last combat operations flown in late April 1945. Closed August 1945.
- **Celone Airfield** – Abandoned German fighter base, located approximately 1km west-northwest of Foggia. Semi-permanent heavy bomber airfield used by the 15th USAAF. Bult by the COE in early 1944, with one 6,000-foot-long PSP runway with extensive taxiway and hardstand parking areas. Steel control tower. Opened 15 February 1944. Last combat operations flown in late April 1945. Closed October 1945.
- **Cerignola Airfield** – Abandoned, located in the vicinity of Cerignola. The airfield was captured and then operated by the 12th and 15th USAAF heavy bombers and tactical fighters. Also, major command and control headquarters. Opened late 1943. Last combat operations mid-1944. Used by 526th Air Service Group until July 1945 as a support base, then closed afterwards.
- **Foggia Airfield** – Now Foggia-Gino Lisa Airport. Located approximately 3km southwest of Foggia. Captured airfield and used by 12th and 15th USAAF by both for operational aircraft and as a major command-and-control headquarters. Inactivated in February 1946 and turned over to Allied Italian Co-Belligerent Air Force. Today it is a commercial airport.
- **Giulia Airfield** – Abandoned, located approximately 6km northwest of Cerignola. Semi-Permanent heavy bomber airfield used by the 15th USAAF. Built by the COE in late 1943. One PSP runway with extensive taxiway and hard standing parking areas. Steel control tower. Opened January 1944. Closed in late July 1945.
- **Lesina Airfield** – Abandoned, located approximately 22km east-southeast of Campomarino. Temporary airfield used by the 12th and 15th USAAF fighter units. Built by COE early 1944 with a single main PSP runway with large parking area. Possible steel control tower. Large containment area for personnel. Last combat operations in September 1945. Closed and dismantled soon afterwards.
- **Lucera Airfield** – Abandoned, located approximately 13km west-northwest of Foggia. Semi-permanent heavy bomber airfield used by 15th USAAF. Built by the COE inn late 12943. One PSP runway with extensive taxiway and hard stand parking areas. Steel control tower. Opened early February 1945. Last combat operations flown in late April 1945. Closed October 1945.
- **Madna Airfield** – Located approximately 5.5km southeast of Campomarino, on the Adriatic Coast. Temporary airfield used by 12th and 15th USAAF fighter groups, starting in November 1943 until the end of the war in May 1945. Built by COE with PSP runway with parking area, blister hangars. Closed May 1945 and dismantled.

- **Pantanella Airfield** – Abandoned, located approximately15km south of Cerigmnola. Semi-permanent heavy bomber airfield used by the 15th USAAF. Built by the COE in early 1944. Single PSP main runway with extensive taxiway and hard stand parking areas. Steel control tower. Opened March 1944. Remained in use until the end of the war, closing in July 1945.
- **Ramitelli Airfield** – Abandoned, located approximately 9km south-southeast of Campomarino, on the Adriatic Coast. Temporary airfield used by 15th USAAF 332d Fighter Group. PSP runway with parking area. Built by COE in early 1944. Closed in October 1945 and dismantled.
- **Salsola Airfield** – Abandoned, located approximately 17km north of Foggia. Temporary airfield used by the 15th USAAF 1st Fighter Group. PSP runway with parking area. Built by COE in late 1943. Used by 1st FG until March 1945. Closed in April 1945 and dismantled.
- **San Giovanni Airfield** – Abandoned, located approximately 9km west-southwest of Cerignola. Semi-permanent heavy bomber airfield used by the 15th USAAF. Built by COE in late 1943. Single PSP main runway with extensive taxiway and hardstand parking areas. Steel control tower. Opened January 1944. A very large and expansive facility used by two heavy bomb groups, six operational squadrons. Capacity up to 150 heavy bombers with large support facilities to east of airfield c/w blister hangars as well as wooden structures. Stayed operational until the end of the war. Closed in October 1945.
- **San Severo Airfield** – Abandoned, located approximately 40km north-north-west of Foggia. Temporary airfield used primarily by 12th and 15th USAAF reconnaissance units. Built by COE in late September 1943. Last combat operations flown in March 1945. Airfield closed in September 1945.
- **Spinazzola Airfield** – Abandoned, located approximately 13km east-southeast of Spinazzola. Semi-permanent heavy bomber airfield used by the 15th USAAF. Built by COE beginning in September 1943. Single PSP runway with extensive taxiway and hardstand parking areas. Steel control tower. Opened January 1944. Airfield operational until the end of war. Closed August 1945.
- **Sterparone Airfield** – Abandoned, located 11.1km south-southwest of San Severo. Temporary wartime facility. Built by COE beginning in September 1943, after Allied forces seized control of the Tavoliere plain around Foggia, Apulia, Italy. The only known use of the airfield was by the 15th USAAF 483rd Bombardment group, arriving from Tortorella Airfield, Italy on 22 April 1944. Single 6,000 ft x 100 ft with two perimeter tracks with hardstand parking. Personnel were housed primarily in tents. Steel control tower. The 483rd departed after the end of the war and moved to Pisa Airport on 15 May 1945. Closed and dismantled.
- **Stornara Airfield** – Abandoned, located approximately 14km west of Cerignola. Semi-permanent heavy bomber airfield used by the 15th USAAF. Built by COE beginning in September 1943. Single PSP runway with extensive taxiway and hardstand parking areas. Steel control tower. Opened January 1944. Airfield in operation until the end pf the war. Closed in 1945.
- **Torretto Airfield** – Abandoned, located approximately 14km southwest of Cerignola. Semi-permanent heavy bomber airfield used by the 15th USAAF. Built by COE beginning in September 1943. Two PSP runways with extensive taxiway and hardstand parking areas. Steel control tower. Opened in February 1944. Airfield in operation until the end of the war. Closed in August 1945.
- **Tortorella Airfield** – Abandoned, located 9.4km east-southeast of Foggia. A temporary wartime facility built by the COE. Work started shortly after Allied forces seized control of the Tavoliere plain around Foggia, Apulia, Italy. Airfield used by 99th Bombardment Group, which arrived from Oudna Airfield, Tunisia on 11 December 1943. Tortorella was a shared facility of the USAAF and the RAF. A single, 6,700 ft x 100 ft asphalt runway laid over PSP. A second (unfinished) runway east of the main runway was used as a crash strip. Two perimeter tracks with several loop taxiways containing 50 aircraft parking hardstands. Personnel were housed primarily in tents. Steel control tower.

- **Triolo Airfield** – Abandoned, located approximately 8km southeast of San Severo. Captured *Regia Aeronautica* airfield used by 12th USAAF fighter units. Repaired by COE in September 1943 and put into use immediately. In operational use until August 1945 when the USAAF turned over the facility to Allied Italian Co-Belligerent Air Force. Dismantled after the war.
- **Venosa Airfield** – Abandoned, located approximately 9km west-southwest of Barletta. Temporary airfield used by the 12th USAAF fighter and light/medium bombardment units. Built by COE beginning in September 1943. One PSP runway with extensive taxiway and hardstand parking areas. Wooden control tower. Opened 14 March 1944. Last combat operations flown in late April 1945. Closed on 4 July 1945 and then dismantled.
- **Vincenzo Airfield** – Abandoned, located approximately 9km west-southwest of Barletta. Temporary airfield used by the 12th USAAF fighter and light/medium bombardment units. Built by COE in late September 1943. Last combat operations flown in February 1945. Used by the 542nd Air Service Group until October 1945, then closed.

Abbreviations:

USAAF – United States of America Air Force
COE – US Army Corps of Engineers
PSP – Pierced Steel Plank

Chapter 6

RAF 73 & 39 Squadron's AIR's

A. 73 Squadron's AIR's:
NOVEMBER 1940 through to APRIL 1944:

The following information has been collated from the Squadrons Operations Record Books [AIR's], which are kept at the National Archives – Kew. Due to the level of content, it has not been possible to record every finite detailed daily input in each AIR's daily/monthly report and the following is a snapshot in the days/months of the Squadrons exploits during World War 2, both in North Africa and Italy.

LEGEND: *a/c – aircraft, e/a – enemy aircraft, LG – Landing Ground, MT's– motor transport, PO's – Pilot Officer, Sgt. - Sergeant*

AIR 27/629/27 also AIR 27/638
November 1940:

5 November	Squadron based at RAF Debden. Instructions from Fighter Command, FC/S. 21690/AOA, dated 5/11/1940. The squadron to proceed overseas.
6 November	Flying personnel on leave and ordered to report at noon on 09th at Debden. Other ranks were also given Embarkation Leave.
7 & 8 November	Nothing to record on these days, almost the whole squadron being on leave.
9 November	All flying personnel reported to RAF Debden except for Sgt. Pilot Furneaux.
13 November	RAF personnel boarded SS Franconia in Henderson Berth, West Float, Birkenhead, Liverpool. Set sail and joined the main convoy.
16 November	HMS Furious was observed in the early morning to be in convoy with SS Franconia and HMS Manchester and others of His Majesty's Fleet. The pilots and aircraft of the Squadron were on HMS Furious.
17 to 21 November	SS Franconia and HMS Furious between them carried the whole Squadron were on the high seas in the Atlantic Ocean. No event occurred.
22 November	HMS Furious no longer with convoy. SS Franconia docked at Gibraltar in the early evening. No shore leave granted.
23 November	SS Franconia remained moored in Gibraltar. HMS Manchester lying alongside Franconia, both ships and crew opened fire on hostile aircraft at 12,000 feet. The plane appeared to be a Glen Martin engaged in reconnaissance. HMS Furious continued southwards on her way to Takoradi.
24 November	RAF personnel transferred from SS Franconia to HMS Manchester in four separate parties.
25 November	The first party left SS Franconia at 04:00 hours and by 05:20 hours the whole Squadron had embarked without incident on board HMS Manchester.
26 November	The RAF officers were housed in naval officers' quarters whilst the men were quartered in various parts of the ship.

27 November	At 11:20 hours "Action Stations" was sounded, and HMS Manchester received orders to engage the Italian Fleet off Cape Spartivento. The ship opened fire at around 12 noon and continued for a full hour. However, several salvoes from the Italian fleet fell near the Manchester. No Italian aircraft were seen.
28 November	Still on-board HMS Manchester proceeded to Alexandria. The ship increased speed on the night of the 28th and left behind the accompanying convoy.
30 November	HMS Manchester docked in Alexandria at around 11:00 hours. At 14:00 hours the Squadron disembarked and entrained at 15:30 hours, leaving the dockyard at 16:00 hours and proceeded to Heliopolis (RAF Cairo), arriving at 21:30.

AIR 27/629/27 also AIR 27/638
December 1940:

1 December	Whole Squadron, (except for Pilots and aircraft) at Heliopolis where they proceeded to take over the Headquarters allotted to them and to unpack stores and equipment. The pilots were on their way to Heliopolis via Dessert Route from Takoradi. S/Ldr. Murray, P/O Humphries, P/O Legge, Sergt. Laing, Sergt. Stenhouse and Sergt. Brimble were being escorted across the dessert by a Blenheim, which lost its bearings owing to a W/T failure. All seven A/C forced landed in the dessert due to darkness falling. Sergt. Brimble was killed, one Hurricane written off and remaining four A/C were damaged.
2 December To 5 December	Pilots and aircraft in numbers of six (6) Hurricanes, were flown from Takoradi, escorted by one (1) Blenheim to guide them. Much confusion with stores and equipment, as crates and boxes were not marked properly. The mistakes were on the part of the authorities in England, referred to the Operations Book for November 1940. It is hope similar mistakes will not happen again! Took 3 weeks to sort out. Pilots arrived safely from Takoradi.
6 December	More arrivals from Takoradi. No flying took place from Heliopolis. P/O Bernard went to 103 MU, in an attempt to find our missing stores.
7 December	Three P/O's and three Serg't plots arrived from Takoradi. The first Squadrons Detail Order was promulgated. Nothing else to record.
8 December	S/L Murray, Officer Commanding the Squadron and Four (4) other P/Os arrived from Takoradi. Arrangements were being made to organise some Squadron Sports; Rugby, Hockey and Football all being available. P/O Bernard returned from 103 MU, he reported it would take 14 days to sort out the stores and equipment. He would return in 2 to 3 days.
9 December	All pilots have arrived, except for P/O's Humphries and Legge, Serg'ts Stenhouse and Laing, they are in the Sudan awaiting repair of 4 a/c which crash landed. Rumours of a pending move are rife.
10 December	Instructions received that 'B' Flight detached to the Fleet Air Arm at Dakheila tomorrow. P/O Bernard returned to 103 MU. No flying operations today, just engaged in fitting out in readiness for flying. All keen to get involved in the battle, either Greece or Western Dessert.
11 December	Five (5) pilots flew to Dakheila (Fleet Air Arm) plus three other pilots to which they have been attached. Two of the P/O's and twenty (24) crew travelled by road.

12 December	Fine and clear. P/O Millist flew to Dakheila. Sub-Lieutenants Walsh and Richards posted to Fleet Air Arm Unit at Dakheila. F/O Baker-Harber admitted to hospital, F/O Hoole Intelligence Officer has taken over his duties as Adjutant. P/O Gray has been posted to No. 70 (ME) Operational Training. No flying except practice flights around aerodrome.
13 December	Fine and clear; no flying except ½ hour testing. Serg't Pilot Geyders posted to No. 70 (ME) Operational Training. Five (5) Hurricanes ferried to 102 MU, with pilots returning by rail later in the day.
14 December	Nothing to report today.
15 December	Cold wind but fine; four (4) pilots went by air to Western Dessert (Sidi Hanaish) for attachment to 274 Squadron, ground party went by road. No other actions to record.
16 December	Cold and fine. F/O Couchman arrived from 274 Squadron, he has lengthy experience of Western Dessert conditions. F/O Baker-Harber discharged from hospital and resumed Adjutant duties. P/O Scott, DFC moved to 2nd 10th General Hospital, Cairo, sever attack of colitis, condition serious. Enemy aircraft shot down four plus one probable during patrol round Bardia.
17 December To 18 December	Nothing of importance to record. Rumours of a Squadron move to Amriya persist even when cancellation of the original decision to send the Squadron there, it is understood that is where we are going.
19 December	F/L Baird Medical Officer left to visit Amriya to carry out inspection and plan for the Squadrons move.
20 December	F/L Smith is sick moved from Sidi Hanaish to hospital. P/O Goord flying to Sidi Hanaish to take his place. Practice flying only. Squadron stopped all Operational Flying from Heliopolis.
21 December	P/O Stevens left for Amriya to establish a Mess Bath for Officers and Sergeants. The Squadron has no provisions with which to start a Mess and the £20 allowed by ACC seems very inadequate. P/O Stevens sent to Alexandria to get the bare essentials for our move.
22 December	Move to Amriya seems certain. F/O Hoole along with ten men have gone to Amiya to prepare the station for the arrival.
23 December	P/O Bernard returned from 103 MU having recovered greater part of stores and equipment, but still a number of crates missing. Long distance special fuel tanks fitted to Hurricanes for the Dessert Journey have been removed. All aircraft are now ready to operate.
24 December	Orders arrived for Squadron to move to Sid Hanaish. This will be in two stages, the first to Amriya on 29 December, then on the 30 December move from Amriya to Sidi Hanaish. All ranks delighted because the three weeks inactivity following upon the journey from England have proved irksome.
25 December	XMAS DAY: Squadron personnel had a successful Christmas dinner and entertainment. The Officers waited upon the men, and all had a great time. Sergeants being entertained to alcoholic refreshments in the Officers Mess. P/O Stevens and all the men returned from Amriya.
26 December To 27 December	Two days spent entirely in getting ready for move to Sid Hanaish. Nothing of any consequence to report, arrangements all went smoothly and by the evening of the 27th all in readiness for the Advance Party to leave on the 28th.

28 December	Advance Party left for Amriya and arrived at 16:00 hours, where they spent the night. F/L Baird and P/O Stevena accompanied this party.
29 December	Main Party, Adjutant in charge left for Amriya and arrived at 17:00 hours. The Advance Party left Amriya at 07:00 hours for Sidi Hanaish. These moves were carried out without incident or injury to personnel.
30 December	Main Party proceeded from Amriya to Sid Hanaish by road and arrived around 17:00 hours. Rations were dealt out, almost impossible to eat due to severe sandstorm. The men and officers slept in crowded tents as the Advance Party hadn't had the opportunity to erect all required tents. The Squadron were greeted by 112 Squadron, who would be leaving for Amriya in the morning. 112 Squadron did not take too much notice of what 73 Squadron required and required that the Squadrons Adjutant signed for the stores and equipment before 112 squadron left. Before signing off a fire started at 13:15 hours in the Officers Mess and within ½ hour it was burnt to the ground. The good news was that the contents were saved. The fire had started in the kitchen, presumably by accident.
31 December	Fine and clear. Pilots on detachment to HMS Grek (Dakheila) arrived at 10:00 hours and three of them were ordered to patrol around the Bardia area. Nothing reported. The air party from Heliopolis arrived. Adjutant and Intelligence Officer visited 202 Group to gain information concerning respective duties. Rest of the day spent settling in and into working order.

AIR 27/630/1 & AIR 27/630/2 Pilot Ops Report.
January 1941:

1 January Sidi Hanaish	Clear sunny morning, excellent visibility. "B" Flight took off 08:35 hours to patrol around the Bardia area. No enemy aircraft in sight and landed at Base at 14:00 hours. F/O McColl landing at Siddi Hanaish North, finally returning to Squadron at 16:02 hours. "A" Flight left at 11:48 hours on offensive patrol of the Bardia area, again no enemy aircraft seen. All landed back at base.
2 January	Clear and sunny with slight wind. "A" Flight took off at 08:20 hours to patrol the enemy positions in the Bardia area arriving back at 13:40 hours. The aircraft refuelled at Sidi Barrani as it was quite a flight. It is anticipated that if Bardia falls then the Squadron will move 100 miles Westward. Four to five-hour patrols are hard on the Pilots. "B" Flight carried out the afternoon patrol taking off at 11:30 hours and landing back at 17:00 hours. No enemy aircraft were spotted.
3 January	Clear and sunny; message received last night to the effect that a major move is imminent with the object being to capture Bardia. From 07:30 hours a Hurricane was dispatched from Base every 10 minutes to patrol at Angels 20 on a line Bir-Chleta-Gt, Gambut-Ras Uenna. Hurricanes were instructed when homeward bound to dive over Bardia for a recce purpose and all enemy aircraft to be avoided and ground troops and transport were not to be attacked. Throughout the day much information had been gathered with useful intelligence being forwarded to Group. Later in the day contact with enemy aircraft was made and they were shot down whilst trying to bomb our ships.
4 January	Clear and sunny again. A great of action was taking place throughout the day. It was report that our ground troops had captured 5,000 prisoners on the move toward Bardia. A signal had been received saying that the Army hoped to capture Bardia by the end of the day. However, the pilots reported late in the day that Bardia was still held to the South.

5 January	Fine and clear all day. Single aircraft dispatched at 15-minute intervals to patrol Great Gambut area at Angels 20. 23 patrols were carried out. Pilots were informed to expect enemy air activity and not to attack fighters, only if they escorted bombers. A good number of enemy aircraft were shot down during the day. Bardia was captured along with 20,000 prisoners and that the Armoured Division were pressing on to surround Tobruk. The Squadron received some bad news that the NAAFI in Quasaba had no whiskey and that there was none left in Egypt, also that beer was to be rationed. A great deal of discontent fell around all.
6 January	Fine and clear up until 10:00 hours cloud came down with patches almost down to ground level at Tobruk. Above 4,000 feet it was clear. At 06:20 hours Hurricanes dispatched at 15-minute intervals and set to patrol between Gt. Gambut and Tobruk at Angels 20 with orders to avoid enemy fighters unless escorting bombers. Hurricanes patrolling between 10: 30 and 10:45 hours were to be over Tobruk at 20,000 feet to ensure that the enemy didn't interfere with the Bristol Blenheim's from 113 Squadron, who were taking pictures of Tobruk. During the day, several actions were taken against the enemy.
7 January	Flying operations over Tobruk postponed by order from 202 Group at 06:00 Hours and final abandoned, bad weather. Pilots and ground crew took advantage to rest through the day. The Squadron received orders to move its Advance Party from 79 LG *(Landing Ground)* to an LG some 5 miles NW of Sollum on the main Tobruk Road. Also, the Main Party should make ready to move there on the 10th. As many provisions, etc. from the NAAFI are to be pulled together as these may not be available further West in the forward area.
8 January	Fine and clear with 10 mph winds. Single Hurricanes were dispatch every 15 minutes from 06:30 hours. On return, pilots reported no enemy contact at all, and cloud base was at 2,000 feet in the patrol area. The pending move whilst clear the signal received stated that the Squadron stay put and operate from there. The Cypher Officers only has one set of books, and it is not possible to work in both places and be operational. The Main Party are to move as soon as possible in the morning to LG 5 miles North of Amseat near Bardia. Those carrying out patrols in the morning will remain. A second party of men and the Intelligence Officer along with the two Cypher Officers are to leave on the 10th.
9 January	The Main Party left and only intend to get to 79 LG, they should arrive before dark but did not leave until 10:00 hours. The Equipment Officer has gone ahead with pilot kits to Amseat so that when they arrive their kit will be waiting for them. On one of the patrols a C.M. 81 with Red Crosses painted all over the fuselage as well as upper and lower wings and appeared to be unarmed. The plane was flying at 1,000 feet just off the coast, West of Tobruk. The plane was allowed to continue. ***From AIR 27/638 (1) page 51 of 346: 1012281 AC2 Lamb part of the Main Party.***
10 January Sidi Hanaish	No enemy aircraft encountered during patrols around Tobruk. The Main Party spent the night en-route to Amseat, Second Party left Sidi Hanaish at 09:30 hours. One of the pickups almost u/s, finally "packed up" 15 miles from Sollum. The party spent the night at the roadside. Other incidents were recorded. Extraordinarily careless to send out 2 motor cars across the dessert without one complete set of tools.
11 January Amseat - Libya	Main Party arrived late last night with the Second Party arriving 17:00 hours today. No enemy aircraft sighted during patrols around Tobruk. Shortage of men meant a great number of tents could not be erected, also there are no telephones on camp and exceedingly difficult to operate without them.
12 January	Camp now getting more organised. We have a direct line to Advance Wing Headquarters, still no Internal camp telephone. Tents being put up. Restricted flying today due to sandstorm. No enemy aircraft were seen. Two Hurricanes carried out night patrol, they took after supposedly enemy plane. Later said to be friendly.

13 January	All tents erected, Cypher and Signals up and running. We still do not have a camp telephone making it exceedingly difficult for the Squadron Operations Officer to communicate with both Flights. No enemy aircraft seen whilst patrols were carried out around the Tobruk area. Two (2) Hurricanes were on standby for Night Flying.

14 January	Single patrols continued throughout the day up to 16:00 hours. No enemy aircraft reported. In carrying orders from AWC, Sgt. Garton was shot at by some Italians some 12 miles from Tobruk. AWC *(Advanced Wing Command)* were keen to know the movements of our own troops. Sgt. Garton dropped down to 50 feet and subsequently hit and crash-landed 2½ miles inside our lines. AWC required that recce reports be telephoned (inter alia). Exceedingly difficult when you have crash-landed in the dessert. Pilots according to AWC are to safeguard the Hurricanes, carry out the recce's and look out for enemy aircraft. Extremely dangerous. ***From AIR 27/638 (1) page 54 of 346: 1012281 AC2 Lamb on Guard Duty.***

15 January	No flying today, severe sandstorm from 04:00 to 17:00 hours and visibility nil. CO rang AWC on a matter of operational importance only to find there were no controllers in the Ops Room. AWC thought that the Controller was not required due to the sandstorm.

16 January	Nothing of major importance to report. Sgt. Ellis returned from patrol along the main road to Bardia from El Adam at 50 feet, saw 9 C.R.42's at around 200 feet. He increased to maximum speed and outdistanced from the enemy aircraft. No combat took place. Single patrols continued; no enemy aircraft seen. Very poor visibility.

17 January	Poor visibility. Sole patrols in the Tobruk area continued throughout the day. Having not received any orders from AWC, CO carried on with orders previously received. Communications with AWC broke down around 16:30 hours yesterday. Level of Communications is terrible.

18 January	Three solo patrols got off early but by 09:00 hours sandstorm blew up and no more flying. One patrol attacked enemy gun position at Sidi Mahmoud at 08:35 hours successfully killing several enemy and damaging the position. This was not strafing as he found himself at 50 feet due to the sandstorm and grasped the opportunity. Report and operational issues were being dealt with during the remainder of the day.

19 January	Four solo patrols and no more due to sandstorm. No enemy aircraft seen. Late in the day at 16:15 hours 3 Hurricanes were scrambled to search for a missing Blenheim, which was later confirmed as being at another LG. Lost flying time and fuel on this venture.

20 January	P/O Humphries return in a Blenheim (piloted by the CO from 113 Squadron) from Sidi Barrani. Every effort was made to start up his Hurricane to no avail. Whilst on patrol he was unable to find this aerodrome and struck the coast East of Sollum. Landed safely at Sollum. Visit from GC Speakman of 258 Wing to give the CO his instructions. Also, a visit from an Army Liaison Officer from 202 Group who gave details of the allied troop position. All duly copied and noted. CO held afternoon conference with pilots to explain the objections of the morrow.

21 January	First patrol of 5 aircraft due to take off at 06:30 hours were delayed owing to 9 Blenheim's of 55 Squadron having to go first. The last Blenheim dropped 2 small bombs just off the LG, we all thought we were being raided. Seconds later the Blenheim crashed and burst into flames, no one survived. It appeared that the two bombs had been loaded incorrectly and their release and explosion affected the aircraft. The patrol of 5 planes took off at 10:30 hours and West of Tobruk ran into two G.50's, which were chased Westward, the two G.50's was joined by 5 more. Air fight ensued (Wainwrights) Hurricane was seen going down in flames, 2 G.50's damaged and out of control. P/O Legge was hit from the ground, landed at El Adam with engine on fire, which was eventually put out. Great job.

22 January	More clarification received on communications and a specimen Daily Operational Summary (well prepared), was also received. Not sure how the Traffic and Cypher Officers can be deal with this when you're busy. Today 6 different sorties of 4 Hurricanes each took place. No enemy aircraft seen, or opposition encountered.
23 January	202 Group telephoned to confirm that 2 Hurricanes damaged by A/A on the 21st and that fighters are not to fly below 12,000 feet unless absolutely necessary. This order conflicts with the one from 258 Group, which stipulated that aircraft could fly at 6,000 feet. Two Wellingtons and 6 Hurricanes on route to Malta due to land for t. Doing our best to get some accommodation together. All had arrived by 11:15 hours. Between 07:30 and 15:30 hours patrols took place, five of which took off for Acroma – Ras El Mahita. Communique received from 258 Wing, Tobruk was now in Allies hands. All ground East of Derna has been taken. ***From AIR 27/638 (1) page 68 of 346: 1012281 AC2 Lamb on Guard Duty.***
24 January	Nothing of any importance to record. Two patrols of 3 A/C and 2 A/C took off, no enemy a/c seen.
25 January	The 6 long range Hurricanes took off for Gazala on their way to Malta with 2 Hurricanes as escort. They are to refuel at Gazala and then wait for the Wellingtons, last above the LG. The first Wellington broke its tail wheel whilst taxying and a replacement had to be sent for. The second Wellington was flown to Gazala with blankets and kit for the 6 Hurricanes pilots, but burst a tyre on landing, which meant that both planes were out of commission. The 6 Hurricanes return here. Patrols were carried out, no enemy a/c were seen. ***Today is the birthday of 1012281 AC2 Lamb's wife, Mabel.***
26 January	Replacement Wellingtons have arrived. Flight to Malta still on hold. Some pilots stranded at Gazala. Having to get a Vickers Valentia to fetch them back. Five Hurricanes patrolled over Mechili – Martuba. At the end of the patrol the Flight Commander noticed a plane was missing, saw some black smoke and investigated. It was smoke from a crashed C.R.42 and on climbing away over a Wadi at 2000 feet one of the planes flown by Sgt. Stenhouse was hit and controls locked. He managed to straighten and get to 2000 feet before parachuting to ground. He was midway between the enemy and allied troop positions.
27 January	Maximum patrols were put up over Mechili – Derna, orders stated major battle developing. The Squadron was short on planes, but 'A' Flight sent up 7 aircraft. They will need to refuel at Gazala prior to patrol, then return here and rearm and taken by another 7 pilots on the same patrol. 'B' Flight sent off 4 aircraft at 08:30 hours. The Vicker Valentia left at 07:45 hours to pick up Hurricane guns and pilots. Subject to its return the expedition to Malta is planned for noon. Other patrols took place and news back that Stenhouse was in hospital with a broken leg. Good news.
28 January	Six Hurricanes of 'A' Flight and four from 'B' Flight (all we could muster), carried out one patrol each over Mechili – Derna area no enemy in sight. Pilots reported that this area now seems to be in our hands. Intermittent sandstorm prevents Malta flight from taking off. Orders came that 'B' Flight was to move to Gazala tomorrow.
29 January	The Malta planes were set for take-off, 6 Hurricanes at 09:00 hours, refuelling at Gazala and the 2 Wellingtons at 11:00 hours. They will rendezvous over Gazala. The third Wellington had returned to Delta yesterday. The furth took off with Officers and sergeants at 10:00 hours. The fifth Wellington is still at Gazala waiting repair. Considerably more action and patrols took place during the remaining hours of the day.

30 January	Small sandstorm developed during the morning. Only 6 Hurricanes could be mustered for patrol over Derna – Mechili line. Four replacement Hurricanes are at Aboukir waiting pick up. There are no planes available to take pilots to get them and one pilot has flown a Hurricane with a cracked cylinder head which will be left for repair.
31 January	Fine sunny day with everyone up at 05:30 hours and getting ready for our move to Gazala West. The first convoy was due to set off at 08:00 hours, in fact set off at 08:30 hours. The move was carried out smoothly, unlike previous moves. By 18:00 hours most of the Squadron had arrived at Gazala. Each section allocated and most of the tents erected. On arriving at Gazala we found 'B' Flight rather excited as they had spotted about 300 MT's and some 5,000 troops ready to escape the area. Operations were limited; however, 'B' Flight would take off early find the retreating convoy and shot it up. They caused considerable damage and killed many of the enemy. Gazala presented many good buildings that included various messes and that we shall all feel better off here than in Amseat.

AIR 27/630/3 & AIR 27/630/4 Pilot Ops Report

February 1941:

1 February El Gazala West	Great day in every way; 6 Hurricane under command of S/Ldr. Murray took off at 07:10 hours to ground strafe enemy MT's near Barca. CO, F/O Storrar (DFC) and P/O Warsham attacked Apollonia Aerodrome destroying 3 Ghiblis and a Caproni 310. All returned safely. The other three pilots under F/Lt. Beytagh shot up MT's. Many vehicles destroyed with heavy casualties inflicted. During the remainder of the day other sorties were undertaken which destroyed enemy aircraft, numerous lorries and many enemy troops killed. Satisfactory days' work.
2 February	Clear and sunny. The whole day was spent machine gunning enemy troops and MT's retreating to Barca on the road through Tobruk. 30/40 lorries destroyed or put out of action. No e/a seen but heavy A/A from Barca Aerodrome.
3 February	Another sunny day. Hurricanes despatched to machine gun MT's near Barca, continued all day. No e/a seen. All pilots returned safely. P/O Wareham took advance party to Apollonia, P/O Humpreys a party to Derna. The enemy retreat is rapid, HQME concentrating on getting petrol and oil to advanced positions asap to increase fighter range.
4 February	Four Hurricane patrols West of Barca. First patrol the only group to have combat. P/O McColl (Canadian) shot down a Caproni 133 at 500 feet, P/O Goodman (DFC) destroyed in flames a C.R.42. P/O Millist missing in action. P/O Eiby gone on leave, P/O McFadden went on leave on the 2nd. Both to return with new replacement Hurricanes.
5 February	CO (S/Ldr. Murray), F/O Storrar (DFC) and Sgt. Marshall flew to Derna last night and left that Aerodrome at 06:15 hours to attack Benina Aerodrome. About 8 enemy bomders destroyed on the ground, pilots with no opposition. Other patrols flew around Benghazi, no e/a, or troops seen. Four lorries left to move petrol from Derna to Marana. This left the squadron short on serviceable vehicles – an awkward situation.
6 February	A complete blank day. Sandstorm raged all night and all day. A Wellington force landed, undamaged. Four Swordfish, which took off at 19:00 hours on the 5th had a very difficult time; two returned safely, one crash landed at Ain El Gazala and the fourth is missing, the planes unable to contact any enemy shipping. P/O Millist no news either killed or captured.

7 February	Sun but wind at 40 mph. One patrol of 3 aircraft took off in the morning but saw nothing. All patrols cancelled for the day. Benghazi area taken except for Glerrines. Lunch time saw P/O Millist walking into the Mess with P/O Wareham, who brought from Derna. He had been shot down by a C.R.42, force-landed in enemy territory 10 miles NE of Benina. On the 4th he walked and hid, he had no compass or revolver. Spotted by an Italian but eluded him. Tried sleeping n bushes, but too cold so carried on walking. He saw what appeared to be retreating Italian troops marching towards Benghazi. They didn't see him. On the 5th at 14:00 hours he met an Australian Sergeant who gave him food and water. He reported that he bolted as soon as he crashed, many enemies about. Celebration in the Mess. CO took him to 202 Group, and they stayed for dinner. FAA detachment to go to El Adem.
8 February	Very windy and cold. No operational flying at all. CO flew to El Adem in a Hurricane to check on detachment there. Return of pilots from leave or sick, they brought new Hurricanes. The beer, oranges, etc., brought back were very welcome.
9 February	Cold wet morning after night of severe rainstorms. It was nice to hear and feel the rain. No flying at all. Under orders to withdraw advance parties from Benina and Derna. It is unclear as to why the withdrawal. Officers see fit to tidy up and repair some equipment. At 15:00 Leiut. Lea of the FAA landed safely with the missing Swordfish. Crew and machine all OK after their force-landing at El Mechili. Engine would not start.
10 February	Strong gusty wind but fine. No operational flying at all. Strong rumours afloat of move to Greece, our EO had been told at 202 Group plus pilots were told the same at El Adam. CO went to Group to find out definite information, no luck. GC Guest told him that the Squadron was to move East very soon.
11 February	Fine, sunny, but cold day. Group ordered that 3 Hurricanes make ready to escort Mr. Menzies, PM of Australia to Benghazi. All pilots returned from their patrol escort Message received that ACC in C, Air Chief Marshall Longmore to visit Squadron at 08:30 hours tomorrow. Squadron may get more details about pending move. Very poor, misleading communications received, in particular the agreed use of words not being adhered to.
12 February	Fine sunny morning. The ACC in C arrived at 10:30 hours (not 08:30 hours) with WC Chichester and a S/Ldr. Air Commodore Coulishaw arrived later by plane. Meeting took place, then ACC in C toured the camp and left at 12:30 hours. Continuous patrols all day, escort duty to 11 Naval Ships from Tobruk to Benghazi. AC Coulishaw lunched in the Mess before leaving for 202 Group. The ACC in C had no update on the Squadron moving Eastward or remain in Libya.
13 February	Hot and sunny. At 07:40 hours F/C Storrar and P/O Lamb took off to continue patrol of Naval Convoy. F/Lt. Castles arrived in a Lysander and told the CO of Benghazi being badly bombed over each of the last two days. CO flew to Group to request that patrols over Benghazi are set up, this request was granted. 202 Group to move from Benghazi back to Tobruk.
14 February	S/Ldr. Murray and two others took off at 06:00 hours to Benghazi, despite flying over the are no enemy a/c where found, the Italians were not in the area. The 3 men had breakfast in a Cafe with AC Coulishaw in Barca, then returned to Gazala. Visit from official press photographer, an official artist and journalist looking to do a piece P/O McColl who had shot down one of the largest aircraft used by the Italians. Orders were received that one Flight to be detached – half to Benina and half to El Adam. Order not clear regarding self-contained units or under another unit. CO motored to Group to get clarification.

15 February	Windy and slight sandstorm in the morning. The morning was used to make arrangements for the two detachments as self-contained units. Late order cancelled the Benina detachment. Three pilots flew to El Adam and three went by road. On their arrival 4 pilots are to return. Squadron to remain here on stand-by to move to Area 26, understood to be Delta Area. Personnel returned from leave and others went on leave.
16 February	A fine sunny day. No operational flying. Notification received that as from midnight tonight 202 Group will cease control of Squadron operations. In future this will come from RAF Headquarters, Cyrenaica, at Barca. Three of the Palestinians comprising the Pioneer Corps Detachment on Camp caused some trouble, so the CO had them all march at the double for 20 minutes in full kit. No further trouble anticipated.
17 February	Instructions received that a Squadron was to arrive at El Adem during the day and protective patrols were to be maintained over the aerodrome, for as long as the Squadron might remain. CO and S/Ldr. Murray flew to HQME to get details concerning future movements of Squadron. Orders received that one flight and HQ Flight to move to Delta Area. During CO absence order received for one flight to move to Amirya in preparation in going overseas, all carried out by the Adjutant.
18 February	All necessary vehicles loaded and started off on their long journey to Amriya. On instruction from HQME tents left and only minimum equipment was taken. "A" flight remained at Gazala, awaiting further orders. No flying took place. Early rumours of move to Greece were confirmed when orders that an experienced Hurricane pilot was to go to El Adem and from there flown to an aerodrome in Greece to advise on its suitability for Hurricanes. The Amriya convoy spent the night just West of Bardia near a large MRS, the officers of which put up the Officers and entertained them.
19 February	Fine and sunny. Three pilots were ordered to Benina to reinforce No. 3 Squadron, RAAF in defence of Tobruk. When on Patrol over Benghazi F/O Storrar intercepted several ME 110's, damaged one, while P/O Lamb chased a JU88 outb to sea. 'B' Flight detachment at El Adem maintained patrols in defence of Tobruk. The Amirya convoy proceeded on its way with the majority of vehicles reaching Mersa Matruh, there were some that didn't due to breakdowns.
20 February	Fine and clear. No air activity at Gazala as patrols were carried out from El Adem by 'B' Flight detachment. No e/a were seen. The Amriya convoy arrived in the evening only to learn that orders for Crete had been cancelled and it was to return asap to Gazala. Cancellation no doubt due to the German and Italian bombed of Benghazi and Tobruk. The kit being carried by the broken-down lorries was loaded on to alternative transport for return to Gazala. The Amriya base had been made ready with new tents and a hangar by the Station Adjutant, all well received.
21 February	No flying at Gazala; El Adem detachment carried out dawn and dusk patrols over Tobruk, but no e/a seen. At Amriya the Station Adjutant tried to get new MT's along with other vital equipment to enable the Squadron to return. Pay Parade arranged and all personnel went on liberty runs to Alexandria, a privilege richly earned. S/Ldr. Rule of HQME to meet with the Station Adjutant at Amriya to discuss equipment for the return of the Squadron to Gazala.
22 February	Three pilots from 'A' Flight were attached to No. 3 Squadron, RAAF Benina in the morning. A Lysander took their kit. 'B' Flight detachment at El Adem carried out patrols of Tobruk Area.

23 February	The detachment at Benina had several scrambles over Benghazi Area, no e/a were seen. No flying from Gazala, El Adem detachment carried out defensive patrols of Tobruk Area. The first portion of the Amriya convoy left Amriya for Gazala. Station Adjutant and EO were successful in obtaining 5 new MTs for the Squadron. Desperately needed.
24 February	All day standing patrols maintained over the convoy leaving Benghazi for Tobruk. No e/a seen. Dawn and dusk patrols of 2 aircraft were put up over Tobruk. Two pilots returned to Gazala from El Adem.
25 February & 26 February	Benina detachment maintained defensive patrols over Benghazi Area. Similar patrols by 'A' Flight from Gazala and 'B' Flight detachment from El Adem over Tobruk Area. E/a were said to be in the area, but none seen.
27 February	The Benina detachment to return to Gazala and a further 3 a/c being sent tom El Adem. This will mean all of 'B' Flight will be at El Adem, whilst 'A' Flight will remain at Gazala, both Flights will share the duties of protecting Tobruk. At Gazala 2 a/c were at readiness throughout the day and in addition the usual to dawn and dusk patrols were put up. Two scrambles during the day one at 08:05 Hours and one at 15:15 hours.
28 February	Windy and intermittent sandstorms all day. Dawn patrol over Tobruk carried out by P/O Wareham and P/O Legge at 06:30 hours. They saw enemy aircraft. P/O Wareham attacked a JU 88, but no results observed. P/O Legge attacked a Heinkel 111, but no results observed. The enemy aircraft returned fire, but no damage was recorded to the two Hurricanes. Dusk patrol carried out in awfully bad weather; no e/a seen. Sandstorms prevented further flying operations.

AIR 24/630/5 (2) & AIR 27/630/6 Pilot Ops Report
March 1941:

1 March El Gazala	Very windy and intermittent sandstorms. 2 a/c patrol took off at 06:15 hours, patrolled area over Tobruk nothing seen. No fly until evening, dusk patrol took off at 17:30 hours patrolled over Tobruk no e/a seen. The Adjutant, F/L Baker-Harber admitted to sick quarters, intestinal trouble. P/O Harnett GAC arrived with money for airmen's pay. A few cables and even less letters. Receipt is welcomed, feeling rife among men, someone has blundered as some men have not had any mail since leaving England on 15th November last.
2 March	Windy again, sandstorms abated. Dawn patrol over Tobruk carried out, on return reported still very bad for flying. Two aircraft at readiness all day. Communication by telephone with 258 Wing at El Adem still chaotic. The line in camp is correct, not sure if Wing have done anything their end? When contact is made its very poor, impossible to hear. Pay, now sometime overdue to the men arrived today. Pay parade arranged. Hurricane arrived back from El Adem for servicing.
3 March	Fine but windy. We learnt today that Sergt. Leng 'B' Flight took off at 21L45 hours from El Adem on 'B' Flight patrol line near Tobruk and had not returned. No R/T contact or beacon at El Adem. Under the circumstances inadvisable to send any pilot out to do a night patrol on such a night. Dawn patrol carried out. S/Ldr. Murray admitted to sick quarters, intestinal trouble, not serious. After 3 pilots were detached to N. 3 Squadron, this left squadron with only 9 pilots inclusive of CO. Aircraft at readiness cancelled and replaced with a standing patrol of one a/c over Tobruk. 'B' and 'A' Flights provide the required patrols, including dusk patrol. P/O's Beytagh and Millist returned from Crete and have joined 'B' Flight at El Adem.

4 March El Gazala	Fine sunny day. The wind has at last subsided. News received in signal from 55 Squadron at 09:00 hours that Sergt.Leng was in Tobruk hospital suffering from exhaustion. This means he is safe and news very welcome. He is an old member of the squadron with much expertise. His loss would be a severe blow. At 12:15 hours unidentified plane heard over camp. Two Hurricanes took off to intercept. Climbed to 20,000 feet and circled Tobruk, could not locate, no doubt e/a. Single patrols carried out from 12:3 0 hours until 18:15 hours. The CO and Adjutant discharged from Squadron sick quarters. At 18:30 hours a Blenheim from 55 Squadron landed owing to dark setting in, had been reconnoitring over Tripoli. Sergt. Leng discharged from hospital and returned to his flight at El Adem. His a/c found some 15 miles from Sidi Mahmoud. Seemed he could not find aerodrome and bailed out. This is his third time with two at night. Had a visit from GC Guest, of HQ RAF Cyrenaica and Padre Cox on their way to Heliopolis. They stayed the night.
5 March	Fine and sunny. 55 Squadron Blenheim took off this morning. Patrol of the Tobruk convoy carried out one at 08:30 hours and again at 10:00 hours. Convoy to be patrolled all day with two plots at 'readiness' until dusk. Squadron should be moving to Sidi Mahmoud. Dusk patrol over Tobruk no e/a seen. No other operational flying took place.
6 March El Gazala	Fine and windy. P/O Legge left in a Lysander with AC Kent for Heliopolis. Hopefully, the Hurricane left by S/Ldr. Murray, 18th February will be ready to fly. Dawn patrol reported no e/a seen. Pilot from El Adem reported at 09:30 hours sighting a JU 88, which was out of range. On seeing the Hurricane, the e/a climbed into cloud, not found. Sergt. Leng has gone on a well-earned brake. At 13:52 hours a despatch rider from the 19th Australian Brigade brought a signal saying three enemy bombers had bombed a MT Column about 25 miles West of here. The attack took place at 12:52 hours. Squadron informed 258 Wing but took 5 minutes to pass on the news. We asked do we proceed with action the answer came back negative, much to the disgust of the pilots at readiness. CO and Adjutant visited Sidi Mahmoud to inspect our next camp.
7 March	Fine and clear. Two Hurricanes carried out the dawn patrol, while two other a/c maintained a standby patrol from 07:15 hours to 12:00 hours over a convoy travelling from Tobruk Harbour. From the MT bombings of yesterday three aircraft, instead of 2, at readiness. Signal received, Squadron to move to Sidi Mahmoud asap. Aerodrome currently occupied by 55 (Blenheim) Squadron and is 10 miles South of Tobruk. Sorry to leave Gazala with the lovely sea views.
8 March	Very sunny and clear. Two pilots from 6 Squadron arrived in a Lysander at 10:15 hours with orders to fly two Hurricanes back as the Squadron were to equip with Hurricanes. The pilots were given time to fly their hurricanes. They flew back in the Lysander at 16:00 hours. Received word that GC Brown, OC HQ Cyrenaica would pay us a visit at about 09:45 hours to make an inspection. CO and P/O McFadden went to Tobruk then to Sidi Mahmoud to make further arrangements for the Squadron move. Usual dawn to dusk patrols maintained plus the addition of one standing patrol on the 'A' line north of Tobruk between 13:00 hours and 17:00 hours. Nothing was seen.
9 March	Very fine and sunny. GC Brown piloted by S/Ldr., arrived in a Proctor at 10:00 hours. CO met their guest and accompanied him on his tour of inspecting the camp. Two a/c on dawn patrol, no e/a seen. Squadron under orders to move to Bu Amoud (Sidi Mahmoud) asap. Advance party left yesterday with the main body leaving tomorrow morning.
10 March Bu Amoud	Fine. Day spent moving ground personnel and equipment. Due to shortage of transport most vehicles had to make return journeys. The distance of the move is short and the whole move should be completed in 3 days. Pilots carried out standing patrols until 17:00 hours, P/O Humphreys was left at Gazala in charge of the rear party. On arrival P/O Bernard SEO found waiting for us. After being discharged from Amriya sick quarters he went to Heliopolis looking for stores and equipment for the Squadron.

11 March	Fine but slight sandstorms. 'B' Flight at El Adem carried out dawn patrol with dusk patrol carried out from here. Nothing else to report other than settling into our new quarters. None of which appeal to the Squadron like.
12 March	Sandstorms again. Dust and sand very prevalent here. Three pilots carried out dawn patrol over Tobruk, no e/a reported. Three pilots carried out dusk patrol without incident. Further tents arrived from Gazala but still not enough, some without quarters. F/O Scott, DFC returned yesterday from Benina – the last member of the original detachment. He was delayed due to a broken tail wheel.
13 March Bu Amoud	Our sleep was disturbed at 03:00 hours, heavy explosions in progress. It was not Tobruk so must be ElAdem, which was correct. Raid continued for 2 hours. Our aerodrome was not targeted. 'B' Flight returned and confirmed that the bombing had been severe. Had it not been for the sturdy buildings the Squadron would have sustained casualties. Only casualties, two prisoners and one Palestinian soldier. P/O Millist made a heroic effort to reach the dead men, and afterwards took off looking for the e/a. he damaged one of the e/a. Dawn patrols comprised three a/c but saw nothing. F/O Mason, DFC from 274 Squadron arrived to discuss the moving of 6 long range Hurricanes from El Adem (on their way to Malta) to Bu Amoud as he felt they would be safer here, Sandstorms, in varying intensity evident throughout the day. Major discomfort to the Squadron.
14 March	Violent sandstorm all day. F/O Mason and his Hurricanes still with us. The Wellington escort has not arrived yet. Dawn and dusk patrols were carried out. As from now the patrols at dawn to 13:00 hours will cease. 6 pilots will be on 'readiness'. The other Flights will do similar readiness from 13:00 to dusk, with 3 plots doing night 'readiness'.
15 March	Fins and sandstorms have stopped. A 'scramble' order received at 12:30 hours to attempt to intercept a recon aircraft and the section sent up did not see anything. No further operational flying took place. P/O Legge has gone to hospital. F/L Smith and Sergt. Leng each arrived in Blenheim's from Heliopolis.
16 March Bu Amoud	Fine and clear. At 05:00 hours aircraft heard. The pilots in OR identified as a Wellington once correct signal had been received. A convoy escorted from Tobruk going Eastwards until noon, no e/a encountered, 274 Squadron pilots under F/O Mason, DFC still with us, the Wellington not yet arrived.
17 March	Fine and clear. From 06:25 to 10:55 hours patrols over a convoy approaching Tobruk were carried out. Two Hurricanes forming the flight in each case. At 11:30 a 'scramble' order to intercept e/a presumed to be approaching the area. No interception was made. Immediately on landing at 12:15 hours 'scramble' order received to intercept e/a, none seen. Large case of 'Comforts and Games' arrived from HQME. They are badly needed, much appreciated by the Squadron.
18 March	First Hurricane off at 11:00 hours to patrol convoy near Tobruk. 'Scramble' orders at 12:20 hours as e/a plotted moving towards Tobruk. Two Hurricanes took off, attached never materialised, no e/a seen. Fine and sunny. Patrols continued throughout the day until 18:25 hours. The new camp is shaping up nicely.
19 March	Defensive patrols of the Tobruk area commenced at dawn, 'scramble' order received and cancelled before the planes took off. Footballs arrived and a game was played between Officers and Airmen. Strong wind much in evidence as was the fact that the officers were 'rugger' players. The airmen won 4 – 0. G booster for all.

20 March Bu Amoud	Gale – dust rising. Despite the adverse weather conditions, a patrol commenced at 06:25 hours and continued until 11:30 hours. No further flying. CO went to Group HQ Barca, arrived back after lunch. 'A' Flight defeated HG 2 goals to 1 at 'soccer'.
21 March	Strong wind and sand rising. Convoy patrolled from 06:10 hours until 11:40 hours. Convoy moving Westward patrolled from 14:00 hours until 17:35 hours, rather late considering the weather. Successful 'whist drive' held in the airmen's dining hall, over 60 in attendance.
22 March	From dawn until 10:0 hours a standing patrol was maintained over a convoy approaching Tobruk. 'Scramble' order at 13:25 hours but no e/a seen. Sandstorms for the rest of the day and all flying cancelled. Third week without fresh meat, practically no goods at the NAAFI. Difficult to understand when convoys are going to and from Delta almost every day.
23 March	Violent sandstorms all day. One Hurricane carried out a defensive patrol from 07:25 to 08:25 hours. All further patrols wiped out due to the weather conditions.
24 March	S/Ldr. Whitehead paid us a visit and was well impressed with our medical arrangements. Standing patrols over a convoy in Tobruk Area were maintained from 06:10 hours until 13:25 hours. 'Scramble' order received but unlucky again, no e/a seen. They seem to fly remarkably high and turn back before we can make contact. Officers accepted a challenge from the Senior NCOs to a soccer match, with the officers being favourite. The result was a draw, 2 goals each. The camp is well defended with slit trenches in evidence everywhere, as well as sandbagged gun posts.
25 March	Standing patrols maintained again over convoy moving West towards El Gazala. Two 'scramble' orders resulted in no better luck than before; no e/a seen. The weather improved and much good work in cleaning the camp up was carried out. Practice Air Raid Alarm was carried out in the afternoon. F/O Lewis and F/O Hoole have not returned, and a search party is being suggested. Stocks extremely LOW.
26 March	F/O Lewis and F/O Hoole returned late last night just before dinner with their pick-up fully laden with fruit, drinks, and other luxuries. They were given a good welcome as stocks were extremely low and all at a low ebb for a week or more. From 10:40 hours to 16:00 hours standing patrols of two aircraft were maintained over a convoy 7 ships approaching Tobruk from the east. No e/a seen. Weather poor again with rising sand. Work continues to beef up the defence of the camp. The station prisoners have been found very useful.
27 March	Clear morning, severe sandstorms developed after lunch. Patrols over ships approaching Tobruk were maintained regardless, up to 14:00 hours. No 'Scrambles' again.
28 March Bu Amoud	Sandstorms again. This is the worst camp for sand that we have yet encountered. Ships leaving Tobruk in an Easterly direction were escorted as far as Raz Azzaz. The stocks in the Airmen's Canteen is giving cause for concern and much anxiety. CO visited Tobruk to obtain supplies and has been told your next. The Australian Canteen at Tobruk is well stocked and is not going down well with the airmen. There is plenty of beer at Mersah Matruh.

29 March	Clear sunny morning with a resulting risen in the spirits of all. Local flying by both Flights. S/Ldr. Murray to HQ Cyrenaica at Barce in a Hurricane. Protection of the Ops Room continued using Station Prisoners. From noon onwards protective patrols over ships leaving Tobruk for Alexandria carried out. Noe/a seen. F/L McLachlan, DFC, formal 'B' Flight at Castle Camps who volunteered at the end of October with P/O Eliot, to go to the Middle east arrived yesterday with F/O Storrar in a Magister from Alexandria, F/L McLauchlan not only obtained a bar to his decoration since going to Malta, but also his promotion to Flight Lieutenant has shot down 8 e/a is his short stay on Malta. He was wounded in his last engagement and lost an arm. Under orders to return to the UK. He is still keen to get back into Hurricanes if the Ministry will permit. He can fly Magisters. All pleased to see him, charming, well-mannered and are proud of his success.
30 March	All proud this morning as our CO is to be awarded a DFC by HM the King for his courageous leadership and determination in the leading of the Squadron. He was showered in congratulations when he entered the Mess after leading a practice Squadron formation flight. Throughout the day standing patrols were carried out over ships leaving and entering Tobruk. No e/a seen. Two 'scrambles' were given out in the afternoon but in each case a/c plotted proved to be friendly. Football matches proved to be popular. Last night 'B' Flight beat HQ Flight 2 – 1 after a good game. 'B' Flight building up a good reputation.
31 March	Dawn patrols over a convoy approaching Tobruk were carried out. Two 'scrambles' were ordered, both proved friendly aircraft. 'A' Flight carried out a formation 'Balbo' which was well executed. Postings came through for P/O McColl (Canadian) pilot and Cpl. Le Vesconte – Orderley Room NCO; both will be much missed, and we all wish them well. 'Chip' McColl is much envied he is proceeding to the UK. News arrived that 148 Squadron are joining us at Sidi Mahmud.

AIR 27/630/7 & AIR 27/630/8 (1) Pilot Ops Report
April 1941:

1 April Bu Amud	Very quiet day. Single Hurricanes carried out patrols over convoy leaving Tobruk at noon. No e/a seen. A.M. Todder of HQME visited the camp and left at 18:00 hours. Unclear for the purpose of his visit.
2 April	Further shipping escorted during the morning without incident. At 16:15 hours we had a scramble. Two Hurricanes sent up to 15,000 feet some 15 miles West of Tobruk, e/a were said to be approaching Tobruk, they were then vectored to El Adem at 19,000 feet, no contact made with e/a. One e/a was heard over the camp a JU 88 at 10,000 feet. A hurricane took off to intercept. Better opinion says it was a Blenheim. The camp was in readiness for a raid during the night, but the night was devoid of incident. 148 Squadron are to use the Northern side of the aerodrome, and some have arrived. 'B' Flight has gone to Benina to re-enforce No. 3 Squadron RAAF until further notice.
3 April	A minesweeper near Tobruk gave protection for some two hours in the early morning. Things were quiet up to 12:00 hours. 'Scramble' was ordered of 2 a/c over El Adem at 20,000 feet. F/O Scott and P/O Joubert were the pilots. P/O Joubert obtained permission to return, engine trouble. P/O Humphries ordered to take his place. e/a seen at 20,000 feet over the camp, pilots unable to locate and no encounter took place.

4 April	Fine and sunny. Two single patrols ordered to protect two ships approaching Tobruk Harbour. The patrol flew around the designated area but found no ships. At 09:50 hours first patrol relieved by second patrol (who also could not find the ships) ordered to 'pancake' as Wing (258) had made a small blunder. Three a/c 'scrambled' at 14:45 hours at Angels 20 West of Tobruk, the a/c was friendly. Confirmation received that Benghazi had been evacuated. Around El Adem the RE are busy destroying Italian bombs. No news forthcoming about 'B' Flight since they left on the 2nd instant. The CO proposes to fly to Barce tomorrow to make enquiries. Another 'scramble' Angels 20 West of Tobruk at 19:40 hours but no e/a seen. Other flying checks were made but found to be friendly. Several Officers on their way from the front, in the mess and confirmed that Benina had been evacuated and that HQ were about to leave Barce.
5 April	Very hot and sunny. A troopship and two minesweepers escorted into Tobruk in the morning without incident. First 'scramble' of the day at 10:00 hours produced nothing, but F/O Scott, DFC on patrol at 10: 15 hours saw a JU 88 half a mile away, unable to get within 600 yards he fired long bursts, which he noted hit the target. No visible result observed, only that the e/a made out to sea. Further 'scrambles' over Tobruk at 10:40 and 13:05 hours but no e/a were seen. Naval ship going Westward from Tobruk escorted beyond Gazala Point and two ships going East from Tobruk were also escorted in the afternoon. As the day wore on it became clear it was going to be a busy day. A good number of unescorted JU 87's was spotted, and a good number destroyed by the Squadron.
6 April	A very busy and exciting day. News from the front not too assuring, 148 Squadron ordered to return to the Canal Area. Message received at 07:15 hours that there was firing at Acroma, 2 Hurricanes were sent to investigate nothing visible. Later the controller confirmed that parachutists were dropped in that district. All gun posts manned, and extra guards put out along with lookouts. The scare died down later. Enemy recco planes over the camp, Hurricanes sent to intercept but too far away. At 12:15 news came that the small outpost at Acroma had been encircled by enemy troop's it appeared that some escaped Italian and a German soldier had captured the outpost. Steps were taken to send out troops, at 13:00 a minor engagement ensued, and the remainder of the attacking party were taken to Tobruk. Much to and froing throughout the afternoon.
7 April Bu Amud	Orders received for us to move. The Main Squadron is to go to Mechili and then to Bug-Bug. The pilots, Intelligence Officer and Servicing crews to continue operating from here for as long as possible, then go to Mechili then onto Bug-Bug. A sense of excitement prevails but everyone is calm. Italian bomb dumps were blown up in the area. All u/s aircraft that could take to the air were flown to Bug-Bug. Ground strafing patrols over Mechili destroying several vehicles. The remainder of pilots at Gazala returned here and several patrols over Tobruk were carried along with four shipping patrols over the coast. Two enemy raids over Tobruk took place, Sergt. Souter damaged a JU 88 over Tobruk around08:00 hours. The move to Bug-Bug is cancelled. F/O Scott flew down with a message for the Adjutant in charge of the convoy but unable to contact him. His message was left at Monastir - Sollum – and Bug-Bug. They are to return Westwards to El Gubbi asap.

8 April	Two morning ground strafing patrols around Mechili took place, several MT vehicles destroyed. Two patrols over Tobruk produced no results. Severe sandstorm midday put an end to operations except for special flight to Bomba flown by F/O Storrar, DFC with four message bags to drop on our detachments. He found one group and dropped one bag. On his way back he destroyed a JU 87 SE of Derna, near Matuba, he did not return to base. Spotted aircraft on rough landing ground 30 miles East of El Adem. Varey light fired, he landed. The Lockheed Lodestar with General Wavell as a passenger on way back to Sollum from the forward area. Landed due to lack of oil pressure. Plane took off without further steps to get oil. F/O Storrar was fired at by locals and could not start his engine, compelled to leave his plane, and walked to the Bardia Road and got a lift with RASC vehicle to El Gubbi. He then returned to Bu Amoud. Preparations to move to El Gubbi were completed.
9 April	El Gubbi move started at 07:00 hours, enemy raid on Tobruk. By midday Bu Amoud party had all arrived. No news from the Bug Bug convoy. At 11:00 hours heavy enemy raid on Tobruk CO took 3 pilots to their planes and took off. A ME 110 shot down near Derna Road, ground strafing near Mechili late afternoon. One pilot did not return. One aircraft crash landed and is a 'write-off'. Maintenance Section arrived from Bug Bug on the end of an armoured division that was moving up from Sollum. The General in charge of the Armoured Division forbade any further such moves to dangerous. The Adjutant made several journeys to persuade him otherwise. Essential ground staff were moved.
10 April	Two Hurricanes took off and attacked enemy vehicles South of Gelul Ahmer, much success. Blenheims had report they were undefended and shot them up, Sgt. De Scitivieux (Free French0 was shot down, he crash-landed but was seen walking away. Sgt. Websters machine was severely damaged by enemy ground fire, he managed to land back at Bu Amoud. Concern for his whereabouts. He returned later having walked back. Ground strafing continued with much success, enemy MTs destroyed, and many troops killed in the Derna – Gazala area. Pilots browned off with all this ground strafing as we are losing too many machines, which we can ill afford to do. Remainder of Squadron arrived in the afternoon. Some 96 vehicles including 16 – 4" guns protected by the 12 Australian MTs with anti-tank guns. They had a few scares on the way and near Bu Amoud they had to stop whilst Italian bomb dumps were blown up. Also, enemy aircraft attacked the convoy, but all vehicles arrived safely.
11 April	Sandstorm – no flying.
12 April	Siege of Tobruk now serious, recco's returning stating enemy in various degrees of concentration surrounding Tobruk. At 07:30 two Hurricanes took off to carry out ground strafing in the El Adem area, Sgt. Wills was shot down and believed killed. Ground strafing continued with enemy MT's hit along with one carrying around 60 troops were destroyed at Gadd El Ahmar. Bad sandstorm on the way and planes finding it hard to locate the aerodrome. Sgt. Marshall made a safe landing at Mersa Matruh but F/Lt. Ball, DFC failed to return, and no contact has been made.
13 April	Sgt. Marshall returned to El Gubbi with his plane and was congratulated by the Group Captain Brown for saving his machine. Sgt. Marshall had been awarded a DFM for 'knocking down' (confirmed) 12 enemy aircraft. F/Lt Ball, DFC still missing. Thirteen sorties carried during the day along with various attacks. No e/a were seen. Intelligence Officer F/O Hoole is looking tired and ill, but he is still carrying on during these exciting and anxious days (and nights).

14 April	Day started with a most determined attack on the Fortress by 70 e/a. JU 87's accompanied by ME 110's and G 50's as a fighter escort. Dived bombed the harbour with little success. F/Lt Smith exceedingly popular guy was killed whilst attacking 5 G 50's, he destroyed 2 and damaged another. Sgt. Webster was also killed, a bad day. Plus, P/O Lamb ('Kiwi'), the joker failed to return after attacking a mixed formation of JU 87's, ME 110's. Total Squadron bag for the day, 1 Henschel, 2 G 50's, 6 JU 87's all destroyed along with 2 probably destroyed and many others damaged. We had 2 Hurricanes damaged and 3 lost. In spite the achievements from the day we only had 6 serviceable a/c after 34 sorties. One of the saddest days in the Squadrons History.
15 April	'Jerry' has been remarkably quiet with only one formation passing over the defences. Thirteen defensive sorties carried out. And some pilots managed a well-earned rest. P/O Lamb's machine was found. It was stated by A/A observers that the machine dived in from 3,000 feet. The padre came along, we buried 'Kiwi', 'Smudge' and Sgt. Webster by their a/c.
16 April	Severe sandstorms all day. No attacks by e/a on the defended area and no operational flying by Squadron.
17 April	Further sandstorms and no flying all day.
18 April	Defensive patrols carried out; no e/a encountered. Patrols took place over shipping entering the harbour. No interceptions made.
19 April	A busy day. Defensive patrols and 'scrambles' almost continually all-day dawn to dusk. P/O Spence destroyed a JU 88 over the town and destroyed a ME 109 near Gazala. Enemy raid on the harbour in the afternoon but little damage caused.
20 April	A quiet day. Two patrols over Tobruk, no e/a seen. From 11:15 to 13:15 hours 5 Hurricane patrolled our forward troops to protect against dive bombers while engaged in 'mopping up' near the perimeter defences. Ground strafing of enemy positions carried out. S/Ldr. Wykeham-Barnes replaced S/Ldr. Murray who was off to Delta for a well-earned rest. High hopes for the continued success of the Squadron in the existing difficult conditions. The Western Desert experience gained by our new CO will bring confidence to us all in the future and it is felt that the Squadron is in good hands. The Adjutant and some 100 personnel have gone on leave.
21 April	There were 4 'scrambles' in the day with the last encountering 5 ME 109's with no conclusive result. One Hurricane badly damaged on landing and the pilot broke his arm with the plane a write off. From dawn to 10:30 hours shipping patrols provided. Heavy enemy attacks on the harbour and aerodrome, early morning. Squadron now reduced to 5 working Hurricanes: position serious. Morale of Squadron could be better and pilots showing strain and fatigue. If only more planes were available. Day to day pilots cannot be expected to take on 20 to 60 e/a with just five serviceable planes. Morale bound to be lowered.
22 April	Hectic day with 6 'scrambles' together with patrols covering the perimeter troops and shipping approaching Tobruk. Determined attack by the enemy 30 JU 87's escorted by 12 ME 109's and 12 G 50's carried out over Tobruk and the Squadron. A goodly number of e/a shot down and destroyed. Highly satisfactory day.

23 April	A fine day again. First 'scramble' at 07:05 hours over Tobruk. More 'scrambles' took place, and it was agreed by all that there were some 20 JU 87's, 30 ME 109's and 10 ME 110's engaged against our 7 Hurricanes. Several e/a was destroyed during the air fight. We lost P/O Haldenby, shot down in flames by a ME 109 as he tried to land. F/O Martin, DFC bailed out and was safe. The CO bailed out in full view of the camp shot at by ME 109's. A few other pilots received injuries. The enemy ground strafing was severe but no lasting damage. Evening saw another large enemy attack of some 20 ME 109's escorting 20 JU 87's.

24 April	A quiet day. One or two enemy recce machines over the aerodrome.

25 April	At 07:00 hours 258 Wing needed a muster count, possible move. The Squadron back to only 5 serviceable aircraft, GC Spackman of 258 Wing had received answer from 204 Group. We had 8 aircraft available; they took off at 18:00 hours flew to Sidi Hanaish.

26 April	No operations. Aircraft arrived from Gerarba safely. Three pilots left in Lysander for Cairo for a rest and then bring back additional aircraft. Down to 6 serviceable Hurricanes. Six further pilots left for Delta, two pilots to see the Medical Boards after their injuries on the 23rd.

27 April	Dust storms all day. Only 6 pilots available and all on 20 minutes availability all day. No operational flying. Without exception officers in need of rest. All have performed admirably in difficult situations. It is hoped that the Squadron will be sent for a well-earned rest. Of the Squadron total manpower only 40 have had leave since the Squadron arrived in the desert in December 1940. CO has tried without success. Cannot go on leave until other Squadrons become available to take their place.

28 April	Fine. One Hurricane undertook shipping patrol going West in late afternoon. Three Hurricanes on 20-minute availability all day. Sad news that W/C Johnson, S/Ldr. Bardy and the Rev. Cox were killed when their Blenheim was shot down by ME 109's just after take-off from Tobruk. All will be sorely missed.

29 April	Fine. Order received at 06:00 hours that all available aircraft to patrol Tobruk, refuelling at Sidi Barrani East. Only four took off, leaving 3 her to carry out shipping patrols all day. Patrol ordered to abandon, and all returned to base. Two pilots recalled back from Delta: Squadron too short on pilots. A scheme is being prepared where the Squadrons in the desert will have an Operational Landing Ground, a Base Headquarters in the Delta Area, and a dispersal Landing Ground on mud flats for night use. This is so that the men on a rotation can get rested away from the day to day. Eight pilots posted to HQME for a rest.

30 April	Fine. At dawn 4 Hurricanes at 1-hour intervals were sent off to ground strafe moving MT's between Gazala East, Gambut and Sollum. A good number of enemy vehicles spotted and strafed plus 1 Henschel 126 shot down by P/O Pompei (Free French).

AIR 27/630/9 & AIR 27/630/10 Pilot Ops Report

May 1941:

1 May	Fine and clear. Intense enemy activity over Tobruk. At 07:45 hours, all available aircraft took off to patrol the area. Could only muster 6 aircraft. Two went unserviceable at Sidi Barrani and the other four saw nothing at all. Yet 10 minutes earlier 274 Squadron shot down 4 ME 109's over Tobruk but lost 1 pilot and 3 aircraft.

2 May	Fine. Two single patrols from dawn onwards over Fuka Satellite without incident. More 'scrambles' but these appear to be in most cases friendly. CO went to Amriya to contact the Adjutant to get Base Headquarters moved from Helwan to Amriya.

3 May	Ground strafing of enemy MT's between Tobruk, El Adem and Sidi Assies, which started last night continued today. Some good results. Three ME 110's near Bardia were engaged outcome inconclusive.
4 May	Five Hurricanes along with 274 Squadron patrolled Tobruk and met 1 JU 88 coming back. They all thought it was a returning Glen Martin and the 'Heaven sent gift' let to go. Other patrols took off but nothing to report.
5 May	Early ground mist. Considerable chaos this morning. Two pilots took off at 06:00 hours to patrol Fuka, where Bleheims were refuelling. The pilots rang from LG 60 as they could not find the Squadrons 'mud flat' last night. Apart from these patrols over Fuka and one 'scramble' over Mersah Matruh, no flying took place. Around 60 of the Squadron personnel arrived by train Helwan. We shall be glad to see them as men servicing our aircraft know little to nothing about Hurricanes. The 120 men in Tobruk are still there.
6 May	Very severe sandstorms all day. The worst experienced since arriving in the desert.
7 May	A very quiet day. One patrol over Fuka Satellite where Wellingtons were refuelling. Four pilots arrived on posting.
8 May	A fairly busy day. We still have not seen our first e/a from this aerodrome. Three 'scrambles' over Mersah Matruh, nothing seen. Seven single patrols over Fuka Satellite carried out to protect the Wellingtons there. Sergt. Guillou (Free French0 arrived today, we now have four Free French pilots. Two other pilots arrived from ME Pool.
9 May	Severe sandstorm all day and no flying. Two pilots arrived back, one from leave and one from the Hospital in Heliopolis.
10 May	Five scrambles over Mersah Matruh, nothing seen of e/a. Some destroyers coming into Mersah Matruh were patrolled in the afternoon. Sandstorm blew up and stopped all flying. One pilot landed at LG 21 and stayed the night.
11 May	A wonderfully clear day with no sand. At around 11:00 hours our pilot returned from LG 21. Three aircraft at readiness throughout the day. We now only have 5 operational aircraft with one further aircraft arriving making 6.
12 May	Morning patrols were carried out over Fuka and Mersah Matruh, no contact with e/a. We had two 'scrambles' in the afternoon, again no contact. Three aircraft flown to 'mud flats' for dispersal, pilots baffled as to the position of our 'Night Club'.
13 May	Sergt. Berridge killed during the early morning, he was circling the 'mud flats' and spun it off a steep turn. There were 3 'scrambles during the day and a single patrol over Fuka Satellite in the afternoon. No e/a seen.
14 May	Lysander finally repaired and flown back from 'mud flats' to base to the relief of the CO. Blank day operational wise.
15 May	A patrol over Sofafi area was made with no result. The CO and one other flew to Amriya in the Lysander. Eight aircraft carried out ground-strafing of concentrated enemy positions.
16 May	Early patrol of the Fuka Satellite carried out. The remainder of the day spent ground strafing enemy positions, aircraft taking off at twenty-minute intervals. Two full operational orders carried out. P/O Irwin, whilst attacking 2 ME 109's at El Adem was shot at and hit with shrapnel. He landed at Quassha safely. Injuries are not serious.

17 May	Five 'Scrambles' all fruitless. An operational order carried out by 6 Hurricanes to strafe enemy MT's between Tobruk, and Capuzzo was successful.
18 May	An early patrol over Fuka and LG 09. W/C Ballatore took the Lysander to Alexandria and returned with a passenger. One 'scramble' over Matruh – result nil. Late patrol over Fuka and LG 09.
19 May	Early patrol over Fuka and LG 09. 'Scrambled' four times, no result. Sgt. O'Byrne landed en route from Crete to Heliopolis. CO took Hurricane to visit forward refuelling grounds. Two pilots arrived from 103 MU.
20 May	Quiet day. One patrol over Fuka at dusk. Party of three Americans visited the Squadron.
21 May	Early patrol over Fuka. Operation order to attack enemy MT's on Tobruk – Capuzzo Road was carried out. The Strafing was ill feted for the Squadron with a number of aircraft being damaged. ME 109's encountered and P/O Pompei was seen to go down. Some enemy trucks had been shot up. Sgt. Guillou strafed a large camp and destroyed a fuel dump. Down to 7 serviceable aircraft. There were 2 'scrambles over Matruh and a defensive patrol over Hurricanes on Matruh LG. Busy day. Army and RAF MTs were dispersed over the aerodrome at dusk.
22 May	Squadron maintain a patrol by 1 Hurricane over Matruh from dawn until dusk. Patrols were sent out to intercept enemy aircraft but by the time they got there the e/a had gone. Other patrols were sent out, but no e/a seen.
23 May	Two Hurricanes flown back to RSU. Apart from one early 'scramble' over base it remained quiet. Lull before the storm. At 11:00 hours orders came to send 6 Hurricanes in company with a Blenheim escort to Crete. Land at Heraklion, refuel and proceed to Maleme aerodrome, carry out strafing of German troops landed there by parachute, JU52's and troop-carrying gliders. Reported that the JU 52's was coming over unescorted. The flight took off only to return 2 hours later, having been fired on by British Naval Ships, which scattered the flight.
24 May	Sand whipping up at 07:00 hours and by 08:00 hours a moderate dust storm blew. Visibility 200 yards. Out of the dust a plane arrived with two pilots one of which came from Crete. They reported that the reached Heraklion at 17030 Hours the previous day and found a raid by 20 JU88's was taking place. The flight attacked the JU 88's but owing to fuel shortage had to break off from the engagement. The LG had been badly damaged, craters to runways along with enemy troops firing from behind rocks. Once fuelled some of the Hurricanes took off to carry out patrols. Some aircraft were strafed by JU 88's. The remaining pilots were to carry out ground strafing of the German parachutists. All the aircraft managed to take off. It was reported that two pilots were missing, and it was hoped they had returned to Crete.
25 May	Six pilots from 213 Squadron arrived flying non-tropicalised Hurricanes for use by the Squadron over Crete One Squadron plane was flown to RSU, and a non-tropicalised plane flown to get spare tail wheels. A further 5 Hurricanes arrived from Delta. Our 2 serviceable Hurricanes were at readiness all day. Not called upon.

26 May	The Valencia arrived to take 5 pilots to Delta to fly 5 Hurricanes back to base. Instructions from Group received at 15:00 hours. All aircraft to be brought up to readiness including non-tropicalised aircraft. Orders received to provide defensive patrol over the damaged aircraft carrier 'Formidable' approaching Matruh from Crete, 70 miles out at sea. Patrols were carried out and JU 88's was spotted and attacked, only damaged. Two aircraft at readiness scrambled five times, no e/a encountered. The days flying caused havoc with the planes in particular the non-tropicalised aircraft, which will need to go back to base. Too many issues to solve. The Squadron are down to 7 serviceable aircraft.
27 May	Sgt. Guillou took off to search for a trawler off Ras El Monastir after a long search he came across 3 empty lifeboats and some wreckage, no e/a seen. Five 'scrambles' with no result. Two aircraft flown to RSU. Ground crew have worked wonders on the u/s machines rendering all the non-tropicalised serviceable along with three of our own.
28 May	Instructions received to attach 5 pilots to 274 Squadron with experience of long-range Hurricanes. The duly appointed pilots were flown over by Magister. During the day we received instructions to send over any L/R Hurricanes to 274 Squadron also to send two pilots back to base by Lysander to out two L/R hurricanes. Other instructions were received and duly complied with. Later in the day 213 Squadron had received orders to fly 3 L/R Hurricanes to Crete in order to carry out attacks on 150 JU 88's reported to be due at Heraklion. By the time they were ready to go it was too late and the order cancelled.
29 May	A quiet day for us, but we are informed that our detachment pilots to 274 Squadron are working extremely hard over the Fleet. Last night they had to go to Sidi Barrani in readiness to take of at dawn, nowhere to sleep; slept under the wings.
30 May	From 06:00 until 10:00 hours the Squadron maintained a defensive patrol over Sidi Barrani East where the L/R Hurricanes were refuelling. P/O Donati took the Lysander to Bagush to search for a crashed aircraft. The search continued all day but no sighting. Three pilots carried out a patrol in company with a Blenheim over 4 cruisers and 6 destroyers 100 miles North of base, no e/a seen. Instructions received to send a further 3 pilots to 274 Squadron. This leaves the Squadron with 5 pilots plus 6 from 213 Squadron. The Australian A/A doing our aerodrome defence have been replaced today by 37 Battery.
31 May	F/) Goodman carried out a patrol over two ships reported to be off Sidi Barrani, SE. He found heading SW. Wreckage was spotted in the Gulf of Sollum, which the pilot pointed out by circling, the ships altered course nothing picked up. P/O Moss carried on with the search unaware it was to the SW. At times like these the deficiencies in our R/T apparatus is felt. Sgt. Ellis was directed to patrol over HM destroyer Vendetta, not found. Reported cargo boats heading to Matruh. Other patrols sent out but could not find ships. Other activity took place with some success, JU 88 shot down and badly damaged a Cant 1007.

AIR 27/630/11 (1) & AIR 27/630/12 (2) Pilot Ops Report

June 1941:

1 June Sidi Heneish	Several differences of opinion as to whom shot what down which plane. Group have clarified that the credit to the parent unit. Shipping patrols continued in the Gulf of Sollum. Urgent signal received, patrol needed over SS Calcutta, no e/a seen. Patrol over Vendetta was carried out once she was found, 40 miles from position given. More often than not the shipping positions are not accurate, and time wasted trying to find them. Group informed the Squadron that the L/R Hurricanes (brought up by 213) are to return to Delta.

| 2 June | Two pilots carried out defensive patrols over shipping; again, hard to find. Three pilots carried out defensive patrol over photographic Hurricane doing recce over Capuzzo area. All successful. A little A/A fire encountered but no e/a. Pilots returned from attachment to 274. |

| 3 June | Further defensive patrol over recce aircraft carried out, no e/a seen. Continuous patrols carried out from 10:00 until 17:00 hours over shipping approaching Tobruk from Mersa Matruh. Three a/c on patrol at height ordered, one pilot saw a stick of bombs drop from above, which dropped near the ships. Search undertaken but the hun (abbreviation for German) had gone. Orders given to send 3 non-tropicalised Hurricanes to 102 MU using 213 Squadron pilots. Planes due for 30-hourly inspection to be sent to BIG. Everybody interested in the arrival of PAC defence gear, should prove affective check against enemy ground strafing. |

| 4 June | Exodus of planes from here today. 213 pilots took down the 6 mentioned, plus the 30 hourlies. Orders received to send remaining aircraft to dispersal bar 2 two for disposal of 258 Wing. The only flying carried out was that of calibration tests. Six pilots arrived on posting. |

| 5 June | Defensive patrols over shipping from Mersa Matruh to Tobruk. G/Capt. Spackman paid us a visit to inspect our R/T, rumoured we might get new R/T microphones – we do need new. |

| 6 June | Today, R/T transmitter packed up completely. Orders received, all a/c to be on ½ hour notice. Everyone looking forward to some eventful orders. We all know the importance of the shipping patrols. Orders received to maintain one patrol over shipping. Later on, the planes on ½ hour notice ordered to escort Marylands carrying out photographic recce" over Tobruk. Recce's completed avoiding e/and planes returned to base. |

| 7 June | Shipping patrols continued. At 06:55 hours Sgt. Laing set out to patrol two ships off Barrani owing to 6/10 cloud, base about 1500 feet was unable to locate them. Eventually cloud improved and ships intercepted and patrolled over. Afternoon standing patrols maintained over Matruh where 229 Squadron had just landed en route from aircraft carrier to Delta. Patrol maintained until dusk. Maryland landed, Group sending it to all Squadron's, so no mistakes are made identifying the plane. New E/M microphones arrived. Far better communications using these. |

| 8 June
And
9 June | Two flights carried to allow tests to be carried out by the RA to test some instruments. Orders received to re-arm all Hurricanes with MK VIE incendiary and 8 planes to Barrani before dusk. Planes used to destroy e/a on Gazala aerodrome. One Maryland escorted by 4 Hurricanes to proceed to Gazala North to carry out bombing of aerodrome with the Hurricanes flying low to machine gun the dispersed e/a. Additional group to carry out the same at Gazala South. Due to poor light the attacks went awry as the Maryland's failed to format with the Hurricanes. Action eventually took with machine gunning of ME 109's and G 50's. German A/A went into action immediately. E/a took off but were not engaged due to petrol shortage. On the flight back, as they neared the coast severe A/A fire came from coastal gun positions one of which was silenced by F/Lt. Green. Signal received stating that 2 aircraft engaged in fight, one of which crashed into the sea and the other one just inside the Tobruk defences. One pilot found, now safe in Tobruk, the other pilot lost believed to be P/O Tovey. |

10 June	Orders received to provide escort of 3 Hurricanes over 2 Blenheim's who were to convey GCC in C and GCC WDC from Bagush to Barrani. Another raid over Mersa Matruh last night; we put up usual recce patrol no e/a seen. A patrol was maintained over minesweeper proceeding from Matruh to Tobruk from 15.15 until dusk. The CO obtained permission from Group to take a Hurricane up and attempt to intercept e/a should they try to bomb Matruh again tonight. As we were all of course the bomber didmn't arrived.
11 June	Two a/c taken to BIG for their 30-hourly checks. They are to bring back two Hurricanes for those lost on the 9th. F/Lt. Burles arrived from Rear 204 Group H to check current position of our a/c – we are 3 below requirements. Patrol maintained over 2 destroyers Matruh to Tobruk.
12 June	'Scrambles' all day. It started at dawn with plots over Matruh and Fuka and it was decided to keep the standing patrols going until all the a/c were all back at base. 'Scrambled 7 times but no interception made. The A/A defence people change over like it is going out of fashion. One minute 37 Battery, then 38 Battery, then South African detachment with Lewis guns arrived. Enemy bombers active over Matruh. Plans put in place to get up early at 03:00 hours when bombing started. Nothing happened, enemy intuition is arousing suspicion.
13 June	At 05:00 hours our Czechoslovakian ground defence moved out. Sorry to see them go. Ten pilots of 229 Squadron along with their Hurricanes arrived on detachment. Seven pilots from 33 Squadron landed and will be attached to 274 Squadron. Tomahawks have arrived. 250 Squadron to operate from Sidi Haneish South. It will be interesting to see how the Tommies cope with the ME 109's. Extensive operations received for tomorrow to make a big push froward to relieve Tobruk. Fighter Squadrons along with 274 & 73 to provide fighter protection over the forward troops. In addition, strafe enemy plans at Gazala aerodrome similar to the 8th/9th to take place at dawn plus provide patrols to shipping from Matruh to Tobruk.
14 June	Five pilots to carry out strafe over Gazala. Patrols of 3 a/c commenced at dawn and being sent every 40-minute intervals, which means 12 a/c in the air and ground crew frantically refuelling as they land. We also carried out shipping patrols, some 21 a/c in the air, not one on the ground. Of the strafing groups 3 returned unscathed, 3 other a/c did not come back. Reported as downed in enemy territory due to the lack of fuel. Patrols over forward troops in the Capuzzo area reported little action from e/a. On the CO's return he was informed that Sgt. White, DFM had died of his injuries having crashed at the aerodrome. Patrols over troops continued until dusk. Squadron worked extremely hard throughout the day.
15 June	Repeat of orders from yesterday – little further forward today. Ground forces are to try and cross the Bardia – Tobruk Road. Early patrols, not a great deal of movement. At 10:00 hours patrol saw 2 ME 109's, one shot down. Other attacks took place, initially 4 ME 109's then a further 8 more. They were attacked with a number of ME 109's damaged or shot down. Some of our pilots were shot down. Later, more patrols encountered enemy ME 109's, which were attacked with some success. Taking stock, we were down to 6 serviceable planes. Group orders came to confirm that the planes are to run past their 30-hour service, which meant we had 17 a/c. P/O Chatfield returned with a right Royal welcome. He had walked 25 miles before being picked up.
16 June	We learnt that Capazzo was captured, and our patrols had effectively protected troops from enemy air attack. S/Ldr. Wykeham-Barnes, DFC discussed with Group how difficult it was to maintain patrols using sections from numerous Squadrons. They need to be Squadron by Squadron. In one case we had one section of three against 12 ME 109's and communication were not good. Orders received to discontinue patrolling in sections and to patrol by Squadron.

17 June	Rumours filter through about the position up to the wire. The hun is driving up from the South with large force of troops trying to drive through the Halfaya pass. Around midday a bombing raid with fighter escort organised, objective to bomb the head of the column. Twenty-five bombers and escorts from 229 and 33 Squadron. 73 Squadron sent up 13 aircraft to strafe enemy MTs on the High Capazzo and the Bardia Road. They returned and reported that P/O Reynolds was missing. The patrol split into two groups. One attack destroyed 10 MTs on the Bardia Road and the other strafed the High Capazzo column (approx. 1 mile long) destroying 20 to 30 vehicles. Our troops are falling back. News received that P/O Pound is safe, he was picked up with shrapnel wounds in the knee. 229 Squadron set off on strafing mission but came across a concentration of dive bombers, JU 87's, plus some G 50's and ME 109's, a number of which were shot down or damaged.
18 June	Our troops are back where they were before the push. The Squadron continues with protective patrols. Lt. Bruen of the FAA arrived with five pilots of B06/33 Squadron, they are to operate with us. Dust starting to rise just as orders were received to carry out strafes on Gambut. Finally, at 15:00 hours 10 a/c with 3 a/c of the FAA took off, later 'C' Flight (229) in comp-nay of 3 a/c from FAA took off to strafe enemy M/Ts in the Sidi Omar area. Visibility very poor and strong winds blew the a/c way off course. The a/c were told to refuel at Barrani before attempting to fly back. The a/c of the FAA thought they were over enemy territory shot up the wrong groups. Hurricane damaged along with some M/T's.
19 June	Feverish activity of the last few days has died down. The FAA pilots are to proceed to Palestine immediately. Dust storms blow nearly all day. P/O Reynolds arrived back with a badly cut eye, he had crash landed near Salum after losing contact and being shot in the radiator. He was picked up by forward troops.
20 June	Being quieter some of our a/c are going for their 30-hourly inspection. No operational activity today. News that P/O Pompei (the Free French) pilot shot down a month ago is safe at Liva. How he travelled 300 miles from where he was shot down will be interesting. Confirmation of P/O Logan's death, apparently, he bailed out and his scute did not open. Still no news of F/O Goodman, DFC sadly missed in the Squadron.
21 June	One 'scramble' over Matruh with no result. Sent up a patrol of 9 Hurricanes on the Barrani – Matruh Road trying to intercept 9 ME 109's as being report being there.
22 June	S/Ldr. Rosier, 229 Squadron visited his contingent here. Took the Lysander to 6 Squadron to see some more of his detached flight, afterwards flying the Lysander back to Amriya.
23 June	Three 'scrambles' over Matruh, shipping patrol over vessels proceeding from Matruh to Tobruk – no e/a seen. Still send a/c to BLG for their 30-hourlies.
24 June	Things very quiet, no operation orders. F/O Temlett, DFC organised some ground strafing on aerodrome. P/O Sands went to Sidi Barrani to take over from F/O Donati as officer in charge of 05 refuelling ground.
25 June	Morning patrols maintained over shipping around Tobruk. Orders received to carry out patrol over bombers. Around 50 fighters and 25 bombers taking part in operation. Gamala enemy aerodrome to be bombed, hopefully destroying e/a. Great enthusiasm within the Squadron. Unfortunately, all went off 'half-cock', only a few bombers reached the target, fighters continued to Tobruk, but no e/a seen. The Valencia arrived and took 4 Sergeants of 213 back, no doubt the rest will be going back. Not good news as we are short on experienced pilots.

26 June	Today, yesterday's orders were repeated, this time with success. As our fighters approached Tobruk a JU 88 flew over the formation, which was chased as he discarded his bombs. He moved away too fast for our fighters to catch. Other JU 88's attacked with some success. Other encounters took place with P/O Ward now missing. The remaining patrol, whilst at Sidi Omar were short on fuel, were dived upon by 5 ME 109's and P/O Leach hit with cannon fire through his starboard wing. His evasive action took him to ground level where he carried strafing of some MT vehicles. The ME 109's did not pursue their attack.
27 June	Quiet day again – practise flying. No operational flying. Three pilots flew to Delta on leave. Midday Group rang up – they reported some 30 e/a passed over Tobruk going East – later a further 10 more were reported. Dusk attack on forward drome's as a reprisal. We learnt that 6 aircraft destroyed in the air and 6 on the ground. No attack materialised.
28 June	Things still quiet. Patrol over shipping and one 'scramble' nil result. More practise flying. Recce aircraft flew over in the evening.
29 June	Practise flying order of the day. Two French pilots arrive. Put up standing patrols to try and cope with recce aircraft – they did not come.
30 June	Shipping going from Matruh to Tobruk being dived bombed. Group organised patrols over shipping, which continued until dusk. Just before dusk a large formation of JU 87's escorted by MER 109' and G 50's appeared to which 250 Squadron – Tomahawks, whilst on patrol accounted for a good number of e/a casualties. The ships were unfortunately subjected to dive bombing whilst fighters were fighting above.

AIR 27/630/13 (1) & AIR 27/630/14 Pilot Ops Report

July 1941:

1 July Sidi Heneish	At dawn the CO and one other took off on a patrol over a destroyer towing a gunboat, reported a few miles shore near Matruh. After two hours search no sign of boats and returned to base. Later transpired that the boats were never there. Four a/c taken to BIG for 30-hourly inspections. A few bombs were dropped, in the evening, in the Matruh Area.
2 July	Extremely bad weather conditions today, meaning extraordinarily little flying operations were carried out. One a/c taken to RSU for desert camouflage, one a/c taken to BIG, four pilots returned from BIG. Two 'scrambles' in the evening, nothing seen. Orders to disperse our a/c to mud flats during the moon period.
3 July	Day started with 3 patrols over Fuka with last patrol returning to base at 09:00 hours. Sand started to rise making it impossible for a/c to take off. Later in the day it cleared, and 8 a/c took off on practice flights. Whilst in the air visibility reduced to 50 yards and pilots had to land at LG 60. Fortunately, the storm cleared, and the pilots arrived back just in time for tiffin-time.
4 July *USA - Day of Independence &* *LAC Lamb - 1012281 Birthday – 29 years old*	Kept busy with 'scrambles' for most of the day, but no e/a encountered. Two pilots had quite a busy time and spent most of their readiness period in the air. The CO left for Bagush to try and organise some night flying for the coming Moon-period.

5 July	Group have installed R/T Transmitter in the control room and have asked for two R/T tests to be carried out. After lunch two Press Correspondents and News Real Representatives arrived and filmed a 'scrambled' take off at dawn. The film starts with the Operations Officer in a state of nudity dashing up the steps leading to the Ops Room. He eventually jumps into a Commer, which is kept just outside for such emergencies then drives off to the flights. Pilots take off with patrol details. The take-off film by the Lysander as were some of the air manoeuvres. After filming was completed, orders were received and Squadrons 1, 73, 229, 238, 350 & 274 to carry out sweeps as far as Tobruk & on return journey 73 guarded by 229 to strafe Gt. Gambut or Amseat. At 17:15 hours 7 a/c of 73 & 5 a/c of 229 left the base for Sidi Barrani. On arrival at Sidi Barrani insufficient equipment to refuel all the a/c so the operations were cancelled. All a/c returned to their bases.
6 July	Little operational activity today. In the evening 9 a/c were sent to patrol two lighters. No e/a seen. Two pilots arrived in the evening.
7 July	Air of despondency in the Officers Mess. The CO departed for Delta on a well- earned rest. Around lunch time orders received to repeat the orders of the 5th at 15:45 hours. 6 a/c from 73 & 5 from 229 to take off for Sidi Barrani. At 19:45 hours we saw No. 1 SAAF & 250 Tomahawks returning, rang 250 to ascertain outcome of sweeps. Owing to failure of the refuelling equipment they were unable to take off at the appointed time. After taking off could not make contact with 73 & 229 Squadrons a/c. Many discussions took place about what was happening, suffice to say that enemy positions had been strafed on the ground. Heavy A/A encountered on the way back North of the Barrani Road. It is hoped that down pilots will get back. However, the 5 pilots shot down would be in enemy territory. A 'BLACK' day for 73 and rather a blow to the Squadron.
8 July & 9 July	Reports state that Bagush Satellite was strafed, and a train machine gunned this morning by Heinkels and ME 110's. Extent of damage unknown. Several 'scrambles' during the day, but no interceptions. P/O Shelley returned from BIG and reported 5 a/c ready for collection. Arrangements made to pick them up. S/Ldr. Rosier went to Group to finally obtain permission for night flying until the end of the moon-period. During the night bombs were dropped over the aerodrome and personnel bombs in the nearby wadi.
10 July	At 02:25 one of our bombers circled the drome at about 2,000 feet with navigation lights on the 3.7 guns opened fire. Pilot started sending 'abc' signal but carried on towards Fuka. At 04:00 hours control decided to have a machine on patrol until dawn. Single enemy aircraft dropped a stick of bombs in the Matruh Area. By the time our patrol had got to Mersa the hun had gone. During the day we had a run of bad luck. Pilots at dispersal ground LG 65 at time of take off a thick mist rolled in, and they damaged their a/c. In the afternoon 10 a/c patrolled shipping, no e/a seen. Group rang through to know more about the incidents that happened at LG 65. Several incidents happened throughout the evening. Group rang through to say that the AOC would like to speak to CO & the 5 pilots in the morning.
11 July	Order received at 09:00 hours to send 6 a/c to patrol a destroyer that had been bombed and likely to be bombed again. Patrol was later changed but the destroyer had been severely damaged and later sank between Sidi Barrani and Ishailia Rocks. CO and pilots returned from Group Hands slapped and clean start again. Just after tiffin one of the new French pilots when taking off tipped onto the plane's nose.
12 July	CO had meeting with all pilots in the ops room and spoke about careless flying and beating up the aerodrome. W/Cdr. Hallshan is taking over 258 Wing and that 229 were heading back to Delta to re-group. Some long-range Hurricanes landing but are due to go to 102 MU the following day.

| 13 July | The long-range Hurricanes were taken to 102 MU. Later in the day the Squadron received 7 long-range Hurricanes from 274 in exchange for 5 short-range Hurricanes. There were some 'scrambles and patrols during the day but all uneventful. |

13 July — The long-range Hurricanes were taken to 102 MU. Later in the day the Squadron received 7 long-range Hurricanes from 274 in exchange for 5 short-range Hurricanes. There were some 'scrambles and patrols during the day but all uneventful.

14 July — Throughout the morning usual patrols and 'scrambles. Sgt. Ellis was sent out to look for a Wellingtons dinghy in the vicinity of Salum Bay. Afternoon shipping patrols delayed due to sandstorm. No e/a seen during the patrols.

15 July — Dawn saw our pilots out on patrol. One between Fuka Satellite & LG09 and two over LG 60. Long-range Hurricanes patrolled over shipping, 4 hours constant flying. The afternoon brought fresh orders and 12 a/c took off at 15:15 hours for Sidi Barrani. At 21:30 hours Wing informed us that our pilots had seen action and accounted for a number of e/a.

16 July — Quiet day. Only one patrol. Two pilots were sent out to find a Lighter, which was damaged the previous evening, they only found wreckage. Full report given of the raid on the ships. Our pilots going out on their second patrol saw bombs falling near the Lighter. An ME 110 was spotted and the whole formation chased him. The ME 110 led them to 15 JU 88's P/O Johns remained as guard a goodly number of e/a were destroyed or damaged. Our casualties, 2 pilots missing and 1 a/c damaged.

17 July — Four patrols during the morning, afternoon was very quiet. In the evening we rushed 6 a/c in readiness to take off and patrol some ships reported to have been bombed. A further 6 a/c were dispersed but neither patrol found the ship. P/O Wareham for whatever reason flew towards Barrani, found the ships some 50 miles West of given position.

18 July — No operational work carried out and practice flying cancelled owing to dust storms. At 10:00 hours visibility dropped to 25 yards and remained for the rest of the day. In the afternoon the pilots went swimming.

19 July — A plane was delivered to Group for use by W/Cdr. Hallshan. Twelve a/c carried out two shipping patrols in the afternoon and evening. Just before end of the evening patrol, 12 e/a ME 109's appeared at 2,000 feet above our patrol 1 pilot lost and 2 others damaged a/c.

20 July — We had 6 a/c at readiness and 6 a/c available until 18:00 hours. There were no 'scrambles and no engagements. Having released at 15:00 hours orders were received to send 12 a/c to Sidi Barrani. They were stay there for the night to carry out dawn shipping patrols.

21 July — The dawn patrols returned, had nothing to report. No operational flying during the day, pilots went swimming in the afternoon. In the evening Officers visited 250 Squadron.

22 July — Two a/c lent to No. 1 SAAF to carry out shipping patrols. There appears to be preparations for a big move tomorrow. P/O Johns flew to BIG, to muster up maximum number of machines for tomorrow. Orders arrived for tomorrow's operations, we are to be ready at 7;00 hours with 12 a/c, 6 a/c to carry out mid-day patrols and 12 a/c to patrol at 17:00 hours. Just after midnight F/Lt. Smith phoned Wing to complain about 73 Squadrons 'raw deal'. All too late to change orders.

23 July — All orders carried but no interception during either patrol. No. 805 Squadron assisted in the patrols over the fleet and their machines the Grummen Martletts awakened the interest of everyone. The fleet consisted of 21 ships, a thrilling sight.

24 July — No operational flying during the day. Squadron formation practice carried out and during this taking place a piece of wing fell off the machine flown by F/O Johnson. He landed without further damage to the a/c. Squadron received a visit from Mr Woods, Rolls Royce specialist.

25 July	At 06:00 hours a patrol took place over Bagush where a/c were refuelling. There were 2 'scrambles but no interception made. In the evening 12 a/c were sent out to patrol over ships & 2 a/c to patrol over Barrani. All a/c stayed the night at Barrani.
26 July	Our a/c carried out a dawn patrol over Halfaya area and all returned safely. No e/a encountered but intense & accurate A/A fire was met, which damaged one machine. In the afternoon Squadron & Wing formation practice was carried out. The latter was most impressive.
27 July	A rather laid-back day for the Squadron. 6 a/c sent to Burg Elm Arab for modifications and 2 a/c to BIG for inspections. P/O Horstman went to Barrani to relieve P/O Irwin of CO duties to one of the LGs there.
28 July	Squadron at 06:15 hours had 3 a/c at readiness. There was 1 'scramble' during the morning, which proved uneventful. After lunch 1 a/c went to 53 RSU & 4 a/c to BIG. 2 a/c returned from Burg El Arab. Our operations officer was posted to Delta, sorry to see him go. We expressed our hope that he would get his 'Sunderland' or 'Catalina' he cried out for.
29 July	No flying during the morning. 1 a/c returned from 103 MU, 2 a/c were flown to MU for modifications, 5 a/c were loaned to us for shipping patrols by 274 Squadron. One was found to be U/S and replaced by one from No. 1 SAAF. At 14:00 hours 12 a/c left to carry out shipping patrols, 2 a/c returned with leaks. A number of e/a encountered with a good number destroyed or damaged. Our casualties 2 a/c missing.
30 July	In the morning we returned the a/c to 274 Squadron, but later on 3 a/c were loaned to us again along with 4 a/c from No 1 SAAF. To help with shipping patrols. At 17:30 hours, 13 a/c took off on shipping patrols and after the patrol they landed at Barrani where they stayed for the night.
31 July	Ten of the a/c took off for morning shipping patrols whilst the 3 a/c returned to base. After the patrols were completed all the loaned a/c were returned to their Squadrons. F/Lt. Smith & P/O Ruffhead returned with 2 a/c from 51 RSU, in the evening 5 a/c sent to BLG.

AIR 27/630/15 & AIR 27/630/16 Pilot Ops Report

August 1941:

1 August Sidi Heneish	Quiet day, only one operational sortie carried out in the morning. Sgt. Tiffin and S/Ldr. Rosier returned from BIG. In the evening P/O Johns went to Bagush to get instructions on dropping messages, unfortunately the mechanism failed.
2 August	Early morning F/Lt. Smith dropped previous days message over Tobruk. Four a/c returned by No.1 SAAF. Two a/c were flown to Alexandria to be fitted with IFF. Four a/c carried out patrol over Sidi Barrani. Night flying tests being carried out.
3 August	At 00:20 hours S/Ldr. Rosier was scrambled to point A – he returned at 01:00 hours when night flying stopped. Four a/c, which carried the patrol over Sidi Barrani yesterday, returned to base. In the afternoon, 3 a/c loaned to 274 Squadron; 4 a/c returned from BIG in the evening and 2 a./c at readiness for night flying. There were two uneventful 'scrambles' carried before midnight.
4 August	At 01:00 hours and 02:20 hours patrols were carried out, they were uneventful. Three L/R Hurricanes were exchanged for 4 S/R of 274 Squadron. Three a/c went to BIG in the evening. Two patrols carried out by night flying a/c.

5 August	Two-night patrols took place without any result. Night flying ceased at 03:00 hours. From dawn to 09:15 hours a patrol of 2 a/c was maintained between Fuka Satellite and LG 09. In the afternoon 12 a/c carried out shipping patrol with a further 2 a/c patrolling Barrani. They landed at Barrani and stayed the night.
6 August	No operations during the day. Night flying started at 22:00 hours. Two patrols carried out with no result.
7 August	Two further night patrols were carried out, night flying ceased at 02:00 hours. No further operations until 16:20 hours when 16 a/c went to nearby aerodrome for an operation, which did not materialise. One-night patrol carried out no contact made.
8 August	At 06:15 hours a/c took off to patrol over ships. 3 ME 110's was encountered, 2 damaged. We had 1 a/c damaged. In the afternoon 8 a/c went to BIG. Patrols over LG 60 took place, and nothing reported.
9 August	Five-night patrols carried out over point A, P/O Johns on the fourth patrol destroyed e/a. Dawn, 4 readiness a/c took over patrols from the 2 a/c over LG 60 and between Fuka Satellite and LG 09. Search patrols took place in the afternoon. Four replacement a/c arrived from 51 RSU.
10 August	Three-night patrols operated. At 09:00hours 3 a/c went top patrol Barrani. In the evening 12 a/c carried out patrols over ships then landed at Barrani and stayed the night. During the day 5 a/c came back from BIG whilst 3 a/c went to BIG.
11 August	There were 3-night patrols. We had one 'scramble' of 4 a/c in the afternoon no interception made.
12 August	Two-night patrols carried out. In the evening 12 a/c left to patrol ships, they landed at Barrani and stayed night.
13 August	Our 12 a/c left Barrani on shipping patrols then returned to base at 07:15 hours. Two patrols of 2 a/c over LG 60 and 2 patrols of 2 a/c between Fuka Satellite and LG 09.
14 August	One patrol of 12 a/c and two of 11 a/c carried out over shipping, all uneventful.
15 August	Only one operation carried out during the day. Six a/c patrolled Barrani in the afternoon.
16 August	At 16:00 hours 2 a/c left to search for a pilot in the Sollum Bay – they landed at Barrani at 18:30 hours. Ten a/c left base and were joined by the previous 2 a/c, all 12 a/c carried out a patrol over shipping.
17 August	Five a/c went to base, 5 a/c loaned to No.1 SAAF to help with patrols. Four a/c arrived from BIG in the evening.
18 August	No operations carried out during the day.
19 August	No operations until 18:00 hours, when 2 a/c were scrambled over base – no interceptions.
20 August	We had 3 'scrambles during the day. At noon 4 a/c were ordered to patrol Matruh and later 2 a/c patrols of 2 a/c over base. Six a/c loaned to No.1 SAAF.
21 August	The 6 a/c returned but one was damaged on landing. In the evening 12 a/c were sent to patrol shipping.
22 August	We received 1 'scramble' of 2 a/c during the day. Five a/c were loaned to No.1 SAAF and 1 a/c to Naval Squadron.

23 August	No operations carried out.
24 August	No operations during the day. At 18:10 night flying tests carried out. Practice was continued from 20:00 – 22:10 hours.
25 August	Four a/c returned, and 4 a/c loaned from No1 SAADF. In the evening 12 a/c left to patrol shipping, 3 a/c returned, the remainder stayed at Barrani. Night flying practice carried on until 23:30 hours.
26 August	At 07:15 hours 8 a/c returned from Barrani. In the afternoon 12 a/c were on shipping patrol and stayed the night at Barrani. No interceptions.
27 August	12 a/c returned from Barrani. In the afternoon 13 a/c were sent to No.1 SAAF.
28 August	No operations carried out.
29 August	No operations carried out. 4 a/c went to BIG.
30 August	No operations carried out. 3 a/c arrived back from BIG.
31 August	No operations carried out.

AIR 27/630/17 (1) & AIR 27/630/18 (2) Pilot Ops Report

September 1941:

1 September Sidi Heneish	The Squadron left Sidi Heneish in convoy for Amriya and arrived safely. 3 a/c, the only ones remaining at Sidi Heneish accompanied the Squadron.
2 September	An advance party under P/O Irwin went to Gamil. The rest of the Squadron stayed at Amriya until the 5 September.
3 & 4 September	No records entered.
5 September	Six a/c left Amriya for Gamil and the Squadron again left in convoy spending the night at Heliopolis.
6 September Port Said (El Gamil)	The Squadron duly arrived at Gamil to find the advance party and the 6 a/c.
7 September	First operation flight took place from Gamil. The CO taking off at 20:25 hours on a RED Warning, but sortie was abortive and was ordered to land within 15 minutes.
8 September	At 16:00 hours one defensive shipping patrol was flown by 2 a/c. This will become a daily routine till further notice. Night flying practice between 19:25 and 20:15 hours.
9 September	Two a/c at readiness dusk till dawn and the usual 16:00 hours patrol.
10 September	One a/c of the protective patrol was flown by W/C Mermigan but no e/a encountered.
11 September	At 11L35 hours 2 a/c were ordered to patrol Port Said but were recalled within 10 minutes as it proved a false alarm. Usual afternoon patrol was uneventful.
12 September	During the day four patrols were flown. The first at 11:40 hours to intercept e/a reported as JU 88's, turned out to be friendly. In the afternoon 3 patrols of 2 a/c gave cover to shipping between 14:30 and 18:00 hours. No e/a encountered.

13 September	At 11:25 hours 2 a/c were ordered to 'scramble' to deal with Heinkel, which was plotted up from the South. E/a never seen as the plane had changed course. Afternoon patrols continued. Night flying practice carried out 20:00 until 21:30 hours in cooperation with a searchlight exercise.
14 September	At 02:30 hours 1 a/c flown by F/Lt. Wellman ordered to patrol. No e/a seen, but un-askingly he became the target of the A/A, luckily without damaged. During the morning there was 1 'scramble' and in the afternoon the usual shipping patrol – in the evening a Hart was added to the strength of the Squadron.
15 September	Little activity during the day. Usual shipping patrols were in operation and 1 a/c 'scrambled' for 10 minutes unidentified a/c was a Hurricane. P/O Grant joined Squadron as Adjutant. The evening aw 6 new Hurricanes and 2 Tomahawks arrive from Faiyum, great addition. Night flying cancelled until a/c are fitted with IFF.
16 September	A little local flying indulged with by Hurricanes and Tomahawks. One operational flight ordered to protect cruiser coming into harbour. The patrol soon found out that the cruiser had docked one hour before patrol was ordered.
17 September	Much practice flying carried out during the day and in the evening 9 a/c took off to carry out formation practice. Operational activity uneventful. Two a/c sent to investigate an explosion at sea and report traces of oil a separate patrol carried out shipping patrol.
18 September	Operational flying, three patrols of 2 a/c – two mid-days onwards from Ismailia to Geneifa, a third carried out shipping patrol. Nothing encountered. In the day and evening a fair amount of practice flying took place. F/Lt. Devlin left Squadron to take up S/Ldr. post at HQ, RAF ME.
19 September	Four patrols flown during the day all uneventful; two from Ismalia to Geneifa and two shipping patrols all false alarms. From 18:30 hours until 21:30 hours night flying practice.
20 September	Repeat of previous days operations – one shipping and the Ismalia to Geneifa patrol. From 18:30 hours until 20:30 hours night flying practice.
21 September	Uneventful day. Three shipping patrols were ordered up and one Ismalia to Geneifa patrol, nothing sighted. Practice flying carried out.
22 September	A further 8 Hurricanes delivered to the Squadron in the afternoon. We had one 'scramble' and one Canal patrol. No e/a seen. From 18:30 hours until 21:30 hours night flying practice.
23 September	An active but fruitless day. Two patrols, one over shipping and one over the Canal also one 'scramble' which turned out to be a non-event. Night flying practice again, one a/c crash landed with no injury to pilot.
24 September	Not a great deal of change in the operations on day-to-day basis. Three 'scramble' and one patrol over the Canal. Night flying practice resumed, and one a/c crash landed, flaps problem.
25 September	One operational flight took place; a 'scramble' was ordered but returned after 15 minutes. Quiet day. Local flying practice and layer patrol practice in the evening. Interfered by low cloud, planes returned after 45 minutes.
26 September	Usual El Firdan to Geneifa patrol flown from 12:00 to 14:00 hours. In the evening from 17:15 to 18:00 hours shipping patrol. No e/a seen. No night flying practice.

27 September	Active day. Two Canal and two shipping patrols, plus one 'scramble'. No e/a seen during sorties.
28 September	Seven a/c and patrols left for Shalufa on temporary duty and protection of important convoy in the Red Sea. Two shipping patrols. One pilot and a/c arrived from 2374 on attachment whilst our a/c are at Shalufa.
29 September	Further five a/c left for Shalufa and 4 a/c arrived from 274 on attachment. One shipping patrol in the afternoon flown by 274 Squadron a/c. Our 12 a/c detached to Shalufa carried out 11 patrols over shipping. No e/a seen.
30 September	Six a/c detached from the 12 at Shalufa to operate from Ras Gharib. One patrol over shipping was flown by 274 Squadron.

AIR 27/630/19 & AIR 27/630/20 Pilot Ops Report

October 1941:

1 October El Gamil, Port Said	No operational flights from Gamil today. 'A' Flight, from Shallufa made 7 shipping patrols – 'B' Flight the same number from Ras Gharib no e/a seen. S/Ldr. Ward left Gamil to take over as CO to the Squadron.
2 October	From Gamil there were 2 'scrambles' and 1 shipping patrol, each with 2 a/c, a/c one from 73 and one from 274. 2784 provided the extra a/c. At Shallufa 3 uneventful shipping patrols flown by 'A' Flight. Three pilots being posted to Squadron.
3 October	A very quiet day no operational flights and an uneventful 'scramble' by 274 over the base.
4 October	One patrol by 274 over shipping from Gamil. 'A' Flight 7 patrols and 'B' Flight 5 patrols, none of special interest – 'A' arrived back in the evening from Shallufa.
5 October	No operational flying and 'B' Flight returned from Ras Gharib.
6 October	Only 1 shipping patrol at 08:00 hours undertaken nothing to report.
7 October	Two patrols over shipping were provided between 12:30 and 14:45 hours. Nothing to report. Evening night flying practice carried out. Ten pilots from SAAF report for duty, on attachment.
8 October	No operational flying today. However, there was some practice day and night carried out.
9 October	An inactive day, no flying except practice. F/Lt. Wellmon left on posting to 71 OUT. F/O MacDougall went with advance party of 'A' Flight to KILO 8.
10 October	Only on operational shipping patrol flown in the afternoon. Four pilots from 'A' Flight went on detachment to KILO 8.
10 October to 31 October – KILO 8 - Nr Heliopolis	*'A' Flight undertook a whole load of flying and practice carried by the pilots at various times through the days. The details of KILO 8 is not being included in this section suffice to say that KILO 8 was a very busy place.*
11 October	No operational flying. One more pilot went to KILO 8 making 6 on detachment.
12 October	No operational flying. W.C Mermagen did co-operation with searchlights in the evening.
13 October	No operational flying. Some practice flying took place both day and night.
14 October	No operational flying. Some practice flying took place both day and night. Layer patrol practiced at night. ***Our Wedding Anniversary.***

15 October	Only 1 shipping patrol in the morning otherwise no operational flying. Some practice flying during the day.
16 October	No operational flying. Night practice flying took place.
17 October	No operational flying. Only 1 shipping patrol took place.
18 October	No operational flying. Two shipping patrols took place. Night flying practice (Layer Patrols). W/C's Malloy and Riley arrived from Heliopolis and stayed the night. W/C Mermagen carried Searchlight Co-Operation.
19 October	W/C's Malloy and Riley left for Heliopolis. Two a/c 'scrambled' over base. No night flying.
20 October	Three shipping patrols carried out during the day. Three NEW Mark II Hurricanes arrived for the Squadron. Night shadowing practices carried out.
21 October	No operational flying during the day, but at night 2 a/c 'scrambled' without result.
22 October	In the morning Squadron visited by G/Spt. Turton-Jones and the ACC, 202 Group. Two 'scrambles' and 3 shipping patrols but no interceptions.
23 October	No operational flying. In the morning Lt. Jalliffe of FAA landed in a Walrus on his way to Aboukir from Lydda. In the W/C Mermagen carried out searchlight co-operation in the Blenheim with F/Lt. Helsby and F/Sgt. Ellis on practice interception in a Hurricane.
24 October	Morning: Four operational flights carried out. Three shipping patrols by a single a/c and 1 'scrambled' Forward Base West. Afternoon: Six Hurricanes took part in local formation practice. As 1 a/c taxied it collided with tractor and roller, no injuries and plane removed in time for 2 a/c to take off on interception evening flight.
25 October	Eight a/c in both morning and afternoon undertook formation practice. F/O Scade carried out shipping patrol for little over an hour. Evening activities were 4 a/c practicing dusk landings.
26 October	F/O Worrell carried a shipping patrol for 1 hour 10 minutes. S/Ldr. Ward led a practice formation of 8 a/c, F/L. Powel was ordered to 'scramble over Damietta. At 17:00 hours S/Ldr. Ward and P/O Gallagher left for Heliopolis, they returned at 22:45 hours. F/O MacDougall carried out night flying practice.
27 October	Morning: S/Ldr. Ward led a formation of 10 a/c for practice. This was repeated in the afternoon. In the evening W/C Mermagen flew a Hurricane for searchlight co-operation, during which Sgts. Coussens and Henry pratcie interceptions. No operational flying.
28 October	Sgt. Maryut landed from Sidi Heneish and left to go back at 08:50 hours. Later on, formation practice was carried out, then 2 'scrambles' each of 2 a/c took place. These were followed by a shipping patrol by F/O Bellamy. W/C Mermagen flew the Blenheim for Searchlight co-operation.
29 October	F/O Worrall and Sgt. Henry took off on a 'scramble' at 12:48 hours. The only operational activity of the day. A quiet day except for local tests.
30 October	No operational flying af any description. F/Lt. Helsby flew to Heliopolis, returned at 22:20 hours. Six Hurricanes took part in local formation flying with S/Ldr. Ward as leader. Lt. Howey landed in a Walrus left again for Lydda. At 14:55 hours W/C Birch landed in a Hurricane from 108 MU. No night flying.

| 31 October | Early 'scramble' at 06:10 hours saw Sgt. Henry take off for North Foreland. W/C Birch returned to 108 MU at 06:40 hours. Later in the morning Sgt. McPherson took the Blenheim to Palestine. Rest of the day was quiet, only local test flights and practice. |

73 Squadron - AIR 27/630/21 & AIR 27/630/22 (3) Pilot Ops Report
39 Squadron – AIR 27/407/25 & AIR 27/407/26 Pilot Ops Report

November 1941:

From 1 November to 30 November – KILO 8 - LG Heliopolis	*'A' Flight undertook a whole load of flying and practice carried by the pilots at various times through the days. The details of KILO 8 are not being included in this section suffice to say that KILO 8 was a very busy place.*
1 November El Gamil, Port Said	Operational flights over shipping took place, 1 'scrambles' at 12:35 hours with 4 a/c taking part. They were air-borne for 25 minutes at 10,000 feet over North Foreland, and no results. Sgt. McPherson returned from Palestine with the Blenheim. P/O Wareham arrived from KILO 8. Just before mid-night a 2 a/c 'scrambled' to fly over Forward Base West. Again, no results.
2 November	At 02:05 hours 1 'scramble' over Forward Base West, no results. A number of arrivals and departures were the name of the day. Sgt. Barlow arrived from 237 Squadron, Amriya with a new a/c, a Hurricane Mark II No. 3514. F/O Duncan was here for 2½ hours from Amriya in a Tomahawk. F/Lt. Young reported to KILO 8.
3 November	Other than shipping patrols there were no operational activity today. Sgt. McPherson went to Amriya and back again in a Blenheim. Sub/Lt. Baring passed through with a Walrus, from Nicosia to Dekheila.
4 November	Fairly busy day started with a 'scramble' involving 3 a/c at 01:10 hours. A/c were 'scrambled' again at 03:07 hours over Forward Base South for 45 minutes also a flight at 03:10 hours over Forward Base West. Additional 'scrambles' took off, but no e/a were incepted e/a.
5 November	Generally, a quiet day. There was 1 'scramble' of 2 a/c at 10:30 hours over North Forland with no results. Two a/c were on shipping patrols and some flying between bases.
6 November	Orders received throughout the day to carry out patrols over the base were carried out. Some general flying between bases. F/O Worrall and Sgt. Ellis di the return trip to Aboukir toady.
7 November	Throughout the day the Squadron received 'scrambles' along with flights to patrol the shipping. No e/a seen. Two pilots went over to Amriya in the Hart, Sgt. Barlow returned later with a Tomahawk. P/O Scott arrived from Helopolis in a Lysander with despatches, proceeding later on to Dekheila. Two pilots went to Lamailia and stayed the night.
8 November	The Start of the day, a 'scramble at 08:40 hours to 'Angels 10'. A further 'scramble was received but proved false alarm. Two pilots again air-borne at 14:00 hours, there were no results. F/Lt. Powell and F/O Worral returned from Lamailia at 07:45 hours.
9 November	Quiet day. There was only 1 shipping patrol and Sgt. Packham arrived from KILO 8.
10 November	Early at 02:50 hours 1 'scramble' of 2 a/c over Forward Base South at 10,000 feet, nil to report. Shipping patrol was carried out, and transit movements between bases and KILO 8 took place.

11 November	No operational flying today. Transit movements took place. W/C Mermagen to and from Rumani with a Blenheim. One Tomahawk and one Hart flew to Amriya. Other flight took place to and from Ismailia and Heliopolis.
12 November	Momentous day with only movements to report. It's quite a while since 'combat forms' have been completed by any pf 73 Squadron. Other movements were recorded.
13 November	Two pilots were 'scrambled' at 03:32 hours over Forward Base West. These were the only operational flights done today. Other flights between base and KILO 8 took place.
14 November	Only one operational flight today. Shipping patrol carried out. A Magister a/c landed here en route from Mariut to Lydda. S/Ldr. Ward returned from Ismailia at mid-day. F/Lt. Young was in KILO 8 for a few hours.
15 November	A very quiet day again. No operational flights. Other transit flights took place between bases. W/C Bryan landed for a while en-route from Aquir to Meriut.
16 November	Only 1 operational patrol over shipping. Again, a number of other flights seen throughout the day. There was great excitement in camp later this afternoon when it was heard that a Battle Flight was being formed to proceed to the Western Desert. Farewell parties could not be arranged due to the speed at which ops were being set up.
17 November	With every good wish, the following details took-off for the Western Desert; S/Ldr. Ward and 6 other pilots took off on their deployment. Other transits took place during the day.
18 November	A day worthy of note, it records the commencement of the second large-scale offensive by British and Imperial troops against the enemy – a combined German-Italian Force, in the Western Desert. No operational flights today. Other movements were carried out during the day.
19 November	No operational flights today. Only 1 transit took place throughout the day. From base camp to KILO 8.
20 November	An exceptionally quiet day. No operational flights today. Only 1 transit took place throughout the day. From base camp to KILO 8.
21 November	One patrol over shipping carried out. A number of transit flights took place today.
22 November	No operational flights today. It appears that the activity in the Western Desert is keeping e/a busy than usual. G/Capt. Turton-Jones landed in a Gladiator. There has been no news regarding the Battle Flight of 73 Squadron from the Western Desert.
23 November	Again, no operational flights. Patrols from other stations were carried out, including KILO 8. A number of pilots returned from other bases. S/Ldr. Ward returned from the Western Desert at 17:10 hours.
24 November	The base recorded 10mm of rain just before dawn. This is considered a heavy rainfall for this part of the world. Large areas of the aerodrome were unserviceable for 24 hours. However, this did not deter flying practice. We had just the 1 'scramble' over North Forland at 7,000 feet, with no results. Some toing and froing occurred at KILO 8.
25 November	Shipping patrol carried out by 2 a/c in the morning period for 1 hour 17 minutes. F/Lt. Roebotham flying a captured ME 110 escorted by F/O Worrall along with two other Hurricanes arrived from Heliopolis. Sgt. Brooks took off in the Blenheim for Aboukir at 13:45 hours. WE received news that when he took off at Amriya he crashed and died of his injuries. Sad news, he was a popular pilot and well known in the Middle East.

26 November	A number of operations were carried out today with 'scrambled' patrols shipping patrols. There were also transit flights taking place.
27 November	The only operational flight was a 'scramble of 2 a/c to Angels 10 over Forward Base West and Forward Base East respectively at 15:48 hours for 35 minutes. No e/a seen. A number of transit flights took place.
28 November	This morning Sgt. MacPherson reported out again to the Western Desert, there were also some shipping patrols. Some transit flight took place.
29 November	Operational flights consisted of 1 'scramble' at 04:49 hours plus a shipping patrol at 05:00 hours. Nothing to report from either. The Battle Flight returned for refitting. They reported a very successful 'strafe' rendering 13 e/a unserviceable (waiting on confirmation). G/Capt. Turton-Jones, W/C Bayne and F/O Temlett landed in Ismailia – returned an hour later.
30 November	A very quiet day with no operational flights. Some transit flying between base and KILO 8 plus other flights took place. W/C Mermagen flew to Ismalia in the ME 110 and returned later. F/Lt. Roebotham flew the ME 110 escorted by Sgt. McLeod to Heliopolis.
	<u>GENERAL:</u>
	S/Ldr. Ward departed for the Western Desert to take up 1/c of the Battle Flight, F/Lt. Powell appointed CO, F/O Grant is to be Adjutant with Medical Officer being F/Lt. Baird. Pilots arriving during the month for flying duty are F/O Sir J. A. Kirkpatrick on the 07/11/41, 2 on the 20/11/41, 4 on the 22/11/41 and 2 more on the 24/11/41. During the month some 315 flying practice flights took place.
	Rain and subsequent misty weather towards the end of the month curtailed flying practice, particularly searchlight co-operation.

NOTE:
1. *LAC Lamb L. B. 1012281 along with other ground crew were sent on detachment to 39 Squadron during November 1941 through December 1941 to January 1942. In the Operations Record Books of 39 Squadrons AIR 27/407/25 to AIR 27/407/33 the detachments that were carried out are not recorded.*
2. *AIR 27/407/26 Operations Record Book covers 39 Squadrons operations albeit in 'General' terms during the month of January. When requested 73 Squadron would send some of their pilots and ground crew personnel to help out on shortages.*

73 Squadron - AIR 27/630/23 (1) & AIR 27/630/24 Pilot Ops Report
39 Squadron – AIR 27/407/27 & AIR 27/407/28 Pilot Ops Report
December 1941:

From 1 December to 31 December – KILO 8 - LG Helioplois	*'A' Flight undertook a whole load of flying and practice carried by the pilots at various times through the days. The details of KILO 8 is not being included in this section suffice to say that KILO 8 was a very busy place.*
1 December El Gamil, Port Said	At 09:00 hours the Battle Flight left for the Western Desert. Sgt. McLeod returned from Heliopolis after escorting the captured ME 110 there. No operational fights in the morning. Two shipping patrols in the afternoon. New pilot arrived and carried out some practice circuits and bumps. Sgt. Coussens carried out searchlight co-operation for 1 hour 10 minutes.
2 December	Some pilots practiced interception flights. No operational flying and no night flying.
3 December	During the morning non-operational local flying. 1 'scramble' at 14:49 hours over base was carried out. Practice flying interceptions took place. Lt. Howey, RN flying a Walrus landed from Lydda at 15:54 hours.

4 December	The Walrus departed flying from El Gamil to Aboukir. S/Ldr. Louis took off for Ismailia and F/O Wyatt-Smith arrived from Maryut in a Tomahawk. At 14:30 hours Sgt. Joyce patrolled shipping; the only sortie carried out. Evening searchlight co-operation was carried out.
5 December	F/L. Powell went to Heliopolis, F/O Wareham flew to KILO 8 and later F/o Chatfield landed from Maryut in a Tomahawk. No operational flying during the day or night.
6 December	Two a/c ordered to 'scramble'. At 12:50 hours and 15:40 hours 2 /ac carried out shipping patrols. Pilot, F/O McFaddon returned to Squadron after a long absence.
7 December	No operational flights, a quiet day. Some local flying was carried out and Sgt. Mohar did some night flying tests.
8 December	Sgt. McPherson landed from the Western desert. F/Sgt. Ellis took part in an R/T range test. One operational shipping patrol at 12:41 hours was carried out by F/O Kiby. F/Sgt. Ellis co-operated with Port Said searchlights in the evening for practice purposes and F/O Kibt carried out a weather test.
9 December	Sgt. McvPherson took off for the Desert, and two pilots flew to KILO 8. At 15:06 hours two pilots were ordered to 'scramble' to vector 170 deg., angels 16. No e/a seen. Sgt. Buckand landed in a Tomahawk from Maryut and F/Lt. Bellway flew to KILO 8. Three-night tests were carried out and P/O Irwin did searchlight co-operation from 17:48 to 19:00 hours.
10 December	The day started with F/Sgt. Ellis doing a pip-squeak test. Day to day flying in and out and across to KILO 8. F/O Bellway took off for gun co-operation at 11:07 hours. At 11:56 hours S/Ldr. Campbell-Shaw arrived from Fayid, he returned at 4:57 hours. One a/c shipping patrol off Port Said took place. No e/a attempted an attack.
11 December	Two pilots and a/c took off at 08:35 hours for formation practice. G/Capt. Turton-Jones came from Ismailia in a Gladiator and W/Cdr. Anderson in a Fulmar. Six pilots and a/c took off at 11:00 hours for formation flying practice. There was 1 operational shipping patrol. At 15:30 three pilots arrived back from the Western Desert. Remainder of the day was quiet except for some test flights.
12 December	At 09:35 hours F/O Kirkpatrick patrolled ships. W/Cdr. Bayne and S/Ldr. Louis went to Ismailia in Hurricanes and returned at 13:00 hours. 1 a/c landed from KILO 8 and a Blenheim arrived from Ismailia. At 11:29 hours the second 'scramble' received, 2 a/c to patrol over base at Angels 10, vectors given but no e/a seen. Two our pilots proceeded to 'shoot-up' the Army ack-ack post to give them some practice. Some more interaction between bases took place. At 16:47 hours the final operational order was received 2 a/c 'scrambled' to Angels 5 over base. There was no result.
13 December	Three pilots with their Hurricanes practice battle formation flying. Sgt. Packham arrived from KILO 8. F/Sgt. Ellis left for the Western Desert. Sgt.Tackaberry carried out the only operational flight patrolling shipping in the Port Said area. There was one-night flight practice and two pilots landed after completing their air firing practice.
14 December	The only operational flying in the day was a shipping patrol flown by F/Lt, Powell. G/Capt. Turton-Jones landed from Ismalia in a Gladiator and left again at 16:12 hours. S/Ldr. Dudgeon flew to Heliopolis and returned at 17:50 hours. S/Ldr Dudgeon landed from KILO 8 in a Tomahawk and went back at 15:59 hours. There was some local flying during the day.

15 December	Four of our pilots 4 – Hurricane I's to the Western Desert and flew back with 4 – Hurrcane II just before dark. There was one 'scramble' in the afternoon but no interception. There was some general flying during the day. There was no night flying or any operational flying nor co-operation.
16 December	Rather an easy day. Some local flying in the morning. S/Ldr. Ward flew to Heliopolis at 11:50 hours. There was one shipping patrol in the afternoon. F/O Eiby and Sgt. Mcleod delivered 2 – Hurricane I's to Wadi Natrun then proceeded to KILO 8 to collect 2 – Hurricane II's. P/O Irwin and Sgt. Joyes flew to Fuka in the Hart to collect Hurricane II's also. At dusk two-night readiness pilots carried out night flying tests. No night flying.
17 December	No operations in the morning. Four pilots arrived with Hurricane II's. In the afternoon Sgt. Laing flew to Fuka to collect another Hurricane II. At 16:45 hours orders received for a shipping patrol to take place. No e/a seen. Night readiness aircraft were tested and proved serviceable.
18 December	The day started with a shipping patrol, and this proved to be the only operational flight during the day. There were a number of visiting aircraft today plus some top brass. There was a considerable amount of ferrying today.
19 December	Another ae day. A great deal of movement, we had 15 pilots carrying out cross-country flying, flying a range of a/c to numerous locations. F/O Worrall went Shandur, F/Lt. Johnston was back from Shandur in time for him to accompany F/Lt. Wyatt-Smith on a 'Scramble at 16:12 hours. This being the operational flight of the day, with no result. The highlight of our day was the arrival of Air Marshal Todder (ACC -in-c) in a magister from Heliopolis at 10:30 hours.
20 December	A good deal of movement again today. A goodly number of pilots and machines took off to tackle the ongoing threats by the enemy. Just before 10:00 hour two pilots were 'scrambled' over base by the Sector Controller, plus going on to carry out shipping patrols. At 10:59 hours F/O Rushton landed in a Bombay from Khanka and left at 11:51 hours. F/O Tremlett came from KILO 8 in a Gordon and Sgt. Chambers in the Hart.
21 December	The Gordon took off. The day was a little quieter than the 19th and 20th. There was a Battle Flight Formation Practice in which 6 pilots took part.
22 December	There were two operational flights one over shipping and the other on interception, but nothing seen. There were a number of machines booked on cross-country flights today and there was an average amount of local test flying.
23 December	A fairly quiet day. Apart from a 'scramble' and a shipping patrol there was little flying. W/Cdr. Bayne flew to Ismailia and S,Ldr. Ward to Amriya. There was some local flying between base and KILO 8. Mention should be made of a Squadron dance held in Port Said to celebrate the festive season. It was held in the evening and was attended by all personnel fortunate to be off duty.
24 December	Christmas Eve was a little more active. F/Lt. Marchbell landed in a Bombay to take off a number of other ranks, who are necessary to service S/Ldr. Ward and six other planes in the Western Desert. S/Ldr. Ward and the six other pilots left for the Western Desert at 10:25 hours. G/Capt. Turton-Jones arrived from Ismailia in a Gladiator.
25 December	Christmas Day: A very quiet day. One of our F/O had to return to Base after his Hurricane developed engine problems whilst he was flying to the Western Desert. S/Ldr. Louis went to Ismailia and returned, and F/Lt. Bellamy came landed from Shandur.
26 December	There were no operational sorties today. Three pilots flew to Shandur and one of the pilot's F/O Kirkpatrick returning at 12:03 hours.

27 December	F/O Kirkpatrick and Sgt. Baker practiced interception flying and soon after, took off on instructions from the Sector Controller to 'scramble' over base. A second 'scramble' was ordered and at 14:21 hours when F/Lt. Wyatt-Smith and Sgt. Sands had to go to Angels 18. No interception made. Three pilots arrived from Dekhelia.
28 December	St. Sands and F/O Duncan went to Shandur, and P/O Bennett left for Dekhelia left in the Gladiator that arrived at 11:45 hours yesterday. F/Lt. Wyatt-Smith and P/O Chatfield also took off for Dekhelia. Just before 17:00 hours a Beaufighter flew low over the aerodrome. The Sector Controller was expecting the a/c to land so two Hurricanes took off to tell hm it was safe to land. We had, had quite a lot of rain and it is perceived that the Egyptian Authorities had put up warning signs, Ground Unserviceable. The Beaufighter did not land.
29 December	S/Ldr. Lean came from Heliopolis in a Magister. Five pilots did some local formation practices and whilst this was being carried out 5 pilots returned from the Western Desert. F/O Duncan and F/Sgt. Price took part in the only operational flight of the day, a 'scramble' over base at 10,000 feet. There were no interceptions.
30 December	Ten pilots (including W/C Bayne) took off for formation practice. At 11:50 hours P/O Kirkpatrick and Sgt. Packham went to 20,000 feet during a 'scramble' over base both pilots landed at 12:05 hours without intercepting any e/a. In the afternoon a similar exercise to that of the morning took place and two pilots had to breakaway to investigate an unidentified a/c. Atb16:22 hours S/Ldr. Ward re-joined the Squadron, having flown from the newly captured Benghazi.
31 December	There was no operational flying today. F/O Kirkpatrick took off at 10:37 hours for some gun co-operation. An Albacore flown by S/Ldr. Phillips landed from Fayid in the afternoon and then left for Heliopolis. The last flight of 1941at El Gamil proved to be a night flying test, which was carried out by Sgt. Baker in a Hurricane. **(The day on which L. B. Lamb 1012281 received promotion to AC1.)**

NOTE:
1. *This month, besides being a memorable one in view of the activities of our Battle Flight in the Western Desert has produced the 'first' edition of our Squadron Magazine. The magazine has been named 'Tutor et Ultor', after the Squadron's Moto. Owing to the printing in these parts and the fact that the printer's knowledge of English left a lot to be desired, much midnight oil has been burnt in checking proofs and correcting mistakes. The idea for the magazine came about from the very week of December. The committee that was set up are justifiably proud of what has been achieved and it is hoped this may long continue.*

2. *AIR 27/407/28 Operations Record Book covers 39 Squadrons operations albeit in 'General' terms during the month of January. When requested 73 Squadron would send some of their pilots and ground personnel to help out on shortages.*

73 Squadron - AIR 27/631/1 & AIR 27/631/2 Pilot Ops Report
39 Squadron – AIR 27/407/29 & AIR 27/407/30 Pilot Ops Report
January 1942:

1 January El Gamil	The day began with a shipping patrol at 08:10 hours. The only operational flying was a 'scramble' carried out by 2 a/c to cloud base. During the day pilots came and went, one to Aboukir and one from Ismailia. Sgt. Belcham arrived from Shandur and returned later accompanied by Sgt. Baker. Night Flight tests carried out by the 15-minute section.
2 January	No operational flights at all, nut there was a considerable amount of movement. During the day pilots came and went, two arrived from Aboukir, S/Ldr. Dudgeon from Abu Sueir in a Kittyhawk, one from Shandur, one left for Aboukir and one for Shandur. Little local flying apart from 1 hour's formation practice by Red Section in the morning.

3 January	The day started with a 'scramble' for the Readiness Section and lasted only 15-minutes and no e/a. Further 'scramble' at 12:14 hours, two pilots spending 1 hour over base, again no e/a. Third 'scramble' much as the earlier ones. Very little movement during the day except for one crash landing 10 miles from base due to engine issues while returning from Shandur. No serious damage to pilot or plane. Not much happened and days end.
4 January	Operational flying limited to one 'scramble' of 48-minutes duration carried out by 2 a/c. A few movements happened throughout the day: S/Ldr. Ward to Shandur, P/O Ellis to Helwan, F/Lt. Wyatt-Smith from Amriya and F/O Duncan from Heliopolis. The AOC arrived late in his Magister from Lydda. Some local formation practice by two sections was the only flying for the day.
5 January	Operational flying occupied the first and last flights of the day. Sgt. Joyce shipping patrol, 1hr 13mins duration; at 23:50 hours F/Lt. Young and Sgt. Belcham patrolled base at 14,000 feet. Sgt. Belcham landed after 8 minutes owing to engine trouble. The AOC left for Heliopolis at 08:05 hours. More movements to and from during the day with F/O Kirkpatrick carrying out a search for Sgt. Joyce's machine along with doing an R/T test at the same time.
6 January	The day started with operational flying, 'scramble' over base at 10,000 feet, a shipping patrol at 10:58 hours, a second 'scramble' resulted in only an 18-minute flight. Search by 6a/c carried out for a launch, which included some local practice. General movements continued to and from base.
7 January	Blue section was twice 'scrambled' over Damietta, first flight at 13:19 hours and the second flight at 15:32 hours. Both bogies were friendly a/c. Some local flying and again general movement to and from base.
8 January El Gamil	No operational flying and very little local flying. Visitors were G/C Turton-Jones in a Gladiator, a Beaufighter which remained for 15 minutes; S/Ldr. Ward left for Lydda at 06:30 hours; P/O Ellis went to Aboukir at 10:40 hours; Sgt. McPherson to Burg el Arab in the Hart returning with Sgt. Laing as a passenger. Some general flying to and from base plus searchlight co-op. was carried out for 50 minutes by F/Lt. Young at 19:03 hours.
9 January	The only 'scramble' of the day was cancelled 5 minutes after the signal not in time to stop 2 a/c taking off. Very little movement and local flying. General movements to and from base. Only other flying was 'A' Flight carrying out formation practice.
10 January	The one 'scramble' was mirror image of the 9th Blue section being airborne for 5 minutes. There was considerable movement to and from the base as in previous days. Local formation practice and test flights completed the day's flying.
11 January	Practice interceptions were twice successfully completed. First 'scramble', taking all three sections into the air, the interception being made by Green and Black sections. Second 'scramble' at 11:25 hours; Yellow of at 11:30 followed by Blue at 11:38, interceptions made over base a/c landed at 12:15 hours. There were a number of movements similar to that of previous days. One incident was the Hart flown by F/O Worral force-landed 15 miles S.W. of Damietta due to engine trouble, no damage to pilot or a/c. The remaining flying was several R/T and air tests.

| 12 January | In the morning Blue Section – F/Lt. Young and F/Sgt. Price were 'scrambled' over base patrolling for 50 minutes. In the afternoon F/Lt. Young carried out a shipping patrol of 1 hour 8 minutes. A number of movements to and from base took place; W/Cmdr. Baynes left for Ismailia, Sgt. Laing returned to Burg el Arab, F/O Worrall brought the Hart back from its forced-landing ground. Local formation, air and R/T tests carried out and at the close of day practice interception flight. |

| 13 January | Very little flying as only 3 a/c were serviceable in the morning. A 'scramble' at 11:05 hours for Blue Section, which lasted 55 minutes. A number of local movements to and from with an interception was made, 'bogie' but was found to be friendly. Three Free Greek Officers arrived in an Anson from 39 Squadron to collect some gear for the high-speed launch, they all left at 14:35 hours for Burg el Arab, captain was F/Lt. Dinitriadis. At 16:47 hours Sgt. Packham arrived from Fayid. No more flying. |

| 14 January | Total operational flying for the day consisted of a 'scramble' for Blue Section, F/O Kirkpatrick and Sgt. Joyce took off at 11:32 hours and orbited Danietta for 40 minutes. No interception was made. Sgt. Packham returned to Shandur; P/O Laing went to Heliopolis and F/Lt. Johnston arrived from Shandur. No other flying took place. |

| 15 January | There were only 2 shipping patrol operational flights in the day. At 14:42 hours F/O Kirkpatrick for a 1-hour patrol in the vicinity of the harbour. At 15:25 hours Sgt. Joyce took off but returned after 3 minutes with R/T trouble. The fault was repaired, and he took off at 15:40 hours for the harbour area. Not a great deal of local flying as visibility was poor. F/O Laing arrived from Kanka. |

| 16 January El Gamil | There were no operational flights as the morning was taken up with interception practices for Red, Yellow and White Sections all being 'scrambled' in rotation and all practice was very successful. A number of movements took place during the day. Sgt. Henderson and Sissons arrived in Lysander6879 from Aboukir to collect machines. Poor visibility prevented them leaving although the Lysander returned. Weather conditions not good. |

| 17 January | There was very little flying today. The total number of sorties for the day was eight. |

| 18 January | At 09:47 hours F/Lt. Wyatt-Smith left Gamil for Heliopolis in the Hart, and board as a passenger was the Adjutant. The Hart decided to play up with engine trouble and was forced to land. Sgt. Henderson took off for Kanka and F/O McDougall went on a 'recce' to locate the missing Hart. At 11:00 hours F/Lt. Young lead a formation of 7 a/c on a local practice. This took place again in the afternoon, followed by 2 operational flights, both shipping patrols. |

| 19 January | F/Lt. Young 'shot-up' the local ack-ack post and the gunners no doubt dislocated a wrist or two in following his machine with their Bofors! F/O Scade arrived from Shandur and there followed some local flying by W/Cmdr. Bayne and Sgt. Joyce. P/O Ellis came from Heliopolis and F/Lt. Wyatt-Smith went to Samaku and returned. In the afternoon formation practice took place and later night flying tests and searchlight co-op. No other actions. |

| 20 January El Gamil | The missing Hart, having been located, F/Sgt. Price flew with rations, which he dropped near the crashed aircraft. During the day there were several movements to and from the base. One particular was that of F/O Auckland arrived from Shandur in a Maryland to pick up a number of Flight personnel, who were going on detachment. Several night tests were carried out and co-operation with Port Said searchlights. |

| 21 January | Very busy morning: The Squadron carrying out practice 'scrambes', controlled by Sector Ops. Red, Yellow and White Sections all took part. There were no operational flights other than some interception flying. |

22 January	The day started with F/O Kirkpatrick carrying out a 'pipsqueak' test. W/Cmdr. Bayne and F/Lt. Young went to Ismailia. At 12:15 hours the first of two 'scrambles' took place and vectored to Damietta and the second 'scrambled' over base. All friendly. Later on, shipping patrol was carried out by Sgt. Joyce with no enemy action. F/Lt. Wyatt-Smith did searchlight co-op.
23 January	The day started with an hour's shipping patrol. Sgt. Henry, taking the air again after a long spell in hospital, did thirty minutes local flying, to get in practice again. The two 'readiness' pilots were 'scrambled'. They were vectored 180 deg., but no interception was made. Sgt. Joyce carried out a shipping patrol over Port Said. A number of movements to and from base during the day. One of note was Lt. Braithwaite RN landed at Gamil on his way to Fayid from Gaza in a Tiger Moth. Local flying continued and two pilots on night 'readiness'.
24 January	There were no operational sorties. Several movements to and from the base were booked in. There was some local flying and night flying tests, but no night 'scrambles' were ordered.
25 January *Mabel Lamb - LAC Lamb's wife's birthday today.*	Relatively quiet day except for a formation practice by 8 Hurricanes, headed by the CO. F/O Reynolds landed in a Fulmar, of the Navy from Aboukir, bringing back an old pilot of the Squadron who had been in hospital after being wounded in a previous battle flight in the Western Desert, namely Sgt. Barlow.
26 January	Only one operational sortie took place, a shipping patrol. Practice formations were carried out and Sgt. Barlow did some local flying. Further practice formations were carried out and the day closed with some night flying tests.
27 January	Two new pilots Sgts. Farley and Foster joined the Squadron and carried out some 'circuits and bumps' in the morning. Formation practice flying of 6 a/c at 11:15 hours, formed the prelude for the 'mass attack' by Kittyhawks, which occurred in the afternoon. This was practice at aerodrome defence. At 15:50 hours S/Ldr. Ward and seven of his pilots were 'scramble' by Sector Controller to intercept 20 e/a approaching from the south. Air raid Alarm Sounded at Gamil, and as ground personnel took cover in the shelters, the Controller was vectoring the 8 a/c of 73 Squadron in order to intercept the bandits. Interception was made near Gamil bridges, and 'Tally-ho' came over the air at 16:25 hours. 13 e/a straffed the aerodrome, presumably they were driven off! The all clear sounded 'return to work' for the Squadron at 16:45 hours. Searchlight co-op flights were carried out.
28 January	The morning started with formation practice, Sgts. Foster and Farley went up for firing practice. Four pilots from 213 Squadron arrived to take over 'readiness', news spread round the camp that 73 Squadron was going 'up in the blue' again. There were no operational flights during the day. There were 5 pilots who returned from Shandar, and preparations for the move were in hand. Two pilots did searchlight co-operation.
29 January	There was very little flying, except arrival and departure of 213 Squadron pilots.
30 January	Today the majority of 73 Squadron moved out of Gamil. The long convoy of lorries was the last the inhabitants of Port Said saw pf the Squadron as it passed through on its way to Cairio. The capital was reached at dusk, and the night of the 30th was spent at Mena, a 'stone throw' from the Pyramids.
31 January	This day was spent in travel by the Main Party. Daba was reached in the evening, the convoy having passed through the usual sandstorm at Amiria!

1. *73 Squadron Shandur Detachment: The squadron had a large detachment at Shandur, which operated throughout the month of January with the days being made up of patrols, formation, practice, night flying, searchlight co-operation, reconnaissance, interception practice, 'scrambles' as well as interceptions and a range of Tests.*
2. *AIR 27/407/30 Operations Record Book covers 39 Squadrons operations albeit in 'General' terms during the month of January. When requested 73 Squadron would send some of their pilots and ground crew personnel to help out on shortages.*

73 Squadron - AIR 27/631/3 & AIR 27/631/4 (1) Pilot Ops Report
39 Squadron – AIR 27/407/31 & AIR 27/407/32 Pilot Ops Report

February 1942:

1 February Gazala	12 pilots, with S/Ldr. Ward did an offensive patrol over the enemy, leaving Gazala at 14:50 hours. F/O Kirkpatrick joined his fellow pilots, having arrived from Matten Bagush, and later took part in a battle flight with F/O McDougall, P/O Laing, Sgt. Henry, W/C Price and the commander of 'A' Flight, F/Lt. Young. The ground personnel of the Squadron were still on their way up into the 'blue', and in the evening arrived at Sidi Barrani.
2 February	No recording of any operations made on this day.
3 February El Adem	The a/c were flown to El Adem and landed at 09:05 hours. Later in the day, 13 a/c were used to escort Blenheims. S/Ldr. Ward, F/Lt. Young, F/O's Kirkpatrick, and McDougal straffed enemy columns in the afternoon. The main party, still on its weary way, spent the night near Gambut, having moved during the day from Bardia.
4 February	Two raids were made on the enemy, and lorries in a convoy were destroyed and casualties caused among troops leaping for shelter from the convoy.
5 February	P/O Ellis and Sgt. Coussens carried out a recco for bombing targets. At 05:15 hours 3 pilots were 'scrambled to intercept e/a which were raiding he aerodrome. There was quite a large force of Huns around, but come dawn there was not a great deal of damage caused, just a load of noise. Sgt. Sands was chasing a ME 110 towards Gazala, eventually saw it fall to his guns near Tmimi. Being short on fuel he had to land at Gazala, fill up by hand and back at El Adem for 07:50 hours. Not content with this Jerry sent a JU 88 to have a 'shuftie' and using low cloud as cover dropped a couple of bombs near No. 1 Squadron SAAF. 4 a/c took off to intercept, but low cloud made it impossible to find it. Sgt. Baker was one of the pilots who took off on this occasion but only just. He was at around 50 feet when his engine cut out and he crashed. A/C was wrecked (CAT III), Sgt. Baker fortunately was thrown clear and escaped with injuries. There was other 'scrambles' in the morning and in the afternoon, soon after 'tiffin', JU 88's again attacked the aerodrome. All available a/c were 'scrambled', but no e/a destroyed. On the ground, we were less fortunate as on previous raids; 2 pilots were hit by bomb splinters and taken to hospital, P/O Laing was badly injured, and 1 pilot needed some First Aid. Squadron learnt later that both injured pilots were responding well. Sgt. Sands and W/O Price straffed the enemy later in the afternoon.
6 February	F/Lt. Young and three other piots carried out early morning patrols, taking off by moonlight and landing at dawn. At 08:40 hours Sgt. Sands went in pursuit of a single e/a, which had dropped a stick of heavy bombs on the aerodrome. The afternoon saw W/O Price and Sgt. Joyce take off to carry out an offensive patrol.

7 February	Before dawn 4 pilots took off on a patrol [one being Sgt. Sands], and later Sgt. Sands took off on a 'scramble'. At 07:30 hours 2 pilots took off on a recco. The morning was quiet, then at 12:20 hours a single hostile e/a, flying very high passed over the landing ground. W/O Price took off to intercept, but the enemy was too high. At 14:45 hours 10 a/c left El Adem for a cover patrol. These landed at 16:05 hours. S/Ldr. Ward and 2 other pilots arrived from El Gamil.
8 February.	At 07:50 hours F/O's McDougal and Irwin carried out a sector recco, soon after at 08:00 hours 3 pilots were 'scrambled' but no interception made. F/O Scade was coming into land with only one wheel down and many a breath was held as he touched down. It was a perfect landing with only slight damage to the a/c. During the morning nearly every plane was 'scrambled' but no results. At 13:35 hours the Squadron escorted Blenheims on a raid and was attacked by ME 109's, Sgt. Sand's a/c was hit and developed a glycol leak. He crash-landed 10 miles South of aerodrome, Sgt. Sands was uninjured. F/O Irwin damaged 1 e/a and F/O McDougall credited with a probable.
9 February	Enemy aircraft raided El Adem at dawn. S/Ldr. Ward went off to intercept. He destroyed 1 He 111, which fell into the sea North of Tobruk. In the CO's own words: My approach was observed, and the e/a dived down to sea-level. I carried out a n astern attack with no apparent result, there was continuous gun fire from the top twin-machine guns. I carried out a further astern attack hitting the Port and Starboard engines, both damaged. Oil came back and covered my windscreen. The e/a belly-landed on the water and four men climbed out onto the fuselage, one injured. At 10:10 hours 4 pilots took off on a high patrol and intercepted a number of ME 109's, 1 e/a destroyed and 1 e/a severely damaged. Extract from F/Lt. Johnsons combat report reads, 'I climbed to 16,000 to 20,000 feet and placed the flight in the sun and waited for the e/a, which were being fired on by A/A. Finally picking them up I led the attack down out of the sun. I shot their leader down who was leading 5 e/a in line astern'.
10 February	Before light, 5 pilots took off to attempt to intercept e/a but no "huns [slang for Germans]" were engaged. The same happened in the afternoon. During the day the Squadron suffered a sad loss, Sgt. Foster was to ferry a Hurricane to RIG, Sidi Heneish, but failed to arrive. His a/c was eventually found, burnt out, near Gambut, presumably shot down by hostile fighters.
11 February	W/C Price and Sgt. Sands were 'scrambled at 08:55 hours and during the morning and afternoon several pilots took off when e/a were in the vicinity. Sgt, Joyce and F/O Duncan both had engagements with ME 109's, but neither made any claims.
12 February	A sweep was carried by 12 a/c led by S/Ldr. Ward. During the flight they engaged with ME 109's, one being claimed by W/O Price as probable. In the afternoon a further 9 a/c took off and again encountered enemy ME 109's. No claims were made on this occasion. On returning to base the a/c flown by F/O Kirkpatrick developed engine trouble and had to force land some 7 miles West of Acroma Fort. The engine trouble was down to enemy action.
13 February	At 09:03 hours 9 a/c were 'scrambled', which was to prove a veritable "jamboree"! E/A, bombers escorted by large number of ME 109's, were intercepted over Tobruk, and the bombers were forced to drop their bombs before reaching their proper objectives. On landing S/Ldr. Ward expressed the opinion that he had never seen so many aircraft in so small a space! It proved a bad morning for the Germans, for all our a/c returned to El Adem safely with the exception of 1 a/c. The following claims were made: -All Probable's – 2 ME 109's; 1 He 111 and 1 JU 88. Moreover, we soon got news that our missing pilot F/O Eiby was in Tobruk Hospital with superficial leg wounds. He had landed near the Bardia Road. There were 2 more 'scrambles' during the day but no combats recorded.

14 February	There were a few 'scrambles' during the day, but no combats worthy of note took place. Sgt. Joyce carried out a patrol, taking off at 17:45 hours. Two new pilots to the Squadron, P/O Fraser and Sgt. Hill did some local dusk flying.
15 February	Nine Hurricanes of 73 Squadron were used as escort for Blenheims. In the afternoon S/Ldr. Ward led 5 a/c on a straffing raid, all our a/c returned safely at 18:15 hours. P/O Fraser carried out dusk flying again.
16 February	There was 1 'scramble in which 6 a/c took part, but no action was reported. F/O Chatfield landed from BIG at 15:15 hours. Dusk flying was carried out by Sgts. Farley and Reading.
17 February	The day was very quiet. No flying took place except when Sgt. Sands left for Gambut, and S/Ldr. Ward took off for the same place and returned later.
18 February	The ground personnel having previously moved to Gasr-el-Ariyd, the pilots flew their a/c to the new landing ground. No other flying recorded.
19 February Gasr-el-Ariyd	S/Ldr. Ward and F/Lt Johnson did a recco of Derna and Martuba, and during the flight F/Lt Johnson damaged a ME 109. There was some local flying by 7 new pilots to the Squadron. Afternoon, heavy rain hampered operations, and many tents blew down. Low spirits were relieved by the arrival of bags of mail.
20 February	There were no operational flights in the morning. In the afternoon 11 pilots took off for El Adem to do readiness there. They remained in one of the few huts that boasted a roof, the original ops. Tent had been wrecked by the high winds. The pilots returned to Gasr-el-Ariyd without having to 'scramble'. The Squadron, true to its nomadic form, of late, was again informed of a move. This time to Gambut satellite No. 2.
21 February	The morning comprised of local flying. 'B' Flight moved in the afternoon, and at 18:00 hours 6 a/c were brought to readiness, and a little earlier 6 a/c did local formation practice.
22 February	12 'Standby' a/c were 'scrambled' over El Adem, but no action was reported. The second party moved to the new landing ground, followed closely by the a/c.At noon, a recco JU 88 passed over the aerodrome at about 4,000 feet. S/Ldr. Ward took off to intercept, but as he closed in 4 Kittyhawks dived out of the clouds and attacked the e/a. Later, confirmation was received that the JU 88 had been shot down. By15:00 hours the last vehicle left Gasr-el-Ariyd. Sgt. Sands landing at satellite 2, taxied into a Kittyhawk, with both a/c badly damaged.
23 February	In the afternoon 12 a/c took off on an offensive sweep, landing at Gambut Main. At Gambut Main, the a/c were used for readiness, and although nothing happened during the afternoon, they were vectored out to sea on their return flight to satellite No. 2. This was due to the fact that a ship was being attacked by e/a.The e/a were not intercepted.
24 February	There was early morning standby, 2 a/c being used, until 08:15 hours. 12 a/c were on 30 minutes available and should have come up to readiness at 13:00 hours, but as the weather was bad 'rising sand and poor visibility', they remained at 30 minutes. There was no actual flying.
25 February	*The scanned document **AIR 27/631/3** does not include the Operations Record Book for this day.*
26 February	*The scanned document **AIR 27/631/3** does not include the Operations Record Book for this day.*

27 February	*The scanned document **AIR 27/631/3** does not include the Operations Record Book for this day.*
28 February	*The scanned document **AIR 27/631/3** does not include the Operations Record Book for this day.*

NOTE:
1. AIR 27/407/32 Operations Record Book covers 39 Squadrons operations albeit in 'General' terms during the month of January. When requested 73 Squadron would send some of their pilots and ground personnel to help out on shortages.

AIR 27/631/5 & AIR 27/631/6 Pilot Ops Report
39 Squadron – AIR 27/407/33 & AIR 27/407/34 Pilot Ops Report
March 1942:

| 1 March
Gasr-el-Arid	Sandstorms started during the early hours of the morning and continued until shortly after mid-day. At about 09:00 hours a Kittyhawk landed here, the pilot having lost his way. During the afternoon night-flying tests were carried out and the 'Kitty' took off for 3 SAAF Squadron. At 16:45 hours 10 a/c left for El Adem. On arrival they refuelled and then took off at 18:15 hours to carry out operations that they had to abandon the previous night. Once again fate was against us. The a/c having reached Gazala had to return due to low cloud and thick haze. After landing at 19:15 hours, the pilots went to the Mess for the rest of the evening. The a/c stayed at readiness the whole night.
2 March
Gasr-el-Arid	At 06:00 hours 6 a/c were brought to readiness for one hour, but no 'scrambles' took place, and the Squadron were stood down for the day. In the afternoon at 14:00 and 15:00 hours R/T tests were carried out on the a/c that were to be used in the evening. About half an hour before dusk 11 a/c took off for El Adem. Leaving El Adem at 18:20 hours they proceeded to Maturba but on reaching Gazala they encountered 10/10 cloud. Not being able to find the target the CO decided back to base. Whilst the above operation was ongoing, some of the pilots were engaged in night-flying training. Later in evening the CO gave a demonstration on how to carry out alternative methods of straffing enemy aerodromes. Upon landing Wing informed the CO that there was a large concentration of e/a at one of the enemy aerodromes near Tmimi and it was decided to ground-straff. Method of attack was sections of 2 a/c every 30 minutes, the CO and one other took off at 23:57 hours but couldn't find the location from the details given by Wing. The two pilots had become separated with one returning to base at 01:32 hours on the 3rd.
3 March
Gasr-el-Arid	The CO after being separated turned for base but now short on fuel he opted to land at El Adem at 02:00 hours. Meanwhile at base the second pair took off at 00:24 hours but returned within 25 minutes due to the oil cap not being fitted correctly on 1 a/c. The third pair prepared to take off but suddenly noticed that an 'Eclipse of the Moon' was happening, and it would be too dark. They decided to step down until early morning. Back at El Adem, whilst the CO's plane was being refuelled an Army Type in a car steered too close, hit the Port wing against the refuelling lorry, which left the a/c with both wings damaged. The CO flew his a/c back to base albeit damaged. The eclipse pass but the weather deteriorated, operations were suspended. At 06:00 to 08:00 hours 6 a/c were brought to standby, but no 'scrambles' were made. Some evening flying practice took place and F/Lt. Young took off at 21:40 hours for an offensive recco of Tmimi Satellite but could not locate it. During which he saw what appeared to be MT vehicles and reported back. S/Ldr. Ward and W/O Price took off at 23:30 hours and Sgt. Sands at 23:50 hours on the same duty.
4 March
Gasr-el-Arid	The CO returned at 01:35 hours, having straffed a number of tents and vehicles at a point 18 miles NNW of Tmimi. Price and Sands landed 20 minutes later having straffed some MTs without visible result. Two other a/c took off on same duty. Operations ceased at 07:30 hours. There was no further flying due to heavy rainstorms.

5 March Gasr-el-Arid	The rainstorms continued, which prevented any flying. At around 23:00 hours the rain ceased but by this time the landing ground resembled the Serpentine or a miniature Mediterranean and would not be serviceable for 24 hours.
6 March Gasr-el-Arid	Weather has improved a great deal and, in the evening, when the ground appeared o have hardened a little, one of the pilots tested the surface of the aerodrome. He had taxied just a short distance when the a/c sank into the ground almost covering the wheels.
7 March Gasr-el-Arid	Good weather continued throughout the day, but still no flying. The ground of the aerodrome was tested again in the evening. The CO decision was that the ground was unserviceable for normal night operations and informed Wing of this. He added that he would have four pilots available, if it was absolutely necessary to 'scramble' any a/c during the night.
8 March Gasr-el-Arid	At 05:50 hours the CO took off to attempt to intercept raiders over Tobruk, and five minutes later was followed by F/O Scade, F/Lt Young and F/O McDougall. No interceptions were made, and three of the pilots landed at base at 07:00 hours. F/Lt Scade landed at El Adem and returned to base at 08:20 hours. P/O (Monty) Ellis left camp in his buggy in the early hours to locate suitable site for laying flares to guide the pilot's home at night. By lunchtime he had not returned, and F/O Irwin took off to locate him but failed. There was no more flying until 18:00 hours, when the first a/c took off for El Adem. In total 11 a/c went to El Adem for offensive operations and local readiness
9 March Gasr-el-Arid	At 01:15 hours S/Ldr. Ward and Sgt. Sands took off from El Adem on a straffing raid on Martuba. There was no cloud and visibility good over the target area and they straffed the dispersal areas. A/c gun fire was seen hitting about 6 of the dispersed e/a, and the extent of damage could not be confirmed. The second pair, F/Lt Young and F/O Irwin took off at 01:30 hours but were ordered back due to bad weather. At 03:00 hours F/Lt Young and F/O Scade took off to continue the straffing at Martuba. Unfortunately, heavy cloud was encountered which prevented them from seeing their objectives. However, on their return journey they came across some tents and MTs along the Derna Road, which they straffed. There were no further offensive patrols but prior to returning to base they covered 2 'scrambles' over Tobruk. No interceptions were made, and the a/c returned to base at 06:50 hours. At base the morning stand-by a/cowing to the operations from El Adem were reduced to 2 a/c. At 07:40 hours 10 minutes before they were due to be released, the stand-by a/c were 'scrambled'. They patrolled over base for an hour and a half without making contact and then pancaked. No further operational flying only tests carried out at 15:00 hours.
10 March Gasr-el-Arid	At 01.55 hours the first two pilots, P/O Fraser and Sgt. Sands left for El Adem, at 02:30 hours followed by 7 more a/c. Previous arrangement was that Fraser and Sands carry out a free-lance patrol but only Sands could who took off at 02:45 hours. The 7 a/c were to concentrate on Martuba LG's. Leaving El Adem at 03:45 hours. The CO, Sgt. Coussens, F/Lt Scade and F/Sgt Henry went to Martuba, they straffed dispersed e/a, a Breda Gun and MT vehicles along the Tmini Road then returned to base. Sgt. Coussens landed at base and the other 3 a/c at El Adem at 05:30 hours. Some anxiety about Sgt. Sands as he should have been back over an hour ago!! F/Lt Young, F/Sgt. Joyce and F/O McDougall had left El Adem at 04:10 hours, straffed dispersed e/a, a Breda Gun and machine guns at Martuba then returned to El Adem, landing at 05:50 hours. CO was 'scrambled' to Tobruk at 06:00 hours no interception made and returned to base. The 6 a/c left El Adem at 05:45 hours to return to base. Sgt. Sands, young Australian, is our first casualty (hope our last) since night operations started. Still a chance he will turn up. The pilots had their usual morning rest until late afternoon when they carried out an air test.

11 March Gasr-el-Arid	6 a/c went to El Adem for readiness at 04:05 hours, shortly after moonrise, there being no activity they all returned to base at 06:50 hours. At 07:25 hours 4 a/c were 'scrambled' over base and vectored south of Tobruk. They patrolled for 30 minutes at 15,000 feet. They were ordered to return to base and patrol at the same height. Sgt. Henry landed whilst the other 3 a/c patrolled until 08:30hours. No further flying during the day other than a couple of night flying tests. 'B' Flight took off at midday for Gambut Satellite No.1. Three Albacores of No. 826 FAA Squadron arrived at 17:30 hours on attachment to the Squadron. Their role is to co-operate on night offensive patrols.
12 March Gambut Sat. No. 1	The Remainder of the Squadron moved to Gambut Satellite No. 1 during the morning. 14 a/c were also taken over to the new aerodrome before midday and five after lunch. Sgt. Farley arrived in the afternoon with a replacement a/c. At 18:00 hours the HUN paid us a visit; F/Lt. Scade and F/O Mcdougall took off to intercept the e/a. they patrolled over the base for 35 minutes, no contact made, they then pancaked. Three of our new pilots practised dusk and night landings.
13 March Gambut Sat. No. 1	No flying during the morning apart from two trips made by the FAA, Lt. Compton, the CO of 826 Squadron left for Dekheila and a further Albacore arrived from Gasr-el-Arid. The morning brought a very pleasant surprise, namely, Sgt. Sands re-joined us, and what a story he had to tell. Here is a brief summary: After leaving El Adem on the 10th, he flew North Westward across Menelao Bay, then turned Eastwards. He saw a camp of around 50 tents a few miles West of Menelao and dropped his flares. He then dived down to 450 feet and straffed the camp. A machine gun opened fire which he could not avoid with bullets stricking his a/c and the engine spluttered. He climbed to 800 feet, switched to gravity tank, primed the engine with no result. The a/c lost height and at 500 feet Sands 'bailed out'. The a/c crashed and burst into flames. After landing he was chased by about 10 Germans. He ran Southwards for an hour, turned West along a wadi. A Hurricane came straffing along the wadi and Sands crouched behind the wadi bank. On checking he was OK; he then followed the coast for a few miles and hid in a swamp. At dawn two lorries with around 15 German troops arrived looking for him. He spent some uncomfortable hours waist deep in the swamp with a bush over his head. Once the Germans had gone, he started walking again. At sunset he was near to Tmini Satellite and started to walk across the aerodrome when he was challenged by a guard. Sands approached him and when at close quarters fired a couple of shots from his revolver then ran. He found a spot with plenty of shrub and hid. Dawn broke on the 11th, Sands found himself in the middle of a German Camp. He stayed hidden until sunset when he began to walk. At dawn, after crawling through a minefield, he came across a gun-crew of the 1st SA Brigade, they took him to their HQ. Congratulations were showered upon Sands upon his escape "Bloody good show". There were a few incidents later in the day and at 22:35 hours three Albacores took off on a bombing raid.
14 March	The Albacores returned safely from their raid landing at 01:30 and 02:00 hours. We had 6 a/c on readiness between 05:30 and 6:00 hours along with 6 a/c on standby from 06:00 and 08:00 hours. Four of the standby pilots were 'scrambled' over base at 07:05 hours. Patrolled for 40 minutes, no interception made then pancaked. Usual tests were carried out on the a/c in the afternoon. Some new pilots again practiced dusk and night landings. The Squadron has been plagued with misfortune. Sgt. Simpson took off at 20:45 hours and only been in the air for a short time and from some unknown cause, his a/c dived into the ground and burst into flames. The fire and ambulance rushed out to the crash, and on arrival found nothing but a heap of smouldering ashes.

15 March	The day started with 6 a/c at readiness from 05:30 to 06:00 hours standby from 06:00 to 8:00 hours, a further 2 a/c for a patrol. F/Lt. Scade and Sgt. Coussena [who carried out the reconnaissance and patrol of Bomba] took off at 05:55 hours and returned at 07:30 hours. At 13:30 hours a recce e/a JU 88 passed over the aerodrome, 2 a/c took off to intercept but the e/a headed out to sea, so the 2 a/c pancaked. No further operational flying during the day.

16 March	Four Albacores took off for a bombing raid at 03:00 hours. One a/c returned with engine trouble; the other 3 a/c returned at 06:00 hours. We had the usual 6 a/c at readiness. One section 'scrambled' over base just before 07:00 hours, only airborne for 15 minutes. No further flying throughout the day. We did have 2 a/c on standby from 18:15 to 19:15 hours.

17 March	We have 6 a/c on readiness and standby again. One section 'scrambled' at 06:30 hours but returned within 10 minutes. W/O Price took off on an air test at 08:05 hours. Whilst airborne was ordered to patrol over base. Patrolled for 30 minutes and then pancaked. No further flying until 17:00 hours, when 2 air tests were carried out. We had 6 a/c kept on standby from 18:00 hours until dusk but there were no scrambles.

18 March	Wing requested that 12 a/c for readiness and standby for this morning and two more recco of Bomba and Martuba. We only had 11 pilots available. The two recco a/c took off at 05:40 hours, returning one hour later, 3 a/c ere 'scrambled' at 06:45 hours and 4 minutes later 4 more a/c followed them. They were all back down at 07:05 hours, as the Germans had turned back. The pilots should have been released at 08:00 hours but Wing instructed that they remain on standby until relieved by one of the other Squadrons. We had 5 a/c 'scrambled' at 08:25 hours. They patrolled for an hour but unable to sight the e/a. Air tests were carried out on the a/c in the afternoon. In the evening there were 6 a/c at standby from 18:00 to 19:00 hours and between 18:30 to 19:40 hours. P/O Woolley and Sgt. Hill practised night flying.

19 March	We had 4 Albacores take off at 03:00 hours on a bombing raid. One returned at 03:30 hours with engine trouble and the remaining 3 a/c landed at 05:30 hours. Around 30 minutes before dawn 12 pilots came to readiness and at 06:00 hours 6 of them were brought to standby. The others remained at readiness. There was 1 'scramble', 2 a/c over Bu Amud, which lasted an hour with no result. Flying ceased until 16:30 hours when air tests were carried out. In the evening, the CO and Wing arranged for the Squadron to carry out some practice straffing, on No. 2 Satellite as the area was unoccupied. The FAA co-operated by dropping flares over the LG.

20 March Gambut Sat. No. 1	At 05:40 hours P/O Fraser and Beaumont carried out a weather test over Martuba. There was no readiness before dawn but at 06:00 hours 6 a/c were brought to standby for one hour. At 06:45 hours they were 'scrambled' over base, at 07:10 hours 1 a/c returned with engine trouble, the others patrolled for 35 minutes. No interceptions made they pancaked. Pilots released from standby. In the afternoon the a/c were air tested and at 17:00 hours 6 a/c took off for El Adem., they took off from El Adem at 18:25 hours and proceeded to Derna. On arrival they found 7/10 black cloud from 6,000 to 10,000 feet. They had dived down below cloud and found the aerodrome lit up with flare-path and floodlight. They were expecting some a/c there, for as our a/c came down from the clouds someone on the flare-path signalled them in with a green light. The a/c dived low over the aerodrome straffing the flare-path, aircraft, tents, and MTs on and dispersed around the aerodrome. The Albacores should have co-operated with us, were late on taking off due to raiders in the vicinity. Consequently, they arrived over the target long after our a/c had left there. On leaving Derna 1 a/c headed for home landing at 20:00 hours. The remaining 5 a/c refuelled at Gazala on the way home arriving at around 21:30 to 22:20 hours. The Albacores landed at 22:05 hours.

21 March	From 06:00 to 08:00 hours 6 a/c were at readiness but there was no activity. No flying took place until 17:00 hours, night flying tests carried out. At 18:40 hours 6 a/c took off for El Adem to carry out free-lance patrols. When they arrived, the operations had been cancelled on instructions received from AAH and the a/c returned to base landing at 21:50 hours.
22 March	Some local flying during the day and later night flying tests, but no operations restricted by poor visibility.
23 March	P/O Beaumont and Sgt. Baker acted as escort for a DH 86 Ambulance a/c that was going to the aid of a bomber crew. Plane shot down South of Bir Hacheim and Sgt. Baker with P/O Woolley and a Lysander had located it earlier in the morning. Unfortunately, the DH 86 went off its course and eventually landed at Bu Amud, and the Hurricanes returned to base. In the evening 12 a/c went to El Adem and carried out free-lance patrols from there. Tents and -guns were straffed 5 miles Northwest of Menelao Bay and four incendiary bombs were dropped in the Martuba area. MT's, tents, lights were straffed in Martuba area and a further 4 bombs dropped at El Chrebi. A number of machine-guns were silenced, full damage impossible to judge. A fire was started 8 miles East of Martuba, visibility very poor.
24 March	Sandstorm blew all day, no flying.
25 March	Activity hampered by rising sand and only flying was non-operational.
26 March	The weather cleared and the sand settled on the ground, the a/c of the Squadron became visible. Four pilots did early morning readiness and 'scrambled' over base at 07:35 hours. During the day, the a/c were tested ready for night operations. At 18:00 hours 10 a/c were flown to the island just off Gazala, where a German bomber was reported to have crashed. The object of this was to stop rescue operations, which were being carried out, as there were many e/a in the area, so our planes were recalled. Several 'scrambles and patrols took place but no interceptions. The weather was mainly good as was the visibility.
27 March	No flying until the afternoon when air tests took place. 13 a/c went to El Adem, and Derna was main target for the night, although Martuba, Tmimi and a night-flying LG approx. 12 miles Southeast of Derna were also attached. Full extent of damage unclear but a small fire was caused at Martuba. Four Albacores of 826 Squadron assisted by dropping flares.
28 March	Only air tests were carried out during the day, but at 17:00 hours 6 a/c were flown to Sidi Barrani, following a report that the railway there was expected to be raided. Only 3 a/c were on readiness at El Adem, and they were 'scrambled' to a position North of Tobruk, there were no interceptions. At base, 2 a/c were on readiness standby, and e/a were reported 10 miles North of Tobruk. S/Ldr. Ward and F/Lt. Scade took off, but they saw nothing. It was quiet at Barrani and the 6 Hurricanes returned after an uneventful day.
29 March	The Albacores left Bagush Sattelite early in the morning, and the 3 Hurricanes from El Adem and the 6 a/c from Barrani landed back at base. The day was uneventful and at 17:15 hours 6 a/c left for Barrani, again to do readiness, 5 a/c went to El Adem and 2 a/c remained on readiness at Gambut. Free-lance raids operated from El Adem and 2 single engine monoplanes and gun positions at a night flying LG approx. 12 miles Southwest of Derna LG, as well as vehicles along the Derna Road were straffed. Other targets included MT's, gun posts in wadis North of Martuba, tents, vehicles West of Tmimi and the LG's at Martuba. Meanwhile at Gambut, our a/c were 'scrambled' to intercept Hun intruders, but they did not succeed. The full extent of the damage caused by straffing is unknown, 2 e/a are believed to have been severely damaged. Sidi Barrani remained quiet.

30 March	No operational flying during the day and in the evening, readiness was carried out at Gambut. 2 Hurricanes 'scrambled' over base and 2 a/c over El Adem, although several e/a were about, no interceptions were made.
31 March	Early morning readiness was carried out by 6 pilots, and they were 'scrambled' at 07:00 hours. One pilot was unable to take off, the remaining 5 pilots went to 20,000 feet, no interceptions made. The rest of the day was quiet, then at 19:00 hours 6 a/c went to El Adem for operations. The coastline from Ras-el-Tin to Marsa Belaghigh was straffed and 25lb incendiary bombs were dropped on Martuba Main LG, Umm-er-Rzem and Ras-el-Tin. MTs in a wadi East side of Martuba were straffed as well as the roads nearby. Other targets were tents and MT's near Umm-er-Rzem, Ras-el-Tin and Martuba. At Gambut 2 Hurricanes were 'scrambled' at 21:45 hours but no interception made.

AIR 27/631/7 & AIR 27/631/8 Pilot Ops Repor

April 1942:

1 April Gambut No. 1 Satellite	6 pilots did dawn readiness, towards the release time 2 pilots F/Sgt. Henry and Sgt. Wiseman were 'scrambled' at 08:00 hours. They had climbed to 12,000 feet and then ordered to 15,000 feet unidentified a/c was approaching from the East. In the air for over 1 hour, they saw nothing and pancaked at 09:15 hours. Reports were received from pilots returning from free-lance night operations. They had been using El Adem, the usual LG from which straffing raids were carried out. Sgt. Baker had taken off at 00:05 hours and proceeded to Martuba where he bombed the East side from a height of 6,000 feet, straffed the roads from East to West, along with wadis and MT vehicles. No results were noted due to poor visibility and returned to El Adem at 01:20 hours. F/O Irwin took off at 01:00 hours but encountered poor visibility and did not straff. He was also unfortunate whilst attempting to bomb MT's North of Mechili, his bomb failed to drop. F/Lt. Young was luckier dropping his bomb in a wadi at the Signal HQ at Umm-er-Rzem where he observed tents in a wadi. He severely straffed the area and returned to the advance base at 02:15 hours. During the morning there were a number of other operations undertaken by the Squadron. The afternoon saw air tests carried out on a/c to be used for night flying and at 19:40 hours 6 pilots flew to El Adem, 4 remained at Gambut for local defence. P/O Fraser left El Adem at 22:15 hours and straffed the road from Umm-er-Rzem to Menelao Bay. P/O Beaumont went to 6,000 feet over Gazala and then 8,000 feet over Menelao but found 10/10 cloud all the way to Derna. He flew out to sea and followed the coast home. F/Lt. Scade patrolled in the direction of Derna and Martuba but finding 10/10 cloud returned to base. The poor visibility encountered hampered other flights, all returned to base.

2 & 3 April Gambut No. 1 Satellite (two days rolled into one).	The day's flying activity was limited to air tests, except for a sector recco carried out by F/O Pain. At 19:35 hours 6 pilots went to El Adem and 4 remained at Gambut for aerodrome defence. F/Lt. Young and F/o Irwin went Mechili, where they dropped their bombs among MT's dispersed over a mud flat. Sgt. Baker flew to B.Tengeder and saw 5/6 vehicles in a semi-circle and dropped his bombs which started a small fire. He also straffed the lorries. His second trip, he went up the Derna Road saw some lights, which were extinguished as he approached. He went down and straffed a column of lorries; then he saw a red navigation light of a plane but was unable to catch it. F/Lt. Young took off early on the morning of the 3 April, and straffed tents and transport East of Martuba and across the main road tank trap at Tmimi. F/O Irwin on his second trip saw an e/a at 8,000 Feet between Tmimi and Martuba. He fired at it but it broke away and was lost. F/Sgt. Henry left El Adem at 22:35 hours flew to about 5 miles North of Menelao, on the coast and was met with gun fire from 6/7 Breda Guns. He straffed them and dropped his bomb but did not observe results. He then set course for Martuba, where he met much Breda fire, he straffed both sides of the road West of the aerodrome. On his second trip he straffed the Derna Road East of Martuba where there appeared to be MTs in a wadi 8 miles North of Tmimi. He then saw a convoy on the road going North, which he fired at twice. W/O Price made 3 trips over the lines. First, he went to Mechili LG. bombed and straffed dark shapes on its West side. On his second patrol straffed the wadi West of Tmimi, where there were dispersed tents and vehicles. His third and final sortie was a weather test at Gazala. Sgt. Hill left El Adem on an offensive patrol, his compass was out of order and not finding his target flew over Tobruk and soon decided to return to base. At 06:25 hours (3/4/42) F/O Irwin and F/Lt. Young were 'scrambled after a Focke Wulf Condor, which out at sea. The bandit went East, too fast to make interception so both pilots were told to pancake. At Gambut 4 pilots were at readiness and were 'scrambled at 08:15 hours to 12,000 feet West of Tobruk. They orbited the area as bandits were in the vicinity. Two ME 109's came out of the sun and passed very close to Sgts. Goodwin and Wiseman. They turned, but the hun had disappeared into thick haze.
4 April Gambut No. 1 Satellite	In the early morning 3 pilots went on free-lance patrols from El Adem. Sgt. Baker took off at 00:25 hours and flew to Derna, where he saw a flare path alight. Two Red, One Green and One White, star shells were fired over the LG to a height of 10,000 feet. He dropped aflare and the lights promptly extinguished, so he turned out to sea, came down to 500 feet and returned, straffing 3 groups of MTs in a wadi. Sgt. Coussens dropped a bomb in a wadi South of Martuba, 2 machine guns opened fire so he straffed them, they ceased firing. P/O Wooley took off at 02:20 hours and went to Ras el Tin where he dropped a bomb, then straffed a track and the Derna Road near Menelao Bay. Sgt. Sands dropped bombs on buildings between No. 4 E and No. 1 W Martuba Satellites, starting a small fire. He also attacked No. 4 LG E Satellite. The operations were hampered by thick cloud over El Adem and haze Westwards of Gazala. The a/c returned from El Adem in ones and two's landing between 07:00 and 07:30 hours. There was further flying until the afternoon when the a/c were air-tested.
5 April Gambut No. 1 Satellite	6 a/c went to El Adem for offensive operations. F/Lt. Young left base at 00:45 hours and a further 5 a/c followed at 01:45 hours. Free-lance patrols were carried out over Dermna and Umm er Rzem areas from 02:15 and 05:15 hours. The extent of damage unknown but two fires were started one along the Derna Tmimi Road and one a few miles Northeast of Umm er Rzem. 5 a/c returned to Gambut Satellite at 07:15 hours and the 6th a/c at 08:30 hours. There was no more flying until 16:15 hours when the a/c were air-tested.
6 April Gambut No. 1 Satellite	6 a/c flew to El Adem for early morning operations. Incendiary bombs dropped on suspected Night Flying LG's approx. 18 miles East Northeast of Mechili, also on dummy flare path 8 miles Northeast of the LG and on Umm er Rzem. These areas were straffed along with two suspected LG's, one at Got bu Ascher, the other South of Martuba. At Gambut, a/c 'scrambled' over base but no interceptions.

7 April Gambut No. 1 Satellite	At 04:05 hours Sgts. Sands and Goodwin took off on early morning 'scramble'. No results. At 07:00 hours the a/c from El Adem arrived at base and there was no more flying during the day except for local air-tests. In the evening 8 a/c went to El Adem for operations. In the night of 7/8 April only one recco was carried out by P/O Fraser owing to poor visibility.
8 April Gambut No. 1 Satellite	The a/c returned to base with one being damaged when it overshot the LG. Air-tests carried out in the afternoon with F/O Chatfield carrying out a calibration test with 833 AMES and 6 a/c went to El Adem for readiness. No action during the night and no sorties made.
9 April Gambut No. 1 Satellite	The 6 a/c returned from El Adem and the day was quiet except for tests. No a/c went to El Adem in the evening and the night was quiet.
10 April Gambut No. 1 Satellite	Air tests were the day's only activity, but at 19:05 hours F/Sgt. Joyce carried out a calibration test. The same pilot was 'scrambled at 21:00 hours after e/a raiders but was unable to intercept. S/Ldr. Ward went on recco later and saw a few vehicles between Martuba and Carmusa and one vehicle on the Derna – Tmimi Road.
11 April Gambut No. 1 Satellite	S/Ldr.Ward returning from El Adem following his recco noticed anti-aircraft fire at Capuzzo. He patrolled between Gambut and Capuzzo but saw no e/a, he landed at 01:55 hours. No further operational flying during the day. Several tests and P/O Beaumont did a calibration test at 19:15 hours. The night was uneventful.
12 April Gambut No. 1 Satellite	The day's activity consisted only air tests, but at 19:35 hours 10 a/c flew to El Adem for operations. The CO followed at 20:20 hours.
13 April Gambut No. 1 Satellite	First operation, a weather recco by S/Ldr. Ward took place between 00:01 and 00:20 hours. During the early morning and before dawn, Tmimi, Blust el Daba, and a wide area of ground at Tmimi were bombed and straffed. Breda Guns and a battery of heavy anti-aircraft were also straffed as wel las wadis and roads. The a/c returned from their raids direct to base, and all landed between 06:20 hours and 06:40 hours. Usual air tests and F/Sgt. Coussens did a calibration test with 833 AMES, Bu Amud. The night was quiet owing to rising sand and wind. No flying.
14 April Gambut No. 1 Satellite	The weather cleared sufficiently by 12:00 hours for test to commence and in the evening 2 a/c went to El Adem for a recco over the lines, but one flown by W/O Price developed engine trouble and was forced to return to base. At dusk the CO took off to try and intercept an e/a recco that flew over the base but the hun made off before the CO could gain height. At 23:20 hours W/O Price took off again to carry out his recco, but yet again his a/c developed engine trouble and was forced to land gain.
15 April Gambut No. 1 Satellite	F/O Chatfield left El Adem and flew over the lines and observed British shelling South of Gazala. He was the pilot who had left with W/O Price. This sortie was the only operational flight of the day, only tests were recorded for the remainder of the day's flying.
16 April Gambut No. 1 Satellite	On this day, there was no flying as a severe dust storm raged and visibility was extremely poor.
17 April Gambut No. 1 Satellite	Once again, the nomadic race of 73 Squadron packed up its belongings and sallied fourth this time only to Gambut Main, but a Khamain wind began to blow at 10:00 hours the shifting of equipment and kit became very difficult. The Sick Quarters recorded a heat of 121 deg. In the shade, and another indication of the extreme temperature was a swift reduction of the canteen's stock of beer!
18 April Gambut Main	No flying took place on this day as the wind and sand were blowing with increase violence.

19 April Gambut Main	The storm's violence dropped towards the latter part of the day and F/O Selby and P/O Fraser did a calibration test with 833 AMES in the evening. They were the only soties of the day and no flying took place during the night.
20 April Gambut Main	Reasonable weather being experienced again; air test was carried out ready for night operations. F/O Irwin and Sgt. Wiseman took off after 129:00 hours for practice interceptions, and a patrol by 6 a/c was maintained over Tobruk for an hour and a half. No e/a encountered.
21 April Gambut Main	At dawn 6 a/c patrolled Tobruk, and some e/a [bombers] arrived on the scene: F/L Scade managed to get a burst into a JU 88 but unobserved, as a lucky shot (for the 88) entered F/L Scade's Hurricane, causing a glycol leak and he was forced to land at El Gubbi. No other engagements with e/a. Tests were carried out during the day and at 18:445 hours 12 a/c flew to El Adem, followed by S/Ldr. Ward at 19:25 hours. The Squadron was active during the night and the following sorties took place: - 1) S/Ldr. Ward 'scrambled at 20:50 hours but with no result, except that the CO observed a smoke trail between Tmimi and halfway to Gazala. 2) 6 a/c did layer patrols over Tobruk, with layers between 9 – 14,000 feet and 1,000 feet between each a/c. There was no action. Several pilots then took off to intercept e/a returning to their base. No hostile bombers were located but ground lights were observed in many places, and a powerful lights 3 miles Southeast of Derna. One pilot noticed that the line of flight of his a/c was indicated on the ground by flashing lights. The edge of the LG at Martuba was straffed as well as dark shapes by the road near Tmimi. P/O Fraser did a recco of the Derna Road and dropped a flare near Martuba. He saw 3 e/a Macchi 202's but as his flare was extinguished by someone on the ground, and the Italian fighters were lost to sight, he did not straff.
22 April Gambut Main	Operations carried on in the early morning, and at 05:45 hours 6 a/c carried out a dawn patrol of Tobruk, landing at Gambut, much cloud was encountered on this patrol. No combats took place. In the evening 12 Hurricanes were flown to El Adem, but operations had to be cancelled as visibility became extremely poor.
23 April Gambut Main	The day started with 6 a/c from El Adem on a patrol over Tobruk from 06:00 to 07:30 hours. They all landed back at base, an uneventful patrol. All planes returned at first light. Evening brought the next operational flying with 9 a/c flown to the usual advanced base. Unfortunately, the operation was cancelled due to a severe sandstorm which began soon after dark.
24 April Gambut Main	Weather had cleared for a dawn patrol to be carried out over Tobruk, 6 a/c took part leaving El Adem at 05:45 hours and landed at Gambut at 07:20 hours. Some 4/10 cloud was experienced as allow as 800 feet, no sign of e/a. Early part of the evening, 7 Hurricanes flew to El Adem, and P/O Lawford and F/O Irwin cooperated with 833 AMES for a GCI practice. S/Ldr. Ward and Sgt. Sands took off and joined the 7 a/c at El Adem. Mention was made of a pilot who whilst landing crashed into the 'chance light' causing pandemonium on the flare path. Meanwhile 4 a/c had carried out a patrol over Tobruk with nil result. Final sortie of the day was when F/O McDougall was 'scrambled' from El Adem at 21:25 hours to angels 15 North of Bu Amud. He patrolled for 1 hour and 15 minutes, saw nothing and landed at 22:40 hours.

25 April Gambut Main	Hurricanes of 73 Squadron patrolled Tobruk at dawn and this time a party of e/a turned up, 2 JU 88's were claimed as damaged, one by F/Lt. Scade and one by F/O Chatfield. F/Lt. Scade intercepted and e/a flying North at 13,000 feet North of Tobruk. The JU 88 rear gunner opened up with no result and F/Lt. Scade attacked from 300 yards. The e/a dived and was lost in the dark. F/O Chatfield encountered the other JU 88 North West of Tobruk at 7,000 feet, he was flying North but turned West on seeing the Hurricane. F/O Chatfield attacked from the forward quarter at 300 yards, but he too lost the e/a in the dark. F/Lt. Scade saw shells exploding on the wing of the JU 88 intercepted by him, and F/O Chafield damaged the nose of the other JU 88. F/O McDougall and Sgt. Hill took off from El Adem to re-inforce the Tobruk a/c but did not intercept e/a. Air tests were carried out during the afternoon and the force proceeded to forward base with 11 a/c. The evenings GCI practice was undertaken by Sgts. Hill and Jones and a patrol with nil results was carried out by F/Lt. Young and F/O Badger. The CO then left Gambut for a weather recco, landing back at base at 22:25 hours.
26 & 27 April Gambut Main	A layer patrol was carried out over Tobruk in the early hours and gun flashes were observed on the ground South of Acroma by 2 pilots from 7,000 feet at around 06:45 hours. The flashes were checked out, but no importance was attached to them. No other visuals seen, and the a/c landed at base at 07:00 hours. The Squadron undertook further patrols over Tobruk, this time at dusk. 10/10 cloud at 15,000 feet was experienced along with thick haze and no eventful happenings occurred. Flying continued well into the night and following morning, when Martuba Main, Martuba West and tents West of Derna Road were attacked. One pilot, when 12 miles East of Derna saw three balloons North of Umm er Rzem. The Derna Road was straffed, and at Martuba West a 25 lb incendiary bomb illuminated 4 single-engine e/a. P/O Beaumont straffed them from 2,000 feet and saw his high explosive shells exploding across them. The 4 unidentified e/a were claimed as damage, but accurate observations were impossible. All these operations were carried out from El Adem as well as several 'scrambles, but from the 'scrambles' there were no results, except that one friendly a/c was intercepted approaching from the West. At 05:30 hours 7 Hurricanes were used for a layer patrol of Tobruk, no action reported. F/Lt. Young and P/O Pain carried out a dawn patrol North of Gazala, no e/a reported. At mid-day **HRH the Duke of Gloucester** visited the Squadron and each pilot was introduced to him by S/Ldr. Ward. The visit was a brief one as **HRH** had much ground to cover, other Squadrons to see. Later in the day S/Ldr. West and Sgt. Robb plus 2 new pilots to the Squadron flew a local recce. Sgts. Atherley and Wilson and 2 newcomers did local flying. Sgts. Jones and Farley carried out the evenings GCI practice. 9 Hurricanes took off for El Adem, these were followed by S/Ldrs. Ward and West. It was a busy night again with several nil resulting 'scrambles. However, Sgt. Sands in his free-lance patrol straffed an MT from 200 feet near No. 3 LG at Martuba, which caught fire. He also attacked 2 e/a on the Northwest corner of No. 1 LG and 1 e/a burst into flames, P/O Fraser straffed transport at Eluet Basel and saw his HE strikes. On his return journey, at Gazala, an aircraft he believed to be an ME 110 passed below flying Northwest but was unable to catch it.
28 April Gambut Main	Operations carried on well into the morning, terminating with the usual dawn patrol of Tobruk. The a/c were air tested during the day and the El Adem force in the evening numbered 9 a/c. At 20:40 hours 3 pilots led by S/Ldr. Ward straffed MTs in the vicinity of U.1022 (Derna: 1:500,000 Libyan Grid). The railhead was patrolled from base, but no e/a encountered. El Adem a/c were carrying out raids at Martuba and Derna, and there was evidence that e/a were active. An e/a was seen by P/O Fraser straffing the rad 10 miles East of Gazala, using cannon shells from a rear gun. A flare path of about 14 White lights and 1 Red light was seen at the Western approach of Derna LG. One unidentified e/a landed and was promptly straffed by the Hurricane. Results unobserved.

29 April Gambut Main	Operations went on until dawn, when an uneventful patrol of Tobruk took place, all a/c landed back at base. No further operational sorties were carried out until 19:50 hours, when 3 Hurricanes were flown to El Adem. No flying took place from that base; however, a single a/c did a nil resulting patrol over Tobruk. The reduction in flying was due to a sandstorm, which started in the evening.
30 April Gambut Main	No flying took place due to the storm which reached an alarming height in the early morning and continued throughout the day.

73 Squadron at Tobruk:

Extract from:
Rommel and the Defeat of the Allies – Tobruk 1942. Author: David Mitchell Hill-Green

Page 106 paragraph 3
On 9 April 1942, as Rommel's threat intensified, its aerial defence was boosted by the arrival of the Hurricanes from 73 Squadron, joining 6 Squadron (Hurricanes and Lysander tactical reconnaissance aircraft) at El Gubbi, one of four landing grounds inside the fortress. The next day, an additional seven Hurricanes arrived. These aircraft provided invaluable ground support; for example, 73 Squadron undertook twenty-three ground strafing sorties on Good Friday (11 April), destroying eleven enemy transport vehicles and damaged many more. [*Cull, Hurricanes over Tobruk, p102-8]

AIR 27/631/9 & AIR 27/631/10 Pilot Ops Report
May 1942:

1 May Gambut Main	The month started well when S/Ldr. Ward whilst carrying out a straffing raid on Barce with F/Lt. Young and F/O Badger, came across a very large e/a, and shot it down in flames. The 3 pilots left from Gazala the most forward LG at 00:40 hours and reached the target area at 01:30 hours. When they were 3 miles from their objective, a flare path and dispersal lights were switched on. The Hurricanes circled the LG, and an e/a signalled from 2,000 feet with three downward identification lights and a revolving search light in the tail. S/Ldr. Ward went to attack but his number 2 and 3 had commenced to straff the aerodrome, he joined them and attacked the southern dispersal area. The anti-aircraft fire was intense and very accurate and came from all around the perimeter. The CO observed no results of the run but saw the original e/a with tail search light in front of him. It was a very large aircraft, but the taillight was so bright the fuselage could not be seen. He could make out an engine a good halfway along the wing, which made S/Ldr. Ward believed it to be a four-engine e/a. He fired a 3 to 4 second burst from 100 yards and broke away to port. One engine of the e/a gave out puffs of flame and sparks and a second attack from the port beam saw the e/a burst into flames and crashed in a forest causing sheet flame covering a wide area. F/O Badger's a/c had been hit in the port wing by Breda fire. The wing started to burn and continued as F/O Badger climbed to 3,000 feet. The fire expired after 10 minutes. S/Ldr Ward intercepted a second e/a but had insufficient ammunition to damage it. F/O Badger eventually reached base safely and landed with the CO and F/Lt. Young. 9 Hurricanes in all had gone to El Adem and during the night several sorties took place from there. A search was made for balloons in the Menelao Bay area and there were 'scrambles' over Torbruk and El Adem, all with no result.
2 May Gambut Main	In the evening 10 Hurricanes were flown to El Adem for +operations and there were several 'scrambles and patrols. Free-lance raids took place with straffing of the fort at Mechili and a LG approx. 12 miles West of Martuba. The flying hours for the night and early morning totalled 20 hours 28 minutes with the number of sorties being 11.
3 May Gambut Main	No flying until 18:00 hours due to a sandstorm, which reduced visibility to almost nil. In the evening S/Ldr. Ward flew to base LG and apart from an IFF test by P/O Woolley and Sgt. Hill, the remainder of the day was uneventful.

4 May Gambut Main	Sand rising again today, but visibility was good enough at 18:00 hours for tests to be carried out.
5 May Gambut Main	S/Ldr. Ward returned from Sidi Haneish. Early morning patrol carried out by S/Ldr. Johnston and Sgt. Sands. In the afternoon, the weather again grew worse and by dinner time most tents were horizontal than vertical. The storm reached its peak at about 19:00 hours. There was no flying during the day.
6 May Gambut Main	No operational flying during the day or night, and the Squadron learned the heartening news that leave had been granted to one and all.
7 May Gambut Main	Little flying today, and the sorties that took place were non-operational. In the evening, a Squadron Pay Parade was held so that all were well equipped for the leave period. Sgt. Hill flew over the external flare path and dropped a message to the crew regarding the leave.
8 May Gambut Main	In the early morning, the leave party left for Alexandria by road and at 08:30 hours the a/c took off for BLG. The flying for the day following was of course restricted and a summary follows: -
9 May Gambut Main	F/O Irwin arrived from BLG and returned at 16:55 hours in HN.115
10 May Gambut Main	P/O Lawford flew the same a/c to Gambut from Sidi Haneish and went back in the early afternoon.
11 May Gambut Main	There was no flying.
12 May Gambut Main	S/Ldr. Johnston took off on a compass deviation test and flew for 35 minutes.
13 to 15 May Gambut Main	No flying during these 3 days.
16 May Gambut	S/Ldr. Johnston flew to BLG and returned landing at 17:50 hours.
17 May	S/Ldr. Young arrived from Sidi Haneish. The leave party arrived on the camp at dusk, but a few straggling vehicles did not turn up until well into the night.
18 May	The a/c were flown back to Gambut from BLG and S/Ldr. Young left for Edku, having been posted to 213 Squadron to take over the post of Commanding Officer. Sgt. Sands took off at 21:30 hours on a 'scramble' but made no interception.
19 May	Only air tests made up the day's flying, but in the evening 2 pilots did GCI test with 833 AMES at Bu Amud. Sgt. Sands did searchlight co-operation, and the newly installed searchlights round the aerodrome succeeded in picking him upon several runs. At the same time and e/a flew over and dropped numerous flares and a few bombs some distance away. F/O Pain took off but made no contact with the e/a.
20 May	Full scale operations commenced again in the way of a move. The Squadron packed up and moved West to El Adem, the a/c took off at 19:00 hours. No night flying was carried out.
21 May El Adem	Night flying tests were done during the late afternoon and early evening. Operations began with P/O McDougall taking off on a GCI patrol. Several other sorties were made until the moon went down; no interceptions resulted.

22 May	An early morning patrol was maintained over Tobruk by 4 a/c but there was no action. Albacores of 826 Squadron arrived during the day, and night flying tests were carried out on the Hurricanes of 73 squadron. In all, five-night sorties took place, but still no e/a were encountered.
23 May	4 Hurricanes again patrolled Tobruk from dawn until 06:40 hours. Sgt. Jones patrolled Gazala, but no incidents occurred on any of these flights. Night flying tests were done, and an extensive night flying programme was laid on. There were many GCI patrols and 'scrambles but the Hun, as usual, seemed to make a point of evading the Squadron. Intruder patrols took the war into his own territory. However, 6 such sorties were flown during the night and early morning.
24 May	The dawn patrol of Tobruk was carried out by 4 a/c after which no operational flying took place until 22:00 hours when P/O Beaumont took off on a 'scramble'. A number of nights flying hours were added to the Squadron's total, but no e/a were destroyed.
25 May	Operational sorties continued well into the morning and F/O Selby concluded the programme with a patrol of the Tobruk area. F/Sgt. Joyce was next to continue the operational flying, the day having been spent by rest and tests. He and F/O Pain went off on an intruder patrol at 20:30 hours, and the latter pilot engaged and damaged a Macchi 200. A busy night was again spent with GCI patrols and intruder patrols carrying on until nearly dawn. Albacores also operated and co-operated by dropping flares. Pilot P/O Beaumont failed to return.
26 May	Four new pilots arrived from BLG. P/O Colmore, P/O Stone, P/O Fairbairn, and Sgt. Lawes. In the morning there was a low-flying attack by ME 109's and the parachute and cables were operated. No e/a were destroyed by this means; no damage was caused by the raid. The usual night programme was prepared, and the Hun showed unusual activity. The Squadron was kept busy all night with low-flying JU 88's and F/Lt. Scade and F/Sgt. Joyce 'bagged' one each. F/O Selby probably destroyed a CR.42.
27 May	The operations went on until dawn and 4 a/c took part in the usual dawn patrol. Another straffing rai was carried out by ME 109's on the LG and an airman, AC Debono was killed. It was then that it was learned that the Hun had advanced and that a tank battle was taking place some 15-20 miles Southwest. It was decided that the Squadron reached Gambut by evening, but one party proceeded to El Cubbi under the instructions of the Military Police.
28 May Gambut	No flying took place today, but at 20:20 hours a/c were flown to Gasr-el-Ariyd for readiness. Other a/c were prepared for night flying at base and the Hun duly arrived with the aid of a full moon. The enemy force was large but 2 JU 88's did not return to their base; one being shot down by F/Lt. Scade and the other by F/O McDougall.
29 May	Patrols carried on into the morning and flying was still taking place at dawn. At mid-day, the party that had been diverted to El Cubbi arrived, making the Squadron complete again. The next operational sortie was by F/O McDougall, who did a recco of Tobruk, Tmimi and Bomba, taking off from Gambut at 20:20 hours. F/O Pain began a series of intruder patrols and was followed by Sgt. Goodwin and P/O Double.
30 May	The above patrols were interrupted by 3 'scrambles', but on this occasion no e/a were encountered. 9 further intruder patrols were then carried out and completed the night/morning programme. As usual only test flying made up the day's activity. Night flying commenced at 20:00 hours and a/c were on readiness at Gasr-el-Ariyd and Gambut. Intruder patrols were carried out to lower the morale of the Hun.

| 31 May | These patrols went on until 05:40 hours but 2 pilots, Sgts. Atherly and Barrie failed to return. Sgt. Atherly was safe, however, having got lost and came down near the road at Sollum. No news was received of Sgt. Barrie, but it is hoped that he is safe. There was no further operational flying until 22:30 hours, when F/O Selby took off for a weather test. |

AIR 27/631/11 & AIR 27/631/12 Pilot Ops Report
June 1942:

1 & 2 June Gambut Main	F/Sgt. Joyce took off for a weather test at 00:15 hours, followed by 7 a/c (patrolling Hurricanes) which left Gambut at regular intervals to straffe the Hun. Later in the morning F/O Irwin flew to BIG and returned early in the afternoon with a bag of mail. At 18:25 hours S/Ldr. Ward rejoined his Squadron, having flown up to Gambut from Gamil. Sgt. Wiseman began the operational night flying with a recco of the Segnali area, and shortly afterwads, readiness was maintained at base and Gasr-el-Ayrid. There were several 'scrambles' covering the night-morning period and S/Ldr. ward pursued a JU 88. He saw the e/a at 7,000 feet against the moonlight and closed in to attack but the pilot of the JU 88 saw the a/c and took evasive action by weaving, also diving and climbing. Whenever the CO attempted to get on his tail he turned into the darkness. After about 3 minutes, the S/L carried out a beam quarter attack and saw some shell bursts on the fuselage. Return fire was experienced. F/Lt. Scade saw the Hun go down to ground level and followed him down but lost sight of him near the coast. Patrols carried on until 06:00 hours and at between 05:00 and 06:00 hours a recco of the forward areas was carried out by Sgt. Jones, Sgt. Wiseman, Sgt. Hill, and F/O Irwin.
3 June	Night flying tests took place in the early evening and some a/c were flown to Gasr-el-Ariyd, but no operational flying was laid on until: -
4 June	At 01:30 hours Sgt. Hill began the day with a patrol and his flight was followed by 13 other operational sorties which covered the period of darkness. At 11:20 hours a new pilot joined 73 Squadron; F/Lt. Cantrill arrived from BLG
5 June	Activity on the ground in the forward areas being greatly and with the Hun attempting his push on Bir Hacheim, 73 Squadron was added to the day flying Squadrons to assist in a maximum effort. The moon period was over, thus making night interception difficult. The day was spent with battle formation practices and 21 training sorties were made.
6 June Gambut Main	Day flying began in earnest with an offensive patrol by 8 Hurricanes. The sweep lasted until 09:50 hours but no e/a were encountered. A similar offensive patrol was carried out in the evening, but no action resulted.
7 June	The number of a/c on the morning sweep was increased to 12 a/c, but P/O Henry had to land early with an oil leak. Gazala and Acroma were the areas patrolled. A 'dog fight' with a formation of ME 109's and our aircraft returned to base in 2's and 3's. We suffered 3 Hurricanes lost, but the pilots of 2 a/c returned later. The missing pilot was F/Lt. Cantrill. Sgt. Wiseman crash landed after having his airscrew knocked off by an unidentified a/c and Sgt. Wilson bailed out. At 17:15 hours 11 Hurricanes were 'scrambled' but no combat or interceptions occurred.
8 June	The Bir Hacheim area was patrolled by 10 Hurricanes, and ME 109's again made an appearance. The e/a did not do so well, for without loss to us, one was destroyed and another damaged. F/O Selby was the pilot who shot down the ME 109 and P/O Coussens the pilot who claimed the damaged. The time for the second formation to take off was 12:20 hours and 12 a/c took part. No engagements took place on this occasion.

| 9 June | The Free French still holding Bir Hacheim in spite of reported enemy attacks on that position. 13 Hurricanes of 73 Squadron were engaged for escorting Hurricanes of 274 Squadron that were to be used for the dropping of medical supplies, the operation was carried out successfully and no e/a interfered. From BLG came F/T. Robin, another new pilot, together with Sgt. Wiseman and P/o Colmore, another sweep took place between 17:00 hours and 18:30 hours and 11 Hurricanes flew. W/Cm. Fenton led the formation. F/Sgt. Joyce probably destroyed an ME 109 during this sweep. |

| 10 June
Gambut Main | 12 a/c took off from Gambut at 07:00 hours for a sweep of the battle areas, especially around Bir Hacheim. Our a/c were top cover to 2123 Squadron and 'A' Flight was 'jumped' by 5 Macchi 202's. The Hurricanes turned into them 3 times, but the Italians did not fight. Two batches of 20 + e/a Stukas and JU 88's was observed heading West to Bir Hacheim with a/c of 213 Squadron in hot pursuit. 'B' Flight met 3 to 4 ME 109's at 15,000 feet and forced the e/a up. P/O Fraser saw an e/a belching black smoke, diving almost vertically with an a/c following him down and shooting at him. From this operation one of our pilot's F/L Scade did not return and for some hours acute anxiety was felt for his safety. We learned later that he had been injured and had forced landed, but by the time the Squadron learned this news he was safe in Tobruk hospital.
The next operation was carried out between 15:40 and 17:00 hours. It was similar to the last, with the exception that 73 Squadron was bottom cover to 213 Squadron. In spite of this, 12 e/a ME 109's 'jumped' 73 Squadron and in the fight, which followed S/Ldr. Ward claimed the ME 109 damaged, Sgt. Baker one ME 109 probably destroyed, and P/O Henry an ME 109 damaged. One of our a/c was destroyed but the pilot, Sgt. Wilson bailed out and landed without injury. He re-joined the Squadron a few hours later. |

| 11 June | 12 a/c took off at 09:15 hours, acting as bottom cover to 213 Squadron on a sweep of the forward area. On this operation nothing was seen. On the second patrol S/Ldr. Ward's a/c developed an oil leak, and he called on the R/T confirming he was returning. He did not reach Gambut and forced landed near the battle area. He re-joined the Squadron late in the evening. A further patrol was carried out between 18:35 and 19:50 hours by 11 a/c with one returning due to engine trouble. The El Adem area was patrolled but no e/a were encountered. |

| 12 June | 12 a/c were detailed to sweep Southeast of El Adem, but soon after taking off one a/c returned with engine trouble. 3 ME 109's attacked the formation and made off quickly. Sgt. Wilson's a/c was hit in the wing, but that was the only damage suffered. At 13:40 hours 9 a/c were 'scramble' over base and then sent to patrol El Adem and to join 213 Squadron at 12,000 feet. Two unidentified a/c were seen near El Adem at 16,000 feet but no action resulted. A nil resulting 'Scramble' took place at 16:410 hours, but at 19:35 hours 12 a/c took off on a 'scramble' that was to prove the most successful of the very eventful week. Near Acroma a large force of JU 87's and JU 88's with a cover of ME 109's and Macchi's were intercepted. In this resulting fight, P/O Coussens, Sgt. Baker. P/O Henry, Sgt. Hill and Sgt. Jones each destroyed a Stuka and F/O Chatfield destroyed a JU 88. There were also 4 Stukas probably destroyed and a further one damaged. The only damage caused to 73 Squadron was one a/c slightly damaged with the pilot F/O Chatfield being injured in the arm. |

| 13 June | Today continued the almost non-stop flying carried out by a/c of No. 243 Wing, Hurricanes of 73 Squadron went up at 10:25 hours after being 'Scrambled' to El Adem. Nothing was seen there, and they were told to return to base. When about 5 miles West of Gambut, 2 ME 109's came up from behind and a 'dog fight' ensued. P/O Woolley damaged 2 ME 109's, and Sgt. Wiseman's a/c received a few bullet holes. |

14 June	The 73 Squadron, during this period were well and truly in the battle, flying almost all day. Patrols and 'scrambles', mostly of 12 a/c took place and during one of these F/O Selby saw a ship 15 miles North of base going West very fast, also a couple of barges going east about a mile offshore. It was then that we had instructions to leave Gambut immediately. The Hun making ugly advances towards the aerodrome, it was decided to evacuate the place, but notwithstanding a rear party was left, in order to keep the a/c flying until the last.
15 June	Ground crew down to a minimum and pilots with only their flying kit left with them, the Squadron carried on during this day. At 05:45 hours 12 a/c took off for a recce of Acroma, Gazala and the Knightsbridge areas, and on the road from Tobruk many MTs were observed travelling East also some on the Axis Road. There was no activity on the Hun side. A few hours later 12 a/c patrolled Tobruk and acted as top cover to 213 Squadron. At 13:55 hours a further 11 a/c took off on a 'scramble' to the Northwest of Tobruk. A 50-minute recce of El Adem completed the day, which was carried out by F/O Selby and Sgt. Wilson. The battle was raging near El Adem, the Free French having fallen back from their gallant stand at Bir Hacheim.
16 June Gambut Main	In spite of the increased difficulties, serviceability was to a high standard and once again 12 a/c left Gambut in order to patrol Tobruk. On this and on a later patrol of 11 a/c, nothing was encountered. In the afternoon F/O Selby flew over Sidi Rezegh for a recce and saw 6 tanks going West down the escarpment just East of El Adem box. There were also 40 MTs around Sidi Rezegh who fired at him. At 17:35 hours 12 a/c took to the air again led by the CO following instructions to 'scramble' to El Duda. Our formation was jumped by ME 109's and in the battle F/L Robin is believed to have been shot down, 1 a/c was seen to crash with the pilot NOT returning to base. F/L Robin whilst new to the Squadron he had secured immense popularity and will be missed by all that new him.
17 June	A difficult day to record. This was a day which commenced well with a patrol by 11 a/c, was to prove tragic for the Squadron. At 12:25 hours 12 Hurricanes took off from Gambut as escort for patrols. On their way back the a/c were jumped on by 6 ME 109's, F/L Baker, and P/O Coussens both damaged an e/a fighter each, but 4 of our a/c were destroyed. The CO, S/Ldr. Ward and P/O Woolley were killed and P/O Stone and Sgt. Goodwin both had to jump out with their parachutes, both were injured. At 18:00 hours the Squadron were instructed to move away from Gambut as quickly as possible, and the ground personnel were extremely lucky in that they were not captured by the rapidly advancing Hun. The enemy reached the LG that evening.
18 June L.G. 115	The advance party had settled down at LG 115 and there was flying in spite of the fact that the rear party were still on the road. Two sweeps of Sidi Azeiz took place. One at 11:25 hours and one at 13:00 hours. **This is the day on which Tobruk was being hard fought over by the German and Italian Forces.**
19 June L.G. 76	The rear party had by this time joined the main party at LG 115. Then we learned that we were to move a little further East to LG 76.
20 June	'A' Party left soon after dawn, but the a/c with a limited number of ground staff remained until 12:30 hours. No operational flying took place during the day or night.
21 June	Only one operation took place, a recce of the Bardia area. LG recces were carried out by several pilots in the evening should the Squadron be called upon to operate during the night. **The day on which Tobruk Fell to the German and Italian AXIS Forces.**

22 June L.G. 76	In the early morning 12 a/c of the Squadron were used for patrols of the Sollum area, no e/a were encountered. The operation was led by S/Ldr. Johnston who had taken over command of the Squadron.
23 June L.G.76	The Squadrons a/c having been dispersed overnight at LG 155 flew back early this morning. One operational sortie during the day, when F/O vis went in search of a Spitfire that had forced landed near the lines. He observed the damaged a/c on a trailer being driven back to an RSU. At this point the Squadron was waiting for orders to move again; an advance party having gone on to Qassaba. Orders came through from Group HQ at about 17:00 hours and we left LG 76 shortly after.
24 June Qassaba	No operational flying took place during the day, but night flying commenced at 22:00 hours.
25 & 26 June Qassaba	8 patrols in all were carried out, which lasted until 02:10 hours. Ju 88's was in the vicinity flare and bomb dropping, and Sgt. Hill encountered one South of Sidi Haneish and destroyed it. It was seen going down in flames by P/O Henry who also intercepted an enemy bomber and claiming a 'probable'. There was no operational day flying. Night flying began soon after 22:00 hours. Several patrols took place and carried on well into the morning of the 26th with F/Sgt. Joyce destroying a JU 88. In the early evening 5 a/c took off for a recce over the Matruh and forward areas. They encountered a number of ME 109's and F/O Coussens was believed to have been killed. In truth he returned late that night having 'bailed out' West of Matruh. He landed in a minefield and spent some uncomfortable time getting out of the danger area. During the same patrol P/O Fraser was wounded but flew his a/c back to base and landed it safely. Once again, we had word to prepare for a further move towards the East. Loaded lorries stood by all night, and an advance party left for Daba by moonlight.
27 June Daba	The Squadrons two parties met at Daba, the rear party having left Qassaba early this morning. No flying was carried out from Dada other than a party proceeded to LG 20 and night flying took place from here.
28 June L.G. 20	Patrols began from LG 20 at 00:05 hours and lasted until dawn. F/L Bird chased a JU 88 out to sea but lost it, S/Ldr. Johnston was more fortunate and claimed a JU 88 as damaged. Although F/O Selby chased a JU 88 out to sea, he fired at it and saw it dive with engines flaming, he could only claim the bomber as 'probably destroyed' as he did not see it hit the water. The afternoon saw us again moving East, this time as far back as Burg-el-Arab. No operational flying could be done as the Squadron was on the move.
29 June Burd-el-Arab	No day flying took place, but although several lorries had not arrived by nightfall, and they were important units to the Squadron, including a V.H.F. tender and a chance light. Night flying was carried out. Sgt. Jones claimed a JU 88, but loe turn, but Sgt. Baker damaged a JU 88. Flying went on until well into the following morning.
30 June	There was no operational flying, and the next sortie was at 23:05 hours when F/O Selby took off for a recce of the Fuka area. It was a very short trip as visibility was very poor.

AIR 27/631/13 & AIR 27/631/14 Pilot Ops Report

July 1942:

1st Battle of El Alamein – 1 July to 27 July 1942

[For further details of this battle refer to Chapter 5 – D. El Alamein]

1 July L.G. 39	F/Lt. Bird and F/O Selby carried out early morning recce but F/Lt. Bird finding visibility very poor landed after 15-minutes. He flew again later, however landed at LG 91 to report. Special attention was paid to the Southern half of the area, Grid Ref's. 882898 to 852242 where the Hun's main threat was expected. Positions of enemy MT's and guns were recorded. No operational flying carried out.
2 July	At 05:15 hours 4 Hurricanes took off for a recce of the battle area. 120 enemy MTs were seen at 850250 and at 830250 – 840250, 5 groups of 50 to 60 stationary MTs, including 10 heavy tanks. At 09:30 hours there was a 'scramble' and 12 a/c took off. One landed early having lost formation. No e/a were engaged, but one section was detached from formation to chase a JU 109. Th e/a made off swiftly and no action took place. F/O Selby and F/Sgt. Joyce carried out a weather recce between 11:45 and 12:30 hours. 73 Squadron then moved East to LG 89.
3 July L.G. 89	The first 'scramble' at the new LG was extremely eventful. 12 a/c took off at 12:30 hours and proceeded North of the Alamein Line. A 'Stuka' party was on and after the interception e/a were destroyed: - one ME 109 by Sgt. Jones, one ME 109 by F/O Pain and one ME 109 by F/Sgt. Joyce, 3 more e/a were probably destroyed and a further 4 e/a damaged. 2 Hurricanes did not return, F/Sgt. Packham arrived latein the afternoon, having force landed following a spin at Kilo 75. Later the Squadron learned that Sgt. Hill had been killed. A very popular and excellent pilot. Another 'scramble' took place at 16:45 hours with 33 Squadron as top cover, 10 a/c proceeded to the Alamein box. F/lt. Selby damaged a JU 87 by blowing a hole in its side between pilot and observer. P/O Double hit the starboard wing root of another dive bomber and Sgt. Farley saw two hits on another while the e/a went down with black smoke coming from it. F/O Pain claimed one probable destroyed and one damaged, and Sgt. Wilson destroyed a further 2 e/a, one of which blew up in mid-air. S/Ldr. Johnston also one Stuka and probably destroyed another. The total score included the Stuka damaged by S/Ldr. Matthews being 3 destroyed and 3 probably destroyed and 4 damaged. One of our pilots did not return to base at once as he landed at LG 92.
4 July **LAC Lamb -1012281 birthday**	12 a/c took part in a patrol of the Alamein box. Led by S/Ldr. Johnston. E/a were engaged without loss to the Squadron, 2 e/a ME 109's was destroyed and 2 other e/a damaged. The next patrol began at 14:15 hours with the Squadron acting as top cover for 33 Squadron in a sweep of the Alamein Line. One e/a a single ME 109 was seen but too far away to be engaged. The third and final sweep of the day commenced at 19:00 hours and continued until 20:15 hours. On this occasion 33 Squadron was top cover at 13,000 feet. There were no engagements.
5 July	The first operation of the day was a cover patrol over our forward troops, 11 a/c Hurricanes took part. The patrol lasted 1hour 30 minutes but no encounter with e/a. The Squadron was released for training flying and 13 a/c and pilots did local flying practice. The following new pilots took part, Sgts. Carcary, Logan Marsh, Wright, P/O Gill, F/Lt. Miller, F/O Henfry and P/O Laing Measons. Further training was carried out in the evening, this time in the form of interceptions.

6 July	Patrol South down the Alamein Line and cover the New Zealand troops at 8629. If attacked by Macchi's detach a Section to deal with them. These were the instructions for the sweep which left LG 89 at 08:55 hours by 12 a/c of the Squadron. The formation met with no Hun or Italian e/a, landed back at 10:10 hours. The early evening saw the next patrol of the Alamein Line carried out with 73 Squadron being top cover to 213 Squadron. Numbers of hostile e/a were reported by control, but all turned out to be false. In fact, nothing at all was observed.
7 July L.G. 89	The Squadron was released until 08:00 hours and then released for further training flying. Battle formation was carried out by 112 a/c and then a further 6 a/c did a similar flight. The first operational work was at 15:55 hours, when 12 a/c Hurricanes with a/c of 213 Squadron as top cover patrolled the forward area. Evidence of Italian air activity was proved by the appearance of G.R.42's, two of which were destroyed one by F/Lt. Selby and the other by F/Sgt. Joyce. In the afternoon 73 Squadron was at 15-minutes availability and a further sweep was laid on. They took off at 18:15 hours. Soon after taking off R.T. trouble was experienced and as 213 and 145 Squadrons were also airborne the cause of the fault was difficult to trace. One of our a/c flew over the LG for an R/T test to check on any problems and all systems were quite in order. The Squadron was released until further notice.
8 July L.G. 89	A quiet day. We were again released for training and Maintenance and the 'state' persisted all day. 'A' Flight and 'B' Flight both made practice 'formation' Flights of 6 a/c in the morning to train new pilots and 5 a/c were also airborne.
9 July L.G. 89	At 05:30 Hours – Squadron at 30-minutes availability. At 09:50 hours - Squadron called to readiness, 12 a/c and at 10:55 Hours – The Squadron 12 a/c led by F/Lt. Badger was airborne as top cover for 33 Squadron, to patrol friendly territory close to the front. No e/a were encountered but bombing by Bostons was observed. The weather was good with clear visibility. All our a/c landed without incident at 12:10 hours. Channel 'C' was used as R/T instead of the usual Channel 'A'. Readiness at 13:30 hours with instructions to use Channel 'A' if 'scrambled' with 213 Squadron, Informed by AIO of a battle raging 12-15 miles Southwest of El Alamein and warned of e/a Fighter Bomber attack on the LG./ This failed to materialise though the Squadron led by (S/Ldr. Johnston) was 'scrambled' over base as top cover for 213 Squadron at 16:40 hours. Patrol was kept over Burg-el-Arab at 16,000 feet but no e/a seen. The Squadron landed at 17:55 hours. Weather and cloud 'nil' – some haze. After refuelling the State became '30-minutes availability'. The Squadron released with tomorrows form given as '30-minutes' availability from 05:30 hours.
10 July L.G. 89	Squadron at 30-minutes as from dawn until 07:20 hours when with 213 Squadron as top cover and with Spitfires of 145 Squadron above them. 11 a/c led by the CO were airborne to patrol the Sidi Ralman area. Patrolled Northwest to Southwest in this area and observed swirling dust as from a tank battle, about 15 miles Southwest of Alamein, together some spasmodic shelling. Visibility was good but no e/a were encountered and on being relieved by No. 239 Wing the Squadron landed at 08:37 hours without incident. The state was 15-minutes available after refuelling until 10:45 hours when the Squadron came to readiness. At 11:55 hours 11 a/c were again airborne led by F/Lt. Selby and to patrol El Alamein – Sidi Abdel Rahman – Ghazal and near Ghazal saw 5 C.R. 42's at 300 feet above us going East. We engaged them, they dived to avoid but we followed, and the results are 1) F/Sgt. Joyce destroyed a C.R. 42, 2) F/Sgt. Packham destroyed one, 3) F/O Pain damaged one seeing bits fall away from it. Then 4 e/a ME 109's tried to jump us Northeast of Alamein and as we turned into them, they flew away. F/Lt. Selby was forced to land as a result of the engagement – his a/c now Cat. II, he escaped uninjured. The weather was good, clear visibility and no cloud. The a/c landed at 13:00 hours. At 16:20 hours the Squadron led by the CO swept the forward area, but no results or Huns so returned and landed at 17:35 hours. A further sweep was 'laid on' for 19:15 hours, later cancelled, the Squadron released for the day.

11 July L.G. 89	At 05:30 hours Squadron at 15-minutes available from dawn. At 07:55 hours 12 a/c took off to patrol the El Alamein forward area. On the way 6 r/a ME 109's was observed 10 miles West of Burg el Arab heading North, no contact was made. Patrolled out to sea off Rass el Shaqig – 'A' Flight at 8,500 feet and 'B' Flight at 7,500 feet with 4 a/c from No.7 SAAF Squadron below 'B' Flight. 2 e/a ME 109's observed at 2,5600 feet and F/Lt. Badger half rolled on to one as he dived to strafe firing at 200 yards, and after a few bursts of gun fire black smoke poured from the ME 109: as it dived towards the ground. At 09:00 hours pilots of No.7 SAAF confirmed e/a destroyed. Sgt. Jones saw 2 e/a ME 109's and chased one and fired several bursts and black smoke came from the e/a. He did not pursue as ground fire was accurate, he later claimed a 'probable'. The patrol continued by 'A' Flight and 2 a/c of No. 7 SAAF, there was no further action and they all landed at 09:25 hours. Weather – slight haze. At 10:25 hours Squadron state 15-minutes availability and at 12:02 hours 12 a/c led by the CO were airborne with 4 a/c from 145 Squadron as top cover, looking for Stuka bombers over El Alamein box. They patrolled North and South and slightly East of Alamein, but no Huns were visible and so laned at 13:20 hours. At 14:00 hours state at 15-minutes available. At 16:30 hours 12 a/c again led by CO with 145 Squadron as top cover and patrolled the Alamein box and West thereof, to look for JU 87's and 88's. Flew up and down through Alamein and observed 25 large tanks near Bir el Mukheim moving Southwest, 6 miles South of Alamein. A 'dogfight' developed between our top cover Spitfires and ME 109's, we turned North to check out A.A. fire and then South to meet an attack from 3 e/a ME 109's. The attack failed as unable to engage, The Squadron returned as petrol was low. Landed at 17:50 hours, weather very hazy. Squadron released and got ready for state in the morning – 30-minutes at dawn.
12 July L.G. 89	At 05:30 hours Squadron state 30-minutes available, At 07:00 hours state of readiness. At 09:00 state 15-minutes available. At 18:15 hours state 30-minutes available. At 19:10 Squadron called to readiness for local defence. 12 a/c at readiness but not used. At 19:45 hours Squadron released, an uneventful day, no flying largely due to dust storms and little land activity.
13 July L.G. 89	At 05:30 hours state 15-minutes available. At 09:05 Hours12 a/c called to readiness. At 10:30 hours 12 a/c were 'scrambled' over base at 10,000 feet and sent West to check out 6 'bogies' 25 miles Southwest of Burg el Arab. Nothing encountered and patrolled for a further 30-minutes over the area. Controlled informed that 6 bandits at 18,000 feet, 25 miles Southwest of Burg el Arab. The Squadron was at 14,000 feet going East so immediately turned about, then informed that the 6 bandits now at 7,000 feet to starboard. No bandits seen and the Squadron landed without incident at 11:50 hours. Weather, no cloud but slight sand haze. At 11:57 hours F/Lt. Selby was airborne to do a recce of El Magloa Lake and tracks to the West of it. He flew at 50 feet between El Magloa and Matum Sharil but observed no vehicles – he then turned North and found about 2/300 heavy armoured cars moving East by North at 847252. He also observed a Division of British motorised Infantry and light artillery between 8826, 8725, and 8824, did not encounter e/a nor tanks. He landed at 12:53 hours. Squadron at 12:00 hours state 15-minutes available. At 14:42 hours 12 a/c led by the CO were airborne at 10,000 feet, with 213 Squadron as top cover at 14,000 feet plus 8 Spitfires of 145 Squadron above 213. The object was to sweep and intercept Stuka party over El Alamein. The patrol was maintained for some time to try and intercept e/a but no e/a were seen and the Squadron landed at 16:00 hours. Weather hazes up to 8,000 feet. As soon as the a/c were refuelled and at 17:00 hours they were brought to readiness. At 17:42 hours the Squadron was 'scrambled' led by the CO and took off with top cover provided by 33 Squadron to intercept Stuka party over El Alamein with disappointing results. Various vectors were given but no e/a were seen, except a couple on unidentified a/c who dropped bombs 5 miles South of El Alamein, they then flew at deck level. Squadron returned to base at 20:00 and released.

14 July L.G. 89	At 05:30 hours the Squadron was called to readiness. At 07:35 hours12 a/c led by the CO were 'scrambled' over Alamein. A patrol was maintained around Alamein at 12,000 feet but no e/a were encountered, and the Squadron landed at 08:50 hours. Weather – Hazy. At 09:20 hours Squadron state – 15-minutes available and at 11:00 hours at readiness. At 13:00 hours state was 15-minutes available and at 14:10 hours state readiness. At 15:10 hours 12 a/c led by F/Lt. Baker 'scrambled' North of Alamein box with No. 7 SAAF as top cover and with 4 a/c Spitfires right on top. A fire was observed and as we approached saw 5/7 ME 109's dive-bombing the same area. We dived on to them, but they broke away and made off at speed. We then patrolled at 11,000 feet between the fire and Alamein, but no more e/a were seen. Weather was clear and much ground movement was observed. All landed at 16:25 hours without incident. At 17:00 hours the Squadron sate 30-minutes available, at 118:45 hours state readiness and at 20:30 hours released.
15 July L.G. 89	At 08:55 hours the Squadron called to readiness, and at 09:30 hours 12 a/c Hurricanes led by F/Lt. Selby 'Scrambled' to patrol South of Alamein with 4 Spitfires of 145 Squadron as top cover. We patrolled at 7/8,000 feet, then climbed to 12,000 feet as there was a haze at 10,000 feet. There were /in the vicinity but we saw none and returned to base landing at 10:50 hours. At 11:15 hours state 15-minutes available and at 12:00 hours Squadron called to readiness. At 13:00 hours and led by F/Lt. Selby 'scrambled' over base with 4 a/c of 145 Squadron giving top cover. We patrolled Southwest of Alamein at 8,000 feet but no e/a seen. Some spasmodic shelling was observed on the ground. At 14:00 hours Sgt. McPherson left the formation to fly Eastwards and was later heard to say that he force-landing in the desert 6 miles Northwest of base not witnessed by the returning a/c that landed at 14:20 hours. At 14:30 hours state 15-minutes18:00 hours state readiness. At 18:45 12 a/c 'Scrambled' led by the CO with 33 Squadron as top cover and patrolled at 13,000 feet South of Alamein. Control informed us that e/a were approaching from the West. We turned in that direction but could not find them and resumed our patrol to 20 miles East of Alamein then returned to base landing at 20:05 hours. Weather very hazy. At 20:20 hours the Squadron was released.
16 July L.G. 89	At 06:45 hours state 30-minutes available. At 08:35 hours 12 a/c led by the CO airborne for a patrol the El Alamein Line with special attention to pinpoint 847277. Started off South-West for patrol area meeting various friendly a/c, when 12 miles South-East of the pinpoint, 6 e/a ME 109's appeared at 12,000 feet, after making a few turnabouts 1 e/a ME 109 attacked us without result to either side. We were at 10,.000 feet when attacked, we reassembled and returned to base. However, Sgt. Edwards did not return with the Squadron. At 09:05 hours he was heard as saying over the R/T that his engine had 'out-out' and would force-land. He was over enemy territory at the time, and it was feared that he will be taken prisoner. The Squadron landed at 09:40 hours. At 10:00 hours state 15-minutes available, then at 11:00 12 a/c at readiness. In order to improve the time required to 'scramble' from readiness a new system was introduced, whereby a/c are taxied out to 'line-up' position on receipt of readiness order. This should save valuable time in taking off. At 12:00 hours Sgt. McPherson return, his a/c had developed engine problems and he force-landed at 475885 (Cairo sheet), wheels up, a/c Cat. II. McPherson was uninjured and had been picked up at 06:00 hours today by army transport which took him to LF 39. At 13:00 hours 12 a/c led by F/Lt. Badger, accompanied by 4 a/c of No. 7 SAAF Squadron, with a further 4 a/c od 145 Squadron as top cover set off to patrol the area around pinpoint 870300 (Matruh sheet) at 12-15,000 feet. They patrolled North and South a few miles to the east of the pinpoint but saw no e/a. Some gunfire on the ground was observed but too hazy for accurate observation. Squadron landed back at 14:15 hours. At 15:00 hours state 30-minutes available and at 17:00 hours at readiness. Again 12 a/c at 17:15 hours, led by F/Lt. Badger were airborne as top cover to 213 Squadron with 4 a/c Spitfires of 601 Squadron above us, to patrol near pinpoint 882575 where enemy bombing was expected. Weather was hazy and we patrolled at 15,000 feet.

No e/a encountered so returned to base at 18:50 hours. Sgt. Edwards phoned to say that he force-landed, wheels up at pinpoint 466886 (Cairo sheet), his a/c is Cat. II and that a guard for it has been furnished by the OC General Transport 180 RASC. At 19:00 hours Squadron was released.

<table>
<tr><td>

17 July
L.G. 89

</td><td>

At 06:00 hours state 15-minutes available then at 07:00 hours 12 a/c led by the CO and with 145 Squadron providing top cover was airborne on patrol. The patrol area was 10 miles to the South of Alamein, instructions received to keep 5 to 6 miles to the East of the line, out of observation post range and to maintain R/T silence. WE were flying at 14,000 feet with 145 Squadron a/c at 16,000 feet when 4 e/a ME 109's appeared above the formation at 16/17,000 feet and making for the sun. They jumped 145 and one Spitfire was shot down the pilot landing by parachute. The ME 109's then made off at speed. We continued our patrol but saw no more e/a, the Squadron landed at 08:15 hours. Weather clear, visibility good, cloud 1/10 at 2,000 feet.

</td></tr>
</table>

17 July
L.G. 89

At 06:00 hours state 15-minutes available then at 07:00 hours 12 a/c led by the CO and with 145 Squadron providing top cover was airborne on patrol. The patrol area was 10 miles to the South of Alamein, instructions received to keep 5 to 6 miles to the East of the line, out of observation post range and to maintain R/T silence. WE were flying at 14,000 feet with 145 Squadron a/c at 16,000 feet when 4 e/a ME 109's appeared above the formation at 16/17,000 feet and making for the sun. They jumped 145 and one Spitfire was shot down the pilot landing by parachute. The ME 109's then made off at speed. We continued our patrol but saw no more e/a, the Squadron landed at 08:15 hours. Weather clear, visibility good, cloud 1/10 at 2,000 feet.

At 09:10 hours state readiness. At 09:55 hours the CO led 12a/c to patrol 10 miles South of Alamein at 12,000 feet North to South 5 miles East of Alamein Line. We were vector 15/20 e/a coming towards us, we turned to intercept but they turned West before reaching Alamein. We resumed our patrol. No e/a were encountered, and no ground movement observed. Visibility was very good. Squadron landed at 11:25 hours. At 11:45 state 15 available and at 13:25 state brought to readiness. Then at 14:08 hours 12 a/c led by F/Lt. Badger took off with 2 a/c Spitfires of 145 Squadron providing top cover, we were to patrol forward areas. They patrolled at 12,000 feet over the centre of El Alamein Line, but no e/a were seen. Weather was hazy and only slight activity was observed on the ground. Squadron landed at 15:25 hours. At 16:00 hours state 15-minutes available and at 18:55 hours 12 a/c took off, again led by F/Lt. Badger accompanied 4 a/c of No. 7 SAAF with 8 a/c Spitfires of 145 Squadron as top cover to patrol the centre of the Alamein Line. They approached at 15,000 feet and when 10 miles Southwest of there they observed bombs bursting on the ground but could not see any e/a. There was 7/10 cloud at 3,000 feet and visibility poor due to a thick haze. We were told over the R/T that the e/a were below cloud at 3,000 feet, we commence our dive to engage them. Halfway down our leader decided it was impossible to catch them and at the same time noticed 6 e/a JU 88's approaching Alamein from the West at 12,000 feet, so we started to climb to engage the JU 88's and before getting to them they turned for home. We were attacked by 3 e/a ME 109's from 13/000 feet but made off as we turned into them. Continued to patrol Northwest of Alamein but saw no e/a, so we returned to base landing at 20:10 hours. At 20:15 hours the Squadron was released.

During the day much pleasure had been felt around the Squadron at the announcement that *F/Lt. Scade had been awarded the Distinguished Flying Cross [DFC]*. He had joined the Squadron on the 1 June 1941 and between that date and the 10 June 1942, when he was shot down with multiple shrapnel wounds over Bir Hacheim, he had flown 240 operational hours and engaged in 30 combats. His victories include 2 – JU88's destroyed, 1 – ME 110 destroyed, 1 – HE III and 1 JU 88 probably destroyed, and 2 – JU 88's damaged. F/Lt. Scade visited the Squadron yesterday on his discharge from hospital and has now departed on a well-earned rest.

18 July
L.G. 89

At 05:30 hours state 30-minutes available. Again at 09:20 hours state 15-minutes available, then at 10:220 hours Squadron called to readiness. Then at 11:50 hours and led by S/Ldr. Matthews 12 a/c took off to patrol the battle are as top cover for 213 Squadron. We patrolled North and South 5 miles East of Lagoona (420 Eastway Cairo sheet) at 16,000 feet but saw no e/a, or ground movement. The weather was hazy when we landed at 13:10 hours and a bad dust storm was obscuring the LGH. At 13:20 hours the Squadron was released for Maintenance but owing to the dust the Engineer Officer was unable to carry out the desired work. At 16:30 hours the Squadron was called to readiness and briefed for a patrol at 17:15 hours weather permitting. The weather did not permit! Great clouds of dust made visibility about 10 yards at times and instructions were amended for the patrol to take place when visibility improved, but at 129:15 hours the Squadron was released.

| 19 July | At 06:15 hours Squadron at readiness. Then at 07:45 hours 11 a/c led by F/Lt. Miller |
| L.G. 89 | 'scrambled' to patrol the Central Section of El Alamein Line. Top cover was to have been |

19 July
L.G. 89

At 06:15 hours Squadron at readiness. Then at 07:45 hours 11 a/c led by F/Lt. Miller 'scrambled' to patrol the Central Section of El Alamein Line. Top cover was to have been provided by 2313 Squadron but owing to the delay in their take-off we proceeded without them. We patrolled North and South along the Alamein track, but no e/a were encountered. Very heavy ground shelling was observed in the 26 Northing between 87 and 88 Eastings (Matruh sheet). Weather was clear. 1 a/c returned to base at 09:00 hours with oil trouble and another landed at Burg el Arab owing to being low on fuel. The remainder of the Squadron landed at 09:15 hours without incident.

At 10:10 hours state 15-minutes available and at 10:35 hours state readiness. Later at 12:00 hours state 15-minutes available and at 13:45 hours state readiness. Then at 14:27 hours led by F/Lt. Selby 12 a/c were 'scrambled' to patrol El Alamein Line at 12,000 feet, 213 Squadron were to provide top cover, but owing to a dust storm which was obscuring visibility up to 3,000 feet we were unable to join up with them so proceeded independently. We patrolled North and South just East of Alamein track, but no e/a were encountered and due to the poor visibility, no ground movement was observed. The Squadron landed successfully at 15:40 hours. Owing to the LG becoming unserviceable for dust, the Squadron was held at 30-minutes availability from 16:00 hours to 20:00 hours when they were released.

20 July
L.G. 89

At 05:30 hours state dawn readiness, then at 09:00 hours state released for breakfast. At 09:55 hours 12 a/c led by F/Lt. Selby were 'scrambled' to patrol our side of the Alamein Line (Central Section) to protect our own troops whilst a 'BalBo' of our a/c attacked Daba LG. We patrolled as ordered from 10 miles South of Alamein to 15 miles North of El Maghra at a height of 10,000 feet. No e/a were encountered. A small amount of shelling was observed. The weather was clear with no cloud and the Squadron landed at 11:05 hours. At 12:00 hours The Squadrons state 15-minutes available. Then at 15:20 hours 12 a/c led by F/Lt. badger took off to LG 151 to await further instructions from Group. Owing to bad visibility we were unable to locate LG 151 and after a considerable time trying to locate it, so we landed at LG 39 at 16:25 hours. At 18:30 hours 2 a/c returned to base (LG 89) with oil leaks. Then whilst at LG 39 and at 18:55 hours 10 a/c led by S/Ldr. Matthews were 'scrambled to patrol the end of the Alamein Line. We were at 9,000 feet when we arrived at the 'Box' and as we did, we came underneath 15 e/a ME 109's flying at 12,000 feet. They had dived on us several times and we ducked and scrammed finally came down to deck level and came home. Sgt. Baker fired at 1 e/a ME 109 as it crossed his gun-sights and claims he damaged it. 2 of our a/c sustained slight damage but both are Cat. I. The Squadron landed back at LG 89 at 19:55 hours. At 20:00 hours the Squadron was released for the day. During the day a new Hurricane No. 220 was delivered from Base.

21 July
L.G. 89

At 38:30 hours state – Readiness. Then at 12:00 hours the Squadron was released for 24 hours much needed Maintenance. At 14:40 hours 10 a/c were airborne on practice formation flying and shadow firing. This was carried out without incident and the a/c landed at 15:30 hours.

22 July L.G. 89	All the Maintenance work was completed by 11:00 hours and were able to inform Wing that we are ready for operations. The Squadron came to readiness at 11:30 hours and 12a/c led by F/Lt. Selby were airborne to patrol the (Centre Section) of the Alamein Line where intensive ground activity was taking place. We patrolled at 13,500 feet and were 10 miles from the coast over the Alamein Line heading North when 9 e/a Me 109's was seen at 3,000 feet above us heading East. We turned towards them. They also turned heading West and came down parallel to us about 1,000 above. We did several turnabouts and then the ME 109's attacked/ 2 a/c of ours were shot down in the encounter. P/O Hall was seen to bail out about 863270 and the other Hurricane crashed at about 880260. Nothing was seen of the pilot (F/Sgt. Cardary) of this a/c. A 3rd Hurricane was damaged but returned to base and is OK Cat. I. 10 a/c landed at 13:25 hours. At 14:10 hours state0-minutes available. At 14:30 hours the Squadron was released pending a move to Ballah at dawn tomorrow, where we are to undertake night flying. At 16:00 hours Wing Intelligence reported P/O Hall was safe, but his a/c was Cat. III.
23 July El Ballah	At 07:00 hours the Squadron took off from LG 89 for Ballah. The ground personnel arrived at Ballah at 16:00 hours but no operational flying was carried out on this day.
24 July El Ballah	At 20:45 hours 8 a/c took off on a practice layer patrol over Dvur Soir at 6,000 feet. The patrol was successfully carried out and the last a/c landed at 21:51 hours. No e/a were encountered.
25 July El Ballah	At 20:40 hours 12 a/c were 'scrambled', led by the CO on a practice layer patrol over Dvur Soir at 6,000 feet. All the a/c landed at 21:55 hours without incident.
26 July El Ballah	During the day a durable amount of cannon testing was carried out in the air. At 20:50 hours 10 a/c 'scrambled' on practice layer patrol over Ballah at 6,000 feet. All the a/c of the Squadron landed at 21:45 hours without incident.
27 July El Ballah	During the day many air tests were carried out. At 20:43 hours 12 a/c again were 'scrambled', led by CO on a layer patrol over Ballah at 6,000 feet. No e/a were encountered, and the Squadron landed at 21:55 hours without incident.
28 July Shandur	17 a/c took off and flew to Shandur where the Squadron was at readiness during the night of the 23 to the 29 July.
29 July El Ballah	At 09:10 hours all the a/c returned to Ballah from Shandur. At 18:06 hours 12 a/c led by the CO were 'scrambled' on a practice layer patrol over Suez at 9,000 feet. Instead of returning to Ballah they landed at Shandur where they were joined by 4 a/c flown direct from Ballah. The Squadron remained at readiness during the hours of darkness.
30 July El Ballah	At 06:55 hours all the a/c returned to Ballah from Shandur. At 18:05 hours 12 a/c were 'scrambled on a practice layer patrol over Ballah and landed at Shandur. They were joined by a further 4 a/c and stayed at readiness during the night.
31 July Shandur	During the day the remainder of the a/c were flown to Shandur, and the ground staff moved over to this LG. At 12:45 hours 2 a/c were 'scrambled' over base at Shandur to attempt to intercept e/a on a recco over the Suez area. They were unable to gain sufficient height to intercept and landed again at 13:20 hours.

AIR 27/631/15 & AIR 27/631/16 Pilot Ops Report

August 1942:

1 August
Shandur

At 02:55 hours 14 a/c led by the CO 'scrambled' on a practice layer patrol South of Suez at 4,000 feet. Weather was hazy and no e/a were seen. All a/c landed without incident at 04:10 hours. At 18:00 hours 12 a/c were airborne on practice formation and night flying training and all a/c landed at 19:00 hours. At 23:40 hours S/Ldr. Matthews took off on a Sector recce, no e/a were encountered, and he landed back at 00:28 hours.

2 August
Shandur

A large number of practice formations and air tests were flown during the day. 2 a/c were held at readiness throughout the hours of daylight with 2 more a/c available for local defence.

3 August
Shandur

2 a/c at readiness and 2 a/c available for local defence from dawn to dusk. No scrambles.

4 August
Shandur

During the hours of daylight, the usual 2 a/c were kept at readiness and a further 2 a/c available. At 15:30 hours Sgt. Smythe and Hendrey were 'scrambled' over base at 15,000 feet to intercept lone e/a. They received various vectors but saw no e/a they 'pancaked' at 16:30 hours. At 17:55 hours 6 a/c were airborne on practice formation when Sgts. Jones and McPherson were ordered to detach themselves from the formation and investigate unidentified a/c flying 20 miles North of base. The a/c was identified as a Hurricane, so the 2 a/c pancaked at 18:55 hours. Much practice flying was carried out during the day.

5 August
Shandur

The usual 2 a/c at readiness and 2 a/c available maintained from dawn to dusk. At 10:00 hours P/O Ingle and Sgt. Stillman were 'scrambled' to maximum height over base to intercept e/a. They were told the e/a were approaching from Ismalia at 30,000 feet and after receiving various vectors, sighted the e/a, a JU 88 flying 15 miles East of Suez at 28,000 feet. Our 2 a/c were then at 24,000 feet but turned and chased him. The e/a was turning continuously and drew away to the Southwest. Our a/c altered and got within 3 miles of him, but he again altered course to the South and our a/c were unable to catch him so pancaked at 11:00 hours. Weather clear, with no cloud. Much training flying was carried out during the day.

6 August
Shandur

The usual 2 a/c at readiness with 2 a/c available were maintained during the hours of daylight, but no patrols were flown. Much flying training was carried out during the day, and this was marred by the crash and death of F/Sgt. Packham. F/Sgt. Packham had served with the Squadron for about a year, during which time he had performed much good work. At 18:10 hours he was airborne with Sgt. Logan to perform aerobatics over the base. Whilst turning at 9,000 feet his a/c went into a spin. He managed to straighten out at 2,000 feet but the nose again dropped, and the a/c crashed on to the Suez-Cairo Road. He was killed outright.

7 August
Shandur

From dawn to dusk 2 a/c were held at readiness with 2 a/c available. F/Lt. Badger and F/Sgt. Chandler were 'scrambled' over base to intercept an e/a 'Heinkel 111' flying very high. Our a/c climbed to 33,000 feet and after receiving many vectors finally sighted the e/a at 36,000 feet going in a Westerly direction over Suez. They could not climb up to him and so were pancaked at 14:15 hours. A lot more training was carried out during the day.

8 August
Shandur

The usual 2 a/c at readiness with 2 a/c available from dawn to dusk. At 09:58 hours P/O Speck and P/O White were 'scrambled' to maximum height over base. When at 20,000 feet ordered to intercept e/a 60 miles to the West. After flying about 40 miles in this direction and climbing to 27,000 feet they were ordered to pancake as the e/a were still going West. They landed at 10:45 hours. Visibility - very clear. Practice formations and interception practices were flown during the day.

9 August Shandur	The usual 2 a/c at readiness with 2 a/c available from dawn to dusk. At 12:10 hours P/O Ingle and F/Sgt. Chandler were 'scrambled' over base. They climbed to 6,500 feet and were then ordered to pancake as the bandit had turned away. They landed at 12:25 hours. Visibility good. At 16:15 hours P/O Warburton and Sgt. Jones were 'scrambled over base to a height of 25,000 feet. They were informed that a bandit was orbiting Cairo and they were then ordered to pursue another e/a South of Suez. They were then ordered to investigate the first bandit. They climbed to 33,500 feet and identified the plane as a friendly fighter. They both landed back at base at 17:15 hours. Visibility – very clear. Shadow firing and practice day fighting was carried out during the day.
10 August Shandur	14 a/c and pilots were detached today to El Bassa, Palestine. 44 members of the ground staff were conveyed by air to provide maintenance at El Bassa.
11 August EL Bassa	2 a/c were maintained at readiness during the day. At 18:05 hours F/Lt. Selby and Sgt. Farley were 'scrambled' over Heifa at 25,000 feet to intercept an identified a/c. The a/c was identified as a DC 3 and they both a/c landed at 18:35 hours. During the day 2 more a/c with pilots and ground crews were detached to Gaza from Shandur.
12 August El Bassa	2 a/c were maintained at readiness during the day. At 12:27 hours F/Lt. Badger and Sgt. Beard were 'scrambled' to recce a submarine but failed to observe it. They both landed back at 13:15 hours.
13 August El Bassa	2 a/c were maintained at readiness during the day. At 15:47 hours F/Lt. Badger and W/O Baker were 'scrambled' over base to intercept an identified a/c at 20,000 feet. They patrolled for 45-minutes but failed to locate this a/c and landed back at base at 16:30 hours.
14 August El Bassa	2 a/c were maintained at readiness during the day. At 11:10 hours F/Sgt. Chandler and W/O Baker were 'scrambled' over base and climbed to 7,000 feet and were then ordered to pancake and they landed back at base at 11:25 hours. At 14:30 hours F/Lt. Selby and P/O Speck were 'scrambled over Heifa Point to 20,000 feet but observed nothing and were ordered to pancake and landed at 14:55 hours. At 14:45 hours S/Ldr. Johnston and Sgt. Farley were 'scrambled' over base but on climbing to 5,000 feet were ordered to pancake and landed at 14:55 hours. At 17:50 hours S/Ldr. Matthews and Sgt. Smythe were 'scrambled' over Heifa Point to intercept and identified a/c. The a/c was identified as a Liberator and our a/c landed back at base at 18:25 hours.
15 August, El Bassa	2 a/c maintained at readiness during the day. At 19:05 hours P/O Gill and F/Sgt. Chandler were 'scrambled' over base to intercept an identified a/c. Contact was made and both a/c were pancaked and landed back at 19:25 hours.
16 August, El Bassa	2 a/c maintained at readiness during the day, but no 'scrambles' were called for.
17 August El Bassa	2 a/c were maintained at readiness from dawn to mid-day. At 09:16 hours F/Lt. Selby and P/O White were 'scrambled' over base gaining angels to intercept e/a approaching the coast. They received various vectors but were unable to gain sight of the e/a ordered to pancake at 10:20 hours. 11 a/c returned to Shandur landing there at 19:20 hours. The majority of the detached ground crews also returned.
18 August Shandur	During the morning, the remainder of the detached a/c and personnel returned to Shandur and by 13:00 hours 2 a/c were at readiness. Readiness was maintained until dusk.

19 August Shandur	2 a/c were maintained at readiness from dawn to duck. At 15:38 hours Sgts. Wiseman and McPherson were 'scrambled to patrol at maximum height to intercept e/a. The e/a turned away whilst still a great distance away and our a/c laned back at base at 15:58 hours. A great deal of formation flying, and aerobatics were carried out in the evening, but dust storms prevented any practice.
20 August, Shandur	2 a/c maintained at readiness from dawn. F/Lt. Verity and Sgt. Wright were 'scrambled' over base to angels 25 to intercept a bogey. The bogey was identified as friendly, and our a/c were pancaked and landed aback at 08:25 hours. At 10:54 hours Sgts. Jones and Edwards were 'scrambled' over base to maximum height to attempt to intercept a high-flying e/a. Our a/c reached height at 34,500 feet over Ismalia. The e/a was then above them at 36,000 feet and our a/c were unable to climb up to it. They followed it down to Suez and the e/a then made off Westwards. Sgt. Jones developed and oil leak and so landed at 12:05 hours. Sgt. Edwards continued to chase until he was ordered to pancake and landed at 12:25 hours. At 14:11 hours F/Lt. Selby and P/O Speck were 'scrambled' over base to angels 20 to intercept an e/a approaching base. When 40 miles away the e/a turned away and when our a/c (in pursuit) reached 70 miles from base they were ordered to return and pancaked at 14:49 hours. At 15:00 hours the Squadron was released pending a move. Much more flying training was carried out during the day.
21 August, Shandur	The advance ground party left for L.G. 85.
22 August L.G. 85	Our a/c and advance party had arrived at LG 85 by 13:00 hours to reform 243 Wing. The remainder of the Squadron personnel arrived by road before dusk.
23 August L.G. 85	Air tests in preparation for the night flying were flown during the day. At 21:45 hours the first a/c was airborne on intruder patrols over the German support area of the Alamein Line and was followed at intervals of 20-minutes by a further 5 a/c. Visibility was good, and all patrols were carried out at a low height. Particular attention was paid to the two tracks running Southeast and South-South-East from Daba but no movement of enemy transport was observed. Some tents and small encampments were strafed during the patrols but with no visible effects.
24 August L.G. 39	All our a/c had landed by 01:15 hours. At 19:50 hours 11 a/c were airborne for Burg el Arab where night readiness was to be carried out at LG 39. At 21:45 hours W/O Joyce D.F.M. was airborne to investigate A.A. and photographic flares over the coast to the Northeast of Burg el Arab. He could find no e/a over this position and so flew 8 to 10 miles Northwest of LG 85, where he discovered an e/a dropping bombs 15-16 miles to the Southeast of his position. This e/a too was lost, but when approaching Burg el Arab at 22:50 hours, he saw a JU 88 about 16 miles East of Burg el Arab at 7,000 feet going Northwest towards burg el Arab. W/O Joyce manoeuvred until he got 2/300 yards behind the e/a, which took evasive action. He closed to 40 yards and gave the e/a gun burst causing it to explode in the air. The e/a crashed at 23:10 hours at 490905 (Cairo sheet). W/O Joyce landed at 23:15 hours. At 22:05 hours 9 more patrols of single a/c were flown over the Alamein Line and covering the Fuka and Daba areas.
25 August L.G. 39 & L.G. 85	At 01:55 hours Many tents and MTs were strafed without visible results. A train was observed just West of Daba but very intense light A.A. prevented an attack being made. 2 a/c were sent to investigate point 878262 (Matruk sheet) where 200 MT's stationary were found on a new track leading East to West below the escarpment. The same track was examined earlier and found empty. This force appears localised on a front 1 mile with a depth of 2-3 miles. The MTs were seen further West than 3 miles. All a/c returned to base by dawn. At 21:40 hours F/Lt. Verity was airborne for Burg el Arab from where he made a local patrol without results. At 22:40 hours S/Ldr. Matthews and W/O Joyce were airborne on a local patrol. They flew at 8,000 feet over Alamein, but nothing seen, and no e/a encountered. They landed at Burg el Arab at 23:55 hours.

| 26 August | At 04:35 hours P/O Speck was airborne on patrol. He went along the coast as far as Ras Gibeisa then came in and searched the railway line for a train. Squirted a building near Sidi Abd el Rahman without visible effect, then patrolled South down the Alamein Line for a distance of some 20 miles and returned on a parallel course 5 to 6 miles to the West of the line at a height of 300 feet. No movements or concentrations were observed, and he landed back at 05:55 hours. At 19:35 hours 7 a/c were airborne for Burg el Arab for readiness from there. At 19:58 hours F/Lt. Selby and P/O Speck were airborne for a recce of the Central and Southern Sectors of the Alamein Line to look for a southern movement of enemy transport. The recce was carried out at 300 feet, but no movement was seen. They landed at Burg el Arab. The 7 a/c at Burg el Arab carried out intruder patrols over Alamein and the Daba area, strafing tents and MT's, some Ack/Ack opposition was encountered. Another 6 patrols were flown during the night from base with some results. All our a/c returned to base by dawn. |

27 August
L.G. 85

Between 21:15 Hours and 04:30 hours 7 intruder patrols were carried out from LG 85 and LG 39. Sundry camps, tents and MTs were strafed, and a Breda Gun was silenced. Despite the Full Moon no e/activity took place over the area and 6 a/c held at readiness were not used.

28 August

With the rising of the moon came the Hun to indulge in some fairly intense bombing of neighbouring LG's, 8 a/c 'scrambled to intercept but no visuals were obtained, 7 of the a/c landed at Burg el Arab from where intruder patrols were flown over the Alamein and Daba area and much strafing carried out. The Hun paid a return visit at 04:00 hours and another 9 a/c were 'scrambled' to intercept. P/O Joyce D.F.M. got a visual of an e/a at 6,00 feet going West. He chased him climbing to 12,000 feet where he shot him down 6 miles South-South-West of base. At about the same time F/Sgt. Johnson was shot down by a single engine fighter aboutn8 miles Southwest of base. F/Sgt. Johnson bailed out and escaped with shrapnel wounds and burns. Despite an intensive search, no wreckage of an e/a was discovered, where W/O Joyce claimed his victim crashed, and it is reluctantly concluded that the supposed e/a was in fact F/Sgt. Johnson. No damage resulted from bombing on the LG.

29 August
L.G. 85

12 a/c made intruder patrols during the night of the 29th to 30th August over Alamein and Daba. The usual strafing of tents and MTs was carried out. Large clouds of dust from the movement of large numbers of transport were observed towards the South of the Alamein Line, these were strafed without any visible results.

30 – 31 August
L.G. 85

At 19:25 hours 6 a/c took off for Burg el Arab for readiness from there. A further 6 a/c were held in readiness at base.
At 03:30 hours the Hun again paid a visit in some strength to the neighbouring LGs in this area. Our a/c took off to attempt to intercept. P/O Joyce D.F.M. was patrolling LG 39 at 7-9,000 feet when he saw bombs dropping near LG 85. He observed tracer from this e/a so went towards it. The e/a passed beneath him at 7,500 feet and he recognised it as a JU 88. He carried out a rear attack and the JU 88 burst into flames and crashed. The CO, S/Ldr, Johnston was patrolling over base at 7,000 feet when he saw a JU 898 passing on a shallow dive. He turned after the JU 88 and, closing, gave it a short burst. He saw strike on the port engine and behind the cockpit. The JU 88 spiralled away to the left and crashed on the ground bursting into flames. A third pilot was unlucky in that although he obtained two visuals of a JU 88, each time he turned into it they approached head on and passed within yards of each other. No bombs fell on the LG and no doubt the loss of 2 – JU 88's will teach the Hun to respect 73 Squadron Base. The enemy land forces commenced to attack in the southern sector of the Alamein Line at 04:00 hours.

AIR 27/631/17 & AIR 27/631/18 Pilot Ops Report

September 1942:

1 September L.G. 85	At 03:30 hours there was a slight attack by e/a on neighbouring LGs and 12 a/c took off to intercept them. The raid was short lived, and no visuals were obtained. A weather recce was carried by F/Lt. Selby over the Alamein positions.
1 & 2 September L.G. 85	During the night 10 interception patrols were flown without any visuals being obtained. 2 a/c carried out a weather recce over the frontal areas at first light. No cloud, visibility clear.
2 & 3 September L.G. 85	At 19:15 hours 8 a/c, led by the CO were airborne to patrol North and South of Burg el Arab station. No e/a were encountered, and all a/c landed without incident at 20:20 hours. We now had 6 a/c at readiness at base and another 6 a/c at readiness at Burg el Arab. There was some slight bombing over this and adjoining LG's during the night, and between 03:00 and 06:00 hours 5 interception patrols were flown. P/O Joyce D.F.M., whilst patrolling Burg el Arab at 04:30 hours, saw an ME 110 immediately below him going east. He closed to 150 yards and gave a 1 second burst observed 'strikes' along the left wing. He suddenly had doubts as to whether the a/c was a ME 110 or a Marauder and so withheld his fire, he claims that during the next 2-minutes he could have destroyed it had he been certain. The a/c returned fire and escaped by diving away into the darkness. F/Sgt. Jones also encountered a JU 88 and fired from quarter head on. He observed strikes on the fuselage but the JU898 broke away and lost sight of it.
3 & 4 September L.G. 85	A dawn weather recce was flown. Weather – no cloud – only slight haze. At 19:35 hours 6 a/c took off, led by P/O Joyce D.F.M. and patrolled along the coast to 8 miles West of Burg el Arab at 4,000 feet. No e/a were seen and nothing on the ground except a battle away to the Southwest. Between 03:05 and 06:15 hours, 7 patrols were flown between base and the Alamein Line, but no visuals were obtained. Weather hazy.
4 & 5 September L.G. 85	4 a/c were kept at readiness for the dusk period, but no intruding e/a visited us. 6 a/c kept from readiness but were also unused. At 03:30 hours F/Lt. Selby carried out a long-range intruder patrol over Sidi Heneish and Mersa Matruk LGH's but observe no ground activity and returned to base at 06:00 hours without incident. Also, at between 03:30 and 06:15 hours 7 interception patrols between base and Burg el Arab were flown without visuals being obtained.
5 & 6 September L.G. 85	A great deal of Light Flying Training was carried out after dusk. Readiness was again maintained by 6 a/c for the morning period and 6 a/c carried out interception patrols between base and Daba without obtaining visuals. Cloud 5/10 at 3,000 feet along the coast and 15 miles inland.
6 & 7 September L.G. 85	More Light Flying Training was carried out and the usual morning readiness maintained. Interception patrols over the Alamein – Daba area were carried out by 4 a/c piloted by newly trained night operational pilots. No visuals were obtained.

7 & 8 September L.G. 85	6 a/c having been adapted for long-range patrols; it was arranged to use them for the first time over Sidi Heneish LG's. At 21:10 hours the CO S/Ldr. Johnston flew the first patrol. He proceeded along the coast at 3,000 feet arriving over the target at 22:15 hours. No activity was visible, and he landed back at base at 23:30 hours. At 22:00 hours F/Sgt. Chandler patrolled over the coast to Sidi Heneish at 5,000 feet. He also found no activity and landed back at base at 00:30 hours. At 23:00 hours F/Lt. Selby took off and whilst proceeding to Sidi Heneish via the coast, at a height of 3,000 feet, he observed a flarepath of some 20 lights at Matru Bagush. He continued to Sidi Heneish but finding nothing visible there returned to Bagush. The flarepath was still alight and as he approached, a yellow flare was fired from the air over Fuka Point. This was followed by 3 Red and 4 White verey lights from Bagush Satellite. At that moment, an e/a landed on the flarepath and taxied away. Another e/a approached to land and as it was about to touch down F/Lt. Selby strafed the flarepath from end-to-end scoring hits on the landing e/a. There was an explosion from the e/a with all its lights going out. F/Lt. Selby circled the LG and as he did so, a verey cartridge was fired from the ground and another large e/a put on its lights just 250 yards ahead and 200 feet below him. He attacked observing one strike and as he pulled away all its lights went out. He made another circuit of the LG, and this time met an e/a head on. He finished all his ammunition on this one but observed no strikes. The search lights then exposed him, so F/Lt. Selby decided to return to base, being helped in his decision by very intense Breda fire from the LG and Fuka Point. He claimed 2 e/a as damaged, and as he states that the Breda fire was directed at all the other e/a in the circuit, except hm, it is hoped that other casualties may have occurred due to their own Ack/Ack fire. He landed back at base at 01:15 hours. At 00:01 hours P/O Fairbairn went to Sidi Heneish via the coast at 4,000 feet. As he arrived over target at 01:00 hours he saw an e/a with lights on making an approach to the lighted flarepath at a height of 1,500 feet. He dived and carried out a beam attack as the e/a was holding off. The e/a landed, and P/O Fairbairn made another attack across the flarepath as the e/a slowed up. He observed a flash on the e/a which did a ground loop. The lights on the e/a plus the flarepath went out at the same time and intense accurate Light Ack/Ack fire was directed at P/O Fairbairn, 3 lights also exposed but failed to pick him up. He turned for base at 01:20 hours on account of petrol trouble. He claims 1 multi-engine e/a damaged. He landed back at base at 02:20 hours.
8 & 9 September L.G. 85	Night flying training and moon readiness was carried out as usual, but no interception or intruder patrols were flown during the night.
9 & 10 September L.G. 85	Another quiet night. Only night flying training and morning readiness being carried out.
10 & 11 September L.G. 85	All flying had to be abandoned tonight owing to very bad visibility caused by dust storms.
11 & 12 September L.G. 85	Some night flying training was carried out and the usual long-range readiness. At 23:35 hours P/O Henry patrolled the Ghazal at 3,500 feet. Visibility was very poor with cloud 6/10 at 3,000 feet and he had considerable difficulty in finding a target. He dropped a 30lb incendiary from 3,000 feet but was unable to see any results. He then dived down to 1,500 feet and strafed East to West on what he thought was the road, he then turned North and strafed tents across the beach. He returned to base landing at 00:35 hours.
12 & 13 September L.G. 85	Night flying training and the usual long-rage readiness was carried out during the night. No patrols were flown. A practice formation of 4 a/c was flown at dawn.
13 & 14 September L.G. 85	The usual night flying training was carried out and 2 a/c maintained at readiness during the night. In addition, 4 a/c carried out long-range patrols over Sidi Heneish during the night between 22:00 and 03:40 hours. No ground activity was observed either at Heneish or Fuka and no visuals were obtained. A 30lb incendiary bomb was dropped 10 miles West of Daba but failed to explode. Cloud 5/10 at 200 feet.

14 & 15 September L.G. 85	3 short-range intruder patrols were flown between 19:45 and 22:00 hours but no e/a were encountered. Another 30lb incendiary bomb, which was dropped near Ras Abu el Gurub failed to explode. Moon readiness of 4 a/c and long-range readiness was carried out during the night. Cloud 4/10 at 3,000 feet. Visibility Fair.
15 & 16 September L.G. 85	3 short-range patrols were made over Alamein and Daba. No good targets were obtained, but the enemy Ack/Ack was more active than of late. 6-8 searchlights were strafed without visible results and a bomb was dropped on the road. 5 large ships were reported 3 miles offshore from Ras Abd el Gurub. Cloud 1/10 at 3,000 feet. Visibility good and moon set at 22:30 hours. Moon readiness and long-range readiness by 4 a/c was maintained during the night.
16 & 17 September L.G. 85	Moon readiness and long-range readiness was maintained during the night. Training in dusk landings was carried out by 3 new pilots. Between 21:00 and 23:00 hours 3 intruder patrols were made over Daba and Fuka. Some strafing of tents, searchlight positions etc was carried out resulting in a strike on a searchlight. Between 01:40 and 03:45 hours 2 patrols were flown to attempt to locate a suspected enemy LG at 845250 (Daba sheet). Various odd lights were seen on the ground, but no definite traces of an LG were observed. Visibility was poor on account of haze with 10/10 cloud at 2,000 feet.
17 & 18 September L.G. 85	Between 20:15 and 23:50 hours 4 a/c went on patrol of the Fuka, Daba and Alamein areas. The first 3 a/c flew along the coast to Daba and Fuka. 1 a/c saw some shadows on the beach West of Daba and strafed the area but saw no results. The fourth a/c flew to Alamein but returned due to haze and bad visibility. The usual readiness was carried out at base. **Note: All the co-ordinates given are taken from the Daba sheet.**
18 & 19 September L.G. 85	7 a/c operating singly, carried out patrols over Daba, Alamein and Ghazal. No e/a were seen. A truck in the Daba station and 40 MTs to the North of the station were strafed without observed results. MTs were also strafed on a track running South from Daba and strikes were seen on one MT. Another a/c strafed shadows in a wadi near the depression without observed results. Much heavy Ack/Ack was encountered over Ghazal. The usual readiness was maintained at base.
19 & 20 September L.G. 85	1 Flight proceeded to Burg el Arab for readiness and intruder patrols, while the other Flight carried out readiness at base. During the night 7 independent sorties were carried out over enemy territory covering the areas around Ras Abd el Gurub and Sidi Abd el Rahman, all along the Alamein Line and 20 miles inland. 1 a/c flew along the North line of the depression. No movements of importance were seen, but at 845250, there were about 6 groups of 12 stationary MT's about 200yards apart, A further 20 vehicles were seen stationary and well dispersed at 868607 (Daba sheet). P/O Jones dropped a 30lb incendiary bomb from 3,000 feet on a camp of 2 EPIP's and 15 smaller tents at 855304. The burst was seen but no fire. S/Ldr. Johnston strafed some tents East of Ghazal and other isolated ones on the way back from the front line. Visibility generally was good.
20 & 21 September L.G. 85	6 a/c did readiness at Burg el Arab and a further 6 a/c at base. 12 individual intruder patrols and one patrol of 2 a/c were flown over the Daba and Alamein areas and as far South as the Qattara Depression. P/O Joyce D.F.M. was also 'scrambled to patrol Marriut at 7,000 feet. An e/a approached at 12,000 feet but withdrew before contact could be made. P/O Warburton made 2 sorties strafing from 5600 feet groups of MTY's on 8425 and 8526. 1 vehicle exploded and caught fire; other vehicles were hit but results were not visible. P/O Double strafed 30 dispersed MTs at 8430 observing 1 hit. Sgt. Wilson scored strikes on MT's widely dispersed in groups of 20 at 8629. F/Lt. Miller who made 2 sorties strafed a light at 837251 where a fire was probably started. He dropped a 30lb incendiary bomb, but this was not seen to burst. F/Sgt. Chandler started 2 fires amongst MTs at 8525. Other groups of MTY's and tents were attacked, but no results were observed.

| 21 September | *The following message was received today from Headquarters, RAF ME "On the recommendation of the Air Officer Commanding in Chief, His Majesty the King has been graciously pleased to award the Distinguished Flying Cross [DFC] to Acting Flight Lieutenant J. J. Badger of 73 Squadron, for courage, determination, and devotion to duty."* |

21 & 22 September
L.G. 85

The usual readiness was carried out at base and at Burg el Arab. 1 a/c was 'scrambled' from base but landed without incident as the plots were false. 7 intruder patrols were flown along the coast to Daba and South to the Depression. Visibility was very poor due to heavy haze, and little was seen. At 8526 some widely dispersed MTs and tents were strafed. Hits were scored and a fire started. A small body of MTs on the move was strafed at 8529 but owing to clouds of dust it was not possible to observe results. Much light Ack/Ack and machine gun fire was encountered at 8424 and near Ghazal.

22 & 23 September
L.G. 85

Readiness was maintained at base and Burg el Arab. 4 a/c were 'scrambled' over base and Burg el Arab on interception patrols, but no e/a were seen, and all landed without incident. 4 other a/c made intruder patrols over the Daba area strafing MTY's at 852282 and 850280. Some hits were observed. Considerable Ack/Ack and machine gun fire was encountered. P/O Fairbairn and P/O Gill carried out an offensive recce of the Daba – Fuka road at a height of 1,000 feet. MTs in groups of 10 were observed parked one side of the road all the way along. MT's and sightings at Daba and tentage at Sidi Abu el Rahman were strafed without observed results. Much Ack/Ack was encountered.

23 & 24 September
L.G. 85

The usual readiness was maintained at Burg el Arab and base. Between 20:55 and 02:00 hours 7 a/c were 'scrambled' on individual interception patrols over Burg el Arab and Alamein. Bombs were seen bursting Northwest of Burg el Arab, but no e/a were seen. F/Lt. Miller and P/O Wiseman were airborne to make a long-range intruder patrol over Sidi Heneish. Wellingtons were bombing the Sidi Heneish LG's and our a/c patrolled 5 miles out at sea until the last Wellington had left the targets. A large fire was seen at LG 13, which our a/c orbited for some time without finding any suitable targets for strafing. On their way back to base they investigated Daba and Fuka without results. Some movement was observed along a track from Southeast towards Daba. They landed back at base at 03:45 hours.

24 & 25 September
L.G. 85

6 a/c were maintained at readiness at base throughout the night with a further 6 a/c at Burg el Arab. Between 22:30 and 00:30 hours F/Sgt. Chandler and P/O Jones carried out a long-range intruder patrol over Sidi Heneish. They arrived over target at 23:25 hours and orbited at 6,000 feet for 25-minutes under heavy Ack/Ack fire. On return to base at 03:00 to 04:00 hours noticed chance light flashing in the Northeast corner of 7730. Took off again to investigate light but ground mist and low cloud obscured target so flew to Italian HQ at Ras Gehensa and dropped bombs with unobserved results. Between 03:35 and 05:05 hours Sgt. McPherson and Sgt. Gadd patrolled the area South of Sidi el Rahman at 500 feet encountering inaccurate Breda fire from one gun, which was silenced. Widely dispersed MT's and tents were strafed under fire from Breda's. Results were not observed.

25 & 26 September
L.G. 85

In addition to the usual readiness at base and LG 39, 4 long-range intruder patrols were undertaken in the Sidi Heneish area. Landing Lights at LG 13 and LG 12 were investigated at 20:30 hours by P/O Warburton and P/O Henry respectively. At LG 12 20 plus e/a were seen widely dispersed on the ground, but offensive action could not be taken at 23:50 hours. Heavy Ack/Ack at Ghazal and Bofor shells were encountered. Between 23:15 and 00:10 hours 1 a/c was 'scrambled to the Waiting Room and received a vector to Alexandria Bay where it orbited until ordered to land. S/Ldr Johnston also took off, but no e/a were seen. Between 02:30 and 04:15 hours 2 a/c patrolled the area between Burg el Arab and Alamein without incident.

26 & 27 September L.G. 85	Readiness at base and Burg el Arab was maintained throughout the night. 8 sorties were made in the Burg el Arab, Fuka, Sidi Heneish areas. Between 21:55 and 23:00 hours Sgt. Beard whilst on a standing patrol was directed to the Waiting Room where he orbited at 8,000 feet. Several vectors were given but nothing was seen. Between 23:00 and 01:30 hours F/Lt. Selby patrolled Sidi Heneish area for 35-minutes encountering heavy Ack/Ack East of Fuka Point. Between 24:00 and 00:55 hours whilst patrolling the roads between Burg el Arab and Alamein Line, Sgt. Wilson was vectored on to a strafing e/a. He obtained a visual as the a/c approached, but was unable to get in a burst before ne lost sight of the e/a.
27 & 28 September L.G. 85	Between 21:25 and 03:00 hours 9 patrols of the roads between Burg el Arab and the Alamein Line were made without incident. Between 20:00 and 22:40 hours in a long-range intruder over Sidi Heneish, F/Lt. Miller spotted various bright White lights 15 miles inland between Fuka and Daba. They illuminated for a few seconds then douse but with no particular frequency. a/c were at readiness during the night both at base and Burg el Arab
28 & 29 September L.G. 85	Between 23:20 and 00:05 hours during readiness, P/O Baker was 'scrambled to investigate a Bogey 10 miles North of the Alamein Line. He identified it as Boston, then continued to patrol the coast on a weather recce. Visibility was very poor due to haze and no further patrols were carried out.
29 & 30 September L.G. 85	The usual readiness was maintained at base and Burg el Arab. Whilst 6 patrols were carried out over the coastal areas as far as Sidi Heneish. Heavy Ack/Ack was met with just East of Daba when F/Lt. Miller went down to investigate some Green verey lights. P/O Fairbairn observed some flare and bombs over Matruk and whilst orbiting Heneish was plotted by a night fighter lights and by searchlights. Nothing of interest was seen in the Alamein area patrols.

AIR 27/631/19 & AIR 27/631/20 Pilot Ops Report
October 1942:
2nd Battle of El Alamein – 'Operation Lightfoot' 23 October to 11 November 1942
[For further details of this battle refer to Chapter 5 – D. El Alamein]

30 September & 1 October L.G. 85	The weather was unfavourable for long-range intruders, but 3 coastal patrols were carried out in the Burg el Arab – Alamein area. Visibility was poor and the a/c were ordered to land at period of flying.
1 October L.G. 85	S/Ldr. Johnson relinquished his command of the Squadron on posting, becoming time expired with effect from October 1st, 1942.
1 & 2 October L.G. 85	a/c were held at readiness both at base and Burg el Arab throughout the night. 3 patrols were made in the area Southwest of Sidi Abdu el Rahman where small groups of MT's and isolated vehicles were strafed without visible results. Further patrols of the coast and road between Burg el Arab and the Alamein Line were made by 4 Hurricanes on individual sorties. There were no strafing activities by the enemy and nothing of note was to be seen. Visibility generally was poor owing to haze at low levels.
2 October *L.G. 85*	*The following message has been received from HQRAFME, "On the recommendation of the AOC in Chief, His Majesty the King has been graciously pleased to award the D.F.C. to F/Lt. J. B. Selby (Now A/Squadron Leader) of 73 Squadron for courage, determination, and devotion to duty".*

2 & 3 October L.G. 85	Weather conditions over the enemy territory were responsible for the recalling of the last 2 of 5 intruders, which were sent out. An electrical storm in the Daba area nullified P/O Henry's patrol in the region. P/O Jones and F/Sgt. Chandler on individual sorties to the tracks just North of the Qattara depression strafed a few scattered transport vehicles, but no results were observed. P/O Jones spotted an e/a showing landing lights intermittently preparatory to landing but was unable to get within striking distance. The a/c held at readiness at base and Burg el Arab were not required during the night.
3 & 4 October L.G. 85	Readiness was maintained at base. Other operations had to be cancelled because of adverse weather conditions.
4 & 5 October L.G. 85	Readiness was maintained throughout the night. P/O Wilson crashed just after taking off on an intruder patrol and sustained injuries to head and hip.6 other intruder patrols were made individually in the area around Daba and to the North of the Qattara Depression. Visibility was poor due to haze and no results of strafing could be observed.
5 & 6 October L.G. 85 ***6 October*** ***L.G. 85***	Readiness on base only. ***The following message has been received from HQRAFME, "On the recommendation of the AOC in Chief, His Majesty the King has been graciously pleased to award the D.F.C. to Squadron Leader G. R. A. M. Johnston of 73 Squadron for courage, determination and devotion to duty".***
6 & 7 October L.G. 85	The weather again was unsuitable for intruder patrols, but the usual readiness was maintained at base. At 05:45 hours S/Ldr. Selbt made a recce of the Sidi Heneish and Quassaba LGs from 1,500 feet. Heneish was waterlogged, Quassaba serviceable. No a/c were observed on either LG or the dispersal pens as they appeared empty.
7 & 8 October L.G. 85	Between 20:20 and 21:25 hours 2 a/c at readiness were 'scrambled' o identify bogey a/c over base, which proved to be friendly. 3 intruder patrols to the West of the Line up to Daba area were made. P/O Fairbairn dropped a flare over LG 20 and saw 1 or 2 e/a; and store dumps close by but was immediately illuminated by 3 searchlights. 5 miles East of the aerodrome he was again picked up by 2 more searchlights. P/O Gill flew over the encampment on the coast to the West of El Rahman encountering light machine gun fire and about10 miles West of Daba was met with Breda fire guarding groups of MT's.
8 & 9 October L.G. 85	5 intruder patrols were made during the night and a weather recce at dawn. At 21: hours F/O McGill scored hits on an MT vehicle and one of a group of 5 lights, the latter in face of accurate Breda fire. 6 searchlights, which failed to pick up Sgt. Smyth Northeast of Ghazal were strafed without results. The dawn recce gave indication of floods at the foot of the escarpment South of Daba.
9 & 10 October L.G. 85	Intruder patrols over Daba and Fuka were made during the night. 1 bomb aimed at Daba station failed to explode and nom results were observed when 8 searchlights were strafed. Heavy Ack/Ack ang bomb bursts were observed in the Daba area and accurate heavy Ack/Ack co-operating with searchlights were encountered Northeast of Ghazal. Plotting lights giving position direction and height of our a/c were used extensively in the Daba area. At dawn F/Lt. Ellis made a weather recce as far as Sidi Heneish.
10 & 11 October L.G. 85	There was no flying due to bad weather.
11 & 12 October L.G. 85	At 19:45 hours 1 a/c took off but returned to base almost immediately as weather unfit for night operations.
12 & 13 October L.G. 85	6 intruder patrols over Heneish and Daba areas were carried out during the night. F/O McGill strafed a group of MT's hitting 3. More plotting lights were observed near Heneish, whilst heavy and light Ack/Ack were in action at Daba.

13 & 14 October L.G. 85	P/O Jones strafed a reported Storch LG at 828319 but saw no results. 6 searchlights from, proximity of LG 20 failed to pick him up. S/Ldr. Selby strafed the road from Fuka to Ghazal causing a bright flash at one point. P/O Wiseman repeated the CO's performance. F/O McGill hit 1 of 10 camouflaged dumps which were illuminated by his flare. P/O Warburton was directed to a store dump at 864289 but low cloud obscured target. P/O Charlesworth patrolled coast as far as Ras Gibesa.
14 & 15 October L.G. 85	First Official news of the push against the enemy was given to the Squadron by AOC Western Desert when he landed in a Fiesler Storch. No date was given but a reminder to the older members of old tracks to be retraced and the consequent hardening of living conditions. He recalled the last time the Squadron was his audience at Gambut and remarked that the faces were much cleaner. 3 a/c piloted by the CO, F/Lt. Miller and P/O Chandler combined in an attack on a group of searchlights at 864310 and though under fire from many light Ack/Ack guns strafed their objectives extinguishing one. More searchlights and heavy Ack/Ack were encountered by F/O McGill at 807320 but he continued on and strafed the camp at 795320. Sgt. Beard did not return from a long-range patrol.
15 & 16 October L.G. 85	News received on the evening of the 15th that Sgt. Beard had belly landed near Fayum. Only 2 intruder patrols were made, 1 as far as Garawla without incident. The other to Fuka area where 2 searchlights at 07320 and 6 searchlights at 807317 were in action.
16 & 17 October L.G. 85	On the afternoon of the 16th a sever sandstorm blew up, curtailing all operations. Heavy showers followed during the night. At daybreak many of the tents were down. A word of praise for the messing staff who excelled themselves under great difficulties.
17 & 18 October L.G. 85	Night operations NIL, after a continuation of sandstorm. Sgt Beard returned to Squadron with a slight bump on his head and an account of his adventure on the night of the 14th. Whilst on his way to Daba he had spotted a JU 88 heading North, given chase and after an hour flying out to sea had closed the distance to 50 yards. By this time the planes were almost at sea level and as he fired and saw strikes on starboard wing group propeller struck the sea. He managed to pull out and the JU 88 had disappeared. Sgt. Beard set course for the coast by the stars as R/T was out of action. He flew on without sighting the coast and did not pick up any landmark until he spotted flashing beacon. A nearby LG had too many dispersed a/c about to land in safety and as patrol was almost finished, he belly landed as near to the beacon. 1 JU 88 was claimed as damaged by Sgt. Beard.
19 October *L.G. 85*	*Today we lose the services of F/Lt. Swinburne who, as adjutant has been greatly appreciated by all. He goes to HQME.*
19 & 20 October L.G. 85	There was little activity tonight on part of the pilots. 3 out of 4 a/c which went out on intruder patrols had to return on account of engine trouble. P/O Warburton patrolled between Fuka and Quassaba but no movements.
20 & 21 October L.G. 85	Several new pilots arrived to make up the Squadron strength, which had been depleted by the posting of F/Lt. Joyce, P/O Henry, Sgts. Farley and Henfrey. F/Lt. Ambrose, F/O's Smith and Leggett, F/Sgt. Phillips, Sgts. Hiltz and Bennett are all welcome. In night operations Sgt. MacKinnon did not return after his second sortie with F/Lt. Miller and P/O Chandler he took off to strafe a camp 2 miles West of LG 20. Shortly after breaking formation, on account of low cloud, Ack/Ack combined with searchlights opened up and Sgt. MacKinnons a/c was seen illuminated in cross Breda fire. Many hits were scored over a wide area on tentage and MT's. A Staff car disintegrated under fire from F/O Pain. Our redoubtable neighbours, The Bostons, were covered by the CO on their return from a bombing expedition.

21 & 22 October L.G. 85	Several camps in the Daba area were successfully straffed; huts, tents and MT's being hit. Meanwhile anti-strafing patrols were carried out behind lines, but no bandits were seen. Sgt. Rawson had to crash land when his a/c developed a glycol leak. Pilot uninjured but a/c Cat. III.
22 & 23 October L.G. 85	Warning was given that the Squadron would be moving to L.G. 89 on the next 2 days. Passes to Alexandria stopped. The offensive id due to begin. Our intruder patrols concentrated attacks in the Southwest of Sidi Abd el Rahman, scoring hits on a light tank, machine guns, many groups of MT's, tentage and 1 light Ack/Ack gun. A bomb was dropped on LG 18 where 4 or 5 Macchi202's was seen. Sgt. Harris who went on an intruder to Daba did not return.
23 & 24 October L.G. 85 and L.G. 89	1 detachment moved off in the afternoon to prepare the camp at LG 89. The Flight operating from Burg el Arab at night returned to the new base in the morning, whilst the remainder followed, and everyone was settled in by mid-day on the 24th. The night operations were highly successful. 26 intruder patrols were made in the coastal area where 5 field guns were damaged, 3 ammunition carriers blown up as well as a small dump. 26 MT's, tents and huts were damaged, 1 fire was started, and 2 Breda's were silenced. This was the prelude to the opening of the Army's offensive at dawn.
24 & 25 October L.G. 89	Despite poor visibility 7 intruder patrols were made and groups of MT's were successfully strafed in the wadi's North of the Qattara Depression by Sgt. Davies, P/O Chandler, and F/Sgt. Marsh. Various 'scrambles' were made but without result.
25 & 26 October L.G. 89	Throughout the night, our a/c operating from a forward base patrolled the line. Several hostiles were chased away from their objectives, During the long-range intruder patrol over Heneish P/O Chandler scored strikes on a HE111 attempting to land at LG 14 and which he claims as a probable. 30 sorties, totalling nearly 52 hours flying, gives point to the message received by S/Ldr Selby DFC from **AOC RAF Western Desert: "You and your chaps are doing grand work at night. Well, done".**
26 & 27 October L.G. 89	A good night's work resulted in Sgt. Gadd destroying 1 - JU 87 and damaging 2 more. Whilst F/Sgt. Marsh damaged 1 – JU 87 before his guns jammed. They had intercepted 12 plus e/a Stuka's orbiting LG 12 with landing lights on and the flare path lit up. F/Sgt. Marsh on a later patrol. Damaged 2 e/a which were landing at Heneish. 7 other hostiles were seen during the night on individual patrols, but only in two instances were contacts made and then without success. Tents and MTs were strafed by the CO South of Ghazal and 4 patrols were made in an attempt to direct the ASRS to a pilot in the sea of Ras el Shagig. In all, 23 sorties were made.
27 & 28 October L.G. 89	Whilst on patrol Sgt. Beard received a vector from Commander, which him on the tail of a JU 88 flying West to Alamein. He was fired at by the rear gunner but closed and fired. The JU 88 went down in a spiral turn and burst into flames when it hit the ground about 25 miles West of Alamein. 9 other patrols of the line were made without result. F/O Thompson was 'scrambled' over Alamein area and got a visual 6,000 feet below but lost sight. 2 a/c were recalled after being 'scrambled'. P/O Gill on an intruder to Heneish got heavy Ack/Ack and Breda fire from Fuka LG and more Breda fire from Heneish line. On his return he had a visual of an e/a going West but lost sight. P/O Chandler strafed 6 MTs on LG 104. 3 other long-range intruder patrols were made over the Heneish area but had nothing to report.
28 & 29 October L.G. 89	High activity was made up of 5 'scrambles', 8-line patrols and 6 long-range intruder patrols. None of the pilots were 'scrambled' over base and Alamein obtained visuals of e/a. P/O Chandler however, whilst on - line patrol chased a JU 88 as far as Daba but was unable to get within range. Several vectors were received during the line patrol and bomb burst and flares were seen but contact could not be made. P/O McGill on 1 of 6 patrols to Heneish area dropped a bomb amongst scattered MT's near Fuka. Little else to report other than heavy Ack/Ack combined with searchlights was encountered at LG 12 and at Matruh, P/O Smyth experienced Breda fire and searchlights.

29 & 30 October L.G. 89	F/Lt. Miller and Sgt. Gadd patrolled LG 14 at Heneish but saw no hostile e/a, though there was some ground activity, and the flare path was extinguished when Red verey lights were fired. Railway tracks at Dabam.T. near Fuka and on the Gazala road were strafed. Light Ack/Ack with searchlights were in operation at Daba. 16 - line patrols were made without result. Heavy artillery fire was seen and 2 bomb bursts on our side. No contacts were made with e/a.
30 & 31 October L.G. 89	Mist and haze curtailed the night operations which consisted of 4 - line patrols and a layer patrol of 6 a/c. F.O McGill was vectored to Daba at 12,000 feet and then told to pancake. Sgt. Gadd also under control of Commander saw e/a exhausts at 4,000 feet when he was at 15,000 feet.

AIR 27/631/21 & AIR 27/631/22 Pilot Ops Report
November 1942:

31 October & 1 November L.G. 89	Several patrols were made over the line without result. For the second night our pilots were subjected to Bofor fire from our own lines. Long-range patrols were sent out over the Heneish are tom intercept possible e/a JU 87's but no activity was seen except our own bombers attacking Heneish station. Some MTs was strafed on the road East of Daba.
1 & 2 November L.G. 89	No e/a activity was observed during our patrols over the line. Sgt. Edwards reported that our army had broken through the enemy lines in the Northern Sector and was pushing West and South.
2 & 3 November L.G. 89	Line and layer patrols were maintained throughout the night. A twin-engine a/c was seen but not contacted by F/Sgt. Phillips. During long-range intruders to Heneish flares and bombs were being dropped on Daba without opposition.
3 & 4 November L.G. 89	A good night's work of strafing MTs in the Fuka area was marred bythe failure of F/Lt Miller to return. F/O Waechter was also reported missing but returned to the Squadron the following day. The controls had seized, and his a/c burnt out after crashing. S/Ldr. Selby, DFC. F/O McGill. P/OP Jones and P/O Gill were all successful in strafing MTs, tents, and huts. **The days on which Tobruk was recaptured from the German and Italian AXIS Forces by the Allied Forces.**
4 & 5 November L.G. 89	2 a/c were 'scrambled' at dawn over Alamein line but saw no e/a. In the morning "A" party move off to unknown destination. All pilots and a/c remain behind with "B" party to continue operations.
5 & 6 November L.G. 89	Gala Night – All a/c were fitted with long-range tanks ready for a dusk and dawn straffing attack on the retreating enemy. 12 a/c operating in pairs arrived in the Garawla – Fuka area just before dusk and straffed hundreds of MTs on the roads, many were carrying troops. Heavy and light Ack/Ack also intense Breda fire was encountered – various gun positions were straffed and at least 1-Breda silenced. All a/c returned to base but 2 were minus long-range tanks, another had been hit in the wing and another in the main tank. The dawn effort was not nearly as successful. Our army had pushed so rapidly that it was impossible to distinguish enemy troops near Garawla. Layer patrol was operated by 2 a/c along the coast to Heneish but no hostiles were seen. The pilots reported everything quiet as far as Fuka. Orders came in the morning for "B" party to be one, one hour's notice Tents were struck, and everybody was straining at the leash. The move was delayed, and night operations went forward as usual.

6 & 7 November L.G. 89	The first long-range patrol however encountered heavy rain cloud before reaching Daba and had to return. Meanwhile another patrol had taken off and was recalled. At midnight a weather recce was made which confirmed the above report but at dawn the weather had cleared, and 6 a/c went on a layer patrol Heneish to Matruh. No hostiles were seen.
7 & 8 November L.G. 21	Orders were received for the a/c to proceed to L.G. 21 where "A" were established. "B" party after seeing the a/c off proceeded in convoy to L.G. 13 near Sidi Meneish. Movement in convoy was slow and tedious, particularly along the coast road where jams occurred every few minutes. Night operations were limited to 3-line patrols and 2 scrambles. No e/a were seen. The tightening of belts was already in force, water also being rationed. Beer became a memory and cigarettes a highly rated acquisition. But spirits are high because we are no longer stagnating. There is plenty of work for everyone and no time to brood. Evidence of the enemy's rapid retreat is seen everywhere. Burnt out tanks and lorries littered the roadside and scores of planes, many of which were serviceable, had been abandoned on the LG's.
8 & 9 November L.G. 21	Another night of anti-strafing Patrols passed uneventfully and by morning "B" party had reached L.G. 13 and were ready to receive a/c. "A" party were quickly on the move for L.G. 155 away South of Barrani. The wreckage of F/Lt. Miller's a/c and his grave close by were seen near Fuka.
9 & 10 November L.G. 13	Opportunities arose during the day for a swim at Heneish. A great refresher. 2 mines exploded on the LG but did not cause any damage to the Squadron. During the night 4 a/c carried out a dusk patrol between base and Sidi Barrani in anticipation of e/a strafing then road but there was no hostile activity. At dawn a smaller patrol of 4 a/c but again there was no enemy activity.
10 & 11 November L.G. 13	3 a/c carried out a dusk layer patrol between base and Sidi Barrani but there was no enemy activity. In the morning "B" party were on the move to L.G. 155.
11 & 12 November L.G. 155	3 a/c carried out a dusk patrol over Halfaya but found no enemy activity. Between 05:15 and 07:25 hours 12 a/c flown by the CO, P/O Chandler, F/O Thompson, |P/O Smyth, F/Lt. Ellis DFM, F/O Pain, P/O Wiseman, F/Sgt. Phillips, and Sgts. Davies, Wright and Beard and F/Lt Ambrose DFC strafed the road between Tobruk and Gazala. Much MTs was found travelling West at least 3 fires were started. Tobruk was being evacuated by the enemy who was setting alight very many of his abandoned dumps and vehicles.
12 & 13 November L.G. 155	"B" party arrived in the morning and were straightaway re-directed to Gambut West. 11 a/c took off shortly before dawn to strafe the rad between Gazala and Tmimi but did not find many targets. There was, however, some MT activity on Tmimi LG and this was attended to. On returning to base, they found a thick mist over the LG. 7 a/c landed at other aerodromes where conditions were better.
13 & 14 November Gambut West	On the13th the remainder of the Squadron started for Gambut West and arrived in the evening of the 14th. The Squadron did not operate
14 & 15 November Gambut West	At 04:30 hours 4 a/c flown by the CO, W/O Plenderleith, F/O Maechter and Sgt. Davies took off for Benghazi area and strafed MTs on the roads in that area.
15 & 16 November Gambut West	At dusk F/O/Thompson took off to patrol the Sollum area but had to abandon patrol as cloud was 10/10 at 1,500 feet and much haze, He took off again at dawn accompanied by P/O Gill, Sgt. Gadd, and F/Sgt. Marsh to patrol between Sollum and Gazala but there was no e/a activity.

16 & 17 November Gambut West	The Squadron maintained continuous patrols over Sollum and Tobruk between dusk and dawn, 10 a/c participating. No enemy activity was seen. In the morning, the Squadron moved to El Adem aerodrome for the purpose of talking over the night defence of Tobruk
17 & 18 November El Adem	Did not operate. No ground controls.
18 & 19 November El Adem	At17:35 hours 4 a/c took off and carried out a layer patrol over Tobruk at 2,000 – 8,000 feet. There was no enemy activity. At 19:20 hours FG/Sgt. Phillips and Sgt. Hiltz took off to strafe El Magrun aerodrome but could not locate it. At dawn 4 a/c patrolled Tobruk but again no enemy activity.
19 & 20 November El Adem	At 17:20 hours 4 a/c carried out a layer patrol over Tobruk at 2, 4, 6 and 8,000 feet. No enemy activity Sgt. Beard crashed on landing. At 23:00 hours 6 a/c 'scrambled' after e/a reported in the Gazala - Tobruk area. Flares were seen over Gazala, but no other evidence of the enemy's presence was encountered.
20 & 21 November El Adem	Between 00:55 and 05:00 hours 4 a/c carried out a layer patrol off Tobruk without incident. The Squadron carried out dusk and dawn patrols of Tobruk. Each patrol comprising 4 a/c. There was no enemy activity. During the night 1 a/c was 'scrambled' North of Tobruk but did not make contact with the intruder.
21 & 22 November El Adem	4 a/c took off and patrolled Tobruk without incident. During the night, 3 a/c 'scrambled' after an intruder who was strafing the road North of Gazala. 1 pilot, P/O Jones got a visual of a JU 88 and closed the range to 20 yards where he opened fire. Unfortunately, only one of his cannons worked and immediately afterwards he lost sight of the e/a. P/O Wiseman patrolled the Tobruk – Gazala road between 00:35 and 01:15 hours, but there was no enemy activity, P/O Jones saw an e/a strafing underneath him. He followed the strafing as far as Derna, but could not see the e/a, so re-joined the patrol which was completed without incident.
22 & 23ʳNovember El Adem	2 a/c took off at 16:40 hours and patrolled above a convoy North of Tobruk. They received several vectors but were unable to make contact with the hostile e/a. 2other a/c carried out a patrol of Tobruk between dusk and dark without incident. During the night 1 a/c was 'scrambled' over Tobruk but did not see any enemy activity. In addition, 7 a/c maintained a continuous patrol over Tobruk – Gazala road during the night without seeing any hostile activity. Except for P/O Charlesworth, who got a visual of a low flying JU 88 strafing the road. He gave chase, but the e/a disappeared rapidly to the North Werst and was lost sight of.
23 & 24 November El Adem	At 05: 05 hours 3 a/c carried out a patrol over Tobruk at 2, 4 and 6,000 feet without incident. 1 a/c was 'scrambled' and vectored 80 miles Northwest of Tobruk but did not see the hostile e/a. At 17:15 hours 4 more a/c took off simultaneously and carried out a layer patrol without incident, F/Lt Ambrose DFC crashed on landing, a/c Cat. II. A similar patrol of 4 a/c maintained a continuous patrol of the Tobruk – Gazala road without seeing any e/a.
24 & 25 November El Adem	4 a/c carried out a dusk layer patrol of Tobruk and 3 a/c a dawn layer patrol. In both cases the duty ended without incident. Continuous patrols by 6 a/c over the Tobruk – Gazala road between dusk and dawn were similarly uneventful. In addition, there were 3 'scrambles' of 1 a/c during the night but nothing was seen of the e/a.
25 & 26 November El Adem	3 a/c carried out the dusk patrol and 4 a/c the dawn patrol of Tobruk. The patrols ended without incident, except that Sgt. Wright crashed on returning at sunrise, a/c Cat. II. In addition 2 a/c patrolled the Tobruk – Gazala road without seeing any e/a.

26 & 27 November Detachment: Bu Amud	A detachment of 7 a/c and pilots flew to Bu Amud providing dusk to dawn patrols of 3 a/c each of Tobruk and also a patrol of Tobruk – Gazala road. The night was uneventful. The detachment consisted of F/Lt. Ellis DFFM as CO, F/O Waechter, P/O Wiseman, P/O Jones, P/O Warburton, F/Sgt. Marsh, and Sgt. Hiltz. The remainder of the Squadron at El Adem did not operate.
27 & 28 November Detachment: Bu Amud	The detachment carried out dusk and dawn patrols of Tobruk, 3 a/c in each case, and also 3 patrols of 1 a/c over the Tobruk – Gazala road and a standing patrol over El Adem between the 21:30 and 01:00 hours while a force of 40 Wellingtons was taking off to bomb Marble Arch aerodrome. All the patrols were without incident.
28 & 29 November El Magrun	2 a/c from Bu Amud went to on dusk patrol and 1 a/c on dawn patrol of Tobruk. No e/a was seen. At El Magrun where the strength of the Squadron was now established, 3 a/c were 'scrambled' at dawn when bombs were dropped nearby. Sgt. Davies saw road strafing as far as Aghelia but could not make contact with the e/a. F/O Davis and S/Ldr. Selby DFC both saw bombs exploding but did not obtain a visual. F/O Smith closed with an ME 110 which was road strafing from 2,000 feet and attacked from astern at a range of 300 yards. He saw strikes on the fuselage and then gave a final burst as the e/a turned out to sea.
29 & 30 November El Magrun	The detachment put up dusk and dawn patrols of 2 a/c over Tobruk and in addition 2 a/c were 'scrambled' and given vectors. No e/a were seen. The defiles Werst of Agheila were the objective of 4 strafing patrols, one of which returned early with engine trouble. The only car seen was hit by F/Sgt. Phillips. Otherwise, there were no other objectives seen. 2 a/c which were on readiness at Benina were 'scrambled' at dawn. Flares and strafing were reported by F/Lt. Ambrose DFC, but he did not get visual. F/O Davis saw bombs exploding, then contacted a JU 88, 3 miles out to sea off Tocra. He closed to 150 yards at 7,000 feet, fired and saw a strike on the port wing. He received return fire and lost sight, but the e/a was seen to burst into flame and crash Northeast of Benghazi. 3 road patrols were made at dawn between Benghazi and Agedabia. Flares strafing and bombing were seen but no e/a could be contacted.
30 November & 1 December El Magrun & El Adem	At Bu Amud 2 a/c did dusk patrol over Tobruk without result. P/O Jones was 'scrambled' before dawn and F/O Waechter did the dawn patrol. Neither of these pilots saw any e/a. 2 a/c which were at readiness at Benina did a dawn patrol of Benghazi and the area North of Tocra but saw no e/a. 4 a/c from base strafed the roads from Agheila to Marble Arch. A few lorries were seen and 2 were hit. Tentage was also strafed. P/O Smyth had a visual of a JU 88 but lost sight when it entered cloud. Breda fire was encountered at various points along the road. A road protection patrol was made at dawn by 4 a/c between Benghazi and Agedabia without signs of enemy activity.

AIR 27/631/23 & AIR 27/631/24 Pilot Ops Report

December 1942:

1 & 2 December El Magrun & Bu Amud	Atb Bu Amud F/Lt. Ellis DFM and P/O Jones made a dusk patrol of Tobruk without incident. P/O Warburton and F/Sgt. Marsh were 'scrambled' at 04:25 hours but saw no e/a, they continued to patrol Tobruk until 07:00 hours. F/Sgt. Marsh saw a stick of incendiaries dropped across the road 8 miles Northwest of Gazala but doid not get a visual of the e/a. 3 strafing patrols on the roads West of Agheila. No transport was seen but tentage and huts were strafed, and 2 fires were started. Very accurate Breda fire from the defiles. 6 a/c patrolled the rods from Tocra to Agedabia but saw no enemy activity.

2 & 3 December El Magrun & Bu Amud	2 a/c made a dusk patrol of Tobruk and in addition 4 a/c were 'scrambled' at 18:25 hours to intercept 6 e/a. These e/a were seen to come in South of Tobruk, but contact was not made. Later P/O Wiseman and Sgt. Hiltz saw an e/a in the light of flares, but no contact was made, On the dawn patrol of 2 a/c P/O Jones was vectored on to returning Liberators. Operations from Magrun were restricted on account of bad weather. 1 road patrol as far as Benghazi was flown between 17:10 and 19:10 hours but no e/a were seen. At 02:00 hours 2 a/c took off to strafe Ras el Aali; 1 a/c returned early owing to the weather but the other continued and reached the target which he duly strafed apparently successfully. The target, a jetty was well defended, and he received much accurate Breda fire, a projected dawn patrol was cancelled because of heavy rain.
3 & 4 December El Magrun & Bu Amud	At Magrun a dusk patrol was carried out between Benghazi and Agedabia, but no enemy activity was seen. At the same time 4 a/c provided protection for a convoy which was then 560 miles out to sea from Benghazi. At 04:50 hours 4 a/c took off and were ordered to proceed to Tocra to intercept e/a. Flares were seen over Benghazi and also 3 to 4 bombs were dropped but the e/a themselves were not seen. At 06+:00 hours another a/c took off on seeing flares and Ack/Ack over Benghazi, but this had ceased by the time he reached there, and no e/a were seen. The detachment at Bu Amud, 2 a/c carried out a dusk patrol over Tobruk and a dawn patrol of 3 a/c without incident. Later on, in the morning when the detachment was off duty and resting a JU 88 was seen and 3 pilots were in the air within 3 to 4 minutes. The JU 88 however pulled away fast and was not seen again.
4 & 5 December El Magrun & Bu Amud	2 a/c patrolled the road between Benghazi and Agedabia at dusk and at dawn and a further2 a/c patrolled from Magrun to Benghazi. Both patrols were without incident.at 23:55 1 a/c was 'scrambled' after an e/a dropping flares over base and to the North, but no visual was obtained. At dawn 1 a/c patrolled Benghazi but saw nothing. A further a/c patrolled the coast 30 miles North of Benghazi and investigated a dozen small explosions but did not get a visual on an e/a. Dusk and dawn Patrols over Tobruk were made by 2 a/c in each case. At 20:00 hours 1 a/c was 'scrambled' but without results.
5 & 6 December El Magrun & Bu Amud	3 dawn strafing patrols were made on the road West of Agheila and past Marble Arch. A convoy of 20 MT's were strafed, and strikes were scored; also, a single vehicle was hit. 2 or more a/c operating from Benina made a dawn patrol of the road from Tocra to Benghazi without seeing any signs of enemy activity. At Bu Amud 2 a/c made a dusk Patrol over Tobruk without incident.
6 & 7 December El Magrun & Bu Amud	Operating base 4 a/c strafed the road from Agheila to Marble Arch at dawn. There was much MTs on the road and some Breda fire was experienced. Also, at dawn 4 a/c patrolled Benghazi and to the North of it. There were some hostile e/a about and visuals of 2 JU 88's were obtained but our pilots were unable to close the range before they disappeared. The detachment at Bu Amud carried out dusk and dawn patrols of 2 a/c each over Tobruk without incident.
7 & 8 December El Magrun & Bu Amud	At Magrun 2 a/c carried out a patrol over Benghazi at dusk and 10 a/c carried out a patrol at dawn in layer formation between 2 and 4,.000 feet; no e/a were observed on either occasion. At dawn also 1 a/c made a tactical recce of the road West of Agheila as far as Ras el Aali and saw only 2 small convoys of MT's one of 6 vehicles and the other 4 vehicles going Wets, nothing going East. The detachment at Bu Amud carried out a dusk patrol of 2 a/c over Tobruk and a dawn patrol of 3 a/c over the same, without seeing any e/a, or enemy activity. During the day, 2 a/c which were at readiness with 80 Squadron were 'scrambled' at 14:00 hours but no contact was made with e/a.

8 & 9 December El Magrun & Bu Amud	Operating from Magrun 4 a/c took off at 17:00 hours to provide protection for a convoy which was then 25 miles North of Benghazi. On the way to pick up the convoy, one of the pilot's F/O Smyth saw 2 – JU 88's but was unable to intercept either of them. A little however, another JU 88 passed close overhead and P/O Smuth was able to get within 250 yards of him from which rang he gave him 2 – 1 second bursts and saw strikes on the porty engine and fuselage. A large piece flew off from close to the wing root and a cloud of smoke appeared. The pilot turned to make another attack but lost sight of the e/a so he went down to 1,500 Feet and saw a large patch oil spreading on the water and dark objects floating in it. The pilot was credited with a JU 88 destroyed. At dusk also 1 a/c patrolled over an MT convoy between Agedabia and Mersa Brega and a similar patrol was flown at midnight without incident on both occasions. At dawn 1 a/c carried out a recce of the road West of Agheila and saw only about 5 MTY's going West and a similar number going east near Ras el Aali. Also, at dawn, a layer patrol of 9 a/c between 2 and 11,000 feet was carried out over Benghazi, flares and bombs were seen near Tocra but no e/a. The detachment at Bu Amud at dusk put up a patrol of 2 a/c over Tobruk but no e/a seen. During the day of the 9th 2 a/c at readiness with 80 Squadron were 'scrambled' but no engagement took place. The detachment did not operate again from Bu Amud and re-joined the Squadron at El Magrun on the 11 December.
8 & 9 December El Magrun	At 17:00 hours 4 a/c did a layer patrol over Benghazi but did not see e/a. Sgt.Rawson did a dawn recce West of Agheila as far as Marble Arch and back along the road to Mersa Brega, but there was not much to be seen except for a handful of MT's moving West.
9 & 10 December El Magrun	7 a/c did a dawn layer patrol over Benghazi, but the results being the same as the previous evening, no e/a seen.
10 & 11 December El Magrun	4 a/c took off on a patrol of Benghazi, no enemy activity seen though the weather was excellent for the enemy to take advantage of. At 05:35 hours the CO took off and patrolled the road at 500 feet between Ras el Aali and Mersa Brega, saw no MT's. He then went to see if there were any ships alongside Ras el Aali pier but saw none, on the way home he got some Breda fire from one-gun East of the defiles. At dawn 8 more a/c took off to keep a watchful eye on Benghazi, and a sharp look out for any e/a that tried to approach, but nothing was seen.
11 & 12 December El Magrun	4 a/c patrolled South of Agedabia and 4 a/c over Benghazi, on both trips no enemy activity was seen. Weather very poor with 10/10 cloud at 2,500 feet.
12 & 13 December El Magrun	The weather being very bad during the morning and afternoon and owing to the very heavy rainstorm which made the aerodrome unserviceable, all operations were cancelled.
13 & 14 December El Magrun	At 4 a/c took off on a layer patrol over Benghazi, and 4 more a/c at dawn, on both occasions no enemy activity was seen. At 19:50 to 20:30 hours 5 a/c were 'scrambled over Benghazi the CO, Sgt. Thomas, P/O Smyth, P/O Wiseman, and F/Sgt. Logan. Flares were seen being dropped North on Benghazi but could not make out any interceptions. F/Sgt, Logan got a visual of a JU 88 going into cloud, he gave it a few seconds burst and also sprayed the cloud, later on an e/a was reported to have crashed at the same time and place and he was credited with the destruction of a JU 88. 5 a/c took off at intervals on straffing patrols to the defiles but found no suitable targets, the road was deserted. One pilot did see some dark objects which he thought were tents so gave them a burst but saw no results.

14 & 15 December El Magrun	At dusk a layer patrol of 4 a/c was carried out over Benghazi at 3, 6, 8 and 10,000 feet. No enemy activity was seen. Between 19:35 and 23:55 hours 7 a/c strafed the road between Marble Arch and Bir el Ahmar, many targets were found amongst MT's and huts and several fires were started in various places. Night accurate Breda fire was experienced. 1 a/c provided protection to a M.T. convoy on the road near Mersa Brega between 22:20 and 11:20 hours. No e/a were encountered. 4 a/c carried out a dawn patrol over Benghazi without incident. At dawn 1 a/c did a recce of the road between Mersa Brega and Nofilia, much enemy MTs was seen moving Westwards ingroups of 15, all along the road the pilot received accurate Breda fire. Marble Arch was found the be evacuated by the enemy.
15 & 16 December El Magrun	4 a/c made a dusk patrol of Benghazi area but no enemy activity. Immediately after their return 6 a/c were 'scrambled' to intercept a formation approaching the coast from the North. This formation however proved to be friendly, and our a/c returned to base without incident. From 18:35 to 00:30 hours 7 a/c made individual strafing patrols West of Nofilia LG. Many hits were scored on MT's and at least 4 fires were started. Very Accurate Ack/Ack was encountered from the coast North of Nofilia along with some machine gun fire. The dawn patrol of 4 a/c over Benghazi had nothing to report. A tactical recce of Nofilia LG and the road East to Marble Arch was made just after dawn by F/O McGill. No e/a were on the LG and only 3 transport and 7 Stukas could be seen. Enemy troops were withdrawing Westwards with a large force West of Marble Arch. Some of our transports were seen about 6 miles inland approx. halfway between Marble Arch and Nofilia. This recce was made at 0 feet in the face of intense Breda fire.
16 & 17 December El Magrun	During and between 17:50, 19:00, 19:05 and 20:30 hours several patrols were carried out. The dusk patrol of 2 a/c over Benghazi saws no enemy activity. 4 a/c were 'scrambled' to intercept raiders over Benghazi but though they saw flares and bombs explosions they were unable to get any visuals except F/O Davis, who confirmed a JU 88 destroyed by F/Sgt. Beard who just returned from dusk patrol and was preparing to land saw Bofor's fire over Benghazi and returned to investigate. He Had a visual on a JU 88 at a range of 20 yards gave a short burst and followed him down in a dive through the barrage to 1,000 feet when after another short burst he saw strikes on fuselage and port engine and the e/a crashed into the sea in flames. During and between 17:30 and 02:15 hours 8 a/c patrolled in the vicinity of Nofilia LG, but no e/a took off or landed there. A dim flare path was seen and a White Beacon to the North of the LG was in use
17 & 18 December El Magrun	During and between 05:00 and 08:05 hours 1 a/c strafed about 200 MTs to the West of Nofilia and saw many strikes. A recce to Sirte was of little use owing to heavy rain and poor visibility. Some MTs was seen on the road to the Southeast of Sirte. Weather continued to be bad during the day and night. 2 a/c on dusk patrol over Benghazi saw nothing. The first 2 strafing patrols over the road West of Nofilia encountered heavy rainstorms though some MTs was seen and strafed. Further operations were cancelled after a weather recce had been to Marble Arch. At dawn Sgt. Davies flew to Marble Arch LG to test the serviceability of the aerodrome.
18 & 19 December El Magrun	During and between 17:30 and 20:35 hours 4 a/c made dusk layer patrols over Benghazi but saw no enemy activity. On their return to base the controller told them there was 1 e/a over Benghazi, which they went to investigate but saw nothing. During and between 21:30 and 23:35 hours 4 a/c were 'Scrambled' over Benghazi and patrolled at height of 4,000 to 7,000 feet, they received various vectors but saw no e/a/ F/Lt. Ellis DFM saw a light out to sea about 20 miles North-North-West of Benghazi, went to investigate and found light appeared to be on the water, he circled it several times losing height each time. He then made a run across it from 20 feet with his landing light on and received MG fire, called up Controller and asked them to plot him which they did. He also requested permission to fire and was told he could with caution. He thought it to be a sub. But did not fire in case it was a crew in a boat.

19 & 20 December El Magrun	During and between 05:40 and 07:30 hours 4 a/c made a dawn layer patrol over Benghazi but saw no enemy activity. Dusk to dawn patrols were made by 4 a/c in each case, nothing was seen. Between 20:30 and 21:40 hours 4 a/c were 'scrambled' over base and told by the Controller bandits going South over base, pilot saw flares dropped about 6 miles Southeast of Beacon also incendiaries but was unable to get a visual. On his return to base saw an explosion, investigated, and thinks it was ammunition.
20 & 21 December El Magrun	At Magrun 3 a/c carried out a patrol over Benghazi at dusk, and 4 a/c carried out a similar patrol at dawn, no enemy activity was observed on either occasion. S/Ldr. Selby DFC made a patrol over Benghazi; whilst on patrol was told by Controller bandits were about 100 miles off approaching Benghazi. They turned into Benghazi, and he saw two very bright lights, went and investigated and found e 2 a/c with navigation lights on. These were so bright that he was unable to get a silhouette of them. He informed Controller who told him to open fire as they were definitely bandits. He then got close to one and gave him a short burst but saw no results. He then flew under him to see if he could identify the a/c and found it to be a Liberator, and tole Controller. The second a/c was also identified as a Liberator.
21 & 22 December El Magrun	The usual dusk to dawn patrols were carried out over Benghazi, in each case 4 a/c did the patrol without incident. At 22:25 to 23:20 hours 1 a/c F/Lt. Thompson was 'scrambled' over Benghazi. When he was 2 miles South of Benghazi and 5 miles out to at 5<000 feet got a visual of a JU 88 beneath him, got within 300 yards range and fired at him, he received no return fire, so gave another burst, and then another one, the JU 88 was losing height all the time. He gave him a 4th burst from 1,000 feet; the aircraft dived down straight into the sea. He circled it for a few minutes and gave a D/F plot to 2.2 Group. The JU 88 confirmed destroyed by No. 89 Squadron (Beaufighter).
22 & 23 December Merduma	The Squadron moved from El Magrun and arrived at Merduma this morning. Owing to the bad condition of the LG the usual operations were not carried out, but 4 a/c, was at readiness all night.
23 & 24 December Merduma	4 a/c were at readiness from the Moonrise. At 23:25 hours 2 a/c were 'scrambled' North of Bask. But saw no e/a. They returned to base and landed at 00:35 hours.
24 & 25 December Merduma	Again 4 a/c were at readiness from Moonrise all through the night, but the Hun failed to turn up.
25 & 26 December Merduma	To-day. Christmas Day, a good time was had by all, thanks to S/Ldr. Selby DFC when things looked black in the morning as the Christmas had not arrived, after a lot of hard work on the part of the CO we had our dinner and a good time followed.
26 & 29 December Merduma	4 a/c were at readiness all night, but nothing came over. Owing to the very bad conditions of the LG the usual operations were unable to take place, but 4 a/c were on readiness each night in case the Hun dared to come over.
29 & 30 December Merduma	4 a/c at readiness from Moonrise, at 05:10 hours 1 a/c was 'scrambled' 10 miles North of base and then given a vector and told bandits in the immediate vicinity at 8,000 feet. He did not see him. Returned to base and landed at 06:15 hours. At between 05:25 and 06:30 hours 1 a/c was 'scrambled' 5 miles South of base and given various vectors, but saw no e/a.
30 & 31 December Merduma	4 a/c were at readiness from Moonrise, but no operations took place. 1 a/c was due to take off on a dawn recce, but owing to heavy rain during the night, which made the LG unserviceable, it was cancelled. **(On the 31 December 1942 1012281 L. B. Lamb, promoted to Leading Aircraftman's - LAC)**

The following records from 27 December 1942 through to 31 December 1943 have been taken from the handwritten diary kept by LAC Lamb L.B. 1012281.

NOTE:
From December 1942 to December 1943 L B Lamb personal diary has been used. The recorded 73 Squadron AIR's during the War in North Africa & Italy (late December 1942 to April 1944) have been referred to and cross referenced, where applicable.

AIR 27/631/23 & AIR 27/631/24 Pilot Ops Report
December 1942:

Sunday, 27 December	Wrote Mabel. Dull day at Merduma. Mr. M Arch F/LT Thompson posted to 601 Squadron. *Refer to the above AIR 27/631/23.*
Monday, 28 December	Still at Merduma. Nothing doing. Air raid at night. *Refer to the above AIR 27/631/23.*
Tuesday, 29 December	Sludging Tunnel. Nothing doing. Air raid 20:00 hours. *Refer to the above AIR 27/631/23.*
Wednesday, 30 December	Very cold day. Wrote Mabel. *Refer to the above AIR 27/631/23.*
Thursday, 31 December	Go to pack, on the move again. Left at 14:00 hours. *Refer to the above AIR 27/631/23.*

AIR 27/632/1 & AIR 27/632/2 Pilot Ops Report
January 1943:

Friday, 1 January Merduma	Passed Nofilia II. Slept out in the blue open skies at 06:00 hours. AIR 27/632/1 covers operations for the day.
Saturday, 2 January Alem el Chel	Arrived at Asaba 20:00 hours in the Blue. Feeling fed up and dirty. AIR 27/632/1 covers operations for the day.
Sunday, 3 January	Issued with B.M.A. money. Just settled. Sandstorm all day. Feeling fed up. AIR 27/632/1 covers operations for the day.
Monday, 4 January	Sandstorm still on. On duty all night. Received letters from Mr. Riley, Mabel & mother. Cable from George. AIR 27/632/1 covers operations for the day.
Tuesday, 5 January Wednesday, 6 January	Very cold feet. Sandstorm stopped. Plenty of work on A/C. Big do tonight on again. A nice hot day, quite a change. Plenty of flying. Wrote to Mr. T and post a letter to Mabel. AIR 27/632/1 covers operations for the day.
Thursday, 7 January	Prepared to move to another drome. Plenty of flying. AIR 27/632/1 covers operations for the day.
Friday, 8 January	Went to matinee of 601 Squadron, 7 Sinners, Marlene Dietrich. First for ages. AIR 27/632/1 covers operations for the day.
Saturday, 9 January	Moved from Assalia on Alem el Chel. AIR 27/632/1 covers operations for the day.
Sunday, 10 January	Slept on the desert what a night. Fed up with travelling. AIR 27/632/1 covers operations for the day.
Monday, 11 January Tamet Satellite	Arrived at Hamaliar, lots of 190 710's about. Stopping for a day. Moved to Wadi Tamet. AIR 27/632/1 covers operations for the day.
Tuesday, 12 January	Air raid just as we arrived then A/C destroyed. Another raid at breakfast. Strafed drome no one injured. AIR 27/632/1 covers operations for the day.

Wednesday, 13 January	Wrote Mabel and Aunty, jerry dropping flares, raid any time. Still why worry. AIR 27/632/1 covers operations for the day.
Thursday, 14 January	Plenty of work on A/C. rained at night. Still at the same drome. Working all night till dusk. AIR 27/632/1 covers operations for the day.
Friday, 15 January	Sandstorm. Had a letter from Mabel [112], feeling quite happy after it. Another raid last night. Make a paper knife out of shrapnel. AIR 27/632/1 covers operations for the day.
Saturday, 16 January	Easy day. Camouflage tanks. Talk from Army Officer on the war out here. Preparing for another raid, hope that it is not. AIR 27/632/1 covers operations for the day.
Sunday, 17 January	Big job on tonight, Cassino Benito & strafed. On duty tonight. Also had a jab, not feeling well. AIR 27/632/1 covers operations for the day.
Monday, 18 January	Finish at 06:00 hours this morning. Arm very painful medication tablets and slept well after time. Hope there is no raid tonight. Wrote Mabel. AIR 27/632/1 covers operations for the day.
Tuesday, 19 January	A really peaceful night, no raids. Wrote to Mrs. E and George. No mail again. B. Flt moving up today, in advance. Dreamt of home. AIR 27/632/1 covers operations for the day.
Wednesday, 20 January	Moving tomorrow to Ber Dufau, perhaps. Operating tonight. AIR 27/632/1 covers operations for the day. AIR 27/632/1 covers operations for the day.
Thursday, 21 January Bir Dufan	Moved to Dufan at 11:00 hours. Passed Buaret, slept out the night. Too cold to sleep. AIR 27/632/1 covers operations for the day.
Friday, 22 January	Started at 07:30 hours. Turned off at Campo-Fortuna, arrived at 10:00 hours, am on N.F. Sent Mabel cable. Worse luck. AIR 27/632/1 covers operations for the day.
Saturday, 23 January	Wrote Bill, nothing much happened today. Feeling fed up and tired. AIR 27/632/1 covers operations for the day.
Sunday, 24 January	Went to communion and mass at our camp and yanks squadron. Wrote Bill and George. AIR 27/632/1 covers operations for the day.
Monday, 25 January	Very little doing, rumours of moving to Tripoli in three days. No flying, thank goodness. AIR 27/632/1 covers operations for the day. Mabel's birthday.
Tuesday, 26 January	Having some rain and plenty of sandstorms. Wrote Mr. Hodges. No mail yet. C/O Relax W/CDR. Hope Monty is C/O. AIR 27/632/1 covers operations for the day.
Wednesday, 27 January	Rain again, not that much. Rumours of a move. Waiting for mail, letter came from Mother. AIR 27/632/1 covers operations for the day.
Thursday, 28 January	Worked on my model. Nothing much to mention. Played tombola won 18/-. AIR 27/632/1 covers operations for the day.
Friday, 29 January	No operations, plenty of rest. Waiting for move. AIR 27/632/1 covers operations for the day.

Saturday, 30 January	Received a letter from Mabel [113]. Plenty of work today. AIR 27/632/1 covers operations for the day.
Sunday, 31 January	Great day today, put my name in for the boat? Longing now for the time to see Mabel (192). Writing Mabel today + John, posted. AIR 27/632/1 covers operations for the day.

AIR 27/632/3 & AIR 27/632/4 Pilot Ops Report
February 1943:

Monday, 1ᵗ February Bir Dufan Gasr Garabulli	Wrote mother and Hubert Ridler. No mail. Lovely sunny day. C.G. Beat A Flt 1-0; Cooks 3 B Flt 1, good matches. Feeling fit as a fiddle. AIR 27/632/3 cover operations for the day.
Tuesday, 2 February	Received a letter from Mabel [114] and an 'airgraph' from mother. Preparing to move. AIR 27/632/3 cover operations for the day.
Wednesday, 3 February	'B' Flt moved up to Tripoli. Plenty of work on A/C 13 daily. Hoping to move tomorrow. AIR 27/632/3 cover operations for the day.
Thursday, 4 February	Left for Castle VERDI and entered the 'green belt'. Posted the music at Liptis Magna and arrived at Castle VERDI at 07:30 hours 100 miles. AIR 27/632/3 cover operations for the day.
Friday, 5 February	Wonderful to wake and find grass to walk on. Received Xmas cards Stan & Edith. AIR 27/632/3 cover operations for the day.
Saturday, 6 February	Lovely sunny day. Not much to do so am writing Phil. AIR 27/632/3 cover operations for the day.
Sunday, 7 February	Mass at 10:00 hours. Lovely day. Rain at night. Wrote mother, and a letter to Sid. AIR 27/632/3 cover operations for the day.
Monday, 8 February	Rained a lot, last night, just like blighty rain, kit very cold. Looking forward to trip. AIR 27/632/3 cover operations for the day.
Tuesday, 9 February	Went to Tripoli for the day. Had a good time but rained all day. Bought a few gifts for home; I am hoping to get them home. AIR 27/632/3 cover operations for the day.
Wednesday, 10 February	Rained all night and still raining. Made a star. Had a good feed. Packed a parcel for Mabel. No mail. AIR 27/632/3 cover operations for the day.
Thursday, 11 February	Sent Mabel parcel and registered it. Rain all morning. Writing Mabel. AIR 27/632/3 cover operations for the day.
Friday, 12 February	Nothing much doing. Made some cakes out of biscuits. AIR 27/632/3 cover operations for the day.
Saturday, 13 February	Rainy day again. Rumours of a move. AIR 27/632/3 cover operations for the day.
Sunday, 14 February	Moved at 12:00 hours. Slept out at night. C/O mentioned on Radio D.S.O. AIR 27/632/3 cover operations for the day.
Monday, 15 February El Assa Castel Benito	Moved off at 09:00 hours. Arrived at EL ASSA at 13:00 hours. Raid as we arrived. Sandstorm, no more grass. AIR 27/632/3 cover operations for the day.

Tuesday, 16 February	Quite a nice day. Not sand again. Wrote Sid. Nothing happened at night. AIR 27/632/3 cover operations for the day.
Wednesday, 17 February Castel Benito	Received L.C. from Bill. B party arrived at 12:00 hours. No ops. AIR 27/632/3 cover operations for the day.
Thursday, 18 February	Sand blowing all day. No ops. AIR 27/632/3 cover operations for the day.
Friday, 19 February	Went to mass at 250S. Still no ops. S/Ldr Ellis out, new C/O arrived. AIR 27/632/3 cover operations for the day.
Saturday, 20 February	A Flt play B Flt at baseball. Had another jab today. No ops. AIR 27/632/3 cover operations for the day.
Sunday, 21 February	Received an air graph from Marie and Ralph. Still no ops. Getting fed up waiting. AIR 27/632/3 cover operations for the day.
Monday, 22 February	Received LP from Mabel, Marie and Mother. Q Griffiths sorted choir last night, quite a success, expecting rain tomorrow. AIR 27/632/3 cover operations for the day.
Tuesday, 23 February	Clock put back one-hour last night. No ops. AIR 27/632/3 cover operations for the day.
Wednesday, 24 February El Assa	Wrote Mabel. Q Queenie G choir practice. Still at El Assa. A/C started ops. AIR 27/632/3 cover operations for the day.
Thursday, 25 February	Wrote Marie. Rotten cold, but lovely day. No mail. AIR 27/632/3 cover operations for the day.
Friday, 26 February	Choir practice tonight. Sand blowing all day. AIR 27/632/3 cover operations for the day.
Saturday, 27 February	Tombola tonight. Still no mail. AIR 27/632/3 cover operations for the day.
Sunday, 28 February	Terry and Joe passed to 37 Sqdn also Ron Daley. A/G from Mabel. AIR 27/632/3 cover operations for the day.

AIR 27/632/5 & AIR 27/632/6 Pilot Ops Report

March 1943:

Monday, 1 March El Assa	Choir practice tonight. Plenty of work. A/C Firing. Getting ready to move again. AIR 27/632/5 cover operations for the day.
Tuesday, 2 March	NAAFI managed to get some goods in. First some Oman. Still no mail, or beer. AIR 27/632/5 cover operations for the day.
Wednesday, 3 March El Assa, Castel Benito	Mass at 14:00 hours. No ops. AIR 27/632/5 cover operations for the day.
Thursday, 4 March	No mail. No ops. AIR 27/632/5 cover operations for the day.
Friday, 5 March	Yanks arrived. AIR 27/632/5 cover operations for the day.
Saturday, 6 March	Played cooks, won 6-1. No mail. AIR 27/632/5 cover operations for the day.
Sunday, 7 March	Played yanks baseball lost 10-5. Good game. AIR 27/632/5 cover operations for the day.

Monday, 8 March	Played cooks lost 3-0. Played tombola lost 5/-. No mail. AIR 27/632/5 cover operations for the day.
Tuesday, 9 March	Sand blowing again. No ops. No pancakes either. AIR 27/632/5 cover operations for the day.
Wednesday, 10 March	Received 2 LC from Mabel and one from mother. AIR 27/632/5 cover operations for the day.
Thursday, 11 March	Concert tonight. Our own gala ROC, very successful. Received letter from G.G. Also played W.T. won 4-0. AIR 27/632/5 cover operations for the day.
Friday, 12 March	Armoury played W.T. drew 1-1. Wrote Gran and mother. Played Tombola won 11/6d. On sick list for 3 days. AIR 27/632/5 cover operations for the day.
Saturday, 13 March	Lovely day. A/C tests. AIR 27/632/5 cover operations for the day.
Sunday, 14 March El Assa	Received L.P. from Mabel. AIR 27/632/5 cover operations for the day.
Monday, 15 March	*No recorded details in his diary.* AIR 27/632/5 cover operations for the day.
Tuesday, 16 March	*No recorded details in his diary.* AIR 27/632/5 cover operations for the day.
Wednesday, 17 March	*No recorded details in his diary.* AIR 27/632/5 cover operations for the day.
Thursday, 18 March	*No recorded details in his diary.* AIR 27/632/5 cover operations for the day.
Friday, 19 March	*No recorded details in his diary.* AIR 27/632/5 cover operations for the day.
Saturday, 20 March Nefatia South	Letter from Mabel. AIR 27/632/5 cover operations for the day.
Sunday, 21 March	Rained all day. Plenty of work. Fed up and worried. AIR 27/632/5 cover operations for the day.
Monday, 22 March	Still, plenty of rain, thunderstorm last night. On duty tonight. Wish it was all over. Wrote Mabel. AIR 27/632/5 cover operations for the day.
Tuesday, 23 March	Had concert in Mess. Q Range 73 quite a success. AIR 27/632/5 cover operations for the day.
Wednesday, 24 March	P/O Chandler shot down JU88 over SFAX. Received paper dated 4th. L.C. from Mabel. AIR 27/632/5 cover operations for the day.
Thursday, 25 March	L.C. from Mabel and mother, air cable from Mabel. On duty all night. Dog extremely ill. AIR 27/632/5 cover operations for the day.
Friday, 26 March	Received Francs and changed. B.M.A. as we are in Tunisia. AIR 27/632/5 cover operations for the day.
Saturday, 27 March	*No recorded details in his diary.* AIR 27/632/5 cover operations for the day.
Sunday, 28 March	Had mass this morning. Also A.G. from Mitch. AIR 27/632/5 cover operations for the day.
Monday, 29 March	Need a ½ B Beer. First since Xmas. Wrote Mabel and Mother. AIR 27/632/5 cover operations for the day.

Tuesday, 30 March	Shot down JU88 over SFAX AIR 27/632/5 cover operations for the day.
Wednesday, 31 March	Received letter from mother. Griffin UK ROC. AIR 27/632/5 cover operations for the day.

AIR 27/632/7 & AIR 27/632/8 Pilot Ops Report
April 1943:

Thursday, 1 April Nefatia South	Received letter and PO from Mr. Leach. Also L.C. from Mabel. AIR 27/632/7 cover operations for the day.
Friday, 2 April	Pay parade. Back to Francs. AIR 27/632/7 cover operations for the day.
Saturday, 3 April	*No recorded details in his diary.* AIR 27/632/7 cover operations for the day.
Sunday, 4 April	Mass said but could not attend. AIR 27/632/7 cover operations for the day.
Monday, 5 April	Mother, Mabel, Nora, Bill, Mitch. On duty all night. AIR 27/632/7 cover operations for the day.
Tuesday, 6 April	*No recorded details in his diary.* AIR 27/632/7 cover operations for the day.
Wednesday, 7 April	*No recorded details in his diary.* AIR 27/632/7 cover operations for the day.
Thursday, 8 April Gabes Main	*No recorded details in his diary.* AIR 27/632/7 cover operations for the day.
Friday, 9 April	Moved from Hafatier, also arrived at Gabes. AIR 27/632/7 cover operations for the day.
Saturday, 10 April	A.G. from Mabel. AIR 27/632/7 cover operations for the day.
Sunday, 11 April	Cable to John, Nelson. Had mass at Gabes. AIR 27/632/7 cover operations for the day.
Monday, 12 April Sfax el Macu	Left Gabes at 09:00 hours to go to SFAX, arrived at 13:30 hours. AIR 27/632/7 cover operations for the day.
Tuesday, 13 April	*No recorded details in his diary.* AIR 27/632/7 cover operations for the day.
Wednesday, 14 April	*No recorded details in his diary.* AIR 27/632/7 cover operations for the day.
Thursday, 15 April	*No recorded details in his diary.* AIR 27/632/7 cover operations for the day.
Friday, 16 April	Shot down 3 – JU52, 3 prob's. But lost one of our best. Pilot P/O Chandler, he was killed in crash. We shall all miss him. AIR 27/632/7 cover operations for the day.
Saturday, 17 April	Walked into Sfax and back, very pleasant. Posted letter to Mabel. AIR 27/632/7 cover operations for the day.
Sunday, 18 April	B Flt moved today to Kairouan nr Sousse. We shot down 4 – JU52. 7th Jerry A/C shot down; 2 probables, and 3 damaged. AIR 27/632/7 cover operations for the day.
Monday, 19 April Alem	Visited my American friends. We got another 2 – JU52. No news. We moved. Total of enemy A/C has reached 100. AIR 27/632/7 cover operations for the day.

Tuesday, 20 April	Arrived at Kairouan. On duty all night, feeling fed up. Wrote mother, Mrs. Griffin, Mabel today. Destroyed 1 – JU52, damaged 1. AIR 27/632/7 cover operations for the day.
Wednesday, 21 April Monastir	Moved to Monastir. Wrote Martin Ekland. Raid at night, bit hot our drome. AIR 27/632/7 cover operations for the day.
Thursday, 22 April	Raid at night, no damage. Received two rabbits off natives. AIR 27/632/7 cover operations for the day.
Friday, 23 April	Natives did my dobi [washing]. Glorious weather. Wrote mother, nelson, Phil Mr. Leach. Rabbits doing fine. AIR 27/632/7 cover operations for the day.
Saturday, 24 April	No recorded details in his diary. AIR 27/632/7 cover operations for the day.
Sunday, 25 April	Went to mass in Monastir. Walked most of the way. No mail. Yet B.7 shot down 1 – JU88. AIR 27/632/7 cover operations for the day.
Monday, 26 April	Lecture by W.O. on the war.B.7 shot down 2 – JU88 and damaged 1. Wrote to Mabel a letter and posted it. No mail. AIR 27/632/7 cover operations for the day.
Tuesday, 27 April	No mail. Wrote Mr. Gardner. R.A.F.R. Played Cover Flt drew 2-2. AIR 27/632/7 cover operations for the day.
Wednesday, 28 April	A.C. from Mabel. Had a disaster at drome, 10 men killed in Hudson. Army Major, 7 personnel and six others, all killed and burnt. AIR 27/632/7 cover operations for the day.
Thursday, 29 April	Played for Cooks, won 2-0. No mail. AIR 27/632/7 cover operations for the day.
Friday, 30 April	Played 285 Wing won 4-0. NAAFI supply in, first half. AIR 27/632/7 cover operations for the day.

AIR 27/632/9 (1) & AIR 27/632/10 (1) Pilot Ops Report
May 1943:

Saturday, 1 May Monastir	Played Cover Flt 2-0. No mail. AIR 27/632/7 cover operations for the day.
Sunday, 2 May	Played French Services at Monastir. Won 4-1. AIR 27/632/7 cover operations for the day.
Monday, 3 May	L.C. from Mabel. AIR 27/632/7 cover operations for the day.
Tuesday, 4 May	Played cricket, won by 20 runs against the rest. AIR 27/632/7 cover operations for the day.
Wednesday, 5 May	Played cricket. Lost by 5 runs against officers and pilots. AIR 27/632/7 cover operations for the day.
Thursday, 6 May	Letter from Sidney. Wrote mother L.C. AIR 27/632/7 cover operations for the day.
Friday, 7 May	Wrote Mr. Leach, Mabel, Phil. Harry Curtis. AIR 27/632/7 cover operations for the day.
Saturday, 8 May	Flew over Bizerta and back today. Wrote Sid. AIR 27/632/7 cover operations for the day.
Sunday, 9 May	Mass at Monastir. AIR 27/632/7 cover operations for the day.

Monday, 10 May	*No recorded details in his diary.* AIR 27/632/7 cover operations for the day.
Tuesday, 11 May	Played 14 C at cricket. Won by 57 runs, a real treat. AIR 27/632/7 cover operations for the day.
Wednesday, 12 May	On duty all night for the last time up here. Still at Monastir. AIR 27/632/7 cover operations for the day.
Thursday, 13 May	Sqdn. played Wing 285, drew 3-3. Had photograph taken **[see pictures below]** AIR 27/632/7 cover operations for the day.

73 (F) SDN Tunisia 13.5.43
[1012281 LAC - L B Lamb, Back Row 1st on the right. Front Row – middle is 'Johnny Johnson' with sandy the mascot]

Signatures on the back.
[Top left signature 'Johnny Johnson']

Footnote: Having researched the name 'Johnny Johnson' I am not sure if this is the same 'Johnnie Johnson' Spitfire Ace of Aces. I have researched and cannot find any reference to the latter flying in North Africa.

Friday, 14 May	*No recorded details in his diary.* AIR 27/632/7 cover operations for the day.
Saturday, 15 May	Received letter from Martin Eklund. AIR 27/632/7 cover operations for the day.
Sunday, 16 May	L.C. from Mabel, L.C. from Nora. AIR 27/632/7 cover operations for the day.
Monday, 17 May	*No recorded details in his diary.* AIR 27/632/7 cover operations for the day.
Tuesday, 18 May	Visit Tunis AIR 27/632/7 cover operations for the day.
Wednesday, 19 May	L.P. from Mother, 2 Mabel. Heavy rainstorm. AIR 27/632/7 cover operations for the day.
Thursday, 20 May	*No recorded details in his diary.* AIR 27/632/7 cover operations for the day.
Friday, 21 May	L.C. from Mabel. AIR 27/632/7 cover operations for the day.
Saturday, 22 May	Visited convent of St Joseph of the L'Aparition at Sousse. Sister Mary of the Child Jesus. AIR 27/632/7 cover operations for the day.
Sunday, 23 May	Went to mass at Monastir. Service in English. Visited convent. Received letter from Mabel. AIR 27/632/7 cover operations for the day.

Monday, 24 May	Expecting Spits replacements. Wrote Mabel L.C. Parted with rabbits. Daniel Garson parted last of my old pals. AIR 27/632/7 cover operations for the day.
Tuesday, 25 May	Visited the convent to see Sister Mary. AIR 27/632/7 cover operations for the day.
Wednesday, 26 May	Received L.C. from Mabel and Uncle George. Writing mother today. AIR 27/632/7 cover operations for the day.
Thursday, 27 May	Visited convent. AIR 27/632/7 cover operations for the day.
Friday, 28 May	Visited Sister Mary at the convent. Moving tomorrow. AIR 27/632/7 cover operations for the day.
Saturday, 29 May	Left Monastir at 10:00 hours for La Sebala at Tunis. Arrived same day. AIR 27/632/7 cover operations for the day.
Sunday, 30 May	Writing Sister Mary at the convent in Sousse. AIR 27/632/7 cover operations for the day.
Monday, 31 May La Seballa	*No recorded details in his diary.* AIR 27/632/7 cover operations for the day.

AIR 27/632/11 (1) & AIR 27/632/12 Pilot Ops Report
June 1943:

Tuesday, 1 June La Sebala	Visited Tunis. AIR 27/632/7 cover operations for the day.
Wednesday, 2 June	Visited Tunis. Bought perfume and powder for Mabel. No mail. AIR 27/632/7 cover operations for the day.
Thursday, 3 June	No mail. AIR 27/632/7 cover operations for the day.
Friday, 4 June	Wrote mother a L.C. AIR 27/632/7 cover operations for the day.
Saturday, 5 June	*No recorded details in his diary.* AIR 27/632/7 cover operations for the day.
Sunday, 6 June	Missed Mass. AIR 27/632/7 cover operations for the day.
Monday, 7 June	No mail. AIR 27/632/7 cover operations for the day.
Tuesday, 8 June	No mail. AIR 27/632/7 cover operations for the day.
Wednesday, 9 June	Wrote to Martin Eklund. No mail. AIR 27/632/7 cover operations for the day.
Thursday, 10 June	*No recorded details in his diary.* AIR 27/632/7 cover operations for the day.
Friday, 11 June	Wrote dad at Nelson, also mother. Mabel's mother died in May 1943; R.I.P. AIR 27/632/7 cover operations for the day.
Saturday, 12 June	*No recorded details in his diary.* AIR 27/632/7 cover operations for the day.
Sunday, 13 June	Went to mass at the Altar, Thamet. Wrote David. AIR 27/632/7 cover operations for the day.
Monday, 14 June	Went to Tunis. AIR 27/632/7 cover operations for the day.
Tuesday, 15 June	*No recorded details in his diary.* AIR 27/632/7 cover operations for the day.

Wednesday,16 June	Went to the theatre to see Cedric Neilson and Q10. AIR 27/632/7 cover operations for the day.
Thursday, 17 June	Formed choir AIR 27/632/7 cover operations for the day.
Friday, 18 June	*No recorded details in his diary.* AIR 27/632/7 cover operations for the day.
Saturday, 19 June	*No recorded details in his diary.* AIR 27/632/7 cover operations for the day.
Sunday, 20 June	Planes to base. Plenty of work. AIR 27/632/7 cover operations for the day.
Monday, 21 June	Wrote Mother. AIR 27/632/7 cover operations for the day.
Tuesday, 22 June	Corpus Christi. Unfortunately missed mass. AIR 27/632/7 cover operations for the day.
Wednesday, 23 June	Wrote Mabel. AIR 27/632/7 cover operations for the day.
Thursday, 24 June	*No recorded details in his diary.* AIR 27/632/7 cover operations for the day.
Friday, 25 June	Received letter from Sister Mary at the Child Jesus, dated 20 June. Visited Tunis. ***[see envelope and letter below]*** AIR 27/632/7 cover operations for the day.

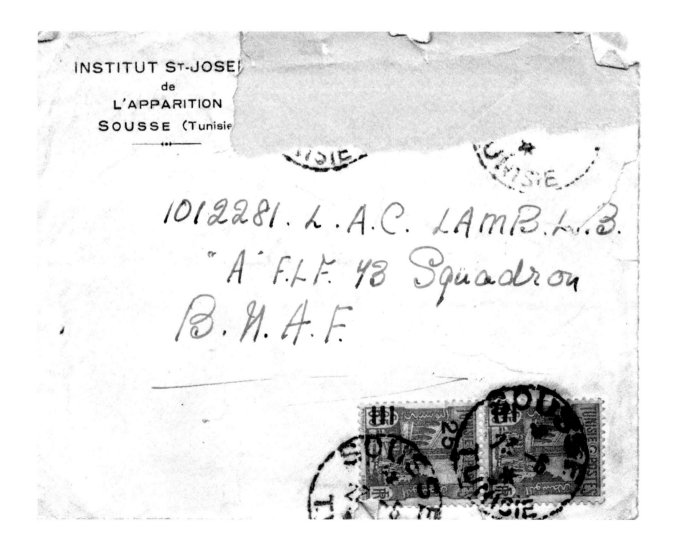

Page 1 of letter

9. M. J.

St. Joseph's C.
Monastir
Sunday 20th

Dear Bernard,

I could not sit down & call you Mr. Lamb could I? How it was a real pleasure to get your letter. I received it last Sunday – Whit-Sunday. I was fairly busy during the week so I put off answering till to-day.

How is Rex and all your pets or had you to leave them all behind you! If so I am very sorry for you. You know I meant to tell you that if ever you had to part with Rex I should be delighted to take him & at the same time I'm sure it would be a consolation to you to know that he had found a British friend. But your going away was so abrupt that I did not think of the dog.

Page 2 of letter

Don't worry about the vases. They're splendid & made a rather grand effect in our little chapel in Sousse; for it was for my own convent in Sousse that they were destined. I am still in Monastir but shall be soon going back to Sousse. Remember me to your friend Frank Smith. I'm glad to know that you are still together.

Now for those French sentences. The first sentence contains "heart" used in its proper meaning, the second in a figurative sense. Word for word: I never slept with such a good heart meaning I never slept so soundly or well. "(de) Bon cœur" also means willingly.

Here now that's enough for chatting & I've plenty of letters to write.

I promise to pray for you until the end of the war.

Yours sincerely in Christ,
S. Mary of the Child Jesus.

Saturday, 26 June	Going to Tunis. AIR 27/632/7 cover operations for the day.
Sunday, 27 June	Went to mass at Sidi Thamet. AIR 27/632/7 cover operations for the day.
Monday, 28 June	No mail. AIR 27/632/7 cover operations for the day.
Tuesday, 29 June	Received some papers from Mabel. AIR 27/632/7 cover operations for the day.
Wednesday, 30 June	Received parcel from Alan Redditch and photo of Mabel. Letter from John. AIR 27/632/7 cover operations for the day.

AIR 27/632/13 (1) & AIR 27/632/14 Pilot Ops Report

July 1943:

Thursday, 1 July La Sebala	Visited Tunis. Received letter from Darrell Craig. AIR 27/632/7 cover operations for the day.
Friday, 2 July	Wrote Mr. Hodges and John at Nelson. AIR 27/632/7 cover operations for the day.
Saturday, 3 July	Paper arrived. Mending a/c. AIR 27/632/7 cover operations for the day.
Sunday, 4 July	My birthday. Went to Mass at Thamet. Waiting for mail. AIR 27/632/7 cover operations for the day.
Monday, 5 July	Nothing to report. AIR 27/632/7 cover operations for the day.
Tuesday, 6 July	Nothing to report. AIR 27/632/7 cover operations for the day.
Wednesday, 7 July	Still no mail. AIR 27/632/7 cover operations for the day.
Thursday, 8 July	Wrote mother. No mail. AIR 27/632/7 cover operations for the day.
Friday, 9 July	*No recorded details in his diary.* AIR 27/632/7 cover operations for the day.
Saturday, 10 July	Received L.C. from Mabel. AIR 27/632/7 cover operations for the day.
Sunday, 11 July	Went to Mass at Thamet. Received letter from Uncle G. AIR 27/632/7 cover operations for the day.
Monday, 12 July	Wrote Mabel. AIR 27/632/7 cover operations for the day.
Tuesday, 13 July	Received L.C. from Bill. AIR 27/632/7 cover operations for the day.
Wednesday, 14 July	Wrote Bill and Uncle George. AIR 27/632/7 cover operations for the day.
Thursday, 15 July	*No recorded details in his diary.* AIR 27/632/7 cover operations for the day.
Friday, 16 July	*No recorded details in his diary.* AIR 27/632/7 cover operations for the day.
Saturday, 17 July	*No recorded details in his diary.* AIR 27/632/7 cover operations for the day.
Sunday, 18 July	Went to Mass. No mail. AIR 27/632/7 cover operations for the day.
Monday, 19 July	*No recorded details in his diary.* AIR 27/632/7 cover operations for the day.
Tuesday, 20 July	*No recorded details in his diary.* AIR 27/632/7 cover operations for the day.

Wednesday, 21 July	*No recorded details in his diary.* AIR 27/632/7 cover operations for the day.
Thursday, 22 July	*No recorded details in his diary.* AIR 27/632/7 cover operations for the day.
Friday, 23 July	*No recorded details in his diary.* AIR 27/632/7 cover operations for the day.
Saturday, 24 July	*No recorded details in his diary.* AIR 27/632/7 cover operations for the day.
Sunday, 25 July	Went to Mass. L.C. from Mabel. AIR 27/632/7 cover operations for the day.
Monday, 26 July	Moving tomorrow. No mail. AIR 27/632/7 cover operations for the day.
Tuesday, 27 July	Moved to Sebala 1, arrived same day. AIR 27/632/7 cover operations for the day.
Wednesday, 28 July	L.C. from Mother. Wrote mother A.G. AIR 27/632/7 cover operations for the day.
Thursday, 29 July	*No recorded details in his diary.* AIR 27/632/7 cover operations for the day.
Friday, 30 July	*No recorded details in his diary.* AIR 27/632/7 cover operations for the day.
Saturday, 31 July	*No recorded details in his diary.* AIR 27/632/7 cover operations for the day.

AIR 27/632/15 & AIR 27/632/16 Pilot Ops Report
August 1943:

Sunday, 1 August La Sebala	Mass at Thamet. AIR 27/632/7 cover operations for the day.
Monday, 2 August	*No recorded details in his diary.* AIR 27/632/7 cover operations for the day.
Tuesday, 3 August	*No recorded details in his diary.* AIR 27/632/7 cover operations for the day.
Wednesday, 4 August	*No recorded details in his diary.* AIR 27/632/7 cover operations for the day.
Thursday, 5 August	L.C. from Mabel. AIR 27/632/7 cover operations for the day.
Friday, 6ᵗAugust	*No recorded details in his diary.* AIR 27/632/7 cover operations for the day.
Saturday, 7 August	*No recorded details in his diary.* AIR 27/632/7 cover operations for the day.
Sunday, 8 August	Mass at the Cathedral, Tunis. A.G. from Fred Grant. AIR 27/632/7 cover operations for the day.
Monday, 9 August	Writing Mabel. AIR 27/632/7 cover operations for the day.
Tuesday, 10 August	*No recorded details in his diary.* AIR 27/632/7 cover operations for the day.
Wednesday, 11 August	Letter from Mabel, Mother and David Craig. AIR 27/632/7 cover operations for the day.
Thursday, 12 August	Writing Mabel. AIR 27/632/7 cover operations for the day.
Friday, 13 August	Wrote David Craig. AIR 27/632/7 cover operations for the day.
Saturday, 14 August	*No recorded details in his diary.* AIR 27/632/7 cover operations for the day.
Sunday, 15 August	Went to Mass at Thamet. Also visit Tunis. AIR 27/632/7 cover operations for the day.

Monday, 16 August	Wrote F. Grant, H. Carter, Marie, and Mother. AIR 27/632/7 cover operations for the day.
Tuesday, 17 August	*No recorded details in his diary.* AIR 27/632/7 cover operations for the day.
Wednesday, 18 August	*No recorded details in his diary.* AIR 27/632/7 cover operations for the day.
Thursday, 19 August	*No recorded details in his diary.* AIR 27/632/7 cover operations for the day.
Friday, 20 August	*No recorded details in his diary.* AIR 27/632/7 cover operations for the day.
Saturday, 21 August	*No recorded details in his diary.* AIR 27/632/7 cover operations for the day.
Sunday, 22 August	Mass at Sidi Thamet. AIR 27/632/7 cover operations for the day.
Monday, 23 August	Away on 'Detachment' AIR 27/632/7 cover operations for the day.
Tuesday, 24 August	Away on 'Detachment' AIR 27/632/7 cover operations for the day.
Wednesday, 25 August	Away on 'Detachment' AIR 27/632/7 cover operations for the day.
Thursday, 26 August	Away on 'Detachment' AIR 27/632/7 cover operations for the day.
Friday, 27 August	Away on 'Detachment'. L.C. from Mr. Langston, Mabel, Mother. AIR 27/632/7 cover operations for the day.
Saturday, 28 August	Away on 'Detachment' AIR 27/632/7 cover operations for the day.
Sunday, 29 August	Away on 'Detachment'. Mass at Sidi Thamet. AIR 27/632/7 cover operations for the day.
Monday, 30 August	Away on 'Detachment' AIR 27/632/7 cover operations for the day.
Tuesday, 31 August	Returned to Squadron. Received letter from Sid and John. AIR 27/632/7 cover operations for the day.

AIR 27/632/17 (1) & AIR 27/632/18 (1) Pilot Ops Report
September 1943:

Wednesday, 1ˢSeptember La Sabala	Wrote Mr. Leach, Mr. Langston, Nora, Mother, Mabel, and Bill. AIR 27/632/17 cover operations for the day.
Thursday, 2 September	Wrote Sid and John, Nelson. AIR 27/632/17 cover operations for the day.
Friday, 3 September	W/O posted to Wing. AIR 27/632/17 cover operations for the day.
Saturday, 4 September	Received L.C. from Mabel and Mother. AIR 27/632/17 cover operations for the day.
Sunday, 5 September	Working could not attend Mass. AIR 27/632/17 cover operations for the day.
Monday, 6 September	No mail. AIR 27/632/17 cover operations for the day.
Tuesday, 7 September	Writing Mabel, Aunt Mabel, and Mother. Working. S/LDR. Adam posted to 52B Group. AIR 27/632/17 cover operations for the day.
Wednesday, 8 September	Italy capitulated at 17:00 hrs. Sqdn. A/C operated from Italy, Par Roso. AIR 27/632/17 cover operations for the day.

Thursday, 9 September	Wrote L.H. 7, received L.C. from Derek Griffith. AIR 27/632/17 cover operations for the day.
Friday, 10 September	Wrote Derek Griffith, Mrs Earningshaw. AIR 27/632/17 cover operations for the day.
Saturday, 11 September	*No recorded details in his diary.* AIR 27/632/17 cover operations for the day.
Sunday, 12 September	No Mail AIR 27/632/17 cover operations for the day.
Monday, 13 September	*No recorded details in his diary.* AIR 27/632/17 cover operations for the day.
Tuesday, 14 September	*No recorded details in his diary.* AIR 27/632/17 cover operations for the day.
Wednesday,15 September	*No recorded details in his diary.* AIR 27/632/17 cover operations for the day.
Thursday, 16 September	Prepared to move. AIR 27/632/17 cover operations for the day.
Friday, 17 September	*No recorded details in his diary.* AIR 27/632/17 cover operations for the day.
Saturday, 18 September	*No recorded details in his diary.* AIR 27/632/17 cover operations for the day.
Sunday, 19 September	Could not attend Mass. AIR 27/632/17 cover operations for the day.
Monday, 20 September	Moved from Sebala to Bizerta. AIR 27/632/17 cover operations for the day.
Tuesday, 21 September	Arrived at Bizerta too late to catch boat. AIR 27/632/17 cover operations for the day.
Wednesday,22 September	Lovely day. AIR 27/632/17 cover operations for the day.
Thursday, 23 September	Moving today. Received letter from Mother, Mabel, and Cecil. AIR 27/632/17 cover operations for the day.
Friday, 24 September	Went to pictures in the hanger at harbour. AIR 27/632/17 cover operations for the day.
Saturday, 25 September	Still awaiting boat. AIR 27/632/17 cover operations for the day.
Sunday, 26 September	Went to Mass at Bizerta. Rained all day. AIR 27/632/17 cover operations for the day.
Monday, 27 September	Went to pictures. AIR 27/632/17 cover operations for the day.
Tuesday, 28 September	Still no news. AIR 27/632/17 cover operations for the day.
Wednesday,29 September	Played bridge all day. AIR 27/632/17 cover operations for the day.
Thursday, 30 September	Moved down to harbour, awaiting to board. AIR 27/632/17 cover operations for the day.

73 Squadron - LAC Lamb 1012281 diary continued:
AIR 27/632/19 & AIR 27/632/20 (1) Pilot Ops Report

October 1943:

| Friday, 1 October La Sabala | Will board, invasion has started. Feeling fed up. AIR 27/632/19 covers operations for the day. |
| Saturday, 2 October | Very calm sea. Still a good sailor, not seasick. AIR 27/632/19 covers operations for the day. |

Sunday, 3 October	Landed at Salerno and moved in land, strange time. AIR 27/632/19 covers operations for the day.
Monday, 4 October	Moved to Foggia Main, awaiting A/C to fly in. Onto C.M.F. AIR 27/632/19 covers operations for the day.
Tuesday, 5 October	Wrote L.C. letters to Mabel and Mother. AIR 27/632/19 covers operations for the day.
Wednesday, 6 October	Went picking walnuts and apples, had a wonderful time. AIR 27/632/19 covers operations for the day.
Thursday, 7 October	Rained all day and what rain. AIR 27/632/19 covers operations for the day.
Friday, 8 October	Rain again all day but cleared up at night. AIR 27/632/19 covers operations for the day.
Saturday, 9 October	Went to Salerno and purchased present for Mabel. AIR 27/632/19 covers operations for the day.
Sunday, 10 October	Preparing to move. Could not got to church. Packed Mabel parcel. AIR 27/632/19 covers operations for the day.
Monday, 11 October	Posted parcel also wrote Mabel. Went to Salerno and bought shoes and stockings – Move cancelled. AIR 27/632/19 covers operations for the day.
Tuesday, 12 October	Posted parcel of shoes and stockings. I pray that they arrive safely. AIR 27/632/19 covers operations for the day.
Wednesday, 13 October	*No recorded details in his diary.* AIR 27/632/19 covers operations for the day.
Thursday, 14 October **Wedding Anniversary**	*No recorded details in his diary.* AIR 27/632/19 covers operations for the day.
Friday, 15 October	*No recorded details in his diary.* AIR 27/632/19 covers operations for the day.
Saturday, 16 October	Wrote Sgt Dan Stevens. AIR 27/632/19 covers operations for the day.
Sunday, 17 October	Went to Mass at Montecorvino. AIR 27/632/19 covers operations for the day.
Monday, 18 October Bizerte	A/C arrived from Sebala. H.A. disappointment, A/C with mail not arrived. AIR 27/632/19 covers operations for the day.
Tuesday, 19 October	Remainder of A/C and mail. Letters from Mabel, Mother, Auntie, Mr. Leach, H. Carter. AIR 27/632/19 covers operations for the day.
Wednesday, 20 October Montecorvino	Wrote Mabel and Mr. Leach. AIR 27/632/19 covers operations for the day.
Thursday, 21 October	Moved to drome at Pontelequano. 18 kites from Salerno. AIR 27/632/19 covers operations for the day.
Friday, 22 October	*No recorded details in his diary.* AIR 27/632/19 covers operations for the day.
Saturday, 23 October	*[Start of the Battle of Alamein 09:40hrs, some 800 guns used to bombard the Germans.]* AIR 27/632/19 covers operations for the day.
Sunday, 24 October	Went to Mass at Pontelequano. Plenty of work. AIR 27/632/19 covers operations for the day.

Monday, 25 October	Plenty of Inspections In. AIR 27/632/19 covers operations for the day.
Tuesday, 26 October	'A' Party Played Wing won 2 – 1. I worked all day. 'B' party arrived today. No mail, Pay Parade. AIR 27/632/19 covers operations for the day.
Wednesday, 27 October	Purchased dress material for Mabel. AIR 27/632/19 covers operations for the day.
Thursday, 28 October	No mail. Letter from Mariann Ekland. AIR 27/632/19 covers operations for the day.
Friday, 29 October	No mail. AIR 27/632/19 covers operations for the day.
Saturday, 30 October	No mail. AIR 27/632/19 covers operations for the day.
Sunday, 31 October	Letter from Bill. Unable to attend Mass. AIR 27/632/19 covers operations for the day.

AIR 27/632/21 & AIR 27/632/22 Pilot Ops Report

November 1943:

Monday, 1 November Montecorvino	Wrote Mabel L.C. AIR 27/632/21 covers operations for the day.
Tuesday, 2 November	Conductor Tior 9237. AIR 27/632/21 covers operations for the day.
Wednesday, 3 November	*No recorded details in his diary.* AIR 27/632/21 covers operations for the day.
Thursday, 4 November	*No recorded details in his diary.* AIR 27/632/21 covers operations for the day.
Friday, 5 November	*No recorded details in his diary.* AIR 27/632/21 covers operations for the day.
Saturday, 6 November	*No recorded details in his diary.* AIR 27/632/21 Squadron released from camp, no operations for the day.
Sunday, 7 November	Working. AIR 27/632/21 covers operations for the day.
Monday, 8 November	Played Com Forces won 8 – 0. AIR 27/632/21 covers operations for the day.
Tuesday, 9 November	*No recorded details in his diary.* AIR 27/632/21 covers operations for the day.
Wednesday, 10 November	Played C.& at Rugby and won 14 – 0. AIR 27/632/21 covers operations for the day.
Thursday, 11 November	L.P. from Mabel. AIR 27/632/21 covers operations for the day.
Friday, 12 November	Xmas Greeting, Mabel Cards, Uncle George, and Mother. AIR 27/632/21 covers operations for the day.
Saturday, 13 November	*No recorded details in his diary.* AIR 27/632/21 covers operations for the day.
Sunday, 14 November	Entered Hospital today. 59 General with wounds in my leg. AIR 27/632/21 covers operations for the day.
Monday, 15 November	*No recorded details, in his diary.* AIR 27/632/21 covers operations for the day.
Tuesday, 16 November	Ken visited me in hospital. AIR 27/632/21 covers operations for the day.
Wednesday, 17 November	*No recorded details in his diary.* AIR 27/632/21 covers operations for the day also states that operations were cancelled due to poor weather.

Thursday, 18 November	Played C.7 at Rugby Sqdn. Won 12 – 0.
Friday, 19 November	L.C. from Mother and Mabel. Ken and Bill came, bought book, at Foggia Main. AIR 27/632/21 covers operational flying for the day.
Saturday, 20 November	Greetings, Bill, George. L.H.F. - R. Tiler. AIR 27/632/21 confirms the arrival of the new CO, S/Ldr. Chase. Operations carried out
Sunday, 21 November	*No recorded details in his diary.* AIR 27/632/21 confirms the Squadrons operations for the day.
Monday, 22 November	*No recorded details* AIR 27/632/21 confirms the Squadrons operations for the day.
Tuesday, 23 November	*No recorded details in his diary.* AIR 27/632/21 states heavy rain and no flying operations all cancelled. Rumours of move to Foggia.
Wednesday, 24 November	*No recorded details in his diary.* AIR 27/632/21 states heavy rain and no flying operations all cancelled.
Thursday, 25 November	Wrote Mabel and Mariann Ekland. AIR 27/632/21 states heavy rain and no flying operations all cancelled.
Friday, 26 November	L.C. from Mabel. AIR 27/632/21 states that the rain stopped in the night and some flying took place.
Saturday, 27 November	Graham Gilbert posted to new base camp, Sorento. AIR 27/6323/21 states that no flying could take place due to the waterlogged aerodrome.
Sunday, 28 November	Released from hospital. Went to Mass before I left, returned to 73 Squadron. AIR 27/6323/21 states that no flying could take place due to the waterlogged aerodrome.
Monday, 29 November	Wrote Mabel, received H.C. from Mr. Etherington, L.C. for Mabel. Letter P.O. Mr. Leach. AIR 27/632/21 confirms that a flying operation's took place today.
Tuesday, 30 November	*No recorded details in his diary.* AIR 27/632/21 covers the daily happenings with the CO returning from Foggia.

AIR 27/632/23 & AIR 27/632/24 Pilot Ops Report

December 1943:

Wednesday, 1 December Montecorvino	Moved to Foggia, arrived the same day. AIR 27/632/23 covers the Squadrons move from Montecorvino to Foggia Main.
Thursday, 2 December Foggia Main	*No recorded details in his diary.* AIR 27/632/23 confirms that the Squadrons aircraft arrived today.
Friday, 3 December	*No recorded details in his diary.* AIR 27/632/23 confirms that 73 Squadrons remaining party arrived. The personnel have billets and not tents.
Saturday, 4 December	*No recorded details in his diary.* AIR 27/632/23 confirms that the Squadrons dispersal tents and other equipment was installed.
Sunday, 5 December	Visited 83 B Sqdn, saw some films. AIR 27/632/23 confirms that sector flying was carried out.
Monday, 6 December	Went to pictures in hanger. AIR 27/632/23 states that a section of Spitfires was at readiness all day.

Tuesday, 7 December	Wrote Mabel letter. Went to stage show in hanger. AIR 27/632/23 some operations undertaken.
Wednesday, 8 December	Went to Mass and F/Sqt John Courage. AIR 27/632/23 some operations undertaken.
Thursday, 9 December	*No recorded details in his diary.* AIR 27/632/23 confirms that 2 Spitfire IX carried out flying operations.
Friday, 10 December	*No recorded details in his diary.* AIR 27/632/23 confirms that 2 Spitfire IX carried out flying operations.
Saturday, 11 December	*No recorded details in his diary.* AIR 27/632/23 confirms that 2 Spitfire IX carried out flying operations.
Sunday, 12 December	*No recorded details in his diary.* AIR 27/632/23 confirms that no flying operations were carried out.
Monday, 13 December	*No recorded details in his diary.* AIR 27/632/23 confirms that no flying operations were carried out.
Tuesday, 14 December	*No recorded details in his diary.* AIR 27/23 records that a number of operations were carried out and one DC3 landed with some VIPs on board.

(Reference made to **Morgan Laboratories**, (Dept F) 59, Gray's Inn Road. London WC1)
Could this be the place where tests were submitted for the allergic reaction he had had to penicillin?

Wednesday,15 December	*No recorded details in his diary.* AIR 27/632/23 some operations carried out along with some local flying practice and recces.
Thursday, 16 December	*No recorded details in his diary.* AIR 27/632/23 some operations undertaken.
Friday, 17 December	Wrote John and Mother. AIR 27/632/23 confirms a good number of operations were carried out.
Saturday, 18 December	*No recorded details in his diary.* AIR 27/632/23 confirms a good number of operations took place.
Sunday, 19 December	*No recorded details in his diary.* AIR 27/632/23 confirms that 'scrambles' took place plus practice flying.
Monday, 20 December	*No recorded details in his diary.* AIR 27/632/23 confirms only calibration tests undertaken today.
Tuesday, 21 December	*No recorded details in his diary.* AIR 27/632/23 refers to a good number of long-range operations undertaken by Spitfires.
Wednesday,22 December	*No recorded details in his diary.* AIR 27/632/23 records No operational flying done.
Thursday, 23 December	*No recorded details in his diary.* AIR 27/632/23 records No operational flying done.
Friday, 24 December	*No recorded details in his diary.* AIR 27/632/23 – Squadron at Foggia Main South Italy equipped with the latest Spitfires.
Saturday, 25 December.	*No recorded details in his diary.* AIR 27/632/23 Christmas day was celebrated as a non-working day and the airmen served a hearty meal by the CO.

Sunday, 26 December	**Final page missing of diary.** AIR 27/632/23 – Squadron at Foggia Main South Italy equipped with the latest Spitfires.
Monday, 27 December	**Final page missing of diary.** AIR 27/632/23 – Squadron at Foggia Main South Italy equipped with the latest Spitfires.
Tuesday, 28 December	**Final page missing of diary.** AIR 27/632/23 – Squadron at Foggia Main South Italy equipped with the latest Spitfires.
Wednesday,29 December	**Final page missing of diary.** AIR 27/632/23 – Squadron at Foggia Main South Italy equipped with the latest Spitfires.
Thursday, 30 December	**Final page missing of diary.** AIR 27/632/23 – Squadron at Foggia Main South Italy equipped with the latest Spitfires.
Friday, 31 December	**Final page missing of diary.** AIR 27/632/23 – Squadron at Foggia Main South Italy equipped with the latest Spitfires.

AIR 27/634/1 (1) & AIR 27/634/2 Pilot Ops Report
January 1944:
Having tried to obtain copies of RAF Medical Records relating to LAC Lamb L. B. 1012281, it appears that they were lost in a fire between 1997 and 2010. NO RECORDS available.

4 January	Transferred from Foggia Main to No.30 MFH.

No details available as to why the transfer took place. It is quite possible that the injuries sustained could be best treated in a hospital, hence his transfer to No.1 General Hospital Naples.

17 January	LAC Lamb L. 1012281 - Flown by Air from No.30 MFH to No.1 General Hospital, Naples. He remained here for the remainder of January 1944.

AIR 27/634/3 (1) & AIR 27/634/4 Pilot Ops Report
February 1944:
1 to 29 February	LAC Lamb L. 1012281 was hospitalised from the 17 January, through February and up to the 19 March 1944 in No.1 General Hospital, Naples.

AIR 27/634/5 (1) & AIR 27/634/6 (1) Pilot Ops Report
March 1944:
Now having to wear a Medical Alarm wristband, which detailed 'Allergic to Penicillin' for the rest of his life.

1 to 19 March In hospital, then *on the 20 of March discharged back to 73 Squadron*	LAC Lamb L. 1012281 (Armourer), who has been in hospital the last few months in NAPLES, returned to the Squadron today and will be leaving tomorrow for the UK. Discharged from No.1 General Hospital, Naples back to 73 Squadron at Foggia Main, Italy. **NOTE:** *He was to be sent back home with immediate effect.*

In the AIR 27/634/5 (1), which covers the Squadrons movements and operations, there is no mention of LAC Lamb L. 1012281 being sent back to the UK – Home Embarkation on the 21 March 1944.

AIR 27/634/7 (5) & AIR 27/634/8 (1) Pilot Ops Report

April 1944:

13 April   Orders for Home Embarkation issued ASAP. ***Dep. P.O.R. 106/44.*** In the Squadron records for April – AIR 27/634/7 (5) There is no record of any diary comment.

22 April   On this date according to the Service Record of LAC Lamb L. B. - 1012281, he duly arrived back in the UK and at RAF St Athan – 32 Maintenance Unit.

22 April   LAC Lamb L.B. was based at RAF St Athan, throughout the remainder of 1944, until 7 March 1945.

May 1944 to March 1945:

May 1944:   The RAF Archive Records held at RAF St Athan now MOD St Athan have been extensively checked by MOD personnel, both military and voluntary and unfortunately due to the age and condition of the records it has not been possible to corroborate the details held on file. I guess when you consider the period of time from 1944 to 2021, it is not surprising that some records have not been found.

March 1945:   At 10 S of TT RAF Kirkham – P.O.R. 149/45

April 1945 to February 1946:

26 November 1945   At 101 PDC RAF Kirkham RELEASED

1 February 1946   Effective Date of Release.

Chapter 7

THE STORIES & MEMORABILIA:

This chapter is set aside to retell some of the stories overheard whilst listening to conversations with old pals and comrades in which experiences were often shared and comparisons made. Also, to the spirit of those men, that, when the time came would give up their jobs and home life to fight in far off countries, and to the memory of those comrades who never returned home.

These are as clear today as they were when first heard. They tell of the apprehension felt, the harrowing experiences experienced and, and if one can dare say, it's light heartedness.

As a young boy, I can remember the times that I would try and find out more about what really happened and the experiences that my dad encountered during the war. Invariably the reply that I would receive was either **"there is nothing to tell"** or **"haven't got time now"**, and that would be the end of the conversation.

The only time that I could find out, would be when all the old friends and comrades would get together, and once together they would start to share and retell some of the things that happened to them whilst abroad, fighting against the German Army, the Luftwaffe, and the Italians who under Mussolini were fighting with and alongside the Germans.

On these very infrequent occasions, more so in later years; I would sit down away from the main group and listen to all that they had to say, it really was an experience, fascinating just listening and trying to understand what they all had been through. It soon became apparent to me why my father had not spoken about these times before.

Until you have experienced the mayhem, death, and destruction that war brings upon us all, then we are all naive to the effect that this had upon those who fought.

Just imagine for a minute that you have suddenly been posted overseas and placed in a hostile environment, little or no news of home and the family; unsure as to your own outcome [live or die] and having to fight against a ruthless force. Not easy, is it? Well, these men and women never really knew what to expect until it hit them; and as to how they would survive not only the battle, but the aftershock is hard to imagine. In today's world and the conflicts being fought it's called **Post Traumatic Stress Disorder (PTSD).**

It became clear why the stories always were kept locked away deep inside each person, and that my father was certainly no exception; this was a time in their lives (in particular, when your best pals were killed) that they wished to forget about. Every now and again however, it helped when reliving the past not because of the sadness of it all but the good times; and there were quite a few of those.

Story No. 1:

The following story has been given more credence after finding out some further details hidden within my father's notes and memoirs written at the time. His records/details relate to the time in May 1941 when Tobruk was under siege from the German and Axis Forces. He recalls that the remainder of the ground crew of 73 Squadron along with others were waiting on the quayside for ships to come alongside and evacuate them away from Tobruk and take them to the safety of Alexandria, Egypt. This was one such occasion, when the allied forces based in North Africa, confirmed as being Tobruk late May 1941, were being forced to retreat and that the men on the ground were to be evacuated by boat by any serviceable ship available. The officers in command were instructed to give the order to make for the quayside and to get their men on board the awaiting boats. On arrival at the quayside, it soon became apparent that there were no boats to get on board. Obviously a 'cock up' in the orders issued.

They waited and waited for the boats to arrive, during which time the enemy were strafing and bombing everywhere and everything; ensuring that the allies could not escape and that they would eventually be taken prisoner or killed depending on how your luck was running at the time.

In the true British spirit, the officers decided that to stay where they were, would be tantamount to suicide and that they should regroup the forces and prepare to try and break out. Just as the order was about to be given an officer spotted a flotilla of boats entering the harbour and that they were heading in their direction, one of the boats being **HMSAS Southern Isles**. Once the boats had docked alongside the quay, the order to embark was given, and as you can well imagine the men only needed telling once and relieved to hear the order to embark. The groundcrew of 73 Squadron and other allied service men clambered aboard **HMSAS Southern Isles.** *★ Refer to details given Chapter 5 - 'Siege of Tobruk', page 63.*

However, my father recalled that he and some of his pals boarded their assigned vessel, but on boarding they made sure that they were ready for any trouble that they may or may not arise. *'When I say prepared; they boarded the vessel armed with hand grenades, pins already removed'.* As they walked around the deck of the vessel, they became decidedly uneasy as they could conversations taking place and not understand the language being spoken. A plan of action had to be decided on, once this had been agreed they would all carry it out. This was typical of the men, the time, and the place. They had made their decision, which was to release the grenades all at once; **"well if we are to be taken prisoner or killed then we will blow the whole place sky-high"**. The very fact of losing their own lives really was not discussed; this was war and the appropriate action needed to be carried out.

As they entered one of the cabins areas, they could hear quite a few people talking and that these people, whoever they maybe were not aware of the pending explosion. What the group of airmen had not realized was that one of their officers was in deep conversation and it was not until he turned around to spot what was likely to happen, that he quickly spoke up and dispelled any doubts that the airmen had about the circumstances they found themselves in and informed them that the boat was now underway and leaving the harbour. As to 'why' they had doubts, was because the ship was manned by South Africans who were speaking in *'Africans'.*

The boat that they were on was one of the lucky ones to get away, there were those that never made it; either bombed or torpedoed with many lives lost. For those being shipped on HMSAS Southern Isles, they were some of the lucky ones, and were being taken to Alexandria, Egypt arriving there on 30 May 1941.

It was on a similar occasion to that above that the enemy sunk one of the ally's hospital ships. This took place in the port of Alexandria, with the loss of many lives. *(Refer to the photograph on Page 195)*

Shipping bombed, ALEXANDRIA, Egypt. Note: Naval and hospital ship at anchor.

Story No. 2:

This story, and a harrowing one at that; was not one where life was lost through being shot or bombed, but where a life was lost through just carrying out the everyday duties and tasks that were assigned to each one of the ground crew.

During the North African campaign, it was quite commonplace for ground crews to move around between the squadrons on what was termed **'*Detachment'*,** and it was on one of these occasions that this incident happened.

A selection of 73 Squadron ground crew were sent on detachment to 39 Squadron, which flew Bristol Blenheim bombers and Bristol Beaufort or Beaufighter's. Their task on their detachment was to prepare the squadrons bombers for take-off. It is quite likely that the type of aircraft was a Bristol Beaufort or Beaufighter one of which 39 Squadron flew.

Having completed all the preparation work to the aircraft in readiness for the aircraft to take off, they would then assist in the planes take off procedure. A job that they had carried out on numerous occasions before and without any problems. Once the pilot had completed his check list and had started the engines, he would signal to the ground crew to take the wheel blocks away *(term commonly known as "chocks away")*. Everything appeared to be OK, and the plane started to taxi towards the runway. What my father didn't realize was that his pal, who was working along beside him had been killed. Instead of walking away to the rear of the plane and away from the rotating propellers; for some unexplained reason, he had walked in the wrong direction and directly into the propeller blades with a catastrophic result.

Everyone, from that day onwards made doubly sure that incidents like that should not happen. In this war, there was no room for complacency. Good men and seasoned campaigners, as this man was, could never be replaced. Such a needless loss of life.

Story No. 3:

One of the more light-hearted moments that now and again would come into their conversations was the time when having just re-captured a previously German held position and finding, to their amazement, underground storage tanks (for fuel or fuel oil) full of red wine.

The story begins just after the allied forces had taken previously held German territory. Having captured quite an important position the allied forces set about rebuilding the airfield and buildings using captured German and Italian soldiers and airmen.

Obviously, the squadron had limited resources and did the best they could under the circumstances. Whilst repairing part of the airfield the ground crew came across some manhole covers and on lifting them found to their amazement that these led to underground storage tanks. They quickly established that the contents were not as they thought (fuel, fuel oil or water), but **Red Wine.** The question asked was, "how the hell did this lot get here?" "Obviously, the Germans and Italians had put it there." Came the reply.
Anyway, no time was wasted, and a sample tasted. **Urika!!!** One can imagine the sheer delight on finding such a find, especially bearing in mind where they were. Comments like "someone up there is looking after us" was the general feeling amongst the pilots and ground crew."

The word soon had gotten around, that an underground tank full of wine had been found, everyone including the officers wanted to be in on the action.

Now you must realize that these tanks are buried in the sand, some distance underground to protect them from the suns' heat and the cold of the desert at night, also to protect them from any possible air attack. To gain access to these tanks there was an access tube with a manhole cover capable of taking a man. *(Refer to the sketch below.)*

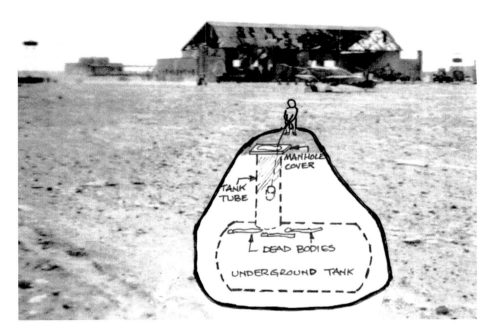

As more and more men became aware of the find the demand for more of the wine became greater. As a result of this they had to resort to using a bucket tied to a length of rope to try and retrieve the tank contents.

You can just imagine what they all must have thought, "a supply of plonk that will last one hell of a long time." 'Well, that is what they thought.'!

After several days had passed by, and everyone enjoying the rich rewards and fruits of their labour; they suddenly found that when the buckets were drawn back up that they only contained small amounts of wine in them. Eventually one of the ground crew shone a light down the access tube, and to his amazement he could see what appeared to be a body wearing a German uniform. On closer inspection, the truth came to light. It was a dead German soldier. Several other bodies were retrieved from the tank. Obviously placed there for a reason, the reason being to try and poison the wine and subsequently anyone who was fortunate to find and drink of it. Well, you can imagine the feeling going around the squadron. The medics were inundated with men wanting to know the outcome of them drinking this infected wine. One of the crewmen came out with a suitable pun "well that wine certainly had plenty of body in it."

After the above experience, needless to say, they all went off the idea of drinking the wine.

The one good thing, if there is a GOOD THING IN WAR, is that they managed to retrieve all the dead bodies from the underground tank and that these were all given a proper military burial in the local mixed German, Italian and Allied forces graveyard. *(**Refer to following photographs.**)*

There are many, many other stories that are of a similar nature to those written about in this chapter. In relating these stories, I have endeavoured to retrace the true feeling of what it must have been like when fighting away from home in far off countries.

Here are some photographs of the typical mixed graveyards that were used for burial, both of Allied Armed Forces, Italian Armed Forces and German Armed Forces.

Shared graveyard for Allied, Italian, and German troops – North Africa

Shared graveyard for Allied, Italian, and German troops – North Africa

These were taken somewhere in the North African desert, circa 1940 - 43
Not only were there graves for burial of dead soldiers and airmen, but there were also graveyard areas for downed German aircraft. *(The following photographs display typical sites along with Italian POW's.)*

Section of plane graveyard [Note: Reference bomb casings) July, August 1943

Remains of German 109F's DABA – August 1942

STUKA dive bomber August 1943, u/s but plenty of Perspex

GAMBUT – July, August 1943. German planes graveyard, taken during Final Push.

Group of captured Italian troops, POW's
TOBRUK 1941/42 – put to work digging trenches.

Chapter 8

ITEMS DISCOVERED, HOBBIES, etc.:

This chapter details and shows some of the memorabilia collected during his service in the RAF whilst stationed in North Africa 1940 to 1943, and Italy 1943 to 1944.

Whilst stationed in the Middle East during World War II it was customary to be paid in what was called **_ALLIED MILITARY CURRENCY_**. A sample of the typical Italian money issued to the Allied Forces at the time is shown below. Unfortunately, a little faded with time but still legible.

      1 LIRA Italian WW 2 Bank Note   **10 LIRA Italian WW 2 Bank Note**

From the limited yet extremely useful information contained within the diaries of L.A.C. Lamb it can quite easily be felt as to the type of life being experienced during the North African and Italy Campaign, and how best they overcame the boredom and sometimes tediousness of the job.

Some remarkably interesting items of discovery at the time were some Russian and German Bank notes. From the investigation carried out these bank notes along with some German, Netherlands, Belgium, and French coins were all found in one of the deserted derelict buildings that had recently been captured from the Germans.

The Russian Bank notes that were discovered are to the value of 500 Roubles _[issued by the Russian State Bank, date 1912]_ and 1000 Roubles _[issued under the name CREDIT MONEY, by the Provisional State Government of RUSSIA, date 1917]_. **_Photographs of these are shown on Page 202._**

500 Rouble Bank Note **1000 Rouble Bank Note**

The German, Netherlands, Belgium, and French coins are all typical of the coins in circulation at the time. It would be fair to say that these were obviously brought to North Africa by one or more of the invading forces and lost during the ensuing battles.

German - 1000 Reichsbaut'note

In addition to the bank notes and coins found, some coins were found in the desert area whilst digging trenches for protection. The coins discovered are of a much earlier period, and it was not until December 1993 to be precise; that their actual date in history was established.

The Ashmolean Museum in Oxford were instrumental in giving precise dates to these coins and from the information and data collated it has been confirmed that these are genuine coins from the ***CARTHAGE*** and ***OTTERMAN*** periods.

There can be no doubt, that like all service men fighting abroad, if the opportunity presented itself by way of collecting souvenirs to bring back home then my father was certainly no exception from anyone else. I would like to think that in bringing these articles back with him it was a way of keeping in touch with the reality that they all faced. Just small fragments of a much larger jigsaw that had been part of their lives during the duration of the war.

However, devastated by the act of warfare and its inevitable destruction of man and his world; these items were a constant reminder to them of not only the bad times but more importantly the good times.

Collection of Coins & Bank Notes set in sand

There were times when the allied forces captured previously held German positions. My father would recall the fact that the first place of call, once they had been made safe from any booby traps, was to inspect the discarded and wrecked planes that the Germans had left behind, to see if any parts were salvageable. Items like, guns, ammunition, Perspex from the cockpit canopies and any item that they could best make use of. Spares of any description were hard to come by especially if the following supply convoys were detained for one reason or another.

From the photographic evidence taken at the time you can get a feeling for the type of life that they all led, and the conditions in which they had to live and hopefully survive.

The Allied troops while stationed in the Middle East would keep themselves occupied in the quieter moments by taking up a hobby. Some of the hobby's that were employed by the troops were making rings and cap badge backings out of Perspex, trick photography and catching desert snakes and skinning them. Once the snake was skinned the skin would then be placed in oils to preserve it. *(Refer to the photograph below.)*

Snake 3' 3" long SIDI AMOUD, March 1941

Unfortunately for my father, his collection of snake skins was stolen and was never recovered. If you can; imagine the feelings that must have been felt at that moment, all that painstaking time and effort in collecting those skins, for what? Well, it may not have been realized at the time, but one positive thing that had happened by way of collecting these skins, and all the other hobby's that were on going at the time, help keep the boredom at bay but more importantly kept the war and all that went with it way in the back of their minds and out of sight!

Chapter 9

Field Hospital, Home Embarkation, Relocation, Demobilization & Family History.

My father. Leo Bernard Lamb – LAC 1012281, enlisted in the RAF in May 1940 and during the period 1940 – 1945 he served in North Africa and, latterly, in the Italian campaign. During this period many of his comrades were either injured or lost their lives, the ultimate sacrifice. We who live in peace today must be extremely grateful for our todays because those who fought and those who died ensured that peace returned, and lives could be lived once again.

A. *Field Hospital:*

In November 1943 my father was admitted into No. 59 British General Hospital (BGH) with injuries to his legs, having been hit by some enemy shrapnel. The hospital was in Mercattella, Salerno, Southern Italy. Official Medical Records for my father cannot be released by the MOD due to all medical records being retained under the 1991 Act. However, during the remainder of his life he had to wear a Medical Alert wrist band, which indicated that he was allergic to Penicillin. This discovery came about whilst being treated for his injuries in the 59 BGGH and an allergic reaction being experienced.

From records prepared by my father he recorded that he was admitted to 59 BGH on the 14/11/1943 and discharged two weeks later on 28/11/1943.

Summary Movement History of 59 British General Hospital:
Peebles 4/41 to 12/41 then overseas.
El Ballah, Eygpt 2/42 to 3/42 then to Gebeit, Sudan.
Gebeit, Sudan 3/42 to 6/43 then to Moascar, Egypt.
Moascar 6/43 to 9/43 then to Tripoli, Libya.
Tripoli 9/43 to 10/43 then to Mercattella, Salerno, Southern Italy.
Mercattella Salerno, Southern Italy 10/43 to 2/44 then to Castellammare, Sicily.
Castellammare, Sicily 2/44 to 8/44 then to Orvieto, Italy.
Orvieto, Italy 8/44 to 11/44 then to Fano, Italy
Fano, Italy 11/44 to 4/45 then to Fortii, Italy.
Fortii, Italy 4/45 to 5/45 then to Forli, Italy.
Forli Italy 5/45 to 10/45 then to Bologna, Italy.
Bolagna, Italy 10/45 to 15/9/46 then disbanded.

No.30 MFH and No.1 GH Naples:
As regards to any further hospitalization; in some of the records there are two dates, which relate to No.30 MFH on the 4 January 1944 and No.1 GH Naples 17 January 1944, this infers that whilst he had been admitted to No. 30MFH he required further and better treatment, hence transferred to No.1 GH Naples, Italy.

On following up my research on the above it became apparent that my father had a long period of time in hospital during the early months of 1944. *This is further reported in the books written by Don Minterne – The History of 73 SQUADRON. In Part 3 and on page 29, 20 March 1944 and I quote 'The field was being resurfaced, so there was no flying. LAC Leo Lamb (armourer) returned from Naples where he had been in hospital for some months. He was ordered to leave for the UK with immediate effect.'*

Whilst carrying out further research into my father's medical history, I received confirmation from the Ministry of Defence (MOD) that his medical records, along with many others were lost in a fire, the date and time of which would not be disclosed.

B. *Home Embarkation:*

The return journey to the United Kingdom for my father took place on 13/4/1944. With further research carried out it was established that he was brought home by troop ship, either on HMT Orontes or Ormonde. The most likely embarkation port would have been either Birkenhead or Southhampton. Actual details are not recorded.

His repatriation saw him arrive on or around the 22 April 1944 at **32 MU**, which stands for 32 Maintenance Unit, RAF St Athan, South Wales, which was part of the then No.43 Group Maintenance Command, Repair Depot.

History of RAF St Athan & 32 Maintenance Unit:

MOD, DDC Brand & Licensing Manager: Pauline Aquiline email 09/02/2022 Approval to use Squadron Insignia/Badges (only inside the book NOT on Front & Rear Covers

The Station opened in September 1938 and was built on a site known locally *[since the time of Henry I]* as the East and West Orchards. The site was purchased by the Air Ministry in 1936, with the intention of establishing a permanent RAF station; however, the URGENT requirement for new training accommodation necessitated the construction of a hutted camp as an interim measure. Those 'interim measures' were still standing on the East Camp until the end of the 1990's. The erection of permanent buildings began in 1939 and these included a cinema, a heated swimming pool (the first in Wales), a huge gymnasium and an indoor drill hall. The airfield, initially with grassed landing area, was situated in the middle of the site, the hard runway system being laid down in 1942.

Station Headquarters opened on 1 September 1938, under the command of Group Captain E B Brice, the Station being administered by No. 24 Group Training Command. The first unit to take up residence was No. 4 School of Technical Training (4SofTT), which was responsible for the training of flight mechanics, riggers, and MT drivers. The school is still situated on the East Camp. In 1939, the scope of the Station's activities began to expand with the arrival of other units, including a fighter group pool, a maintenance unit (MU) and a school of air navigation.

The increase in the size and importance of the Station led to the position of Commanding Officer being upgraded to air rank, and Air Commodore the Honourable J D Boyle was the first air officer to fill the position.

In 1940, RAF St Athan was subjected to air attack several times, sustaining casualties and damage; during one air raid, the large and well-equipped Station Hospital was bombed. As the war progressed, many more units, of diverse nature, were transferred to and from St Athan. Among those were various training units, which were responsible for turning out 22,000 flight engineers and thousands of other trained personnel, including ground mechanics, wireless and radio operators, physical training instructors and navigators. Nos. 19 and 32 MUs handled a great variety of stores and undertook repairs to vast numbers of aircraft and other equipment. For a time, the Czechoslovak Air Force Depot was also situated at RAF St Athan.

At its wartime peak, the Station's working population totalled over 14,000 men and women. With the transfer of ownership of the St Athan site to the Welsh Assembly Government, the introduction of commercial businesses and the arrival of the Special Forces Support Group, the Royal Air Force St Athan was renamed MOD St Athan on 1 HULY 2006. This title more accurately represented the diversity of the personnel based there. No. 4 SofTT, which is part of the Defence College of Electro-Mechanical Engineering, has taken over the RAF Support Unit role, with CO 4 SofTT taking on the post as Senior RAF Officer St Athan or CO MOD St Athan (RAF).

Based Units:

- No. 9 Aircraft Storage Unit (1938 – 7 Feb 1939)
- No. 19 Maintenance Unit (7 Feb 1939 – 1 Nov 1968/7 Apr 1999)
- No. 32 Maintenance Unit (1 Jul 1939 – 1 Nov 1968/7 Apr 1999)
- No. 11 Group Pool (1 Jul 1939 – 9 Mar 1940)
- No. 4 Air Stores Park (26 Aug – 15 Sep 1939)
- No. 5 Air Stores Park (26 Aug – 16 Sep 1939)
- School of Air Navigation (2 Sep 1939 – Jun 1940)
- No. 1 School of Air Navigation (Jun – 12 Oct 1940)
- No. 5 Salvage Centre (18 – 24 Sep 1939)
- Special Duty Fit (14 Nov 1939 – 27 Apr 1940)
- No. 417 Fit (15 Jul – 1 Oct 1940)
- 'U' Fit, No. 1 AACU (15 Aug – 15 Sep 1940)
- No. 1417 Fir (1 – 18 Mar 1941)
- No. 4 School of Technical Training (1 Sep 1938 – Current)
- No. 12 Radio School (1 Sep 1943 – 7 Mar 1946)
- No. 14 Radio School (1 Jun 1944 – 7 Mar 1946)
- Signals Instructor School (1 Jun 1944 - ?)
- No. 68 Gliding School (Mar 1947 – 1 Sep 1955)
- Special Installation Fit)29 Feb 1948 – 5 Oct 1953)
- No. 634 Volunteer Gliding School (1 Sep 1955 – 1 May 1964, 1 Oct 1964 – Current)
- University of Wales Air Sqn (26 Aug 1963 – Current)
- Repair and Salvage Squadron (1991 – Current)
- Aircraft Recovery and Transportation Fit (1991 – Current)

RAF St Athan – 32 Maintenance Unit 1944

In February 1939, St Athan became the home for No.4 School of Technical Training with over 1500 staff and trainees, a number which soon doubled.

No.19 Maintenance Unit (MU) formed in March 1939 as a civilian Aircraft Storage Unit. By January 1940, 280 aircraft were in storage, mostly Fairey Battles and Hawker Hurricanes. These were followed by Bristol Blenheim's, Westland Lysanders, Boulton Paul Deviant's and Bristol Beaufighter's, Supermarine Spitfires, Armstrong Whitworth Whitley's, Vickers Wellingtons, Avro Lancaster's, and De Havilland Mosquitos, taking the total to over 700 by the autumn.

In August 1939, 32 MU were assigned to St Athan and specialised in installing electronic devices such as Air-to-Surface Vessel radar (ASV), Identification Friend or Foe (IFF) and Airbourne Inspection Radar (AI), other work included strengthening Wellington bomber wing spars.
In April 1940, a School of Air Navigation moved to St Athan from RAF Manston, with No.12 Radio School utilising a flight of Avro Ansons from September 1943 - May 1944 under the command of No.27 Signals Group.

When the war ended, the two maintenance units remained, and the base continues with the important functions of repair, overhaul and storage for both the RAF and Royal Navy (DARA). The aircraft that make up the Battle of Britain Memorial Flight are also noted as having been repaired here. Areas of the base are also now used by army units.

St Athan remains an active RAF station with many of the original wartime period expansion buildings and hangars still in use.

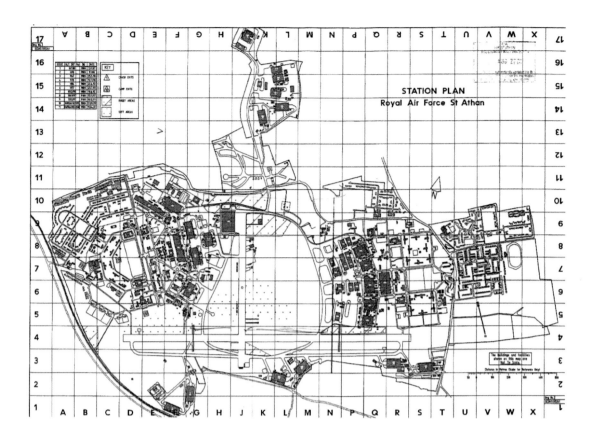

Station Plan – RAF St Athan (photo A)

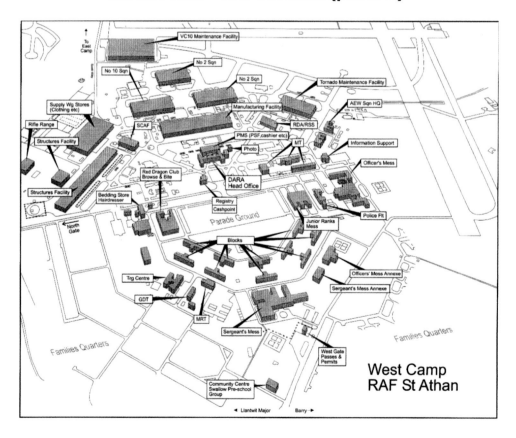

West Camp – RAF St Athan (photo B)

Aerial View of RAF St Athan (photo C)

MOD St Athan/RAF: Wing Commander Mr G. Wedlake Station Commander and WO David Stroud, Station Warrant Officer approved use of Images A, B, C and D from RAF St Athan.

C. *Relocation & Demobilization:*

My father's records further show that on 7/3/1945 he was relocated to No.10 S of TT (No. 10 School of Technical Training) RAF Kirkham, Lancashire, No.24 Group TTC (Technical Training Command).

The next seven months saw him no doubt carry out various training courses to enhance his knowledge, but eventually on the 26/10/1945 my father entered No.101 PDC (No. 101 Personnel Dispersal Centre) RAF Kirkham, Lancashire No.28 Group, Technical Training Command. This unit handled demobilization of ground crew and became the main outlet for all personnel, irrespective of theatre of their origin, sex, or status.

On his return from the war dad had been away for 3 years and 5 months, and as recorded fought in the North African Campaign as well as the Italian Campaign. Now back home he could once again start to enjoy life with his wife Mabel who he had married on the 14 October 1940. After talking to my sister [Dorinda] and from the address on her birth certificate we can establish that mum and dad had set up home in 18, Welford Street, Barry, South Wales. This would make sense as Barry is quite close to RAF St Athan where he was to finish his carrier in the RAF. His effective date of release being 1 February 1946, making his period of service 5 years and 7 months.

D. *Leo Bernard Lamb – Life's History:*

The following dates and Life History set out in brief the life's history of **Leo Bernard Lamb**:

Dates   **LAC Lamb L B, Service No. 1012281 Life's History [in brief]**
The Early Years:

04/07/1912   Date of birth – Born in Gloucester and lived at 11 St Mark Street then at 12 Alvin Street.

03/09/1917   Attended St Peter's School, London Road, Gloucester.

04/07/1920   St Peter's Roman Catholic Church – served as an Altar Server and then when older sang in the choir with his three brothers: George, William (Bill) and Sydney. All the sons started out as altar servers before progressing on to becoming choristers.

01/09/1920   Admission to National School for Boys, London Road, Gloucester. Entry No. 4311

03/09/1920   Local school records indicate the date of his Admission to Widden Street Boys School, Gloucester.

20/09/1920   Further research showed that his Admission to Widden Street Boys School was on this date and not as detailed previously above. Entry No. 52

16/09/1921   School records show that he left Widden Street Boys School and was then transferred back to National School for Boys.

Between the years of 1921 to 1929 it is unclear as to how long he was at the National School for Boys. It would no doubt have been the case that once you had got to the age of 15, 16 or 17 you were sent out to work, and that any further education would have been carried out at Evening Schools. All as detailed below.

Circa 1927   Greengrocers, Gloucester: W. J. Holder – Tredworth, High Street. That is him on the right in dark clothes.

| Session 1929 - 30 | Attended Tredworth Evening Preparatory Technical Classes and awarded a 'Certificate of Merit – Proficiency in the Third Stage in English and Drawing. He attended 122 times out of a possible 132. |

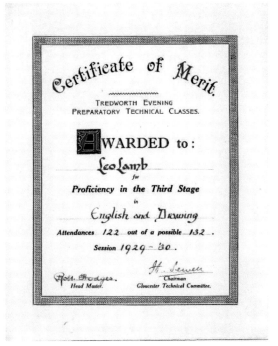

Other places of work:
Cannot confirm the date [circa 1930's], but during his early working life he also worked in a shop, which was called Fearris's – Purveyors of all things Grocery and Game. They had several outlets at the time in the city. The shop he worked in was in the Oxebode, Gloucester.

The Post War Years: [1930 – 1939]
To try and establish what he did before signing up in May 1940 is not the easiest thing to achieve, especially when personal records no longer exist. Several areas of his life have been previously covered, particularly school and work.

What is not covered is his sporting life and how he came to meet my mother (Mabel Broomhead). Having looked through family photographs from this period, what we do know is that he liked playing football, rugby, cricket, and tennis. It was whilst joining as a member of the then Wotton Lawn Tennis Club, off Denmark Road, Gloucester that this was where he was to meet my mother playing tennis.

The War Years: [1940 – 1946]

25/05/1940   Signed up to join the Royal Air Force at the Labour Exchange, Gloucester.

25/07/1940   Transported from Gloucester to RAF Padgate, initial basic introduction to military life.

27/07/1940   Transported to RAF West Kirby for Full Training in Combat, Physical Exercise, etc.

17/08/1940   After the initial training transferred to RAF Debden - 73 Squadron – Hurricanes'. The squadron were being made ready to be posted to North Africa.

14/10/1940   On this day, Dad and Mum married at St Peter's RC Church, London Road, Gloucester. Photographs below of the happy couple. *A bit of trivia (on this day Sir Cliff Richards OBE was born in Lucknow, India. True name is Harry Rodger Webb).*

My Dad & Mum with Dad's Mum, Edith Lamb and
Mum's Dad William H. Broomhead.

The happy couple having just got married.

The happy couple off on a few days' 'honeymoon'.

13/11/1940	Troops and RAF personnel boarded S.S. Franconia in Birkenhead, Liverpool, the ship would transport them initially to Gibraltar before being transferred to HMS Manchester, who would transport them to Alexandria, North Africa.
22/11/1940	S.S. Franconia docked at Gibraltar with NO shore leave being granted.
23/11/1940	S.S. Franconia remained moored in the docks in Gibraltar. In the middle of the day H.M.S. Manchester lying alongside and other ships in the harbour assisted by the ground defences opened fire on a hostile aircraft at 12,000 feet.
24/11/1940	S.S. Franconia remained moored at the quayside all day during which orders were received that the whole of the Squadron personnel was required to transfer themselves to H.M.S. Manchester.
25/11/1940	The orders received on the 24/11/1940 were put in place and the first party left S.S. Franconia at 04:00 hours. The whole Squadron had embarked [without an incident] on board H.M.S. Manchester by 05:20 hours.
27/11/1940	Whilst on board HMS Manchester, the ship and convoy they were travelling with received orders to engage with the Italian Fleet off Cape Spartivento.
30/11/1940	HMS Manchester arrived and docked in Alexandria at 11:00 hours. At about 14:00 hours the Squadron disembarked and proceeded to Heliopolis (RAF Cairo), arriving at 21:30. The Heliopolis station record notes that the arriving party comprised six officers, 17 SNCOs and 230 other ranks (OR).
1940 to 1942/3	North Africa Campaign – Heliopolis, Cairo, Tobruk, El Alamein and many other battles.
1943 to 1944	Italian Campaign – Salerno, Naples, Foggia Main
14/11/1943	Admitted to 59 BGH Mercattella (Salerno) Dep. POR 83/43.
28/11/1943	Discharged from 59 BGH Mercatella (Salerno) POR 86/43
04/01/1944	From Foggia Main, Admitted to No.30 MFH.
17/01/1944	Flown from No.30 MFH to Nr. 1 General Hospital, Naples.
20/03/1944	Returned to 73 Squadron from Naples Hospital where he had been for some months.!! He received orders to leave Italy with immediate effect for the UK.
13/04/1944	Home Embarkation: Transported back to Great Britain from Italy. Dep. POR 106/44

Repatriation to Release Date & Beyond:

22/04/194 4	On this day according to my father's Service Record - LAC 1012281 Lamb L. B., arrived at RAF St. Athan, South Wales – No.32 (MU) Maintenance Unit.

Having now carried out an extensive search/check with MOD St Athan through Warrant Officer David H Stroud and his team of archivists as regard to any RAF Records relating to my father. I have had confirmation from their search of the archived records that due to the age of the paper documents and the number of times that these have been moved, that they are in a very poor state/condition, and on closer examination there doesn't appear to be any further details on file relating to LAC 1012281 Lamb L. B. other than the photograph of 1945 – No. 32 MU Armament, as shown below.

In the above photograph I believe that my father is the one in the 3rd row and the 3rd person in, who is in the middle of the group of five. (Photo D)

MOD St Athan/RAF: Wing Commander Mr G. Wedlake Station Commander and WO David Stroud, Station Warrant Officer approved use of Images from RAF St Athan.

216

| 1944-1946 | Lived in a terraced house, 18 Wilford Street, Barry, South Wales. |

| 07/03/1945 | Transferred to RAF Kirkham – No.10 (S of TT) School of Technical Training. Dep. POR 56/45 and POR 149/45 confirmed arrival at RAF Kirkham. |

| 15/09/1945 | Dorinda [daughter] was born in Barry Hospital. |

| 26/10/1945 | Transferred to RAF Kirkham – No.101 (PDC) Personnel Dispersal Centre. Dep. POR 649/45 |

| 01/02/1946 | Effective Date of Release. Release Class 'A' – Release priority was based on age and length of time in service. |

| 14/03/1946 | Family moved to live at 10, Wern Crescent, Nelson, Glamorgan with my mum's family. |

| 03/1946 | Some information relating to dad's employment!! Grocery Assistant and worked for some time, somewhere in Redditch, England |

| 13/06/1947 | Presentation to Ex-Service Men & Women of the Parish. This took place at The Princes Hall, Gloucester. The service men and women were all presented with 'The Key of Heaven' – A manual of prayer for the use of the Faithfull. |

| 24/09/1949 | Philip [son] was born in Church Village Hospital, Pontypridd, South Wales. |

| 02/1952 | At around this time dad had moved back to Gloucester and most weekends he would travel down to Wales on the Red & White bus service to see us, then travel back to Gloucester for his work. |

03/1952	Started work as a Progress Chaser in No.1 Shop at Rotol Aircraft Corporation, Cheltenham Road, Gloucester, which later became Dowty Rotol. Dad worked here, up to the date of his retirement (as stated later). In the years that followed the name of the company would change several times.
May 1957	My Dad having secured a tenancy on a house ensured that his family could move from Nelson, Glamorgan to live at 9, Tetbury Road, Tuffley, Gloucester.
04/07/1977	Dad retired from the company after 25 years' service.
09/04/1988	Dad passed away on this day, aged 75 years & 9 months. Dad's ashes are buried in the Garden of Remembrance at Prinknash Abbey, near Painswick, Gloucestershire.
23/01/2008	Mum passed away on this day aged 90 years, just two days from what would have been her 91st Birthday. Mum's ashes are buried with in the Garden of Remembrance at Prinknash Abbey with dad's ashes.

Chapter 10

RAF West Kirby Association:

This chapter has been included within the book by way of remembering and commemorating all those service men and women from many countries and of all nationality's, who had joined up in the hour of need, and to fight wherever they were sent to. Also, to commemorate all those who made the ultimate sacrifice, and those who have since passed away in recent years.

Posters like the one shown were displayed all over the country and throughout the commonwealth, which said **'Your Country Needs You'**.

In my search for information relating to the men that signed up to 'Fight for King and Country' at the start and during the World War II conflict, in particular those men who joined the Royal Air Force as raw recruits in whatever capacity. Men and women were needed to as there were ample places to fill and provide the force to fight off the aggressor, namely Adolf Hitler and his armies.

During my investigations I came across some of these men who had received their training at RAF West Kirby. After completing their service in the RAF, a goodly number of them set about arranging an association so that old comrades could renew their friendships and once again reminisce about their time together. Also, to tell the stories about the 'good old day's'.

This band of comrades/brothers eventually set up the **RAF West Kirby Association**. Unfortunately, like many things the years have taken their toll with many of the Association Members are no longer with us. **'Mores the Pity'** and **'Thanks for the memories.'**

When carrying out my research of the West Kirby Camp I happened to come across a book entitled 'West Kirby and Beyond' – written by Dennis Tomlinson (RIP), who himself was a raw recruit and trained at the camp. The book is a great read and gives a wonderful insight into life on the base and around West Kirby itself.

It was at this time I contacted Mr. Alan Carter – RAFWKA Treasurer through the association's website, and I shall be eternally grateful for his invaluable help and assistance. He not only answered all my questions that I posed but more importantly through his association with the RAF West Kirby Association gave me the consent/approval to use the websites images in my book. The use of these images gives an incredible insight into 'Camp Life', and the training that they all had to undergo. Furthermore, he confirmed the following: -

The RAF West Kirby Association held its first gathering on 31 March 2000 at the 'Twelfth Man' in Greasby, which is very close to where the camp was situated. The original organiser was Mrs Ada Stewart (a former NAFFI employee) ably assisted by Mrs. Joan Mackay. Ada had contacted all the people for whom she had contact details of, along with placing advertisements in the local newspapers. Mr Alan Carter was one of those who replied to the advert in the Liverpool Echo. There were no formalities, they simply met in the bar, chatted away and later enjoyed a buffet at £5.00 per head. On the 22 October 2005 an AGM was held, and a Formal Constitution was adopted by the members, the Executive Committee comprised; Chairman - Peter Johnson, Secretary & Treasurer - Terry Barry and Membership Secretary – Bob Oliver who also compiled the Newsletter. Due to dwindling numbers and other factors outside of the Associations control it was decided at the AGM on 28 September 2019 that this would be the associations 'Last Reunion'.

The plaque Image supplied by Mr. Alan Carter – RAF West Kirby Association. Email consent on the 08/03/2022.

The above plaque is located on the church wall, the church being Westbourne Road Methodist Church, West Kirby along with the RAF West Kirby Standard. The plaque commemorates the valued association between the Church and the Royal Air Force at West Kirby during 1939 to 1957.

The church had a significant role in the recruit's life, in that on arriving at your new home for the next number of weeks whilst being trained, you would not be allowed to leave camp. There was of course one exception, that was, if you wished to go to church on a Sunday evening. You can just imagine the take up for going to church, regardless of your religion!

As with some recruits, homesickness played a part in them pining for home. The following day, groups of recruits would be welcomed by the Station Commander and one of the pet sayings was 'If you see any man kneeling down to say his prayers in your billet tonight, don't make fun of him. He's probably got more guts than the rest of you put together.' There never were times when anyone was teased for his religious convictions.

In August 1954 the base was awarded its new badge/insignia, which is detailed below along with a brief description of what the lighthouse and rock signify and history of the forming of the base back in 1940.

No.5 School of Recruit Training

Awarded: August 1954
Blazon: On a Red Rock proper a Lighthouse Sable
Motto: Firm foundations prevail
MOD, DDC Brand & Licensing Manager: Pauline Aquiline email 09/02/2022
Approval to use Squadron Insignia/Badges (only inside the book NOT on Front & Rear Covers)

Link: The lighthouse on a rock indicates this unit's endeavour to provide a firm foundation upon which a recruit may build his service career. The badge also suggests the unit's location on the Red Rocks at the mouth of the river Dee where a lighthouse is situated.

History: Opened as No. 5 Recruits Centre on 25 April 1940 at West Kirby. Re-designated No.1 Personnel Despatch Centre on 17 September 1941. Reformed at West Kirby on 1 September 1946 and was re-designated No 5 School of Recruit Training on 1 November 1948. The final Passing Out Parade took place on 20 December 1957 and West Kirby closed on 1 January 1958.
Sponsored by Bernard and Richard Clarkson and dedicated to all who served at, and passed through RAF West Kirby

APPENDIX

1 – Pictures taken during the Desert Campaign 1940 – 1943

2 – Pictures of Alexandria, Port Said etc.

3 – Souvenir Postcards of Tripoli, Salerno, Pompei and Foggia. All collected during the World War 2 Campaign in North Africa and Italy

4 – Other related Phrase Books, Poems, letters, and the like

5 – LAC Lamb L.B. Service No. 1012281 - His written 1943 Diary

6 – LAC Lamb L.B. Service No. 1012281 - His written Notes & Engineering Data

1 – Pictures taken during the Desert Campaign 1940 - 1943

73 Squadron – Pilots and ground crew. LAC Lamb 3rd from left

Airmen and groundcrew of 73 Squadron, far right LAC Lamb 1012281

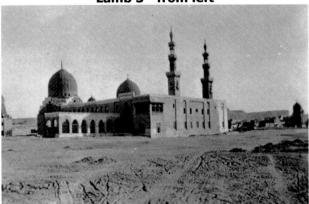

Mosque on the edge of the desert

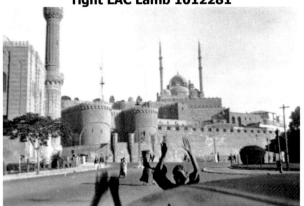

View of Mosque taken from lorry. Local lads endeavour to stop us.

Camped in the desert

Tom Thumb (trick photo)

Hurricane after forced landing -PLT A.D.7C at AIN EL GAZALLA *V7544

Hurricane: Best squadron record for shooting down German aircraft – SIDI AMOUD

Hangers at EL ADEM. What was left after 3 hours of bombing? 13/3/1942 [TOBRUK]

Bristol Blenheim 'fighter-bomber' of 39 Squadron

Hurricane sealed up ready for sandstorm

Blondie, one of my pals [also a plumber] taken in cockpit of his pet kite. Taken at Durna, Feb 17 1941

Footnote:
*Hurricane ref. V7544 – This plane is referenced in 'The History of 73 Squadron Part 2 November 1940 to September 1943, page 237. *-went out to ME on the Furious with 73's Pilots, * 73 [T] flown off Furious, Jas Storrar, 29-11-40. Damaged, repairable, 15-2-41.

SOLLUM from the escarpment, 1941

ABOUKIR – Sunderland flying boats base June 1941

Memorial to the fallen at SIDI BARRANI

L.2 near SOLLUM. Three days of travelling, feeling browned off

Herd of camels in the desert, taken whilst on convoy

Taken at GAMBUT – Eric, Rocky, Fred and me.

EL ADEM, near TOBRUK, May 1942 (Planes in the background)

Arrival at EL ADEM. Building to be used as 'Armoury'

SOLLUM from escarpment, 1941.

Old pal Jean with Smokey Joe – EL ADEM

Ted Ansell, Army. TOBRUK May 1941

Royal Air Force Officers – North Africa

Typical desert airdrome with planes in the background

View of DERNA, taken while on convoy to BENGASSI.

View of DERNA from the escarpment, taken on way to BENGASSI.

SOLLUM from escarpment 1941.

A captured Italian scout tank at BARDIA

Airmen's Mess and NAFFI burning SIDI HENEISH. Totally destroyed

Hurricane ready prepared for take off

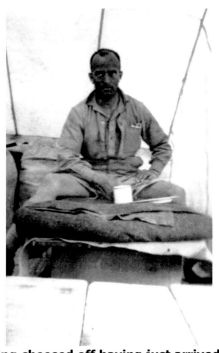

Feeling cheesed off having just arrived and erecting tents. Ain El Gazalla

Camp set up in the desert

Camp set up in the desert

Hurricane already for take-off on air strip

Camp set up in the desert

Party of chums on convoy

One of our happy days

Group of chums at tented base

Chums in what was a base camp – Officers Mess

A lighter moment

My Brother Sidney in Teheran 24/10/1943. It's not known as to why he was in Teheran.

At readiness for a German attack

Sidi Heneish Drome, bungalow behind

Group of Italian POW's TOBRUK 1941.

Pyramids taken on convoy leaving Cairo, bound for desert July 1943

234

Group of Egyptian children 1941.

Bombed Houses, Mursah Matruh

Arab living quarter, taken from Mosque. Typical of that time.

73 Squadron – Birthday Cake

My pet dog, Taken at Aboukir, then month old. November 1942. Best pal I had. Died at Sabala near Tunis, July 1943 R.I.P.

73 Squadron football team. Played game against Wing 285, drew 3 - 3

Airmen and groundcrew of 73 Squadron, LAC-Lamb 1012281 second from the right

Pictures taken during 'Recreation time' the Dessert Campaign of 1940 to 1943

On leave away from the battle of war.

On leave away from the battle of war.

A camel ride to the Pyramids whilst on leave.

Feeding piglets near base

Taken while at Port Said

Taken at Alexandria

Services club Sidi Beesh June. 1942

Sidi Beesh

Pinkner, Paddy & Blondie. Taken while on leave Sidi Beech. During our pleasant stay for a weekend

Swimming pool, Services Club SIDI BEESH 1942.

Promenade and sea wall – Alexandria June 1942

View along sea wall – Alexandria June 1942

Stanley Bay

Stanley Bay

A small party swimming, beach near SIDI HENIESH, July 1941

On leave a long way from the battle of war August, 1941

Taken at Chatby August, 1941

Beach and sea at Sidi Heniesh

Beach at SIDI HENIESH. Just a few hours rest whilst on convoy.

Beach at SIDI HENIESH. Just a few hours rest. LAC Lamb 2nd from left

Chums in what was a base camp – Officers Mess

2 – Pictures of Alexandria, Port Said etc.

Pictures of Alexandria, Port Said, Suez Canal, Sweet Water Canal, Gardens of King Farouk and other related photographs prior to and during the Dessert Campaign of 1940 to 1943.

Port Said

Port said

The Sphinx

The Pyramids at Giza

Palace Gardens - Alexandria

The Suez Canal

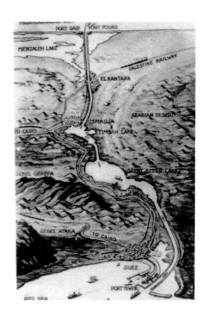

Map of the Suez Canal

Monument a La Défense – Suez 1914-1918

Palace Gardens

Hotel Gardens – Alexandria

Sweet Water Canal to Port Said

Cairo – The Blue Mosque

244

Mosque in Cairo

Services Club - Cairo

The Zoo

Mosque

Gardens in Alexandria

Hotel Gardens

Alexandria – Midan Sead Zagfoul

Palace Grounds Alexandria

Mosque

Ancient Mosque - Cairo

Haifa Palace June 1943

Gardens – King Farouk Palace Alexandria

June 1942 – King Farouk Palace Alexandria

Street scene - Alexandria

Monument of Egyptian Premier Alexandria

Alexandria

Port Said – Entrance to the Suez Canal

Alexandria

Port Said – The Ferry Boat Station

Typical Arab 'Tea seller'

Typical 'Egyptian Lady'

Typical desert scene

The 'Star of Bethlehem'

View of waterway - Palace

Alter – The Church of the Nativity

249

3 – Souvenir Postcards of Tripoli, Salerno, Pompei and Foggia collected during the World War 2 Campaign in North Africa and Italy

North African & Italian 1940 to 1944 WW2 Campaign

Postcard Souvenirs of Tripoli, Salerno, Pompei and Foggia

The following copies of postcards were collected by LAC Lamb L. B. 1012281 during his deployment in the North African and Italian Campaign of World War 2.

The postcards, whilst being around 80+ years old, give a true reflection and indication of the places visited during the conflicts, of how these places looked prior to the war.

TRIPOLI:

Tripoli - Albergo Mehari (E. & A. L.)

Tripoli - Pontile del Re Imperatore

Tripoli - Palazzo del Governatore Generale

Tripoli - Banca d'Italia

Tripoli - Fontana della Gazzella

Tripoli - Tramonto sul mare

252

Tripoli - Albergo Casinò Uaddan (E.S.A.L.)

Tripoli - Bastione del Castello.

Tripoli - Suk el Muscir.

Tripoli - Corso Vittorio Emanuele III.

Tripoli - Palazzo Comando Marina.

Tripoli - Lungomare Conte Volpi.

Tripoli - Parco Principe Umberto.

Tripoli - La Cattedrale.

Tripoli - Piazza Castello.

Tripoli - Casa Littoria.

Tripoli - Corso Italo Balbo.

Tripoli - Panorama Città vecchia.

Tripoli - Strada della Città Vecchia.

SALERNO:

SALERNO   Panorama

SALERNO - Piazza dei Martiri

Polla - Vivaio Forestale del Comando Contà di Salerno

Salerno - Via Roma

POMPEI:

Ai pie' di questo Altare ho pregato per Voi

Chiesa - Pala di S. Michele.

257

4 – Other related Phrase Books, Poems, letters, and the like

MESSAGERIES DE JOURNAUX

LIBRAIRIE HACHETTE

Société Anonyme au Capital de 110.000.000 de francs

AGENCE GENERALE POUR LE NORD AFRICAIN

49ᵐᵉ Rue d'Isly — ALGER

JOURNAUX
PUBLICATIONS
LIBRAIRIE
PAPETERIE
CARTES POSTALES
ARTICLES DIVERS

— Visa C.O.P. 5381 —
— Visa Censure 9274 —
Imp. NORD - AFRICAINE
S. CRESCENZO. — ALGER

E. SIMON
AGRÉGÉ DE L'UNIVERSITÉ

TO LEARN FRENCH
POUR APPRENDRE L'ANGLAIS

METHODE PRATIQUE

A L'USAGE DES FRANÇAIS
FOR THE ALLIED FORCES

GRAMMAIRES
PHRASES USUELLES — PRONONCIATION
DICTIONNAIRES

Préface de M. Charles DUMAS
Inspecteur Général Honoraire
de l'Enseignement des Indigènes en Algérie

Agence Générale
HACHETTE
pour le Nord-Africain

TO ENGLISH SPEAKING READERS

VERY IMPORTANT REMARK

BEFORE USING THIS BOOK, THE READER SHOULD STUDY VERY ATTENTIVELY OUR LIST OF *FRENCH SOUNDS AND SIGNS* PAGES 5 ET 6.

OUR PHONETIC SYSTEM IS VERY SIMPLE : ITS PRINCIPLE IS: ONE SOUND ONE SIGN. EACH PHONETIC SIGN IS PRONOUNCED IN THE SAME MANNER THROUGHOUT THE BOOK. IT WILL NOT TAKE MUCH TIME IN MASTERING AND MEMORISING, AND THE READER WILL BE REWARDED FOR HIS PRELIMINARY EFFORT.

FREQUENT PRACTICE IN SPEAKING WILL PROVE OF THE GREATEST ASSISTANCE, AND NO OPPORTUNITY SHOULD BE LOST OF PERFECTING ONE'S ACCENT BY LISTENING TO THE LANGUAGE SPOKEN BY EDUCATED FRENCH PEOPLE.

AUX LECTEURS FRANÇAIS

AVIS TRES IMPORTANT

AVANT D'UTILISER CE MANUEL, IL EST RECOMMANDE D'ETUDIER TRES ATTENTIVEMENT NOTRE TABLEAU DES *SONS ANGLAIS ET DES SIGNES QUI LES REPRESENTENT* PAGES 7 ET 8.

NOTRE SYSTEME PHONETIQUE EST TRES SIMPLE, LES MEMES SONS SONT TOUJOURS REPRESENTES PAR LES MEMES SIGNES. GRACE A UN LEGER EFFORT PRELIMINAIRE, DONT IL SERA RECOMPENSE, LE LECTEUR LES RETIENDRA FACILEMENT.

IL SE PERFECTIONNERA RAPIDEMENT PAR LA CONVERSATION, AUSSI FREQUENTE QUE POSSIBLE, AVEC DES PERSONNES POUR QUI L'ANGLAIS EST LA LANGUE MATERNELLE.

NORTH AFRICA

North Africa is a very old country which, since French occupation, has gradually awakened, and now (to some extent) assumes the features of a new country.

Without mentioning prehistoric times which have left such curious remains in many regions, the beginnings of the historic period show that the Land of the Atlas — Djezirat el Maghrib the Western Isle of the Arabs — already held intercourse not only with the East through Cyrenaica and Egypt, but also with Europe through Sicily and Gibraltar. From these two directions all through the centuries its civilisation has been moulded by the succession of powers with their various influences.

« The history of North Africa », said Renan, « is hardly anything more than the history of the invasions which the country has suffered» Before the arrival of the French, the Phœnicians, the Romans, the Vandals, the Byzantines, then the Arabs, and the Turks had more or less completely imposed their rule upon the native populations.

The stock of those people is formed by the Berbers, who also used to be called Lybians. They have survived all invasions. Nowadays they are still to be found in Aurès, in Kabylie, in Mzab, in the Sahara (Tuareg) and above all in the mountains of Morocco. In those fastnesses, they still live in closely united communities which have preserved their customs and dialects, but in the remaining parts of the country the majority of the natives who speak Arabic and call themselves Arabs are in fact more or less « Arabified » Berbers. Most of them profess the Moslem religion.

From the political point of view, North Africa now includes three divisions : Algeria, a large colony of settlement conquered between 1830 and 1857, besides, Tunisia and Morocco, two protectorates which have been reorganised by France in conformity with the Treaties of 1881 with the Bey of Tunis and of 1912 with the Sultan of Morocco. Moreover Spain maintains a protectorate over the Rif, and the Tangier area has been placed under an international statute. Those recent and conventional political divisions should not make us forget that all the parts of North Africa are very strikingly alike, and that we have to deal with a well-defined natural region.

Morocco, Algeria and Tunisia, along a general line running from the South West to the North East, are commanded by a range of mountains, the Atlas, which, with great variety in its geological formations and physical features, reaches its highest summits (about 13500 ft) in Morocco, then becomes lower in Algeria, and finally dwindles to a series of hills under 4500 ft in Tunisia.

The Atlas mountains run more or less east and west and on one side slope towards the Mediterranean and Atlantic and on the other towards the Sahara. The northern slopes benefit by their proximity to the sea and the humidity derived therefrom in promoting a high degree of agriculture. Hence the rich plains of Western Morocco and the Sebou, the Riff, the Algerian Tell with its coastal plain and plateau, North Tunisia with its Eastern Sahel.

The Southern slopes however receive the influence of the Sahara with its scorching wind called the Sirocco.

The Sahara forms no impassable barrier but its vastness is an obstacle to communications, and vegetation and human existence are confined to a few wells in oases. Yet, it is through those oases that land communications with the Sudan, West Africa and the rest of Africa are carried out, and great importance is attached to a quick crossing of the Sahara, specially from the Mediterranean to the Niger.

⁂

France found these countries in a state of lethargy maintained through the centuries. The people were divided among themselves and disturbed by constant anarchy. The people were inclined to isolate themselves from the outer world and led a precarious life unworthy of the part they should assume in the world's activities.

They had to be awakened and initiated in the methods of modern civilization so that they could assume the role which should be theirs. With method and perseverance France has successfully achieved her task, improving the condition of the natives and revitalizing the country.

North Africa is separated from the mother country only by a sea which can be crossed in less than 24 hours by boat and in a few hours by air. On the African coast of the Mediter-

ranean, the French settlers have found a climate which differs very little from that of Southern Europe, and they have come over in large families in Morocco and Tunisia, as well as in Algeria. In 1936, among a population of 17,000,000 inhabitants, there were 1,000,000 Europeans, almost 1,000,000 living in Algeria alone. They are a youthful race impregnated by French influence and possess in a remarkable degree the qualities of initiative, authority and endurance which are indispensable in a land where so much was to be done.

The economic life of the country has been completely revived. North Africa still fundamentally remains an agricultural country, but farming processes have been transformed. The cultivation of cereals has been improved by the widespread practice of dry farming; big dams have been built for the irrigation of large tracts of land. Vineyards have been extended, especially since 1880 after the ravages caused in France by the phylloxera. In Algeria, they cover 1,000,000 acres, and their output has amounted to 22 million hectolitres (485 million gallons). The traditional cultivations, such as olive-trees, have been developed. About 10 million olive-trees have been checked off in Algeria, 5 million in Morocco, and the magnificent olive groves in the Tunisian Sahel are a creation of the French. The cultivation of fruit, specially oranges, vegetables and early vegetables is a very thriving industry. Those of tobacco, cotton, and plants used in perfumery should be added to the resources of the country.

The mineral wealth too is very important. Phosphates have been worked in Algeria and Tunisia since 1885, in Morocco since 1912; exports amount to 3 million tons in Tunisia, 1,700,000 tons in Morocco, and 1 million tons in Algeria. There are plentiful beds of iron, lead and zinc.

Commercial intercourse is reflected in North Africa by its good roads of which there are 36,000 kilometers, and about 7,800 kilometers of railroad, as well as efficiently equipped ports. — Moreover, it happens to lie along the great sea routes which, through Gibraltar, run to Suez, the East, the Far East, and, along the Atlantic coast, either to West, Equatorial and South Africa, or to South America. Four fifths of its commerce were carried on with the mother country. Owing to this, the African economy is at present in a critical situation.

The natives have derived great benefit from that prosperity. In Algeria, where the French have been at work for some time their number has trebled between 1872 and 1936, passing from 2 to 6 million. Order and security prevail everywhere; epidemics are becoming scarce : strong action has been taken against such diseases as trachoma, malaria, tuberculosis; a

growing importance is attached to infant hygienics, and the birth-rate being high, the number of the population is increasing steadily.

France does not only care for the welfare of the natives, she gives them an education. In Algeria, in 1939, over 100,000 Moslem children attended the primary schools, where they receive a substantial French teaching, with professional and agricultural training. The young natives also attend the secondary schools, and to the best of them France gives liberal access to the higher forms of her culture in the Universities. She trusts the Moslems, invites them to help in the development of the country, the administration of its interests, and the defence of the Empire. The unshakable loyalty of the Moslems at the time of the most tragic ordeal which a nation may have to endure, the heroism with which the native troops have fought in the past and are fighting in the present war reveal what an unfailing attachment the generous policy of France has fostered in the hearts of her children.

C. DUMAS

(Former Inspector-General of Education for the Natives in Algeria)

———

FRENCH SOUNDS EXPLAINED TO ENGLISH SPEAKING PEOPLE

			Explanations
			shorter than English ee
			same sound, but shorter than in English
			same sound, but much shorter
			very short
			No such sound in English — Lips must be well rounded
			something like the o in oven
			shorter than in English
			Much shorter than in English
			No such sound in English. Like German ü. Round your lips as if to whistle.

Those four nasal sounds have no equivalents in English. They are in large print in the figured pronunciation.

an can best be pronounced as the sound a uttered while keeping the passage between throat and nose closely shut.

on like the sound on in Hong-Kong, Gong (Without sounding the g).

in like the sound of an in hang (Without sounding the g).

un like the sound of un in hung (Without sounding the g).

A Poem Compendium:

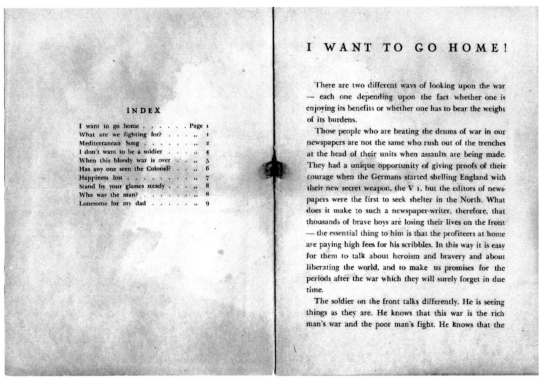

I WANT TO GO HOME!

There are two different ways of looking upon the war — each one depending upon the fact whether one is enjoying its benefits or whether one has to bear the weight of its burdens.

Those people who are beating the drums of war in our newspapers are not the same who rush out of the trenches at the head of their units when assaults are being made. They had a unique opportunity of giving proofs of their courage when the Germans started shelling England with their new secret weapon, the V 1, but the editors of newspapers were the first to seek shelter in the North. What does it make to such a newspaper-writer, therefore, that thousands of brave boys are losing their lives on the front — the essential thing to him is that the profiteers at home are paying high fees for his scribbles. In this way it is easy for them to talk about heroism and bravery and about liberating the world, and to make us promises for the periods after the war which they will surely forget in due time.

The soldier on the front talks differently. He is seeing things as they are. He knows that this war is the rich man's war and the poor man's fight. He knows that the

263

profiteers, politicians and Jews are heaping up money, while he is stuck in the mud. And he knows also that the present advance in Italy will not bring about any change, because he knows the Germans too well, he knows that some day they will settle in new positions, and that the whole affair will start all over again: months of war in the trenches, winter, diseases, the harassing shelling by the artillery and the enormous losses. And who knows what sort of surprises the Germans have still up their sleeves. And because the soldier on the front knows all this, that's why he is fed up with this war. He wants to go home. He does not want that those who remained at home should take away his job, that the rich idlers should turn away his girl, that the magnates of industry should build new palaces with his bones. He does not want it! He wants to go home to put things right there.

And the people at home? The wives and brides and mothers and children? They don't want anything else neither! They have got enough of the worries for their dearest who are constantly in danger, and they absolutely refuse to sacrifice them for some jobbers' wish!

This is the reason why we are publishing these poems written by soldiers of all English speaking nations. They speak the language of the soldier. They call things what they are. And one as well as the other expresses the wish:

I W A N T T O G O H O M E !

I WANT TO GO HOME

I want to go home; I want to go home.
Machine guns they rattle, the cannon they roar;
I don't want to go to the front any more.
O! My! I'm too young to die!
I just want to go home.

WHAT ARE WE FIGHTING FOR?

To free the world from iron chains,
To help our brethren nigh and far,
Or to increase a rich man's gains,
Are these the reasons for this war?

To gain our freedom, was it lost?
Or capture more renown?
To render aid, no matter cost,
And asking thus, no curtains drawn:
What are we figthing for?

- 1 -

Was England's freedom blighted?
Or did we stand alone?
Or were we too far sighted,
With an eye to every throne?

We know now what a war can do,
To make up for years of peace;
And knowing this, the chosen few
provoked a fight that will not cease,
What did they do it for?

No answer can the fighter give,
Just a tool, no more, no less,
To die or, perchance, to live;
There's only God can guess
What we are fighting for.

MEDITERRANEAN SONG

There's some who say the Medi-
Terranean air is heady;
While others, who have stayed there

- 2 -

Are very much afraid there's
A lot more to be said
About the highly vaunted Med.

For instance there's malaria
In the Mare Nostrum area;
And pox in many a guise
Small and cow and otherwise
Can easily be caught
Doing things you didn't ought.

Then there's flies and fleas and
Lice and crabs, that tease and
Make themselves a pest
Always hanging around the test-
Icles; playing hide and seek
In the ballroom, so to speak.

And many more afflictions
That cause a lot of restrictions;
The brothers »dyer« and »gunner«
Are active winter and summer.

- 3 -

264

And dysentry's a damned in-
Convenience notwithstanding.

So I think that you'll agree,
That those who say the sea
Is nearly always blue,
(Which is nearly always true)
Are deliberately misleading
The folks who judge by reading
That the Med for sure and certain
Is the place to do some flirting.
But you and I know better,
And you can bet an old French letter-
Box, that when this war is over
I'll count myself in clover
As long as I've a bed,
And am nowhere near the Med.

I DON'T WANT TO BE A SOLDIER

I don't want to be a soldier,
I don't want to go to war.
I would sooner hang around

- 4 -

Picadilly Underground.
And live off my earnings as I did before:
I don't want a bayonet through my coat tails,
I don't want my buttons shot away.
For I would rather stay in England,
In Merrie, Merrie England
And frolic all the rest of my life away,
Gor' Blimey!
And frolic all the rest of my life away.

WHEN THIS BLOODY WAR IS OVER

When this bloody war is over
O! How happy I should be
When this bloody war is over,
no more soldiering for me.
No more church-parades on Sunday.
No more asking for a pass
Tell the bloody Sergeant-Major
to stick the passes up his . . .

- 5 -

HAS ANY ONE SEEN THE COLONEL?

O! Has any one seen the Colonel?
I know where he is! I know where he is!
                I know where he is!
Has any one seen the Colonel?
I know where he is!
He's dining with the Brigadier.

Chorus
    I saw him! I saw him!
    Dining with the Brigadier.
    I saw him dining with the Brigadier.

Has any one seen the Major?
He's down in the deep dug-out.

Has any one seen the Captain?
He's away on six weeks' leave.

Has any one seen the Subaltern?
He's out on a night patrol.

- 6 -

Has any one seen the Sergeant?
He's drinking up the Privates' Rum.

Has any one seen the Corporal?
He's hanging on the old barbed wire.

Has any one seen the Private?
He's holding up the whole damn line.

HAPPINESS LOST

Whenever I think of happiness
Appears your face, in it I see
A host of love and gentleness
And fond, sweet thoughts of me.
I look towards a future black
Darkened by some jobbers' wish,
But happy memories take me back
To you, your smile, your kiss.
Ever in my thoughts will be
The happiness we've known,
Enjoyed in perfect harmony,
They call it home, sweet home.

- 7 -

STAND BY YOUR GLASSES STEADY

O! Stand by your glasses steady
Though this world be a world full of lies.
And we'll drink to the dead already,
And hurrah for the next man who dies.

Betrayed by the country that bore us;
Betrayed by the land that we love,
Now so many have gone before us,
And they live in the skies up above.

Beneath these low hung rafters
Lie the ghosts of the lads that we love.
And at home live the bloody old bastards
Responsible for this war that we loathe.

WHO WAS THE MAN?

Who was the man who invented the War?
Why did he do it and what was it for?
Ships on the ocean and ships in the air;
Silly old blighter, he ought to be there.

- 8 -

Who was the man who said, "Parade stand at ease,
Carry on with the inspection, Gentlemen, please"
Why should our buttons be shiny and bright,
Can any one tell us what for we should fight?

LONESOME FOR MY DAD

I'm lonesome for my daddy,
Since he has gone to war,
To fight for some men's fancy
Like others, gone before.

We used to be so happy,
And could never wish for more,
Now our only link with Daddy
Is the postman at our door.

I see no great-coat hanging
With shiny buttons on,
I hear no dear voice calling
»Son, turn the radio on.«

- 9 -

Our home and hearts are empty,
We miss the touch of his hand,
Each night our prayers are all for Dad
To return from that other land.

I know other hearts are aching,
And I'm sure they too feel sad,
And though mother's lonesome for
  her sweetheart
I'm just lonesome for my dad.

- 10 -

NOTE BY THE EDITOR:

The writers of the poems published in this booklet are soldiers of the various English speaking nations, who either have died on the battlefields or have been taken prisoners. The multitude of similar poems we have found amongst captured papers make us believe that the feelings and views expressed in the present selection of essays in poesy are those of the soldiers of the Allied Nations in general. A disclosure of the authors' names, therefore, appears to be immaterial.

266

Issued: 1943 to Allied Troops

Letter from Squadron Leader M. W. Smyth DFC FISTC

M.W. SMYTH
24 WHARF ROAD
GNOSALL
STAFFORD
ST20 0LB

TEL- 0785 822143

Dear Mr Lamb,

73 SQDN - WESTERN DESERT, ITALY & JUGO-SLAVIA.

Thank you for your letter. I shall only be too pleased to be of assistance in supplying you will any information that I have regarding the operational activities of 73 in the Western Desert.

Despite flying sluggish tropical Hurricane IIc's most of the time with fitted on long range tank which reduced top speed to 200 m.p.h. or less we were the front squadron to shoot down 300 and also in the desert knocked up a considerable score of 'buntes' transport including due bombing and strafing at night.

73 also known as Selby's Air Force

had quite a unique record - I think
to be Super ground crews and John
Selby we managed to keep fully operational
24 hours per day even when the
Squadron was moving up through
the desert following Alamein.

On we we totally on leave
in the air by the Me 109's Selby
decided to transfer activities strafing
anything that moved on the enemy
side 24 hours round the clock. Our
casualties were not light

If you check on the 'Desert Air
Force' book pages 168 & 169 you
will see extracts included for you may
flying by books which I still have

I was shot in the leg whilst
strafing the Kelibic airfield - Tunisia on
May 10th 1943 and think to in Civil
Service have only recently got a small
pension after all these years.

I was posted as a P.O. to 73
when it moved to PRKOS Jugo Slavia at
the end of the war but was unable
to take up the appointment due to
injuries

Please do not hesitate to get
in touch with me again for if
any of my information that my be of use
to you. Yours Sincerely

maurice Smyth

SQUADRON LEADER M.W. SMYTH DFC FISTC

Maurice Smyth volunteered for aircrew in July 1940. After completing training as a pilot he was posted to No.111 Squadron in August 1941 flying Spitfires on offensive sweeps, Bomber escorts and 'Rhubarbs' over Northern France. During these operations he destroyed one Me 109E and set fire to a large oil storage tank in Dunkirk harbour, when his aircraft was hit by flak.

He was posted to the Western Desert in July 1942 and joined No.73 Squadron. He served throughtout the El Alamein battle and following advance to Tunis. He was hit by a Me 109G in a dogfight over El Alamein and also by flak whilst strafing transport vehicles of the Afrika Korps. He was subsequently involved in the shooting down of Axis bombers and transport aircraft, strafing enemy airfields and night intruder operations. During an attack on an airfield he suffered a direct hit and was wounded.

Following a period as an instructor, he joined No.253 Squadron in Italy, again with the task of ground strafing, in this case the 14 Axis Divisions withdrawing from the Balkans. The targets were troop convoys, trains, vehicles and key positions which were dive-bombed.

In an attack on Mostar airfield he was hit by flak. His aircraft caught fire and he was forced to parachute into the sea. Eventually he reached land where he was hidden by civilians who contacted Tito's Partisans and helped him to evade capture and to contact a British military mission. He was flown from Yugoslavia in a Lysander.

He continued on operations. He led one particularly successful attack by five Spitfires on an enemy assembly park in Greece during which he was again severely damaged by flak. Subsequent photographic reconnaisance confirmed the destruction of 257 vehicles.

He was awarded the Distinguished Flying Cross in February 1945 by which time he had qualified for the G.Q., Caterpillar, Goldfish and Late Return Clubs. After the War he flew jet aircraft with Nos.43 and 66/111 Squadrons.

EXTRACT FROM 1ST DAY COVER
abstract FROM 75th anniversary
of 111 Sqdn

FROM:- M.W. SMYTH
24 WHARF ROAD
NEWTON PARK
BURSALL
STAFFORD

ST20 0DB

P.W.J. LAMB Esq.
55 HAYCROFT DRIVE
St. LEONARDS PARK
GLOUCESTER,
GL4 9XX

270

Letters to and from Museums: [All related to the coins and paper money found.]

L.B. LAMB
9 TETBURY ROAD
TUFFLEY
GLOUCESTER. GL4. OLQ.

AT CRISTIES

Dear Helen.

Enclosed details I mentioned to you, the paper money I do not think are valuable, have been advised by Mr Watkins of the Gloucester City museums Enquiry Service, enclosed is the report he made out for me, together with his reference on each packet of coins.

I collected these when I was in north africa. The Turkish and Greek coines we found in the desert when we were digging trenches, as we required a place to hide when the Germans tried to bomb us, the paper money I found in a bombed building.

I do hope I am not causing you too much trouble, but having had them these years, and not being able to visit the Ashmolean in Oxford to have them valued I would be most grateful. Thank you dear. Yours sincerely

L B Lamb

Name (Mr./Mrs./Miss) A.B. LAMB   Date 25/6/79

Address 9, TETBURY RD, TUFFLEY. GLOUC

Specimen COINS. — Q3 NOTES

Where found COLLECTED (NORTH. AFRICA)

Nature of Enquiry :   IDENTIFICATION   DONATION   LOAN   SALE

REPORT

Notes on the coins are on their respective packets. The largest piece of paper currency seems to be a 500 ROUBLE note of the Russian State Bank, dated 1912, & with the signature of either A. KONSCHIN or I. Schipow as Director. The next largest seems to be a 1000 rouble note issued under the name Credit Money, by the Provisional State Government of Russia in 1917. The third largest is apparently a 1000 MARK note of the German Empire, with a 7 figure serial number issued in 1910.

Acc. No. I 87/1979
P.T.O.

YOUR SPECIMEN AWAITS COLLECTION AT THE   MUSEUM AT YOUR CONVENIENCE.
PLEASE BRING YOUR RECEIPT WHEN YOU CALL.

The two small pieces are examples of Allied Army Money issued in Italy in 1943, a 1 LIRA note & a 10 LIRE note of the "A" series.

I am afraid that none of the pieces I have succeeded in making notes on seems to be particularly unusual.

F. Watkins

272

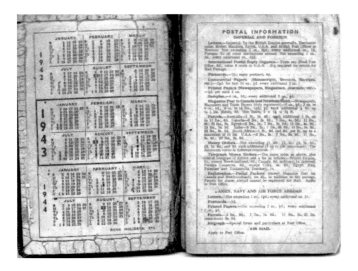

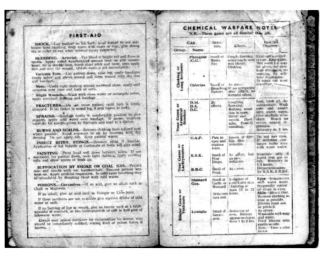

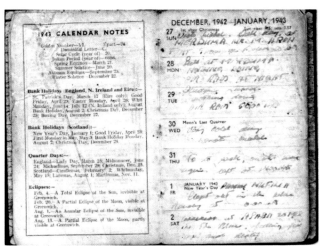

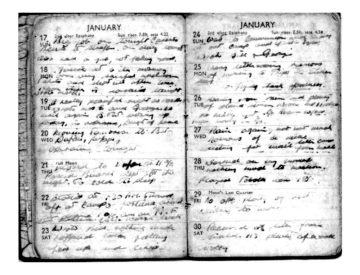

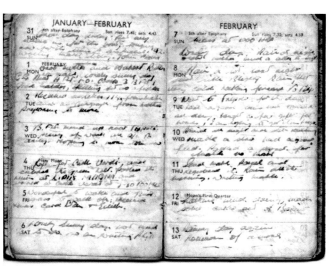

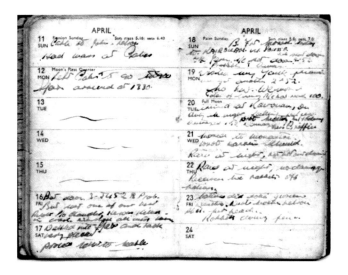

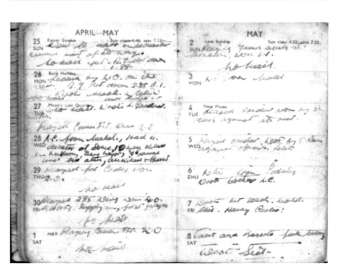

MAY

9 SUN — 2nd after Easter — Sun rises 4.20; sets 7.34	**16** SUN — 3rd after Easter — Sun rises 4.8; sets 7.45
10 MON	**17** MON
11 TUE	**18** TUE
12 WED — Moon's First Quarter	**19** WED
13 THU	**20** THU
14 FRI	**21** FRI
15 SAT	**22** SAT

MAY / MAY–JUNE

23 SUN — 4th after Easter — Sun rises 3.58; sets 7.55	**30** SUN — Rogation Sunday — Sun rises 3.51; sets 8.4
24 MON	**31** MON
25 TUE	**1** TUE — JUNE
26 WED — Moon's Last Quarter	**2** WED — New Moon
27 THU	**3** THU — Ascension Day
28 FRI	**4** FRI
29 SAT	**5** SAT

JUNE

6 SUN — Sunday after Ascension — Sun rises 3.46; sets 8.11	**13** SUN — Whit Sunday — Sun rises 3.44; sets 8.17
7 MON	**14** MON — Bank Holiday
8 TUE	**15** TUE
9 WED	**16** WED
10 THU	**17** THU
11 FRI — Moon's First Quarter	**18** FRI — Full Moon
12 SAT	**19** SAT

JUNE / JUNE–JULY

20 SUN — Trinity Sunday — Sun rises 3.42; sets 8.20	**27** SUN — 1st after Trinity — Sun rises 3.44; sets 8.21
21 MON	**28** MON
22 TUE	**29** TUE
23 WED	**30** WED
24 THU — Midsummer Day, Quarter Day — Moon's Last Quarter	**1** THU — JULY
25 FRI	**2** FRI — New Moon
26 SAT	**3** SAT

JULY

4 SUN — 2nd after Trinity — Sun rises 3.48; sets 8.19	**11** SUN — 3rd after Trinity — Sun rises 3.55; sets 8.15
5 MON	**12** MON
6 TUE	**13** TUE
7 WED	**14** WED
8 THU	**15** THU — St. Swithin
9 FRI	**16** FRI
10 SAT — Moon's First Quarter	**17** SAT — Full Moon

JULY

18 SUN — 4th after Trinity — Sun rises 4.2; sets 8.9	**25** SUN — 5th after Trinity — Sun rises 4.11; sets 8.0
19 MON	**26** MON
20 TUE	**27** TUE
21 WED	**28** WED
22 THU	**29** THU
23 FRI	**30** FRI
24 SAT — Moon's Last Quarter	**31** SAT

AUGUST

1 SUN — 6th after Trinity — New Moon — Sun rises 4.22; sets 7.50
Mass at Foret

2 MON — Bank Holiday

3 TUE

4 WED

5 THU — L.C. from Mabel

6 FRI

7 SAT

AUGUST

8 SUN — 7th after Trinity — Sun rises 4.32; sets 7.40
Mass at the East Farm
A.C. from Fred Grant

9 MON — Moon's First Quarter
Waiting Mabel

10 TUE

11 WED — Letter from Mabel, brother Davies Craig

12 THU — Waiting Mabel

13 FRI — Wrote Dear Craig

14 SAT

AUGUST

15 SUN — 8th after Trinity — Full Moon — Sun rises 4.44; sets 7.24
Mass at Bari
Was mails present

16 MON — Wrote & Cros St Carto
Mass & mother

17 TUE

18 WED

19 THU

20 FRI

21 SAT

AUGUST

22 SUN — 9th after Trinity — Moon's Last Quarter — Sun rises 4.54; sets 7.11
Mass at Lido Sand

23 MON — away on detachment

24 TUE

25 WED

26 THU

27 FRI — L.C. from Mrs Langd Mabel. Mother.

28 SAT

AUGUST — SEPTEMBER

29 SUN — 10th after Trinity — Sun rises 5.6; sets 6.55
Mass at Lido Sand

30 MON — New Moon

31 TUE — Returned to Syda.
pension lette for Sid & John

1 WED — SEPTEMBER — Wrote to Mabel, when Campton shore. Mother Mabel Bill.

2 THU — a note Sid. John Walton

3 FRI — Written to St Mario.

4 SAT — received, L.C. from Mabel & mother.

SEPTEMBER

5 SUN — 11th after Trinity — Sun rises 5.17; sets 6.40
Working could not attend mass.

6 MON — no mail

7 TUE — Moon's First Quarter
Waiting mail. Working
arent south. Mabel
Mail adam joined to 82 River

8 WED — first capital @ 17.00.
from A/C against first day Sept & Brit

9 THU — Wrote L.B.J.
received L.C. from Gerard C.

10 FRI — Wrote Queen Griffith
Miss Cunningham

11 SAT

SEPTEMBER

12 SUN — 12th after Trinity — Sun rises 5.28; sets 6.24

13 MON

14 TUE — Full Moon

15 WED

16 THU

17 FRI

18 SAT

SEPTEMBER

19 SUN — 13th after Trinity — Sun rises 5.39; sets 6.8

20 MON — news from Sebast to Reyate

21 TUE — Moon's Last Quarter

22 WED — lovely day

23 THU

24 FRI

25 SAT

SEPTEMBER — OCTOBER

26 SUN — 14th after Trinity — Sun rises 5.50; sets 5.52

27 MON

28 TUE

29 WED — Michaelmas Day — Quarter Day — New Moon

30 THU

1 FRI — OCTOBER

2 SAT

OCTOBER

3 SUN — 15th after Trinity — Sun rises 6.2; sets 5.35

4 MON

5 TUE — Orete table theatre
L.C.

6 WED — Moon's First Quarter
raining Salerno
and shelling about a weary sun.

7 THU — rained all day, and less of rain.

8 FRI — rain again all day
But cleared up at night.

9 SAT — went to Salerno &
finland present for mail

OCTOBER

10 SUN — 16th after Trinity — Sun rises 6.13; sets 5.21
preparing to move. Only
list go to check — poster
mails parcel.

11 MON — police board all Orete
Mabel. Mail to Salerno and
bought dress and stocking.
Lovely sunshine.

12 TUE — Police Board up Mass &
weddings. I pray may stay
seen again safely.

13 WED — Full Moon

14 THU

15 FRI

16 SAT — Orete Bed Landaverro

OCTOBER

17 SUN — 17th after Trinity — Sun rises 6.25; sets 5.8
first at Mass at
Montegiano

18 MON — A/C arrived from Orate
at 19.0
received from A/C, Sid mail
arrive

19 TUE — Received A/C of A/C and mail
letters from Mabel mother
Mabel & Sid. St Orete.

20 WED — Wrote Mabel, her heart.

21 THU — Moon's Last Quarter
moved to Orete at
Montecagnano. Sid up from SALERNO.

22 FRI

23 SAT

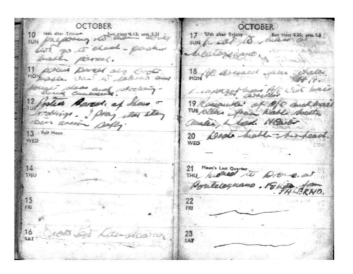

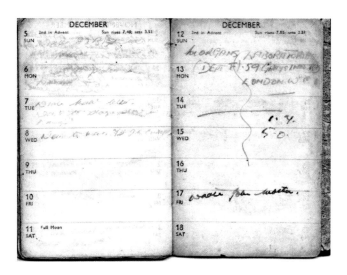

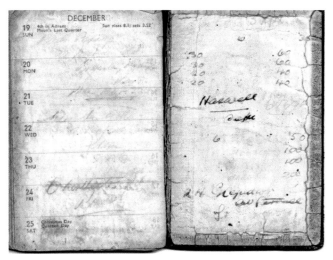

Unfortunately, the FINAL pages to complete the month of December 1943 and the start of January 1944 are missing.

When you think that the diary [in 2022] is 79 years old, it is no wonder that some pages are missing and that some writing has faded with time.

6 – LAC Lamb L.B. Service No. 1012281 - His written Notes & Engineering Data

Jan 1942.

Gambut to Gazala.

Gazala to El Adem.

El Adem to Gambut No I.

Gambut No I to Gazel. El Aried.

Gazel. El. Aried. to Gambut No II.

Gambut no II to Gambut main

Gambut main to El Adem

El Adem to El Gubi Tobruk

El Gubi S. To Gambut main.

June 17. C/o Ward. W/o Woolsey. Killed
WITHDRAWN.

Gambut to Sidi Azeyz

Sidi Azeyz to B.L.G. 75

B.L.G. 75 to B.L.G. 76.

B.L.G. 76 to Sidi Heneish

Sidi Heneish to Quasaba.

Quasaba to Daba.

Daba to L.G. 20.

L.G. 20 to B.L.G. 39.

B.L.G. 39. to B.L.G. 154

---

5 July. (advance w.c.)

L.G. 88. to L.G. 89. 24 Oct.

L.G. 89 to Burgab El. Arab.

Burgab El Arab to L.G. 21. 10 miles W. Daba.

L.G. 21 to L.G. 155 South Sidi Barrani

L.G. 155 to Martuba

Martuba to El Adem

El Adem to Martuba

Martuba to Barché
                  magrun
Barché to W. of Bengazin

---

24 Nov.   Xmas with Regm.
                       but not much of one.
Magrun to Merduma arrived 23rd Dec

Merduma to Amer El Chell. Jan 2. 1943

Amer El Chel to Hamriet Jan 11.

Hamriet to Tarret 13 Jan

Tarret to Dopan 22 Jan
                   NEAR GARRABULLI.
Dopan to Castle Verde   36 miles from Tripoli.
                          Job. L. arrived to rest
leaving Castle Verde. passed through TAGIURA.
VIA. TRIP. ZAURA, SABRATHA.
FEB-15   20th MARCH   ARRIVED 20th
EL ASABRA to NAFATIA
NAFATIA to Gabes.
Gabes to El. NAOU. PFAX.

AFRICA - SICILY - JUNE   July
19 April Passed through El Djem
0900
08.30 21.4.43   ARRIVED Same day
Kairouan to MONASTRE 10-00 NM.
391.5.43 ARRIVED PM.9 DEC 2. 9.33 Kes from Cairo
MONASTRE to. LA. SEBHLANE Tunis NO.II
                          July 27.43
LA. SEBALA. NO.II to LA. SEBALA NO.I.   (HQ)
          20th
LA. SEBALA.I to BEZERTA   1st Oct
BEZERTA to SALERNO   3rd
Palermo   Dec 1st   to Foggia   the same day
Foggia Main to   1630. M.T.II R JAN. 44
30 M.T.M RYAIR to Net G.N NAPLES
                          17th JAN

AFRICA - SICILY - JUNE   July
19 April Passed through El Djem
0900
08.30 21.4.43   ARRIVED Same day
Kairouan to MONASTRE 10-00 NM.
391.5.43 ARRIVED PM.9 DEC 2. 9.33 Kes from Cairo
MONASTRE to. LA. SEBHLANE Tunis NO.II
                          July 27.43
LA. SEBALA. NO.II to LA. SEBALA NO.I.   (HQ)
          20th
LA. SEBALA.I to BEZERTA   1st Oct
BEZERTA to SALERNO   3rd
Palermo   Dec 1st   to Foggia   the same day
Foggia Main to   1630. M.T.II R JAN. 44
30 M.T.M RYAIR to Net G.N NAPLES
                          17th JAN

Letters.   From.   Date.

No. 1.   Anadd   21.5.44

No. 1.   Mother   "   "

No. 1.   Dadan

1004760 CRAIG D

    13 O.T.U.

Trigonometrical Values of certain angles

Degrees	0°	30°	45°	60°	90°
Radians	0	$\frac{\pi}{6}$	$\frac{\pi}{4}$	$\frac{\pi}{3}$	$\frac{\pi}{2}$
Sine	0	$\frac{1}{2}$	$1\frac{1}{2}$	$\frac{\sqrt{3}}{2}$	1
Cosine	1	$\frac{\sqrt{3}}{2}$	$\sqrt{1}\frac{1}{2}$	$\frac{1}{2}$	0
Tangent	0	$1\frac{1}{3}$	1	$\sqrt{3}$	∞
Cotangent	∞	$\sqrt{3}$	1	$\sqrt{\frac{1}{3}}$	0
Secant	1	$\sqrt{\frac{2}{3}}$	$\sqrt{2}$	$\sqrt{\frac{2}{2}}$	∞
Cosecant	∞	2	$\sqrt{2}$	$\sqrt{\frac{2}{3}}$	1

Percentages or as of £1.

$1\frac{1}{4}\% = \frac{1}{80}$ 3³
$2\frac{1}{2}\% = \frac{1}{40}$ 6°
$3\frac{3}{4}\% = \frac{3}{80}$ 9°
$5\% = \frac{1}{20}$ 1-0
$6\frac{1}{4}\% = \frac{1}{16}$ 1-3
$7\frac{1}{2}\% = \frac{3}{40}$ 1-6
$10\% = \frac{1}{10}$ 2-0
$11\frac{1}{4}\% = \frac{}{}$ 2-3
$12\frac{1}{2}\% = \frac{}{}$ 2-6
$15\% = \frac{}{}$ 3-0

$16\frac{2}{3}\% = \frac{1}{6}$ - 3-4
$20\% = \frac{1}{5}$ 4-0
$25\% = \frac{1}{4}$ 5-0
$33\frac{1}{3}\% = \frac{1}{3}$ 6-8
$50\% = \frac{1}{2}$ 10-0

If a bar of any substance is heated 1°C its length will increase by a certain fraction of its length called its Coefficient of linear Expan. Coe. of L. Ex for 1°C of —

Glass = .0000085   Copper = .000017
Platinum = .0000085   Brass = .000019
Iron = .000012   Lead = .000028
Steel = .000012   Zinc = .00003

P.T.O

The Coefficient of Sup: Expansion is double the above
—   —   Cubic Ex. is treble the above.
—   —   —   is used in measuring the expansion of liquids
The Coefficient of Ex. of all Gases is the same
A gas expands $\frac{1}{273}$ of its volume for each degree Centigrade rise in temperature

---

Specific Gravity of some Solids.

Aluminium 2.67   Iron Cast 7.20
Brass 8.00   Iron Wrought 7.79
          Lead 11.35
Glass 1.08   Limestone 2.50
          Marble 2.70
Copper 8.94   Mercury 13.60
          Platinum 21.45
Glass 2.89   Silver 10.51
          Sodium 0.97
Gold 19.32   Steel 7.75
          Tin 7.29
Ice 0.92   Zinc 7.29

To find the weight of a cubic ft. multiply by 62.321 By
number of cub. ft. in 1 ton divide 35.943 S.G.
The S.G. of a liquid is found by means of a S.G.
S.G. of liquids = wt of equal vol of water Bottle

Specific Gravity of some Gases

Hydrogen 1   Oxygen 16
Water Vapour 9   Sulphur Dioxide 32
Nitrogen 14
Carbon monoxide 14
Carbon Dioxide 22
Air 14.4

Sgt Stone.
Sgt Hill
3 French Pilots at Sidi Haneish
F/Sgt. Houghton.
P/O Barret
Sgt Maclean
F/Sgt. Miller   Nov. 42.
Sgt Harris   14.7.42.
Sgt Hopkins DEBRA P.
Sgt Murray 1/81st   20.6.43.
F/Sgt Johnson.

Pilots and aircrew lost in M.E.
                    upto May 24. 43
P/O Lamb   Sgt Dunsopp P.O.W
P/O Woldoney   Sgt Solan
                Sgt Logan P.O.W
Sgt Webster   F/Sgt Johnson
Sgt Willis   Sgt Baker   P/O Sherk U.S
                P/O Chandler   L.A.C. ......
2 French Pilots Sgt Carter   A.C. Bowie
F/Sgt Smith   Sgt Hopkins   Cpl Brown
                P/O Diamond   L.A.C. ......
P/O Green 7   F/Sgt ......   Drowned in
                P/O Thomson   Hospital ships
S/Ldr Wood   F/Sgt Shalloy   sunk off Alex
F/O Dolley   F/Sgt Green   by subs.
                Sgt White   P.T.O

End of Dec. 1940 and 1941
                at Dekheila for ....
Heliopolis to Dekheila. Had .... with navy
Dekheila to Sidi Heneish.
Sidi Haneish to L.G. Solum
Solum 2 to Benina
Benina to Gazala.
Gazala to El Aden
El Aden to Benina
Benina to Martuba

Martuba to Derna
                Retreat.
Derna to Michili
Michili to Gazala South
Gazala South to Benina.
Benina to El Gubi Tobruk
Remained in Tobruk during the siege.
Left Tobruk by S.A.R.N.V.R. Southern Isles
Tobruk to Alex By sea May 28.
..... at Alex May 30.   —

Went to Amiriya. Stayed there for 3 Days
Went on leave to Alex 6 days.
Went back to Sidi Heneish ....
Sidi Heneish to Gamil Port Said. Oct 2nd
Gamil to Amiriya on detachment
                Went flying in Marylands
Amiriya to Marriyut   for 3 Hours
Marriyut to Amiriya.
Amiriya to Edku
                Way for Amara again
Edku to Amiriya Had .... with 53 R.S.U

Amiriya to Gambut left Gamil for Gazala
                                      5 Hours
Went to Heliopolis to go by air, flying
her from Gazala to El Aden.

Acknowledgements:

This book would not have been possible without the help of the following people, and please forgive me if I may have inadvertently forgotten anyone. I wish to thank you all for your continued support, advice, mentoring and assistance over the past 20+ years that it has taken [notwithstanding the fact that some of the research has had to be carried out during the Covid-19 2019 to 2021 pandemic].

The RAF Disclosures, Ministry of Defence – Air Historical Branch, Warrant Officer David Stroud MBA - MOD St Athan (RAF) Archives, Frank Haslam – Editor of 207 Squadron Royal Air Force History Website and, Malcolm Barrass – RAF Historical Society, RAF Museum, Hendon, and Mr. R T L Bickers who like Squadron Leader M. W. Smyth mentioned below gave me his details along with The Spitfire Society, Southampton. Finally, Mr Alan Carter – RAF West Kirby Association.

The staff at various archives and museums deserve a special mention, including those at National Archives (Kew), Ashmolean Museum (Oxford), Imperial War Museum plus many others who have cajoled me into finishing what I started.

Special mention for Squadron Leader M.W. Smyth DFC, FISTC, who kindly wrote to me in 1994, the embryonic stage of starting to compile the book. *[His letter to me is included in Appendix 4 of the book]*. My only regret if I have one at all, is that I never followed up on planning to meet up with him and talk through his experiences of the Western Dessert and beyond. Equally as important, did he recognise my dad?

Also, I would also take this opportunity to thank author, Damien Lewis for his mentoring and support in getting the job done. All very much appreciated.

My family: Jane my ever-supportive wife, my son Mark, my daughter Emma-Jane, and my eldest granddaughter Chloe, all of whom have ensured that as a part of the family history the book required, **NO** needed to be completed. My heartfelt gratitude to you all.

Bibliography

Archives, Museums, Research Organisations

The one prime place for looking at and undertaking research on World War 2 is The National Archives at Kew, which is rich in information when understanding and establishing the build up to war in North Africa and Italy, as well as the movements of squadrons and their personnel.

The Ashmolean Museum in Oxford for their work on establishing the period and age of the coins found in the Western Dessert.

Other sources of information are the Imperial War Museums, RAF Museums, Public Record Office, Census Records, RAF Disclosures, Royal Air Force History website, Royal Air Force St. Athan now MOD St Athan, Ministry of Defence Air Historical Branch (RAF) and Naval Records pertaining to HMS Manchester – Ship's Log.

Unpublished Sources

- Diary and Notebooks written by LAC 2 – Lamb L.B. 1012281
- Photographs taken during the North Africa Campaign
- Purchased Photographs and Postcards
- RAF War Records, held at National Archives Kew Gardens
- RAF Records Cranwell
- RAF Norholt
- RAF Historical Society
- Royal Air Forces Association
- Military Records
- DBS Veterans UK

National Archives Squadron Operational Reports:

73 Squadron:

AIR 27/629/13 (1)
AIR 27/629/15 (1)
AIR 27/629/17
AIR 27/629/18 (1)
AIR 27/629/19
AIR 27/629/20
AIR 27/629/21 (2)
AIR 27/629/21 (3)
AIR 27/629/22
AIR 27/629/23
AIR 27/629/24
AIR 27/629/25
AIR 27/629/26 (2)
AIR 27/629/26 (3)
AIR 27/629/27
AIR 27/630/1 (1)
AIR 27/630/2
AIR 27/630/3
AIR 27/630/4
AIR 27/630/5 (2)
AIR 27/630/6 (3)
AIR 27/630/7
AIR 27/630/8 & 27/630/8 (1)
AIR 27/630/9
AIR 27/630/10
AIR 27/630/11
AIR 27/630/12 (2)
AIR 27/630/13 (1)
AIR 27/630/14
AIR 27/630/15
AIR 27/630/16
AIR 27/630/17 (1)
AIR 27/630/18 (2)
AIR 27/630/19
AIR 27/630/20
AIR 27/630/21
AIR 27/630/22 (3)
AIR 27/630/23 (1)
AIR 27/630/24
AIR 27/631/1
AIR 27/631/2
AIR 27/631/3
AIR 27/631/4 (1)
AIR 27/631/5
AIR 27/631/6
AIR 27/631/7
AIR 27/631/8
AIR 27/631/9
AIR 27/631/10
AIR 27/631/11
AIR 27/631/12

AIR 27/631/16
AIR 27/631/17
AIR 27/631/18
AIR 27/631/19
AIR 27/631/20
AIR 27/631/21
AIR 27/631/22
AIR 27/631/23
AIR 27/631/24
AIR 27/632/1
AIR 27/632/2
AIR 27/632/3
AIR 27/632/4
AIR 27/632/5
AIR 27/632/6 (1)
AIR 27/632/7
AIR 27/632/8
AIR 27/632/9 (1)
AIR 27/632/10 (1)
AIR 27/632/11 (1)
AIR 27/632/12
AIR 27/632/13 (1)
AIR 27/632/14
AIR 27/632/15
AIR 27/632/16
AIR 27/632/17 (1)
AIR 27/632/18 (1)
AIR 27/632/19
AIR 27/632/20 (1)
AIR 27/632/21
AIR 27/632/22
AIR 27/632/23
AIR 27/632/24
AIR 27/633
AIR 27/634/1 (1)
AIR 27/634/2
AIR 27/634/3 (1)
AIR 27/634/4
AIR 27/634/5 (1)
AIR 27/634/6 (1)
AIR 27/634/7 (5)
AIR 27/634/8 (1)
AIR 27/634/9
AIR 27/634/10 (4)
AIR 27/634/11 (1)
AIR 27/634/12
AIR 27/634/13 (1)
AIR 27/634/14 (1)
AIR 27/634/15 & 634/15 (1)
AIR 27/634/16
AIR 27/634/21

73 Squadron: *continued*

AIR 27/631/13
AIR 27/631/14
AIR 27/631/15

AIR 27/637 (1)
AIR 27/638_1 (1)
AIR 27/638_2 (1)
AIR 27/639 (1)

39 Squadron:

AIR 27/400/30
AIR 27/407/25
AIR 27/407/26
AIR 27/407/27
AIR 27/407/28

AIR 27/407/29
AIR 27/407/30
AIR 27/407/31
AIR 27/407/32

Other Related AIR's:

AIR 78/93/4
AIR 29/995 – [32 M.U. St. Athan, August 1939 to December 1945]
AIR 29/1103/1 - [101 P.D.C. Kirkham]
AIR 49/205
RAF Padgate – AIR 29/497
AIR 23/7069 Operations 'Accolade', 'Husky', 'Avalanche and 'Tidal Wave' dated 1943.

AIR 29/116/3
AIR 29/117/3

ADM 1/16815
WW 0222/1568 – [59 B.G.H.]
RAF West Kirby – AIR 29/947

TROOP SHIPS of the British Fleet [AIR/ADM]

HMT Franconia: AIR 29/117/3
HMT Orontes: ADM 1/16815 & AIR 9/119/1
HMT Ormonde: AIR 29/116/13

Town Class – Light Cruiser [ADM]
HMS Manchester:

ADM 53/112669 – 1940 October
ADM 53/112670 – 1940 November
ADM 53/112671 – 1940 December

HMSAS Southern Isles:
Mine Sweeper [ADM]

1941 June - ADM 53/115082
1941 September - ADM 53/115083
1941 October - ADM 53/115084
1941 November - ADM 53/115085

Other Researched Documents:

Catalogue ref: HW 1/672
CAB 121/620
WOP 169/9298
PREM 3/311
CAB 122/1192 Operation Avalanche
WO 234/46 El Adem; WO 234/48 Tobruk; WO 234/49 Tobruk; WO 106/2273; ADM 199/862

Note:
Contains public sector information licensed under the Open Government Licence v3.0

Accreditations to Author's and Image Providers: All as listed.

This book has been compiled using my father's World War 2 Memorabilia, which has been enhanced by documents found on the search engine Wikipedia. The documents found relate to Historical content of the battles fought and their outcome.

The documents used have further enhanced this autobiography and gives the book a greater Historical meaning. It would be remiss of me to not say that if only those that fought in conflicts throughout 1939 to 1945 could have expressed their true feelings of what they endured. My father was one that wouldn't speak about his experiences, only in the company of others that fought in the various battles.

In writing and compiling this autobiography I recognise the great value of those Author's and Image Providers for their storming work that can be found in Wikipedia, and I credit their work, which has helped me in completing the book. The Accreditations are as follows: -

MOD, DDC Brand & Licensing Manager: Pauline Aquiline email 09/02/2022 Approval to use Squadron Insignia/Badges (only inside the book NOT on Front & Rear Covers

MOD St Athan/RAF: Wing Commander Mr G. Wedlake Station Commander and WO David Stroud, Station Warrant Officer approved use of Photographic Images from RAF St Athan.

RAF Padgate: Image Provider: Cheshire Archives & Local Studies Record Office – Cheshire Image Bank c01024. Approval and image received via email from Hannah Bate – Archives Assistant, date 01/03/2022, who have given their consent and approval to use the image in the book.

RAF West Kirby: Image Provider: Peter Jackson-Lee, through the www.warmemorialsonline.org.uk and RAF West Kirby Association. Also, Images from Mr Alan Carter RAF West Kirby Association via email dated 8 March 2022.

RAF 73 Squadron: No restrictions all 'Public Domain'

RAF 39 Squadron: No restrictions all 'Public Domain'

SS Franconia: Australian National Maritime Museum Image Ref: 0017492. Approval given by Inger Sheil – Assistant Curator via email dated 07/03/2022. Credit: Australian National Maritime Museum collection, gift from the Estate of Peter Britz. There being NO Copyright Restrictions.

HMS Manchester: Author: https://en.wikipedia.org/wiki/Battle_of_Cape_Spartivento, & https://en.wikipedia.org/wiki/HMS_Manchester_(15) Image Provider: (pre-1 June 1957 'Public Domain') No Copyright Restrictions.

HMS Furious: Author: https://en.wikipedia.org/wiki/HMS_Furious_(47) Image Provider: (pre-1 June 1957 'Public Domain') No Copyright Restrictions all 'Public Domain'

RAF Takoradi: Image Providers: www.rafkasfareet1953-56.com & alwynstanleyyork@gmail.com

HMSAS Southern Isles: Words: Extract from South Africa's Fighting Ships – Author, Alan du Toit and Image Providers South African Naval Museum, Commander Leon Steyn – Curator, via email dated 17 March 2022.

Italy Invasion: Operation Avalanche – Author: https://army.mil/cmh-pg/books/wwii/salerno/sal-prep.htm. File: Invasionofitaly 1943.jpg Email from susannezoumbaris@nara.gov – 05/04/2022 at 10:44 hours. Providing the credit has been added then consent to use approved.

National Archives:
Contains public sector information licensed under the Open Government Licence v3.0.

Published Books & Media

Reference to and Extracts taken from the following reference books: -

- The Squadrons of the Royal Air Force & Commonwealth 1918 – 88 by James J. Halley.
- The Squadrons of the Royal Air Force by James J. Halley
- The Desert Air War 1939 – 1945 by Richard Townshend Bickers
- African Trilogy by Alan Moorehead
- Middle East 1940 – 1942, A Study in Air Power by Philip Guedalla
- Rommel and the Defeat of the Allies – Tobruk 1942, by David Mitchell Hill-Green
- Royal Air Force St Athan – A History 1938–1988 by S J Bond
- The Second World War by Antony Beevoir
- Finest Years – Churchill As Warlord 1940 – 45 by Max Hastings
- All Hell Let Loose-The World at War 1939-1945 by Max Hastings
- Finest Hours – Churchill as Warlord 1940-45 by Max Hastings
- Finest Hour by Tim Clayton & Phil Craig
- Tobruk The Birth of a Legend by Frank Harrison
- Hurricane -The Last Witnesses by Brian Milton
- The Sky Suspended – A Fighter Pilots Story by Jim Bailey
- Spitfire Ace of Aces - The Wartime Story of Johnnie Johnson by Dilip Sarkar
- Hurricane – The Last Witnesses by Brian Milton
- They Flew Hurricanes – Adrian Stewart
- The History of 73 Squadron Volumes 1, 2 & 3 by Don Minterne
- West Kirby and Beyond – Dennis Tomlinson
- South Africa's Fighting Ships – Alan du Toit

WORLD WAR 2 – BATTLE HONOURS

North Africa – Southeast Europe – Italy

&

- Egypt & Libya 1940 – 43*

- Mediterranean 1941 – 43*

- El Alamein*

- El Hamma*

- Southeast Europe 1943 – 45*

- Italy 1943 - 45

- East Africa 1940*

- Egypt & Libya 1940 – 43*

- Greece 1941*

- Mediterranean 1941 – 43*

- Malta 1942*

- North Africa 1942 – 43*

- Southeast Europe 1944 – 45*

Note: Honours marked with an asterisk* are those emblazoned on the Squadron Standard and were presented to each Squadron by King George VI.

Motto:
Latin – *'Tutor et Ultor'*
English – 'Protector and Avenger'
Insignia:
A demi – Talbot rampant charged on the shoulder with a maple leaf.

Motto:
Latin – *'Die Noctuque'*
English – 'By day and night'
Insignia:
A winged bomb.

MOD, DDC Brand & Licensing Manager: Pauline Aquiline email 09/02/2022 Approval to use Squadron Insignia/Badges (only inside the book NOT on Front & Rear Covers

About the Author:

I was born in Pontypridd, Glamorgan, South Wales on 24 September 1949 in Church Village Hospital (Top Floor). At the time, my Mum and my sister lived with my grandfather and aunty in Nelson, 10 Wern Crescent, to be precise, then I came along and eventually lived there to. My father worked away in Gloucester and would visit us every two weeks, travelling down on what was then the 'Red & White' bus service. During my childhood, which I can honestly say was incredible and one in which I had some wonderful moments with my grandfather otherwise known as (Grondon) on a farm in the Welsh hills above Nelson. When old enough I would ask my dad about his wartime experiences. Never did get the answers I was searching for; he would always say 'best left where they are'. We eventually moved to Gloucester in 1957, when I was 8 years old.

As the Author of this autobiography and having no previous experience in writing other than the English Essay's we had to do at school, then this is my first attempt at putting words together about my father's war experiences. As for myself, I am a retired engineer who over the years has been fortunate to work across many industries. In those years I have always had an interest in the RAF and other military services, which spurred me on to put down in words the experiences/exploits that make up 'One Man's Story', namely my dad. I love reading historical military books and reading about those who gave their service for King & Country and in some cases their lives so that we could live in freedom.

The book is an accumulation of many years work in the compilation of military memorabilia and records from the period during World War 2 - North Africa & Italy Campaigns.

It has been a long, long road in producing the book and giving the chance, one that I would do all again, as the buzz you get when compiling and researching is incredible.

PS:
If I have any regrets, they would be one's of not asking enough of the right questions at the time about his wartime experience when my father was still alive.

Finally, I dedicate this book to all the men and women who took part in the various conflicts of World War 2, the greater majority of which are no longer with us. But through their fortitude and perseverance *'They gave of their tomorrow's, so that we can have our today's'*. God Bless you all and may you all Rest In Peace. I hope you have enjoyed the reading of **'One Man's Story'?**

Philip Lamb